MUSEUM MONOGRAPHS

PIEDRAS NEGRAS ARCHAEOLOGY: ARTIFACTS, CACHES, AND BURIALS

By

WILLIAM R. COE

PUBLISHED BY
THE UNIVERSITY MUSEUM
UNIVERSITY OF PENNSYLVANIA
PHILADELPHIA
1959

Price: $5.00

Please send orders for *Museum Monographs* to:

The University Museum

33rd and Spruce Streets

Philadelphia 4, Pennsylvania

CONTENTS

LIST OF TABLES

Part 1

INTRODUCTION

INTRODUCTION

During the 1930's the University Museum spent eight seasons excavating the famed Maya site of Piedras Negras, concluding its field work in 1939. These expeditions recovered a tremendous amount of information on architecture and monuments, in addition to a very extensive collection of pottery and other artifacts. The latter material together with human and animal skeletal remains, was divided accord - ing to contract with the Museo Nacional de Arqueologia y Etnologia of Guatemala, with the University Museum's share on loan in Philadelphia. The present report is a study of all recovered artifacts, other than pottery vessels and clay figurines; it also includes full data on caches, burials, and skeletal ma- terial.

A general description of the site by Dr. Linton Satterthwaite is to be found in S. G. Morley's volume dealing in part with the Piedras Negras inscriptions (Morley, 1937–1938, v. 3, pp. 5–25). The site is located in the Middle Usumacinta region of northwestern Guatemala (Department of Peten). Draining parts of the highlands and southern Peten, the Usumacinta River flows for the most part in a northwester- ly direction, terminating at the Gulf of Mexico. A large part of it constitutes an international boundary between Mexico and Guatemala, Piedras Negras itself being found on the latter side. The proximity of the river to the site must have been an important conditioner in ancient times, for it not only provided the local population with a perennial water supply (this being a limestone region with marked wet and dry seasons), but, if utilized, it formed a natural route between the highlands of Guatemala and the im- portant estuary region of the Gulf Coast. Thus the river and possible trails that followed it could have served to promote object trade and less tangible diffusions.

Although one of many lowland Maya nuclei of ceremonial activity, it is evident that Piedras Negras ultimately became one of the most important. Architecture and sculpture alone suffice to show this. The center evolved in a tropical forest setting. It enjoyed, along with other Usumacinta centers, the great advantage of a river. Economically it subsisted on the slash—and—burn cultivation of maize; hunt- ing, fishing, and gathering surely occurred but from what is known of Maya economy, were ancillary to agriculture. Excavations were confined to the ruins themselves and thus one can speak only very tenta- tively of the nature and distribution of the center's farming component. It is reasonable to believe how- ever that it occupied a stabilized sustaining area, with periodical return to the old milpas.

A variety of signs point to Piedras Negras having been, as noted, a ceremonial site. Furthermore, the artifacts and other data treated in this report well reflect and in certain ways amplify this conclusion. Inasmuch as their function is primarily ceremonial, it might be well to review here current ideas of Classic Maya hierarchal culture. These ideas in effect supply the context, if not the motivation, for the functioning of much that will be dealt with in the following pages.

Granted the existence of priests, farmers, and maize, one must still consider them in terms of their interaction, especially with respect to cause and effect. The time period has been variously called Old Empire, Initial Series Period, Florescent Period, and Classic Period. This last is used here. It is believed on excellent grounds to have lasted some six centuries. Spatially, Classic Period culture ex- tended throughout the large lowland area north of the mountainous portion of Chiapas and Guatemala. Within this framework, the architecture, sculpture, ceramics, hieroglyphic record, calendrical computa- tions, and other hierarchic traits attained maximum and diagnostic expression.

It is generally believed that the population (resident and sustaining) of large lowland centers like Piedras Negras was triangularly structured with a broad agricultural base, intermediate artisans and other specialists, and, at the top, a small, exclusive, theocratic group (e. g., Brainerd, 1954, pp. 71–75). An obviously vital factor was the lengthy period of availability of the farmer for labor within the ceremonial precincts. Underlying this was the probable actual efficiency and productivity of maize cultivation, permitting surpluses for the support of the priests and their retinue of craft specialists.

Presumably the priestly group had varied functions; essentially religio-governmental, they perhaps extended as well to ritual warfare, trade, and kin-group control. Sacerdotal power in part must have stemmed from an extraordinary ability in calendrical astronomical prognostication—an ability that eventually came to condition, even predestine, all aspects of local life. Functioning almost as time-keepers for the dei - ties, the priests of Piedras Negras, as elsewhere, calculated the evil and auspicious days, determined the seasons of a formalized and god-bound farming year and ritual year, and mapped celestial permutations—all in suitable panoply and clouds of copal incense.

If such inferences are true, one must ask whether the ceremonial contributions of priests were sufficient for the peasant population to have reciprocated with the staggering labor needed for temples, palaces, ball-courts, sweat houses and other buildings, all comprising a center like Piedras Negras. Were such contributions, presumably rain-making and alleviations of natural agricultural fears, enough to have maintained for so long the evident cooperation between farmer and theocrat? It seems reasonable that priest - ly tenure originated and depended in part on their foresight, dramatic ability, and accuracy of observation and record, for a miscalculation as to the time to plant and the predetermined moment to harvest could have had serious consequences. During the summer of 1949, normally a season of heavy rains, British Honduras and parts of the Peten were drought -stricken. A number of successive plantings were lost, one of them due partly to predatory birds. Surely these ancient communities were subject to similiar disasters. And it is not unlikely that these priest-mathematicians were responsible for anticipating and sacrificially forestalling these conditions, as well as for rationalizing their effects when they appeared. With extended drought, life must have been thin despite storage grain.

It should be evident from what already has been said that only on a speculative basis can the nature of Classic Period social integration be treated. For all the appeal of ceremonialism as a primary bond, there are other possibilities. Steward (in Steward et al., 1955, pp. 62–64) has broadly pointed to trade monopoly (production and distribution) and the arbitration of land disputes as additional priestly assumptions. Willey (1956) concludes that lowland Classic social stratification might not have been so severe as generally held (e. g., see Kidder in A. L. Smith, 1950, p. 10)—that, in fact, the peasant possessed social mobility and was a potential participant in the hierarchal sphere. Repressive authority, as Brainerd (1954, p. 75) notes, was probably not a part of lowland Classic culture.

All in all, the quantity and complexity of the results argue for a compound cause. But whatever enabled lowland Classic hierarchal culture to take hold (rain-making, for instance) need not have solely carried it.

The excavations disclosed no architectural signs of occupancy in the Piedras Negras locale prior to what is usually referred to as the Early Classic Period. This might be rephrased to say that no signs of Pre-Classic (Formative, Developmental) ceremonial activity were found. It is entirely possible, but lacking in proof, that outlying areas supported a scattered settlement of farmers during Pre-Classic times. A few redeposited Chicanel sherds from the early strata of Structure R-3 (R. E. Smith, personal communication) attest in a slight way to the reality of that occupation. It is unlikely that a priestly group, carrying an incipient Classic ceremonialism, moved into a vacant area accompanied by a massive retinue of food producers! Rather, as perhaps at Copan (see Longyear, 1952), a group of skillful individuals appeared sometime around the beginning of the lowland Classic era and proceeded to organize the local farmers through the imposition of Classic components. Intensive and continued building, elaborate specialized architecture, the manufacture and importation of quantities of fine ceramics and other luxury articles, the broadening of all trade contacts, secret and semi-public rituals, the erection of monuments at certain intervals and the remarkable concern with time that they imply—these and other Classic components, many actually of Pre-Classic origin, could have been introduced to a community with a relatively static, insular, uncomplicated culture, but one that could not mitigate the profound uncertainties of agricultural life. The priestly group, whether locally foreign or locally derived, appears to have claimed this power and thus was able to extract enormous labor from the countryside—labor that fashioned a context for the power itself.

This hypothesis is no more than provisionally applicable to Piedras Negras. Probably pertinent, however, is the seeming late start of Piedras Negras as a Classic center. Unlike Uaxactun, this site lacks monuments dating from Baktun 8. The earliest known inscription of Piedras Negras falls nearly two centuries later than that of Uaxactun. This apparent lag in monuments has its correlates in architecture and pottery. The earliest known association of the latter (see Appendix) can be shown to be no earlier than Tzakol 3, a pottery phase which at Uaxactun concludes the Early Classic Period. Moreover, a commonly cited Classic diagnostic, the corbelled arch, was apparently not employed at Piedras Negras until an estimated half of the local Classic Period had elapsed (see Appendix). But in spite of its late beginning and its lengthy neglect of a major lowland trait, Piedras Negras came to take an important lead in such innovations as the long gallery type of palace structure. It successfully borrowed a dominant substructural form from the central Peten. And it eventually produced sculpture falling close to if not at the apogee of pre-Columbian art.

The most reasonable guess for the start of Piedras Negras as a ceremonial center is 9.0.0.0.0 in the Maya Long Count system. The basis for this is given at length in the Appendix. Substantial building activity was surely current prior to 9.5.0.0.0 (Stela 30). Altar 3 indicates functioning at 9.19.0.0.0, some 280 years after the erection of Stela 30. Satterthwaite (see Appendix) allows, there being no evidence to the contrary, an extra katun for completion of Classic ceremonialism. The whole of Baktun 9 is thus believed to have encompassed Piedras Negras as it is essentially known. With few exceptions, the material treated in this study belongs within that span of 400 years (A. D. 435—830 in the 11.16.0.0.0 correlation).

There are a few signs of post-constructional life. A late persistence until, but probably not beyond, 10.3.0.0.0 is tenuously indicated by the presence of effigy head supports, Fine Orange ware, Carved Gray and Incised Gray wares, and perhaps grater bowls (*molcajetes*) and formed pottery spindle whorls (see Butler, 1935; 1940, p. 246; Cresson, 1937; n. d.; Brainerd, 1941, p. 179; Satterthwaite, 1943; R. E. Smith, 1940, p. 248; Thompson, 1940a, p. 128; and Wauchope, 1941; 1948, pp. 31, 137). Evidence for human cremation is scanty but does exist (see Burials, Lot 20, p. 129; and Satterthwaite, 1954, pp. 28—40). One must then allow for one or more surface finds pertaining to a time beyond the terminal estimate of the local Classic Period.

Four centuries is theoretically sufficient for recognition of inherent cultural change. Architecture and sculptural style clearly did change (see Satterthwaite, 1938; 1939; 1940; Proskouriakoff, 1950; and Appendix in this study), but evidence of evolution, coordinated or not, in the data treated here is perplexingly scanty. This may be partly due to the fact that ideally the report should have been preceded by a complete analysis of all the local pottery and stratigraphic contexts. Since it is not, we lack the bare periodization (and terminology) that would allow, or at least direct, developmental conclusions on a simplified basis. Kidder (1947), for instance, was able to categorize the Uaxactun material in terms of "Tzakol" and "Tepeu." This is a great convenience and serves to prepare the way for the study of local culture change.

There is no doubt that true Tzakol and Tepeu ceramics existed at Piedras Negras (see Appendix). Risky as it may be, we have been forced by various needs to choose a date in the Maya system to mark the end of one and the beginning of the other—in other words, a divisor between Early and Late Classic Periods. In the matter of caches, alone outstanding for their frequency, such distinctions are believed too gross for purposes of developmental analysis. For one, almost all the caches appear to belong in time to the Late Classic Period. Therefore, an attempt has been made (see Appendix) to apply absolute (Long Count) dates to every cache. As will be shown in the chapter on caches, this attempt, in itself perhaps successful, has perversely yielded good evidence of votive constancy rather than evolution. This finding suggests that the other data of this study might similarly have been subject to some factor like immutability, or, better, conservatism, rather than change. The problem is to place each object in at least one or the other period and ideally in relation to a Long Count date. This can be done on a quite tentative basis for the cache and burial material, but to do so for every other artifact not from these sources would hardly be productive in this case. Surface artifacts, particularly above-floor ones, are presumed to be late. Anything from the fills of the stratified R—3 and, to a lesser extent, the K—5 structures is believed to be early. Objects from any of the Acropolis building fills are likely late yet older than the above-floor material. Objects stemming from test pits are also probably on the late side of local occupation.

An attempt was made to group artifacts as Early or Late Classic; it proved essentially fruitless. The overwhelming portion of the collection fell into the Late Classic category. Once there, no sure way was found to stratify the objects consistently. Paucity within obvious types furthermore discouraged efforts to order temporally what was believed to be Late Classic. These factors of limited quantity and temporal imbalance make the realization of a theoretical organization impracticable.

Noteworthy is the fact that no ductile metal, crystal, turquoise, nor plumbate pottery was found at the site. This would seem to indicate that the center collapsed prior to the fullest impact of militaristic Toltec influence to the north and south. Some sites probably dwindled in the midst of growing disillusionment, while others ended with violence. But all shared in the profound and problem-ridden dissolution of Classic Period achievements. The substance of this basic problem has been reviewed by A. V. Kidder (in A. L. Smith, 1950, pp. 9—10). Also noteworthy are signs at Piedras Negras of deliberate destruction (see Mason, 1938, p. 308; Satterthwaite, 1936b, p. 87; 1954, p. 35; Thompson, 1954a, p. 89). This evidence is integral to what Kidder (*op. cit.*) has termed the "social revolution hypothesis." This sees anarchy and abandonment following on a revolt of farmers against their theocratic masters and particularly against the excessive, exploitive burdens required by their ceremonial complex—a complex that is essentially what is meant by the tag, "Classic lowland Maya culture." The substance of this hypothesis was stated some twenty-five years ago by Thompson (1931, p. 230).

If we believe that the interrelationship of farmer and priest was ultimately motivated by religion rather than economics, this explanation is most apt. The maintenance of hierarchic control, in this view, depended perhaps on a surely impossible condition like ritualistic and mathematical infallibility year in and year out. The required settings imposed an extraordinary load on the farmer. This was tolerable as long as he in turn received assurances as to the agricultural and thus personal dispositions of the deities. Possibly in the remote darkness of temples the farmers' real concerns—the propitiated cycle of planting and harvesting, capricious rains, droughts, and plagues—were gradually lost sight of in priestly contemplation of celestial regularities (see Thompson, 1954a, p. 87). Practical fears grew esoteric; once imminent, influential sky and gods bit by bit left the milpa to become parts and ends of theocrats' ritual. And while in Late Classic times what was already complex became that much more so, the initial novelty of agricultural assurance subsided with a growing realization of endless, impractical burden. An unanticipated disaster perhaps could no longer be successfully rationalized in more clouds of incense and doubled sacrifices. In Mexico at this time the warrior was supplanting the priest. And with the Usumacinta leading to Mexico, the news of turbulent change could travel all too easily to a peripheral site like Piedras Negras. Towards the close of Classic times a class composed of traders and warriors may have emerged in the lowlands. If so, we can only ponder to what extent they might have initiated or participated in the revolt that ultimately came. That it appeared is shown by smashed thrones, defaced sculptures, and the cessation of ceremonial activity in all its prior manifestations. What remained once hierarchic control was lost, is unknown—perhaps milpas and farmers, close uncertainties and less distant gods. In time the farmers evidently disappeared. Yet the center of Piedras Negras oddly recouped some religious meaning when unknown people came to bury the cremated remains of their dead, and still later when the Lacandon journeyed to burn copal in their god-pots and to pray among its ruins (see Satterthwaite, 1946 a).

This explanation, in spite of some solid evidence, is full of conjecture. Willey (1956), doubting the supposed gulf between farmer and priest, notes that the hypothesis receives no support in the form of continued peasant occupation once lowland theocratic control had been broken. He writes: "If collapse occurred—and, indeed, something did occur—Maya priest and peasant collapsed and vanished together." Thompson (1954a, pp. 88—89) however has shown that there is good evidence for post-constructional (i. e., post-ceremonial in the Classic pattern) occupation at a number of lowland sites. But we still lack an explanation of why that too ultimately failed.

Classic cultural development and subsidence, all pivoting on ceremonialism, stand as major problems in American archaeology. One can here only note their existence and hope that data will continue to be gathered to explain the foundation, growth, persistence and cessation of Classic culture. The material dealt with in this study is largely a manifestation, albeit often minor, of that culture. The objects and contexts are heavily ceremonial rather than utilitarian, a fact consistent with the location of the excavations. Along with monuments, buildings, and elaborate pottery, these artifacts, caches, and burials definitely attest to the activity of a highly specialized group whose presence has been tentatively accounted for in the preceding remarks.

The collection, comprising objects of stone, bone, shell, and clay has first of all been empirically divided by substance. Stone artifacts fall naturally into those produced by chipping and those by grinding (and pecking). Further cultural subdivision has been in terms of utilitarian as against ceremonial (and ornamental) usage. When feasible, analysis follows functional headings, but many headings are necessarily formal or technical, for use is all too often uncertain or completely speculative. In short, classification has been frankly patterned on A. V. Kidder's *The Artifacts of Uaxactun, Guatemala* (1947; see p. 4). The two collections, derived from comparable sites, warrant compatable terminology and arrangement if comparisons are not to be hindered. The system facilitates description and further permits categories that not infrequently are presumed to be aboriginally valid.

The system, as used here, is obviously weak in spots, particularly where it allows formal lumping of objects originally distinct in function. Such categories cannot be considered cultural although their components may be culturally significant. This dilemma largely stems from the normal but not necessarily scientific inclination to tie loose ends together. Fortunately in lowland artifactual study there is rarely need of committing this obvious error. Here one recalls Brew's belief (Brew, 1946, pp. 44—46) that types are arbitrary, artificial products of the classifier. This is likely true to a certain extent, but it is hard not to believe that our "obsidian flake-blade," "bone awl," even "eccentric flint," approximate as types what artisans had in mind when making them and what priests and all others had in mind while using them.

In instances where the classification must be arbitrary, it is made in the belief that future excavations will yield a quantity sufficient to permit a cultural and thus useful classification. A subjective factor is also present in various categories, especially in those resulting from fine distinctions (size, peripheral details, etc.). This can only be justified if the results are at present or potentially of cultural value. Perhaps subdivisions have been made at the wrong point of what appears as a continuum. If so, future collections may provide a better basis for division and even grouping.

Caches and burials, being common sources have been included in this report. Caches have led to containers, and burials to skeletal remains and various mortuary features.

A thorough bibliography on Piedras Negras has been assembled by Satterthwaite (1943a, pp. 32a—32b), to which have been added subsequent papers in the series *Piedras Negras Archaeology: Architecture*. Part 1, No. 1 of this series contains the final plan of the site.

"Dedicatory" and supposedly contemporaneous dates of Piedras Negras monuments in this report have been taken from Morley (1937—1938) and Thompson (1944).

Realizing that the present study's worth lies most of all in its potential usefulness as a comparative source in future work, I have made an effort to interrelate objects, their proveniences and illustrations, and finally to allow for easy working from illustrations to descriptions. Field numbers of all objects are given when possible with the illustrations. This will aid correlation of objects with architectural data published and pending in the aforementioned series.

A few irregular abbreviations have been used. "L," "W," "T," and "D" signify length, width, thickness, and diameter respectively, all dimensions being in centimeters. "UM" refers to the University Museum and indicates that the object is presently on loan to that institution. "NM" indicates that a certain object is to be found in the Guatemala National Museum. "Left" and "right" are the observer's. Caches are frequently mentioned; for example, "Cache O—13—1." The designation is a compound of the particular structure (locus) with which it was associated, here Structure O—13, and an entirely arbitrary cache number, "—1." Burial numeration, likewise arbitrary, agrees with previously published references.

With minor changes this study is published from a Doctoral Dissertation submitted to the Graduate School of the University of Pennsylvania. I wish to express my appreciation to Dr. Linton Satterthwaite for the many ways in which he aided, guided, and corrected this study. Factual and interpretive errors are, however, most certainly mine. I especially wish to thank him for allowing me to use his field records and other data and ideas, particularly in relation to Piedras Negras stratigraphy. I am also grateful to Dr. Alfred Kidder II for his general advice; to Dr. Wilton M. Krogman for checking my skeletal observations; to Mr. Robert E. Smith for ceramic identifications; and to Dr. Horace G. Richards for identification of shells.

Miss Geraldine Bruckner, Editor of Museum publications, handled the difficult task of editing the manuscript and supervising its publication. Most drawings of objects are by the writer. Important exceptions are a group of intricately inscribed stingray spines (Fig. 56) and certain other objects from Burial 5 (Figs. 48, 49, 53). These were drawn by Miss Tatiana Proskouriakoff, and some of them have been published elsewhere. Drawings of grave structures are by the writer after field drawings and photographs by Satterthwaite. I owe thanks to Mr. Reuben Goldberg for his precise photo-copies of many line drawings, and to Mr. A. Eric Parkinson for chemical analyses. Finally, I thank the various people who kindly provided information of one sort or another; they are credited throughout this report.

Part 2

ARTIFACTS

OBJECTS OF CHIPPED STONE

UTILITARIAN IMPLEMENTS

I. IMPLEMENTS OF LIGHT-COLORED FLINT

Material. Coarse, occasionally pitted flint, ranging in color from an almost pure white through light pink, cloudy blue, to a dirty gray.

A. GENERAL UTILITY TOOLS, 18.

1. *One end rounded, other pointed*, 12 (Fig. 1 a–k,m). L 11.2–18.5; T 2.3–5 cm. Edges are usually quite sharp. Apart from some peripheral retouching, workmanship tends to be rough. Polished areas on one thick, dull-edged specimen (Fig. 1 d), with chip scars erased, point to possible use as a digging implement. Signs of hafting are lacking on all these objects.
2. *Celtiform*, 1 (Fig. 2 a). L 9.3; T 4.3 cm. Relatively thick, crude, with rounded ends and converging sides. One end is broken and sides are blunt.
3. *Rectangular*, 5 (Fig. 2 b–f). L 6.4–10.1; T 2.9–4 cm. A group characterized by approximately parallel long sides and convex ends. One (Fig. 2 c) has fairly keen edges, but those of the others are dull and battered. No visible signs of hafting.

COMMENT. Essentially core bifaced tools. These heavy, roughly worked implements, particularly the first group (1), closely resemble certain Uaxactun artifacts termed by Kidder (1947, p. 5) "chopping(?), or general utility tools." A number of the Piedras Negras examples, however, are outstanding for their quite sharp, retouched edges, a feature seemingly rare in these tools at other sites. Edges being what they are, these might have served as quite effective chopping implements, though, as noted, no tell-tale hafting scars are observable. Perhaps some were used as hand-axes. A few implements polished like that in Figure 1 d have been found at Uaxactun (Kidder, *ibid.*), Benque Viejo (Thompson, 1940, p. 25), Labna (E. H. Thompson, 1897, Fig. 8), Tenosique (Satterthwaite, verbal information), and Louisville, British Honduras (Chicago Museum of Natural History). Besides Labna, they are common in other Puuc sites (Proskouriakoff, verbal information).

While the Piedras Negras pieces are Classic in date, choppers at Uaxactun extend well back into Formative times (Kidder, *op. cit.*) and continued in use there without noticeable change throughout the site's occupation. It is evident that the chopper, with or without the interrogation point, was a lowland implement and was particularly prevalent in the central part of this region. Kidder (*ibid.*) notes its rarity to the north and its absence at Chichen Itza in Post-Classic times. It is also unknown at Mayapan (Proskouriakoff, verbal information). Interestingly, none occurred at Copan (Longyear, 1952). None, I believe, have ever been reported from highland Maya sites.

It is increasingly evident that these rough and seemingly clumsy artifacts were exclusively a Maya product in Mesoamerica and were actually confined to a rather restricted portion of the Maya area itself. The distribution of these particular tools, quite apart from the definite problem of function, is very puz-zling, but it is really only one aspect of a complex situation in Mesoamerica regarding both ground and chipped implements—a situation as yet far from analyzed. Further remarks on the distribution and problematical antiquity of these choppers have been made elsewhere by the writer (Coe, 1955 a).

For anyone preferring sources functionally cut and dried, the presence of four choppers in a probable sub-stela cache (Cache O–13–56) is disconcerting. Another was found in Niche 3 of Burial 10 together with a possibly unfinished chopper (see Fig. 1,1 and below). Utilitarian implements in ceremonial contexts are not unknown elsewhere at Piedras Negras, as, for example, in the case of the cached broken celts in Figure 43 r–t). Still, one might argue that such celts were employed for ceremonial ends.

B. HAMMERSTONES, 2 (Fig. 2 g,h). D 8.1, 8.2 cm. Roughly spherical tools with extremely battered surfaces.

COMMENT. Evidently lacking at Uaxactun. Piedras Negras, however, did not yield implements comparable to the latter's elongated flint pecking or pounding tools (Kidder, 1947, Fig. 61, 1–o).

C. SCRAPER, 1 (Fig. 3 s). L 6; T 1.1 cm. Core-struck, unretouched flake, one edge slightly work scarred.

D. PROBLEMATICAL IMPLEMENT, 1 (Fig. 3 t). Fragmentary. T 1.4 cm. Elongated, bowed from end to end. Chip scars on concave side, but convexity throughout is secondarily well polished and very smooth with traces of blue paint (?) evident.

COMMENT. Possibly an elaborate pot polisher or even a paint grinder. Gann (1918, p. 89, Fig. 33) has recorded a somewhat similar object from northern British Honduras.

E. BLANK (?), 1 (Fig. 1,l). L 15.5; T 3.9 cm. Apparently an unfinished implement. Approximately triangular in cross-section with lime encrusted cavity on apex. Found with a flint chopper (Fig. 1 a), both within a drum-shaped mass of flint chips in Niche 3 of Burial 10 (Fig. 67, 43).

II. IMPLEMENTS OF BROWN FLINT

Material. Greenish brown to chocolate brown flint, opaque except for slight peripheral translucency. Heavily patinated, in a few cases obscuring flint coloration. In contrast to the flints used for objects described in the previous section, these flints may have been imported.

A. PROJECTILE POINTS, 7

1. *Stemmed*, 3 (Fig. 3 h–j). Complete specimens: L 4.6, 5.4; T .75, 1 cm. respectively. Bifacially chipped, symmetrically triangular bodies with tapered stems. *j* previously figured by Satterthwaite (1933, Pl. VII, E).

2. *Unstemmed*, 4 (Fig. 3 k–n). L 4.6–7.5; T .6–1 cm. Great variation in overall forms and, to a lesser extent, in workmanship as well. Note differential patination in *n*.

COMMENT. Although the number of Piedras Negras points is small and few generalizations are possible, this paucity in itself may be significant. For instance, the lozenge *n* does not occur among the Uaxactun specimens, but, except for this specimen, good form agreement exists between the two sites. No points with expanding stems appeared at Piedras Negras and this is in accord with Kidder's comment (1947, p. 9 ; see also Woodbury and Trik, 1953, p. 228) on the relatively late position of this type in Mesoamerica.

The existence of hard woods in the lowlands and the rarity of stone points (and the quality flint to make them ?) suggest that wood was extensively used for hunting and military weapons. Bone may have been so employed, though no examples came to light at Piedras Negras. The size and weight of these flint points probably precluded use as arrowheads. Some, conceivably, served as lanceheads. Evidence is lacking at Piedras Negras for the spear thrower, or atlatl, but sculptural depictions of them do occur in the general area (see Proskouriakoff, 1950, p. 96; Follett, 1932, Fig. 39).

Hunting was surely an important occupation at Piedras Negras and there may have been considerable prestige in the killing of jaguars, the skins of which were made into ceremonial skirts and throne mats. Traps and snares can only be presumed; codical and ethnological Maya examples are described by Luis (1954). There is no evidence for the blowgun at Piedras Negras, but a Classic polychrome plate from Quintana Roo (Blom, 1950) suggests that it might not have been unknown at that site.

In view of the evidence in the sculptures and murals of the not overly distant Bonampak, warfare was likely an important feature of Piedras Negras ceremonial life. Local signs of this are manifested in Stela 12 which depicts a group of roped, naked individuals over whom stand what are presumably their captors.

Lintel 4 similarly shows bound, subjected personages. Bonampak has amply shown the Classic lowland Maya to have been, at the very least, internally aggressive with regard to ritualistic objectives. The evidence for Classic Maya warfare has been studied by Rands (1952). That Classic culture did not necessarily flourish under entirely peaceful, intellectual, aesthetic conditions is a factor of importance, especially in view of Steward's thesis of pacific cultural development (Steward, 1947, pp. 103–105). Nevertheless, expansionistic wars were likely lacking.

B. PROJECTILE POINTS OR KNIVES, 10 (Fig. 3 a–g, o, q, r). Reconstructed length of *a* is roughly 20 cm.; others 8.2 to 14.5 cm.; T .7–1.3. Majority are double pointed, thin bodied, keen edged, with excellent overall chipping. Specimen in *q* probably represents butt end.

COMMENT. Unlike the laurel-leaf blades from caches (discussed under Ceremonial Chipped Stone; Figs. 19, 20) these specimens frequently are use-scarred. Lanceheads as well as knives are possible functions for them, though it is impossible to assign one or the other in any case. A blade, comparable to those in Fig. 3 a–e, appears as a lancehead on Stela 12; interestingly, the hafting thongs are clearly depicted.

C. KNIFE (?), 1 (Fig. 3 p). Original L ca. 6.5; T .8 cm. Triangular in cross-section, slight lateral convexity on underside. Core-struck and utilized without retouching.

COMMENT. Crudely analogous in form and technique to the obsidian prismatic blades discussed under Obsidian.

This object has been mentioned by Satterthwaite (1933, p. 17), who noted its quite uncommon characteristics. Re-examination lessens the possibility of a former tang. But as he pointed out, it does immediately bring to mind the "hastate and tanged" blades analyzed by Joyce (1932) and more recently by Kidder (1947, p. 19). They seem to appear most frequently in British Honduras and are very scarce in highland Guatemala, are prevalent in lower Central America, and even occur in Haitian archaeology. This distribution and its possible signifance have been treated elsewhere by the writer (Coe, 1957).

D. KNIFE-LIKE IMPLEMENT, 1 (Fig. 3 v). L7.9; T .7 cm. Bifacially worked, but roughly, with occasional secondary chipping. Thin, with heavy white patina. Comparable in shape to previously described choppers. Formed part of a group of objects accompanying Skeleton C, Burial 5 (Fig. 64, *19*).

E. GOUGE (?), 1 (Fig. 3 u). L 3.4; T .8 cm. Small, stemmed, laterally retouched, but with sharp unretouched edge on broad end. If employed as a gouge, presumably hafted.

III. IMPLEMENTS OF OBSIDIAN

Material. Of the roughly 140 prismatic flake-blades available for study, none are of the red variety of obsidian. Only one example of green obsidian (NM) has been noted; this assuredly was a Mexican import. One fragment (UM) is jet, that is, absolutely black along its edges. The commonest variety of obsidian employed at Piedras Negras was evidently the clear (opaque grayish when thick). A clear obsidian with heavy black streaking is also frequent in the collection. A less common variety is opaque gray, even when thin. An excellent distributional study of these and other varieties of obsidian has been provided by Kidder (1947, pp. 10–11).

A. POLISHERS, 3 (Figs. 30 f; 37 d, e). Rather small chunks of obsidian abraded on one side, with the exception of Figure 37 e, which is a re-used core fragment. Interestingly, one of these (Fig. 30 f) was included in Cache R–11–6.

COMMENT. Obsidian rubbing tools did not appear at Uaxactun. These objects, are probably too much abraded to have served as pot polishers. Other examples of abraded obsidians from Mesoamerica have been listed by Kidder (*ibid.*, p. 29; A. L. Smith and Kidder, 1943, p. 163) but the present specimens are perhaps the only ones that can be precisely assigned. The cached specimen conceivably was specially made for votive purposes.

B. GROOVED IMPLEMENT, 1 (Fig. 37 c). A small fragmentary piece, longitudinally faceted, oval in section, with a full groove near remaining end. Surely a re-used, exceptionally exhausted core.

C. DRILL, 1 (Fig. 37 a). L 6.6 cm. Reworked oval prismatic core, striking platform unmodified. Although this object does not evidence great usage, it was very probably fashioned as a drill. Field number is lacking. There is, however, always the chance that this was a cache item and even intended as an eccentric obsidian. The Ricketsons (1937, Pl. 60 b 4) show a remarkably similar object from a Uaxactun cache.

COMMENT. If truly a drill, it adds to the slight list of such obsidian artifacts in Mesoamerica (for listing, see Kidder, 1947, p. 29; also Kidder, Jennings, and Shook, 1946, pp. 121—22), where they are known to occur throughout all ceramic periods but are very infrequent. Locally, apart from Uaxactun, the obsidian drill occurs at Baking Pot (Ricketson, 1929, p. 14).

D. FLAKE-POINT, 1 (Fig. 37 b). Unretouched, small, thin, triangular in cross-section, tapered sides, sharp point.

E. FLAKE-BLADES, at least 110 from general debris. Practically all are broken. Edges of these unretouched prismatic implements are as a rule minutely nicked from use. Length of three unbroken specimens: 4.7, 6.1, 6.4 cm. Widths of all range from .6 to 2.3 cm., majority fall close to 1 cm. Other flake-blades were recovered from caches; these have been treated in the following section devoted to ceremonial obsidian objects.

COMMENT. As to the functional characteristics of these blades, Kidder (in Wauchope, 1948, p. 160) writes that they—"...must have been invaluable tools. Their sharp edges will cut string readily and for whittling soft wood they are practically as serviceable as a steel blade. Held by the two ends and used as a draw-shave they are especially effective, nor are they soon dulled (by the loss of tiny chips) if manipulated carefully. Work across the grain, or even with the grain if the wood be hard, spoils the edge rather quickly."

F. CORES, 2 (Fig. 37 k, l). Two fragments of exhausted polyhedral cores, one round in cross-section, the other oval. Platforms smooth. These, of course, served for the production of the elongate, parallel-edged flake-blades just described. At Piedras Negras few cores have survived due to the custom of fashioning the exhausted nuclei into eccentric shapes. Unaltered examples were however occasionally cached (e. g. Fig. 37 f—j); these and the eccentrics will be discussed in the following section.

COMMENT ON OBSIDIAN FLAKE-BLADES AND CORES. The technique employed in producing these flake-blades, so numerous in Mesoamerica, has been fully described by Kidder (Kidder, Jennings, and Shook, 1946, pp. 135—36; see also Ellis, 1940, pp. 48—49) and much information on their distribution is to be found in his Uaxactun report (1947, pp. 15—16). I might mention here that Piedras Negras, unlike many sites, failed to yield blades in burials. All were from caches, test pits, general debris, and surface collecting.

Since Kidder's writing, excavations in various areas of the New World have done much to amplify the time-space aspect of these implements. One outstanding find was made at Santa Isabel Iztapan, north of Mexico City, where an obsidian prismatic flake-blade was found with other artifacts in direct association with mammoth remains (Aveleyra and Maldonado, 1953, pp. 338—39, Fig. 5,5). The writers suggest an Upper Pleistocene dating of 10,000 to 12,000 years B. P. This estimate is confirmed by a recent radiocarbon date for the geologic matrix (Libby, 1955).

Flake-blades and/or parent cores are to be found in practically all Mesoamerican Formative or Pre-Classic deposits (Kidder, *op. cit.*). Often tremendous quantities of blades are found. In the Maya area their presence in early levels like Las Charcas (Shook, 1951, p. 97), Yarumela Eo-Archaic (Canby, 1951, pp. 80,81) and Uaxactun Mamom (Kidder,*op. cit.*) illustrates the local extent of early utilization. One curious exception to their temporal ubiquity was San Jose, where none were found in Period I (Chicanel-like) deposits (Thompson, 1939, p. 172). Perhaps more significantly, they failed to appear until Late Classic times in the Tampico-Panuco region (Ekholm, 1944, p. 489; MacNeish, 1954). The latter exception was evidently not due to any lack of obsidian, for chips occurred in all earlier levels.

As Kidder (*op. cit.*) has pointed out, the obsidian flake-blade is almost entirely lacking in South America, Costa Rica being its southernmost limit. In recent years increased excavations in Panama and Colombia tend to corroborate this observation. However, while no cores have been found, flint flake-blades, existing in all Haitian periods, evidence knowledge of the technique (see Rouse, 1941, pp. 29—31). Tschopik (1946, p. 79) reports prismatic flake-blades and cores as occurring in the Peruvian Huancayo rock shelter sites—sites which are very probably pre-ceramic. And finally, Ecuador has occasionally been cited in regard to these distributional exceptions (Kidder, *op. cit.*, p. 15; Kidder, in "Tax and others," 1953, p. 48; also Bushnell, 1951, p. 68).

North American localities showing this technique, though culturally and temporally diverse, are more frequent than one would suspect. These include Poverty Point, the Flint Ridge site in Ohio and Hopewell in general, also the Paleo-Indian Shoop site in Pennsylvania, and a "series of small Basket Maker III sites" in Arizona (Haag and Webb, 1953; Griffin, 1949, pp. 89—90; Willey and Phillips, 1955, p. 736; Witthoft, 1952; Kidder, 1947, p. 15; UM collections). Gebhard (1946, pp. 510—11, 674—75, 1151—52) additionally lists two dozen or so sites in the United States yielding flake-blades and conical polyhedral cores. Flake-blades ("lamellar flakes") and small cores (fully and semi-polyhedral) have additionally an impressive Arctic incidence; for one, they form an important part of the Denbigh Flint Complex, for which a dating of "more than 5000. . . and less than 9000 years" has been proposed (Giddings, 1951, Fig. 61 b; 1955). Comparable blades, though no cores, were found in the lowest level of the Trail Creek site in the central Seward Peninsula; a radiocarbon test indicates a date of around 6000 years (Rainey, 1953, pp. 44—45). Comparable artifacts have appeared in the Alaska Campus site (Nelson, 1937; Rainey, 1940, Fig. 15,1—6), the Aleutians (Laughlin, 1951, Fig. 35, 5, 6, 8; Laughlin and Marsh, 1954), and the Brooks Range (Irving, 1951, Fig. 34, 9—15; Solecki, 1951, Fig. 36 e, h) as well as in the Mackenzie River region (MacNeish, 1954 a). Collins (1953, pp. 35,38; see also Knuth, 1954) has noted their existence with Dorset remains as far east as Greenland. Additional bibliography and a discussion of terminology has been given by Solecki (1955).

This brief review of prepared cores and the elongate, parallel-sided flake-blades which they yield has ranged far beyond Piedras Negras, but it serves to reiterate the possibility of their being a true Amerasian inter-connective. Nelson's original inference of Old World origin, based on occurrences of core and blades in Mongolia and Alaska, has lately been reinforced by continued Arctic discoveries. That their presence in the Americas might be explained as diffusion from northeast Asia has received additional support from Rainey (1940 ; 1953), Gebhard (*op. cit.*, p. 511), and Willey and Phillips (*op. cit.*, p. 794).

If one can rely on the few dates and estimates at hand, it is evident that the core-and-blade technique was a component of some early American hunting cultures roughly 5000 to possibly 10,000 years ago. Its oldest known occurrence seems to be Santa Isabel Iztapan. With the possible exception of Huancayo, the early distribution does not include South America. Almost universal in later Mesoamerica, the technique disappears below Costa Rica; the Ecuadoran obsidian specimens, conceivably the result of coastal trade with Mesoamerica, are most perplexing. As plotted by Gebhard and others, the lower North American distribution is lacking in continuity and focus—essentially here-and-there in time and space. The Arctic incidence, though, possesses time depth and direction. But, in view of the apparent chronological precedence of the Santa Isabel Iztapan blade, one cannot now discount local reinvention. Distribution alone would suggest this in the case of the Haitian flint examples.

GENERAL COMMENT AND COMPARISON OF CHIPPED UTILITARIAN IMPLEMENTS

Along with items like metates, these implements largely constitute the cultural remains of the lay stratum of Piedras Negras. They tell something of proficiency and function. The category, comprising as it does both obsidian and flint artifacts, possesses enough characteristics to type it as lowland Maya in origin were its actual source unknown. The presence of choppers is itself sufficient; close resemblances of certain flint points to others from Uaxactun would aid localization. The quantity of flake-blades and obsidian varieties might help in culture area placement, but little more.

The sources of the materials employed were both local and distant, the latter represented by obsidian and presumably dark flints. Surely both were imported in unworked form. These were fashioned into tools for chopping, scraping, killing, cutting, and possibly digging and drilling.

Presuming that this portion of the collection is fairly representative of the chipped tools used at Piedras Negras, it appears deficient alongside the Uaxactun inventory with respect to elongate pounding implements, flint drills (?), scrapers, and scraper-awls as well as obsidian points. The two sites, however, are related by choppers and certain point forms. But, on the whole, the people of Uaxactun appear to have had a more varied assemblage of chipped implements at their disposal. If the sampling factor is assumed to be equal in both cases, then basic, prosaic distinctions emerge for the two despite an impressive uniformity evident in hierarchic art, architecture, and calendrical matters.

CEREMONIAL CHIPPED STONE

I. OBJECTS OF FLINT

This group is made up largely of the so-called "eccentric" flints recovered at Piedras Negras. Since a great many are quite symmetrical, the term "eccentric" is, of course, inappropriate. But it is here retained because it is a traditional one applied in Maya archaeology to impractical, exotic flints of a variety of forms found in votive deposits and very infrequently in burials. None show any signs of use and all were probably fashioned for the ceremonial occasion. At Piedras Negras the majority can be assigned to specific caches; others apparently came from disturbed caches, while unfortunately a great many flints canot be exactly placed because they were burned in an almost disastrous fire which broke out at the expedition camp one season. And, in a few cases, cataloguing deficiencies do not allow precise assignments. If not mentioned in the text, the provenience of an item is given in the caption accompanying its illustration and subsequent reference to the section devoted to caches will show its associations. Tables 1 and 2 will also be of help.

The Piedras Negras eccentric flints have been grouped morphologically with notes on the distribution of cognate flints elsewhere. Many of the flints fall into easily definable categories; others just about defy description, these being more truly "eccentric." The latter have been conveniently lumped under "unclassified," thus underscoring the elementary nature of the classification. It should be kept in mind that all these flints might be broadly divided into a bifacial group and a group to cover flint flakes unaltered apart from peripheral chipping.

Mr. A. Hamilton Anderson kindly provided information on the eccentric forms recently found in two Benque Viejo caches by Mr. Michael Stewart. Presumably Late Classic in date and evidently from structure caches rather than sub-stela caches, these flints are presently in the Jubilee Library, Belize. Photographs of others gathered by Teobert Maler, and now in the American Museum of Natural History, were given the writer by Dr. Gordon F. Ekholm.

Material. Both dark and light-colored flints were employed. Some of the better executed pieces were made of the darker variety. Surfaces are generally patinated and, in a few instances, mottled.

A. ECCENTRIC FLINTS, 255. (Minimum)

1. *Ring*, 1 (Fig. 4 j). D 11.2; T 1.6 cm. From Cache O—13—6. A finely worked piece. Outer edge deeply serrated with plain inner edge. Chipped so as to produce an angular ridge on both surfaces. The making of this flint was probably to a large extent initially facilitated by a deep central pit or natural perforation in the core. Flints with natural perforations are known to have been available, for instance, in Caches J—6—2 and J- 6—4 (Figs. 13 h; 14 e).

DISTRIBUTION. *British Honduras*: Pusilha, one serrated ring from Mound I and a plain edged example from Terrace 3 (Gruning, 1930, Pl. XXII, Figs. 1, 3; Joyce, 1932, Pl. IV, 2 a, 3 a); also two serrated rings probably in Stela E (9.15.0.0.0?) cache (Joyce, Gann, Gruning, and Long, 1928, p. 333, Pl. XXXV, Fig. 1; Joyce, *op. cit.*, Pl. IV, 1 a, 5 a). Benque Viejo, two small serrated specimens (Joyce, *ibid.*, Pl. IV, 6 a, 7 a). *Guatemala*: Tikal, two plain edged rings from beneath Stela 16 (9.14.0.0.0) and Stela A—21 (Kidder, 1947, Fig. 8 h, t); and a serrated example in cache of Stela 21 (9.15.5.0.0) (Berlin, 1951, Fig. 13, 1). None of these flints duplicates the size and excellence of that from Piedras Negras.

2. *Crescents*, 32.

a. Plain edged, 15 (Figs. 4 k; 10 f—h; 11 k; 12 s; 13 e, n, o; 14 d, h; 15 e, r; 17 a; 18 h). W 5.8—17.3; T .95—1.4 cm. While in basic form a relatively homogeneous group, workmanship ranges from the notching of simple, thin flakes (see Fig. 10 f—h) up to one of the finest of the Piedras Negras flints (Fig. 17 a).

DISTRIBUTION. *British Honduras*: Pusilha, two in a sub-stela cache, Stela E (9.15.0.0.0?) and one each from Mound I and Terrace 3 (Joyce, Gann, Gruning, and Long, 1928, Pl. XXXV, Fig. 1; Gruning, 1930, Pl. XXII, Figs. 1, 2, see also Joyce, 1932, Pl. IV). Benque Viejo, Gann (1918, Fig. 40 d) records one example; four in Cache C and one in Cache B, Stewart excavations (Jubilee Library). San Jose, two in a Period IV cache (Thompson, 1939, Pl. 24 b 4, b 6). *Guatemala*: Naranjo, two in cache beneath Stela 15 (9.13.0.0.0???) (Maler, 1908, Fig. 19). Tikal, two from sub-stela caches (Kidder, 1947, Fig. 8 i, u). *Honduras*: One very large specimen so labeled in the Museum of the American Indian. *Mexico*, Chichen Itza, a flint crescent occurred in a Post-Classic grave (E. H. Thompson and J. E. S. Thompson, 1938, Fig. 18 j).

b. Serrated, 16 (Figs. 5 o; 7 m; 8 a, k, l; 11 j, l; 13 f, g; 14 c, i; 16 j; 17 b, h; possibly 15 i and 19 k). W 5.1—16.6; T .8—1.4 cm. Like those with plain edges, some of these are finely made while others are quite poorly done. Outer edge of one from Cache R—9—1 (Fig. 17 h) is exceptionally deeply serrated.

DISTRIBUTION. *British Honduras*: Benque Viejo, six in Cache C and one in Cache B, Stewart excavations (Jubilee Library); three recorded by Joyce (1932, Pl. IV, 2 b, 5 b, 6 b) and Gann (1918, Fig. 44 g, h). One large serrated crescent is labeled as "Cayo District" (Joyce, *op. cit.*, Pl. IV, 2 d). Heye (1925, Fig. 44) shows still another example from the Colony. *Guatemala*: Naranjo, one from Stela 13 cache (9.17.10.0.0) (Maler, 1908, Fig. 19). Among a group of flints collected by Maler and now in the American Museum of Natural History and catalogued as "Ticul" (Yucatan) is a beautiful example of this form; Kidder (1947, p. 27) believes that Maler possibly encountered these flints in the Usumacinta region because of similarities to the Piedras Negras flints. *Honduras*: One enormous example, spiked and relatively open rather than closed nearly in form, in the Museum of the American Indian, is labeled as from "Honduras."

c. Incompleted crescent, 1 (Fig. 13 m). W 10.7 cm. Cache J—6—2. The appearance of comparable flints at other sites suggests that this piece was deliberately left unfinished. It provides good evidence that crescents were fashioned from the center outward, perhaps beginning with a natural hole.

DISTRIBUTION. *British Honduras*: Benque Viejo, Joyce (1932, Pl. IV, 1 c) illustrates a serrated example; and three plain ones were found in Cache B, Stewart excavations (Jubilee Library); one of the Stewart eccentrics however possesses a projection on the base of its inner convexity (as in Gann, 1918, Fig. 42).

3. *Trident-crescents*, 36 (Figs. 4 a, h, 1; 5 e; 7 a–1; 9 v; 11 a, d–i; 15 g, p; 16 d, k; 17 1; 18 b, c, j–m). L 5.3–16.4; T .8–1.6 cm. Essentially a crescent, serrated or plain, with a tridentate lower convexity, with central spike tapered and invariably the longest of the three. Aberrantly related to this group are certain flints (Figs. 7 d; 15 g; 18 k, l) that are composed of a simple crescent on a tapered stem. Trident-crescents, despite their frequency in flint, do not occur as eccentric obsidians (see Table 3).

DISTRIBUTION. *British Honduras*: San Jose, one seeming aberrant specimen in a Period IV cache (Thompson, 1939, Pl. 24, a 5). Nohmul, a tremendous flint of this shape is said to have come from near this site, as well as two smaller examples (Gann, 1918, pp. 88–89, Pl. 15 e; also Gann and Gann, 1939, pp. 22–23). Two other fine flints with this form, exact provenience unknown, have been illustrated by Stevens (1870, Fig. 5) and by Lane-Fox (1857, p. 94). A triple spiked flint ("British Honduras") with a diameter of ca. 35 cm. is shown by Joyce (1932, Pl. V. 2 b). Curiously, trident-crescents have not been recorded at either Benque Viejo or Pusilha, sites prolific in eccentric objects. *Guatemala*: Uaxactun, three very open crescents, probably belonging to this category, are from Stela 4 cache (8.18.0.0.0) (Ricketson and Ricketson, 1937, Pl. 59, b 1, b 3). Two others, each exceedingly well made with finely notched periphery, form part of the group collected by Maler and referred to above. While the quantity of trident - crescents at Piedras adds weight to Kidder's suggestion as to the probable source of the "Ticul" pieces, this pair is on the whole far superior to those of Piedras Negras in symmetry, workmanship, and detail.

4. *Double crescents*, 10 (Figs. 5 c; 10 d, n, r; 11 m, n; 15 q; 17 c, d; 19 c). L 5.2–9.2; T .8–1.4 cm. Seemingly a distinctive type although variable in detail. Edges either plain, tightly serrated, or even spiked. Long sides of a few are centrally notched by eversion. All typified by two crescents with joined bases. One serrated specimen (Fig. 17 c) is asymmetric.

DISTRIBUTION. *British Honduras*: Benque Viejo, one resembling that in figure 17 c is illustrated by Gann (1918, Fig. 44 i). Baking Pot, one with open crescents from a cache in Mound E (Ricketson, 1929, Pl. 13 h). San Jose, a fine example formed part of a Period IV cache (Thompson, 1939, Pl. 24 b 5).

5. *Scorpions*, 11 (Figs. 4 n; 5 f, i, m; 7 r; 9 w; 10 1; 12 e; 17 g, j, k). L 5.5–9.7; T 1–1.1 cm. This naturalistic form is best shown in Figure 17 g with tail and pincers clearly represented. Figure 7 r is exceptionally elaborate. Other flints included here are less realistic and their classification as "scorpions" may be somewhat forced in certain instances, but the hook-tail and suggestions of legs or pincers are always present.

DISTRIBUTION. "Scorpions" from sites to the east are very conventionalized, having been reduced to the diagnostic tail, with other features, such as legs and pincers, represented by a serrated bulb (for discussion of latter, see Joyce, 1932, p. xxi). *British Honduras*: Pusilha, a number of these serrated bulb scorpions are figured by Gruning (1930, Pl. XXII, Fig. 3) and by Joyce (*op. cit.*, Pl. III, 4 a, 8 a). Benque Viejo, perhaps as many as six from non-stela caches and a seventh from cache of Stela 1 (10.1.0.0.0) (Gann, 1918, Figs. 40 e; 41; 44 d, e; also Joyce, *op. cit.*, Pl. III, 5 a–7 a); two other typical pieces in Cache C and one in Cache B, Stewart excavations (Jubilee Library). *Guatemala*: Tikal, Stela 16 cache (9.14.0.0.0) contained one, as did Stela A–21 cache (Kidder, 1947, Fig. 8 e, n); also one from cache of Stela 21 (9.15.5.0.0) (Berlin, 1951, Fig. 13, 3); Joyce (*op. cit.*, Pl. III, 1 a) shows a good example which, among others, might have come from beneath either Stela 5 (9.15.15.0.0) or Stela 10 (9.3.13.0.0?? with a style date by Proskouriakoff [1950] of 9.8.0.0.0 ± 2 katuns) (see Kidder, *op. cit.*, p. 17).

6. *Centipedes*, 12 (Figs. 4 e; 5 j; 9 j; 10 c, k, u; 12 a–c; 15 d; 16 f; 17 i). L 7.5–13; T .6–1.1 cm. Elongate, laterally serrated flints with ends either concave or double notched. That these really do depict centipedes is of course entirely conjectural (for discussion, see Joyce 1932, p.xxi). Figure 4 e is a weak example of this otherwise uniform group.

DISTRIBUTION. *British Honduras*: Benque Viejo, one (Joyce, *op. cit.*, Pl. III 1 c). *Guatemala*: Naranjo, a good example from beneath Stela 15 (9.13.0.0.0 ???) (Maler, 1908, Fig. 19). Tikal, centipedes were found in caches associated with Stela 21 (9.15.5.0.0), Stela 16 (9.14.0.0.0), and Stela A–21 (Berlin, 1951, Fig. 13, 5; Kidder, 1947, Fig. 8, a, q); Joyce (*op. cit.*, Pl. III, 2 c) pictures another centipedal flint from Tikal (see Kidder, *op. cit.*, p. 17 for details of find).

7. *Anthropomorphs*, 2 (Figs. 12 m; 16 a). L 14, 6.7; T 1.2, .7 cm. respectively. Both surely were meant to represent the human form although all details beyond outline have been omitted.

DISTRIBUTION. All known anthropomorphic eccentrics are remarkably similar. *British Honduras*: San Jose, one in a cache dated as Period IV (Thompson, 1939, Pl. 24, c 3). Two other British Honduras flints with this form have been illustrated by Rice (1909, p. 361; also shown in Gann, 1918, Fig. 48) and Joyce (1932, Pl. V, 2 d). The latter may be from cache of Pusilha Stela F (see Joyce, Gann, Gruning, and Long, 1928, p. 334).

8. *Quadrupedal animals*, a pair (Fig. 16 g, h). L 7.3, 8; T .77, .75 cm. From Cache R–9–2. A unique pair that presumably represent animals.

DISTRIBUTION. Apart from scorpions and centipedes, faunal forms have been recovered at sites like San Jose and Baking Pot (see Kidder, 1947, p. 18).

9. *Discs*, 2 (Fig. 7 o, p). One with irregular edge, the other plain. Neither is truly round, Both from Cache O–13–10.

DISTRIBUTION. As might be expected, this simple form, both serrated and plain, has been found at a number of other sites. Joyce (1932, p. xxi) has related the serrated disc to a much "subsided" centipede. *British Honduras*: Baking Pot, one from a Mound E cache (Ricketson, 1929, Pl. 13 f). Pusilha, two from Terrace Hill (Joyce, *op. cit.*, Pl. III, 7 c, 2 d). Benque Viejo, three plain examples in Cache C and one similar one in Cache B, Stewart excavations (Jubilee Library). *Guatemala*: Uaxactun, a plain example in cache of Stela 22 (9.3.10.0.0) (Kidder, 1947, Fig. 67 a 3). Tikal, three discs, one of which definitely came from beneath Stela 21 (9.15.5.0.0) (Berlin, 1951, Fig. 13, 2; Joyce, *op. cit.*, Pl. III, 6 c; VI, 2 a).

10. *Crosses*, 5.
    a. Curved edge, 3 (Figs. 14 l, m; 16 i). D 4.8–7.2; T .75– .9 cm. Deeply notched cruciform discs. Symmetrical. Caches J–6–5 and R–9–2.

DISTRIBUTION. While similar in form, others appear to be somewhat rougher than the Piedras Negras examples. *British Honduras*: Benque Viejo, four (Gann, 1918, Fig. 44 a, b, f; 1896–97, p. p. 316, no. 4; Joyce, 1932, Pl. II, 3 c, 5 c, 7 c); also one each in Caches B and C, Stewart excavations (Jubilee Library). Pusilha, one cruciform flint reported from cache beneath Stela E (9.15.0.0.0 ?) (Joyce, Gann, Gruning, and Long, 1928, p. 333, Pl. XXXV, Fig. 1; also Joyce, 1932, Pl. II, 6 c).

    b. Flat edge, 2 (Fig. 10 m, p). L 3.5, 8.2; T .6, 1.1 cm. Cache O–13–47. Relatively crude pieces with notched corners. Those shown in Figure 19 i, j are probably parts of elaborate eccentrics.

DISTRIBUTION. Rare. Those from a Pusilha cache might possibly be considered representative of this admittedly weak subtype (see Joyce, Gann, Gruning, and Long, 1928, Pl. XXXV, Fig. 1, above crescent in center).

11. *Trifurcate*, 5 (Figs. 4 m; 8 m; 12 d; 13 t; 15 o). A catch-all class for a number of otherwise diverse flints. Some are simply rough discs that have been notched three times.

DISTRIBUTION. *British Honduras*: Benque Viejo, a resemblance is notable in one flint from this site (see Joyce, 1932, Pl. II, 2 c). *Guatemala*: Naranjo, the same is true for a flint from cache beneath Stela 15 (9.13.0.0.0 ???) (Maler, 1908, Fig. 19).

12. *Tridents*, 5 (Figs. 6 b, c; 11 o; 13 i, j). L 7–16; T 1–1.4 cm. A very distinctive form, best represented in the two from Cache O–13–10 (Figs. 6 b, c). One example (Fig. 13 i) is curious in having only one terminal projection rather than three and, in fact, may not belong to this cate-

gory at all. One might note here that the trident feature itself is frequent among the "Unclassified" eccentrics (below).

DISTRIBUTION. Elaborate tridents (e. g. Fig. 6 b) occur as follows. *Guatemala*: Uaxactun, this form is very prevalent among the eccentrics from this site and fine examples occur as early as 8.18. 0.0.0?; these are illustrated by Kidder (1947, p. 16, Figs. 7 c; 66; 67) and by the Ricketsons (1937, Pl. 56 b; 57). One of the Maler flints is a beautiful elongate trident with a uniquely notched stem; as noted, Kidder (*op. cit.*, p. 27) judges the collection to have come from the Usumacinta region. *Honduras*: Copan, one of the rare eccentrics to have been found at this site was a trident which formed part of the Hieroglyphic Stairway cache (Longyear, 1952, p. 110, Fig. 93 f, see also Kidder, *op. cit.*, Fig. 73 e).

13. *Double-pointed blades*, 6 (Figs. 4 g; 6 d, e; 9 b; 16 c; 18 p). L of whole specimens 8—13.4 cm. None show any signs of use and all are surely or presumably from caches. In one instance (Fig. 9 b), a chipped thin brown flint blade fragment was deposited with a number of unmatching flint flakes; it is possible that this is the remains of a utilitarian projectile point or knife that, for one reason or another, was included in a votive deposit.

DISTRIBUTION. Relatively small double-pointed blades of flint have been found in caches of other sites. *British Honduras*: Pusilha, one in a Mound I cache (Gruning, 1930, Pl. XXII, Fig. 2). Benque Viejo, nine in Cache B, Stewart excavations (Jubilee Library). *Guatemala*: Uaxactun, many from stela and structure caches; all seem to date from Early Classic times (see Kidder, 1947, p. 17, Figs. 7 a; 66—68; Ricketson and Ricketson., 1937, Pl. 54 a; also A. L. Smith, 1950, Table 8). Naranjo, Stela 15 cache (9.13.0.0.0???) produced a few of this type (Maler, 1908, Fig. 19). *Mexico*: El Palmar, two were cached beneath Stela 10 (9.15.15.0.0) and one in a second offering (Thompson, 1936; illustrated by Morley, 1947, Pl. 95 b; see also Kidder, *op. cit.*, p. 27).

14. *Notched double-pointed blades*, 25.
   a. Central opposed side notches, 14 (Figs. 4 b; 6 f, g; 8 c; 9 d; 11 b; 12 l; 13 c, d; 14 a; 15 n; 16 b; 18 n, o). L 6.5—13.3; T .6—1.6 cm. Majority symmetrical, some serrated and others plain-edged.

DISTRIBUTION. *British Honduras*: Pusilha, one from beneath Stela E (9.15.0.0.0?) is serrated (Joyce, Gann, Gruning, and Long, 1928, Pl. XXXV, Fig. 1; also Joyce, 1932, Pl. II, 2 b). Benque Viejo, one plain-edged flint (Joyce, *ibid.*, Pl. II, 5 b). *Guatemala*: Naranjo, one serrated in Stela 15 cache (9.13.0.0.0???) (Maler, 1908, Fig. 19).

   b. Offset notches on each side (serpentine effect), 10 (Figs. 4 f, o; 5 n; 6 i; 9 m; 14 f; 19 a; possibly 12 k and 16 m, n). Generally leaf-like in form with abrupt notches staggered from side to side. The two fragments in Fig. 16 m, n probably fit together to give this form.

DISTRIBUTION. The distinctly notched form appears rather frequently elsewhere. *British Honduras*: Pusilha, fairly common in caches (see Joyce, Gann, Gruning, and Long, 1928, Pl. XXXV, Fig. 1; Gruning, 1930, Pl. XXII, Fig. 1; Joyce, 1932, Pl. I, 8 a, 3 b, 4 b; Pl. II, 1 a). Benque Viejo, at least six of this category were included in Cache C, Stewart excavations (Jubilee Library).   San Jose, a Period IV cache contained one example (Thompson, 1939, Pl. 24, b 8). Another good specimen from British Honduras, source not specified, is illustrated by Heye (1925, Fig. 45); this would seem to be the same flint shown by Joyce, 1932, Pl. V, 1 d. *Guatemala*: Uaxactun, at least twelve flints with this form came from various caches (Kidder, 1947, Figs. 66 b 3, d 2; 67 d 3—5); Ricketson and Ricketson, 1937, Pl. 58, a 3—6, b); the majority, if not all, of these pieces seem to date from Early Classic times (see A. L. Smith, 1950, Table 8).

   c. Single offset notch on each side, 1 (Fig. 6 h;). Sub-type differs from previous one in number of notches.

DISTRIBUTION. Beyond Piedras Negras, apparently limited to one large flint from Kendal, British Honduras (Price, 1897—99, p. 342; shown in Gann, 1918, Fig. 38 a).

15. *Triangular bodies*, 7.
   a. Double, 3 (Figs. 5 l; 16 e; 18 i). L 9.3–11.7 cm. Elongated, with parallel sides, and a triangular element on each end. These comparable pieces evidently are confined in distribution to Piedras Negras. They may very well be morphologically related to those described under 14 a (above). The piece shown in Fig. 18 i, might be considered transitional.
   b. Single, 4 (Figs. 6 k; 7 q, s; 19 b). Notched edges on all. Tapered projection on "base." No known incidence of this form elsewhere.
16. *Unclassified*, 94.
   (Figs. 4 c, d, i; 5 a, b, d, g, h, k; 6 a, j, l–n; 7 n; 8 b, d–j, n–p, r, s; 9 c, h, k, l, p, q, u; 10 a, b, e, j, o, s, t, v; 11 c; 12 f–j, n–r; 13 a, b, h, k, l, p–s; 14 b, e, g, j, k; 15 a–c, f, h, j, l, m; 16 l, o; 17 e, f, m, n; 18 a, d–g; 19 d–j). Further classification of form is impractical in view of the often indescribable individuality and uniqueness of most of these flints. Many problematical fragments have been included here. Among those grouped here are handsome eccentrics (see Figs. 6 a; 9 c; 13 h; 14 j), a pair of almost matched flints (Fig . 17 e, f), as well as a number of crudely notched flakes (as in Fig. 8 n–p, r, s). Quite a few of these eccentrics have in common a tridentate element (Figs. 4 c, d; 6 n; 10 v; 13 p; 16 l; 18 a, e). One flint (Fig. 14 e) is naturally perforated; holes such as this were very likely employed in fashioning eccentrics in the forms of rings and crescents (see Kidder, 1947, p. 18 for comment on this particular specimen). Cache O–13–10 contained four unrelated fragments of eccentrics (not illustrated). In passing , I should mention the existence of a pound or so of irreparably shattered eccentric flints that were caught in the camp fire; those shown in Figures 18 j–p and 19 a–k are the most nearly complete of this fire-burned collection.

   DISTRIBUTION. Among the unclassified flints are a few with representatives elsewhere. Included in the large El Baul (Guatemala) cache were two identical eccentrics, each composed of a crescent set with three spikes on its one edge (Thompson, 1948, Fig. 23 h); one Piedras Negras piece (Fig. 6 n), from Cache O–13–10, is similar i n most respects, lacking only the formers' two subsidiary notches at the bases of the lateral spikes and the extreme closure of the crescentic body. A curious J–6–3 flint (Fig. 14 b) is almost duplicated by one from Benque Viejo (Gann, 1918, Fig. 44 l; also in Joyce, 1932, Pl. VI, 3 a), and by another labeled as "British Honduras" (Stevens, 1870, No. 7).

   Circular, tridentate flints, two of which appear in the Piedras Negras collection (Fig. 18 d,e), rarely occur elsewhere: El Palmar (Quintana Roo, Mexico), in cache beneath Stela 10 (9.15.15.0.0) (Morley, 1947, Pl. 95 a; see also Kidder, *op. cit.*, p. 27). The El Baul flints, just mentioned, may also be pertinent. There are, however, a remarkable number of cases where an individual is shown holding an object strikingly like the El Baul, El Palmar, and Piedras Negras flints—*British Honduras*: Caracol, back face of Stela 6 (9.8.10.0.0?) (Satterthwaite, 1954 a, Fig. 11). *Guatemala*: Uaxactun, Initial Series vase (surely Late Classic), two instances (A. L. Smith, 1932, Pl. 5; Ricketson and Ricketson, 1937, Fig. 118 h; Morley, 1937–1938, v. 1, pp. 226–34); Tikal, object appears on Lintel 2 of Temple III, and one seems to appear on Altar V (9.14.0.0.0 i s date of associated Stela 16) (Morley, 1937–1938, v. 1, footnote 228; Follett, 1932, Figs. 31, 32); Naranjo, Stela 30 (9.14.3.0.0); Nebaj vase from Alta Verapaz (e. g., Morley, 1947, Pl. 89 a). *Mexico*, Santo Ton, Stela 1; Etzna, Stela 18 (9.12. 0.0.0); Chichen Itza, Temple of the Jaguars, Room E. The greater part of this distribution has been previously cited (Blom and LaFarge, 1926–1927, p. 310, Fig. 263; Follett, *op. cit.*, p. 388; Kidder, *op. cit.*, p. 28; Morley, 1937–1938, v. 1, footnote 243; Thompson, *op. cit.*, p. 40; Proskouriakoff, 1950, p. 96). It is indeed odd why only an eccentric of this shape should have been selected for depiction over such a wide area. The Piedras Negras specimens add considerably to the meager findings of the actual form.

   GENERAL COMMENT ON ECCENTRIC FLINTS. Twenty-three of these Piedras Negras flints have been previously shown by Mason (1935, p. 542). The majority of flints contained in caches have been accounted for and illustrated here. Unfortunately, a number of eccentrics sent to Guatemala have in time lost their field numbers and, while field photographs indicate that these originated in Structure O–13 caches, exact assignments of them are impossible. Reference to both the illustration and itemized cache listing (Part 3) should disclose whether or not the flint component has been completely located. This difficulty applies equally to the eccentric obsidians described at a later point.

For the most part the Piedras Negras eccentric flints are small compared to those of Uaxactun. Two flints found in Cache R–9–1 (Fig. 17 a, b) are truly exceptional. Workmanship is variable, ranging as it does from wonderfully controlled, meticulous, yet still relatively coarse, bifacial chipping to simple peripheral notching. Some caches, for instance O–13–10, R–9–1, R–9–2 and K–5–6, yielded only beautifully worked pieces. On the other hand, caches like O–13–46 and J–1–2, contained flints of only crude workmanship. Still others were mixed in this respect; for example, such caches as O–13–30, O–13–48, O–13–51, and K–5–1. And, in one case, Cache O–13–27, the flint component comprised a well-made blade fragment and six unworked chips. This technical diversity likewise is a characteristic of ceremonial obsidian objects. The fact that such variation in quality of workmanship appears within a single cache to a certain extent reduces developmental perspective.

Consistent repetion from cache to cache of set numbers and forms has not been noted. A few caches contained only one flint, while others, notably Cache O–13–10, produced large numbers of these objects.

Table 1—LOCAL AND EXTERIOR DISTRIBUTIONS OF ECCENTRIC FLINT FORMS

FORMS	LOCAL DISTRIBUTION (CACHES, ETC.)	OTHER SITES
Ring	O–13–6	Pusilha, Benque Viejo, Tikal
Crescent, plain	O–13–6, 46; O–13 miscellaneous; J–1–1, 2; J–6–2, 3; J–29–1; K–5–1, 8; R–9–1; Str. U–3	Pusilha, Benque Viejo, San Jose, Naranjo, Tikal, Chichen Itza
Crescent, serrated	O–13–10, 16, 17, 24; O–13 miscellaneous; J–1–2; J–6–3, J–29–1; R–9–1, 2	Benque Viejo, "Cayo District," Naranjo, "Ticul"
Trident-crescent	O–13–1, 4, 6, 7, 10, 43; O–13 miscellaneous; K–5–1, 8; R–9–1, 2; R–16–1; R–11–7; fire	San Jose, Nohmul, Uaxactun, "Ticul"
Double crescent	O–13–7, 44, 47, 48; O–13 miscellaneous; K–5–8; R–9–1; fire	Benque Viejo, Baking Pot, San Jose
Scorpion	O–13–6, 7, 8, 10, 16, 43, 47; O–13 miscellaneous; R–9–1	Pusilha, Benque Viejo, Tikal
Centipede	O–13–1, 9, 37, 44, 47, 51; O–13 miscellaneous; K–5–1; R–9–1, 2	Benque Viejo, Naranjo, Tikal
Anthropomorph	O–13 miscellaneous; K–5–6	San Jose, "British Honduras"
Disc	O–13–10	Pusilha, Baking Pot, Benque Viejo, Uaxactun, Tikal
Trident	O–13–10; O–13 miscellaneous; J–6–2	Uaxactun, Copan, "Ticul"
Double-pointed blade	O–13–4, 10, 27; K–5–6; fire	Pusilha, Benque Viejo, Uaxactun, Naranjo, El Palmar
Blade, central opposed side notches	O–13–1, 10, 30, 54; O–13 miscellaneous; J–1–2; J–6–3; K–5–5	Pusilha, Benque Viejo, Naranjo
Blade, offset notches on each side	O–13–1, 6, 10, 16, 38; J–6–4; R–16–1; fire	Pusilha, Benque Viejo, San Jose, "British Honduras," Uaxactun

The lack of quantitative patterns is mentioned because instances of sets of nine have been reported in flint, particularly for Tikal (Kidder, 1947, pp. 17, 28). Instead of nine, the most frequent quantities at Piedras Negras appear to have been seven, five, and even three; these are really meaningless in the light of common exceptions and the confused nature of many Structure O–13 deposits.

The distribution of various selected shapes, both within and beyond Piedras Negras, is summarized in Table 1. The chronological ordering of caches has been deferred to the section of this report devoted to caches.

As this table indicates, Piedras Negras shared a variety of flint forms with other sites; particularly, it would seem, with Benque Viejo, some 230 kilometers distant. Except for the trident, the alternately notched blade, and possibly the trident-crescent, there was negligible form agreement between Piedras Negras and Uaxactun. But Uaxactun, as Kidder has pointed out (ibid., pp. 28–29), is exceptional in that the majority of its eccentric flints came from Early Classic deposits; the opposite is generally true among other sites that have produced these objects. Caches early in date at Piedras Negras include R–9–1 and 2; such caches as K–5–6 and –8 are surely earlier than 9.12.5.0.0 (see Table 4). To take one example, the very prevalent trident-crescent was locally produced from relatively early times through Late Classic times with a maximum frequency in Late Classic Structure O–13 caches. It occurs at San Jose (Late Classic) and Nohmul (probably Late Classic) as well as Uaxactun (Early Classic). The specimens from the latter site, open crescentic flints with small protuberances on their convexities, would point to the possibility of their being ancestral were it not for a few roughly contemporaneous and mature Piedras Negras examples. And, with regard to Piedras Negras, it can be said that at an early date forms and workmanship were comparable to those of Late Classic date.

With the addition of the Piedras Negras data, a few regional emphases are perhaps apparent. Surely, the characteristic Piedras Negras eccentric flint, if only from the quantitative standpoint, was the trident-crescent. In contrast, the outstanding Uaxactun shape was perhaps the trident, and further to the east, at Pusilha and Benque Viejo, it was the stylized, bulbous scorpion. Practically all sites, however, that have yielded eccentric flints, have in common shapes like the disc, plain and serrated crescents, and plain and notched blade-like forms. These common and differential factors are indeed puzzling. Why the comparative prevalency of the trident at Uaxactun and its rarity elsewhere, it having been noted only for Copan and Piedras Negras, two widely separated sites but approximately coeval in this regard? There are no signs of it among the quantities of eccentrics from British Honduras. And why the stylistic peculiarities among the Piedras Negras and Tikal–British Honduras scorpions? Is the noted trait-sharing of Piedras Negras and Benque Viejo fortuitous or really indicative of ceremonial interchange? In this regard, the reader is referred to Part 3 and particularly the discussion of Table 7.

The eccentric flints found at Piedras Negras underscore Kidder's conclusion (ibid. p. 27) as to their quite narrow distribution, namely, within the Peten–British Honduras area of the lowlands. None, I believe, have ever been reported from Puuc sites, nor do they seem to have appeared in recent intensive digging at Palenque. A few important exceptions do exist. The oldest available eccentric flint comes from a Miraflores burial at Kaminaljuyu, thus highland and Pre-Classic in origin (Shook and Kidder, 1952, p. 112, Fig. 79 c); this is a large, peripherally worked flake of a notched but seemingly novel form. On the other end of the time scale is a recently reported eccentric flint from Mayapan (Shook, 1954, Pl. 5 e). If not an heirloom, this is still younger than one occurring in a San Jose V grave (Thompson, 1939, Pl. 24, c 1) and a crescent from the early Post-Classic High Priest's Grave, Chichen Itza (E. H. Thompson and J. E. S. Thompson, 1938, Fig. 18 j). The pair of Late Classic El Baul eccentric flints does of course carry the distribution to the Pacific Coast of Guatemala. But these exceptions do little to alter this picture of time-space concentration. Still they do suggest very early highland eccentric production as well as weak Post-Classic persistence of the trait in Northern Yucatan.

Other distant finds include a few large, gross eccentrics reputedly from Honduras in the Museum of the American Indian, Heye Foundation. Certainly one of the most remarkable flint objects ever produced is contained in the Dieseldorff Collection of the National Museum, Guatemala; its provenience is unknown but northeastern highland Guatemala is a possibility. On the basis of mental notes only, it is composed of brown flint, beautifully chipped all over, about a meter in length, comprising a straight slender shaft surmounted by an ornate element. This monolithic, obviously non-utilitarian object warrants special attention in print.

It should be noted that, despite the frequency and diversity of its flints, Piedras Negras lacked examples of the elaborately branching flints found at such sites as El Palmar and Quirigua (for list of occurrences, see Kidder, *op. cit.*, p. 18). Whether or not these foliated flints were produced at the sites of their discovery is problematical. One of the Quirigua pieces figured by Gann (1930, Pl. 1, Fig. 2, largest) has been acquired recently by the Cleveland Museum of Art (Archaeology, v. 6, no. 3, p. 202, 1954). In addition to those listed by Kidder, the American Museum of Natural History contains a beautiful flamboyant example from Orange Walk, British Honduras. It is odd that, apart from El Palmar, sites which contained common eccentrics in any quantity are entirely lacking in these extraordinary, foliated objects. Their occurrence is entirely eastern.

The distributional consistency of eccentric flints in the Peten–British Honduras area during Classic times is marred by their apparent absence at Caracol (Satterthwaite, verbal communication), and, with one exception (from a burial), among the Mountain Cow sites (Thompson, 1931, p. 314, Fig. 15 g). While Pusilha produced many of these objects, Lubaantun, so close by, seems to have yielded very few.

Apart from having been votive objects, the function of eccentric flints remains very obscure. Although, over the years, a number of investigators have dealt with this problem (see Kidder, *op. cit.*, pp. 18, 28, for summary), results have been far from conclusive, for any proposition only covers a relatively small number of eccentrics. Likewise, this pertains to the eccentric obsidians which often accompany flints in caches (see under Ceremonial Obsidian). As Kidder has shown, eccentric flints have appeared very infrequently in burials and then never in quantity (San Jose, Tzimin Kax, Douglas, all in British Honduras, as well as Chichen Itza and Kaminaljuyu; see also Gann, 1918, p. 103). The usual sources are structure and monument caches, the former being the most common. Naturalism is occasionally apparent, as in the case of the Piedras Negras scorpions, centipedes and anthropomorphs, the birds and other zoomorphs of Baking Pot and San Jose, and so forth. Kidder writes:

"What, if any, symbolic significance the eccentric flints may have had is problematical. Most of them seem to be pure abstractions, and realism was seldom attempted." (*ibid.*, p. 18)

"It is obvious that these flints (and obsidians) served no practical purpose. But their ritual significance and the method of their use in ceremonies are unknown." (*ibid.*, p. 28)

The following positive suggestion by Thompson (1936, p. 318) ought not to be disregarded:

"In recent years no one has had the temerity to suggest a possible function for these eccentrically-shaped objects, but, as an admittedly wild guess, supported by no valid arguments, one might hazard that they represent the names or totemic emblems of individuals or clans. In that case the eccentric flints in a cache might represent the names or totemic clans of the participants in the dedicatory ceremony, while the solitary example buried with an individual might represent his name clan. Judging by the modern Lacandones, the Maya probably had some form of totemism, while animal- and insect-names are common among the Maya to this day."

This hypothesis, admittedly intriguing receives little support from the Piedras Negras data. It must of course be extended to also cover eccentric obsidians. One recalls the quantity and even duplication of forms within a cache (see Table 3), the inclusion of unworked flakes (see Table 5), the mass of votive offerings beneath the temple floor of Structure O–13, and the occurrences of cached eccentrics with stelae, the hieroglyphic contents of which are evidently exceptionally impersonal.

Mention has already been made of rare scenes in which an individual holds a pronged object not unlike those shown here in Figure 18 d, e. It will be remembered that the most common Piedras Negras flint is trident-crescent. Of interest in this regard is the strange ornament worn on the face of a Copan Stela B personage (object illustrated by Proskouriakoff, 1950, Fig. 19 t). In form it seems quite similar to the trident-crescent, and while this individual possesses a beard (frequent at Copan), this ornament might be considered associated with it. The symbolism in flint may seem far fetched. But before it is rejected, a study is really needed on the significance of the beard and beard substitutes in Mesoamerica—a study disassociated from notions of Caucasoid invasions and the like.

One characteristic of the double crescent is the pair of opposing notches at the point where the two crescents join. Lateral notching may be either simple (as in Fig. 10 r) or the result of paired lateral spikes (as in Fig. 10 n). Disregarding minor peripheral details, what results is a quadrupally notched ellipse. Morphologically this is identical to what Thompson (in Kidder, *op. cit.*, p. 22) has treated as celestial or solar discs. The device is illustrated on a number of the Uaxactun and Tikal incised obsidian flakes (Kidder, *ibid.*, Figs. 69—71).

There are a number of scenes in the Madrid Codex where the scorpion or scorpion components appear. The scorpion is shown ensnaring and killing the deer. Black individuals, one of which is God M, have tails segmented in a way common to the codical scorpions. In a few instances, the tail of the scorpion terminates in a human hand. Good linguistic evidence that the Maya related the scorpion to mortification has been presented by Thompson (1950, p. 77). Seler (1910, pp. 276—77) noted this same association for Central Mexico. Hunting, the deer, the hand, and penance are features interrelated by the scorpion, and all, as Thompson has shown (*ibid.*, pp. 76—77) enter into the interpretive context of the day Manik. Incised obsidians from Tikal and Uaxactun occasionally show the scorpion (Thompson, in Kidder, *op. cit.*, p. 23). Depictions of scorpions exist on pottery vessels from eastern Salvador (Longyear, 1944, p. 40) and Nicaragua (Lehmann, 1910, Fig. 3).

The centipede (or millipede) does not occur in any of the Maya codices nor do other Maya sources provide clues as to its esoteric significance. One possible example occurs on a Uaxactun sherd (see R. E. Smith, 1955, p. 69). Seler (*op. cit.*, pp. 273—76), drawing on Strebel's Cerro Montoso pottery collection, rich in representations of this insect, has little to suggest in the matter of interpretation beyond noting its apparent association with Xochiquetzal in the Codex Borbonicus. It is indeed curious that Maya caches included effigies of the scorpion and centipede as well as the viciously serrated spines of the stingray— all animals with the capacity to seriously wound.

These few leads, tenuous and perhaps even far-fetched naturally pertain to only a very few of the eccentric forms known from Piedras Negras and other caches. At the moment, the large remainder seems imponderable. It should be remembered, however, that production of some forms, such as the ring, (e. g. Fig. 4 j), was probably entirely dependent on a natural perforation or deep pit in the initial flake and thus, secondarily, on the artisan's objective.

It remains to note that in the New World extraordinary, non-utilitarian flints are not entirely restricted to the Maya. For example, there is the "Duck River Cache," evidently authentic, from central Tennessee as well as other probably reliable flints from Arkansas and Oklahoma (see Lewis, 1954; Dellinger, 1954; Clements and Reed, 1939). Many of the Spiro Mound specimens would seem to be frauds. The flints of the Southeastern area generally comprise large "batons" or "ceremonial standards" as well as turtle-like objects and fragile branched eccentrics. Of equal interest with respect to comparable developments are the relatively small zoomorphic flints from Point Barrow, Alaska (UM collections; also Murdoch, 1892, Fig. 400). The Alaskan, Mayan, and Southeastern occurrences presumably are unrelated. Still, the appearance of analogous flint objects in Russian archaeology and the Neolithic of northeastern Europe (see Zamyatnin, 1948, p. 122; reference kindly given by Dr. Henry Michael) very vaguely points to a common origin for these American instances.

B. LARGE LAUREL-LEAF BLADES, 5. complete and fragments of at least 4 others .
(Figs. 19 l—o; 20). L of whole specimens 25.1, 25.4, 26.5, 27.9, ca. 30.8 cm. T of all 2.2—2.7 cm. White, presumably local flint. Bifacial rough flaking. None shows indications of use. Function problematical. These constitute the remains of a badly disturbed cache, J—3—1. Two of those shown here were previously figured by Satterthwaite (1936, Pl. V, D). Mulleried (1928, p. 89, Figs. 5, 28; 7, 28) reports a blade fragment collected during a visit to Piedras Negras; it is very similar in size and workmanship to those from Cache J—3—1, and might belong to this superficially scattered deposit.

COMMENT. Blades of comparable size and form seem to be rather infrequent elsewhere. At Piedras Negras they are known only from this one cache. Kidder (1947, pp. 18—19) gives the Mesoamerican distribution of "very fine laurel-leaf blades of dark flint, which have usually, and probably correctly, been referred to as sacrificial knives." Sites like Copan and Quirigua, Guaytan, El Baul, and San Jose have produced such objects. But the general coarseness of the Piedras Negras group contrasts with the keenness and superlative finish of sacrificial knives. In view of their weight, it is unlikely that the Piedras Negras blades served as actual spearheads, although use as ceremonial standards is a possibility. Dr. Carleton Coon has pointed out to the writer the collection's resemblance to the southeast Asian gamelan. There is a noticeable size as well as tonal gradation to the pieces. All this of course recalls the unique "sounding" stones from an Esperanza tomb at Kaminaljuyu (see Kidder, Jennings, and Shook, 1946, p. 144).

C. UNALTERED CACHED FLINT FLAKES AND CHIPS

(some shown in Figs. 8; 9 a, e—g, i, n, o, r—t; 10 i, q, w; 15 k). One or more bulbar flakes (and chips) accompanied the following caches: O—13—26, 27, 30, 31, 32, 35, 36, 37, 38, 39, 40, 41, 46, 47, 49, 51, 52, 53; O—16—1; J—1—1; J—6—1; K—5—2; 7; R—9—1 (see Table 5).

COMMENT. This interesting trait, which at Piedras Negras is duplicated in obsidian (see under Ceremonial Obsidian), has been reported at San Jose (Thompson, 1939, pp. 185, 189), Baking Pot (Ricketson, 1929, p. 5), and Uaxactun (Ricketson and Ricketson, 1937, p. 187). In each of the latter two instances, flint flakes comprised the total cache. The practice, though rare, of depositing stone flaking scraps confuses the attempt to appreciate the ritualistic significance of caches.

II. CEREMONIAL OBJECTS OF OBSIDIAN

The objects treated in this section are eccentrics, polyhedral cores, and the prismatic blades originating from these cores. All come from caches, none from burials.

The camp fire is again responsible for the loss of information for quite a few eccentric obsidians; many, of course, were badly shattered by this fire. Many others have, with time, lost their field numbers; others, known from field photographs to have been excavated, cannot located. The collection further contains a number of eccentrics which, while specifically unassignable, surely are the remains of completely disturbed offerings. Form again is used as a basis for the classification of eccentrically-shaped obsidians. Some types immediately emerge, particularly among the thoroughly chipped core eccentrics. The task becomes increasingly subjective when one is faced with ordering a mass of notched small flakes. The end result may be useful to the reader. At least it offers occasional grounds for comparisons.

Material. Three types of obsidian , all presumably imported, seem to have been used in the production of ceremonial objects: clear (black when thick), cloudy to opaque gray, and black-banded clear obsidian.

A. ECCENTRIC OBSIDIANS, 337. (minimum)

1. *Crescents*, 8 (Figs. 22 1, r; 25 j; 33 n, o; 36 n, o; one [UM, not located] in Cache O—13—10). W 2.4—4.5; T .6—1.2 cm. Coarsely chipped objects, some more crescentic than others.

DISTRIBUTION. *British Honduras*: Pusilha, two, very much finer than those from Piedras Negras; one is serrated, and from Terraced Hill cache (Gruning, 1930, Pl. XXII, Fig. 4; also Joyce, 1932, Pl. II, 6 d, 8 d). Benque Viejo, one (Gann, 1918, Fig. 45 c). *Honduras*: Copan, three crude pieces; one might be considered hook-shaped rather than crescentic (Longyear, 1952, p. 121, Fig. 92 m). *Mexico*: Tres Zapotes, two examples one of which has been bifacially ground (Weiant, 1943, Pl. 78, 7, 8). Teotihuacan, one reported by Linne (1934, Fig. 313). Kidder (1947, p. 30) lists several other examples from Central Mexico which seem comparable to those described here.

2. *Scorpions*, 26 (Figs. 21 a, 1, x; 22 a; 23 b—d, q; 24 o, p; 25 e, v, w, z; 27 h—j; 28 q; 29 d; 30 i; 32 j—n; 34 n). L 2.2—7.8; T .3—1.7 cm. All are conventionalized, the constant feature being the hooked stinger tail. A number of these, for all their smallness, are very beautifully made (for instance, Fig. 32 j) while others are only slightly altered flakes (as in Fig. 27 h—j). One scorpion (Fig. 24 o) retains traces of flaking scars of the prismatic core from which it and other finer specimens were made.

DISTRIBUTION. *British Honduras*: Pusilha, two eccentrics with the shape of a scorpion are illustrated as from this site (Joyce, 1932, p. xxi, Pl. III, 3 b, 4 b). Benque Viejo, a quite realistic piece (*ibid.*, Pl. III, 1 b); another is said to have come from a mound near Benque Viejo (Gann, 1918, Fig. 45 a). *Guatemala*: Tikal, one distinctive scorpion but circumstances of discovery are not given (Joyce, *op. cit.*, Pl. III, 2 b).

3. *Centipedes*, 38.
   a. Standard, 8 (Figs. 25 g; 29 n; 30 b; 32 a, c, d; 35 k).L 4.8–8.8; T .8–1.7 cm. counterparts of the flint centipedes. Tend to have notched ends. Unlike the flint examples, core thickness precluded really multiple notching of sides. One eccentric (not located) in Cache R–9–3 is known to have been a finely made centipede.

   DISTRIBUTION. *British Honduras*: Pusilha, one eccentric obsidian from cache of Terraced Hill has this same general form but edges are deeply notched (Joyce, 1932, Pl. III, 8 b). Benque Viejo, one from a nearby mound (Gann, 1918, Fig. 45 f) is unusual in having one end rounded, the other concave. Caracol , one crude obsidian in lower cache below Altar 14 suggests this form; edges unserrated, concave ends (UM, 51–54–37).

   b. Probably related, 30 (Figs. 21 d, i, s, u; 22 t, u; 23 r; 24 h, w; 25 a, p; 27 e–g; 28 j, u; 29 a; 30 h; 31 t–x; 32 b, e–i; 34 p). Many elongated bilaterally notched eccentrics appeared in caches. Often tapered, these might be considered crude representatives of the centipede motif. Made from both cores and flakes.
4. *Anthropomorphs*, 10 (Figs. 22 m; 23 m; 25 b; 28 h, o, t; 32 q–s; 36 e). L 3.3–6.9; T .5–1.3 cm. Ideally shown by Figure 36 e and, to a lesser extent, by 28 o. Others far less distinctive but they do suggest the human figure. One must confess that the orientation of these and other pieces has much to do with their identification.

   DISTRIBUTION. In the Maya area, obsidians in this form, again particularly as in Figure 36 e, are all but restricted to Piedras Negras. Joyce (1927, p. 183) shows one quite similar obsidian from "Northern British Honduras." Curiously, he did not reproduce this fine figure in his 1932 study, although two almost identical specimens from Teotihuacan are shown (1932, Pl. IV, 1 b, 2 b). Actually, Teotihuacan, apart from Piedras Negras, seems to be the sole source of obsidian anthropomorphs in Mesoamerica (see Gamio, 1922, v. 1, Pl. 87 c–e; Linné, 1934, Figs. 314–18; 1942, Figs. 263, 264; Noguera, 1935, Pl. XXIV; Rubin de la Borbolla, 1947, Fig. 9). At Teotihuacan these are often found in graves.

5. *"Monolithic axes,"* 2 (Figs. 26 g; 36 d). L 4.7, 5.7; T .9, 1 cm. respectively. Extremely fine work. These are practically identical. The first comes from Cache O–7–1.

   DISTRIBUTION. Unique, although they recall an enormous monolithic ax of obsidian from a San Jose V cache (Thompson, 1939, Pl. 28 a), an object infrequently found in North America but relatively common, for example, in the Tairona culture of Colombia: the latter are of pecked and polished stone.

6. *Discs*, 24 (Figs. 21 r, z; 22 j, k; 23 j; 24 k–m; 25 i; 27 b; 29 k, r, s; 34 a–h; 36 p). D or L 1.9 –4.3; T .4–1.3 cm. Discoidal to apsidal, some coarsely chipped all over, others altered flakes. Two eccentrics (not located) in Cache R–9–3 are known to have been discs.

   DISTRIBUTION. Discs of obsidian are quite rare. *British Honduras*: Pusilha, one was in a cache beneath Stela F (9.9.13.0.0??) and another in the Terraced Hill cache (Joyce, Gann, Gruning, and Long, 1928, Pl. XXXV, Fig. 2; Joyce, 1932, Pl. II, 3 d). *Honduras*: Copan (Kidder, 1947, p. 20). *Mexico*: Teotihuacan, three discs, two of them from a grave (Linne, 1934, Figs. 320, 321, 324).

7. *Double-pointed blades*, 19 (Figs. 21 b, j, k; 22 e, f; 23 g; 29 h–j; 30 j–m, r, t; 35 l–n, q). L 2.6– 8.5; T .6–1.8 cm. Essentially what Kidder (1947, p. 19) terms "core knives." At Piedras Negras chip-scars were usually obliterated by secondary working.

   DISTRIBUTION. *Guatemala*: Uaxactun, a total of six were recovered from Early Classic caches (Kidder, *ibid.*, Fig. 68 b, 1, 2; Ricketson and Ricketson, 1937, Pl. 54 a, 13–16); generally these are larger than the run of Piedras Negras specimens. *Mexico*: Teotihuacan, eight finely chipped long slender blades were found in a magnificent cache (Rubín de la Borbolla, 1947, Fig. 39). This list could certainly be extended were one to consider larger non-core obsidian blades (see Kidder, *op. cit.*, pp. 24—25). These, however, failed to appear at Piedras Negras.

8. *Truncated blades*, 7 (Figs. 30 a, g, n—q, s). A catch-all for a number of eccentrics having in common one pointed end, the other being blunted, one (Fig. 30 a) might be considered "stemmed."

9. *Notched double-pointed blades*, 28.

 a. Central opposed side notches, 26 (Figs. 21 g, w; 22 c, d, p, s; 23 k; 26 b, f, r; 28 i; 29 l; 31 a—j; 35 p, r—t). L 2.7—7.9; T .5—1.3 cm. A few of these are crudely snub-ended, while others are double-pointed and quite symmetrical. The pattern of notching is constant. Both exhausted cores and thin and thick flakes were employed and show both hasty and careful workmanship.

DISTRIBUTION. Rare elsewhere. *British Honduras*: Pusilha, one good example and one somewhat indefinite example from Terrace 3 cache (Gruning, 1930, Pl. XXII, Fig. 4; also Joyce, 1932, Pl. III, 6 b, 7 b).

 b. Offset notched, 1 (Figs. 30 u). L 4.3; T 1.3 cm. A unique and carefully chipped specimen with counterparts in flint at Piedras Negras.

 c. Incompleted (?), 1 (Fig. 29 m). L 7.5; T ? cm.

10. *"S"-shaped*, 5 (Figs. 22 b; 23 e; 29 o; 32 o, p). L 5.5—6.7; T .8—1.1 cm. Eccentrics such as these well illustrate the technical ability of local artisans. That in Figure 29 o lacks the curvature common to the others but its shape necessitates that it be included here. No comparative material elsewhere.

11. *Serpentine*, 28.

 a. Standard, 16 (Figs. 21 c, f; 23 a, f; 24 g, q; 25 f ; 26 a; 29 p; 31 m, n, r, s; 36 a—c). L 4—8.3; T .7—1.1 cm. Sinuous in shape, some smoother than others as in Figure 23 a. Many made from exhausted cores, others from elongate flakes. Figure 29 p probably aberrant.

DISTRIBUTION. *British Honduras*: Pusilha, one comparable example from Terrace 3 cache (Gruning, 1930, Pl. XXII, Fig. 3; also Joyce, 1932, Pl. I, 6 d).

 b. "Stemmed," 2 (Figs. 31 l; 35 w). L 7, 5.6; T 1, .9 cm. respectively. Finely chipped.

 c. Crude, 10 (Figs. 21 n, o; 22 g, w; 23 i; 31 k, o—q; 36 i). L 3—8.4; T .7—1.4 cm. Elongate with two sides alternately notched, giving an abruptly sinuous appearance. For the most part, an homogeneous subtype.

12. *Miscellaneous notched cores and flakes*, 138

 a. Two notches along one side (tridentate), 33 (Figs. 21 e, v, y; 22 h, i, v; 23 l; 24 j; 25 k, u; 26 c, i, k, m, o, q, s; 27 k, m; 28 b, g, k, p; 29 q; 33 i—m; 36 h, j, k; two [NM, not located] in Cache O—13—10). L 4.2—7.4; T .6—1.3 cm. A variable and crude subtype perhaps best exemplified in Figure 24 j.

DISTRIBUTION. One of the most frequent shapes at other sites yielding eccentric obsidians. *British Honduras*: Pusilha, at least one was included in the prolific sub-stela deposit of Stela F (9.9.13. 0.0??) (Joyce, Gann, Gruning, and Long, 1928, Pl. XXXV, Fig. 2). Caracol, eleven obsidians notched in this manner were encountered in lower cache below Altar 14 (UM 51—54—34, 36,37). Benque Viejo, one made from a flake (Joyce, 1932, Pl. I, 7 d). *Guatemala*: Uaxactun, five from two sub-stela caches (Ricketson and Ricketson, 1937, Pl. 60 b, l). Tikal, one example shown by Joyce (*op. cit.*, Pl. I, 8 d). Another lacks provenience (*ibid.*, Pl. I, 9 d).

 b. Three to four notches along one side, 22 (Figs. 21 m; 25 c, d; 26 e, h, n, p; 28 a, c—f, r, s, w; 33 a—e; 36 f, g). Crudely fashioned from cores and flakes.

 c. Flamboyantly notched, 10 (Figs. 26 d; 27 a; 28 n, v; 29 e, g; 33 f—h; 36 m). Relatively elaborate, hastily made, diverse eccentrics.

      d. Amorphous, 73 (Figs. 21 p, t; 22 o; 23 h, n; 24 r–v, x–z, a¹; 25 h, n, o, q, x, y; 26 l, t–w, y; 27 n–z, a¹; 30 d, v, w; 34 i–m, o,q–s, u–z, a¹–d¹; 35 a–i; two [NM, not located] in Cache O–13–10). The most frequent of all Piedras Negras eccentric obsidians are these small to large specimens without identifiable forms. Truly eccentrically shaped.

   13. *Miscellaneous distinct forms*, 8

      a. "Stemmed" blades, 2 (Figs. 23 p; 35 v). Bifacially chipped objects, one with short "stem," other tapered and disproportionately long.

      b. Star, 1 (Fig. 32 t). W 3.8; T 1.3 cm. Illustrated side concave between stellar points; underside apical. Remains of a disturbed cache.

      c. Others, 5 (Figs. 22 n; 23 o; 27 l; 34 t; 35 j). Individual eccentrics, two of which (Figs. 23 o; 27 l) are morphologically similar although workmanship differs.

   14. *Fragments of unclassified well-made eccentrics*, 6 (Figs. 35 o, u; 36 l, q–s). Fashioned from cores. Notched and pointed eccentrics probably represented. Broken in camp fire. Presumably from Structure O–13 caches.

GENERAL COMMENT ON ECCENTRIC OBSIDIANS.   As is true of eccentric flints, eccentric obsidians did not occur in any of the Piedras Negras burials. There is every indication that all originated in caches, despite isolated finds in general digging. Table 2 summarizes the cache and exterior distribution of selected Piedras Negras eccentric obsidians.

Table 2—LOCAL AND EXTERIOR DISTRIBUTIONS OF ECCENTRIC OBSIDIAN FORMS

FORMS	LOCAL DISTRIBUTION (CACHES, ETC.)	OTHER SITES
Crescent, plain	O–13–10, 50; O–13 miscellaneous	Pusilha, Benque Viejo, Copan, Tres Zapotes, Teotihuacan and other central Mexican sites
Scorpion	O–13–1, 6, 7, 10, 13, 37, 44, 51; O–13 miscellaneous; J–29–1; K–5–8; R–16–1	Pusilha, Benque Viejo, Tikal
Centipede, standard	O–13–44; O–13 miscellaneous; R–9–2, 3; R–11–1; fire	Pusilha, Benque Viejo, Caracol.
Centipede, related	O–13–1, 6, 7, 17, 24, 25, 36, 37, 39, 47; O–13 miscellaneous; J–29–1; K–5–1, 6, 7; R–16–1	
Anthropomorph	O–13–10, 18, 43, 44; O–13 miscellaneous; K–5–1, 5, 6; fire	"Northern British Honduras," Teotihuacan
Disc	O–13–6, 7, 8, 10, 30, 44; O–13 miscellaneous; J–6–5; R–9–1, 2; fire	Pusilha, Copan, Teotihuacan
Double-pointed blade	O–13–1, 6, 10, 13; O–13 miscellaneous; R–9–1; fire	Uaxactun, Teotihuacan
Blade, central opposed side notches	O–13–4, 7, 10, 16, 17, 54; O–13 miscellaneous; J–1–2; K–5–1; R–9–2; fire	Pusilha
"S"-shaped	O–13–10, 13; R–9–2	None
Serpentine, standard	O–13–1, 4, 10, 13, 29, 37, 44, 54; O–13 miscellaneous; R–9–2; fire	Pusilha

    Kidder (1947, p. 19) has pointed out that the "geographic range of eccentric obsidians seems to lie within that of eccentric flints..." The Teotihuacan small ceremonial obsidians should, he feels (*ibid.*, pp. 20, 30), be treated separately as "odd forms" rather than as "eccentrics." The problem is whether or not the Teotihuacan and Maya practices are related. Kidder believes them to have been collateral developments. It should also be noted that the usual Mexican context, namely burials, does not obtain in the Maya area where eccentric obsidians seem to be exclusively from caches; cases of eccentric flints in Maya burials have been previously cited (see under Eccentric Flints, General Comment). In Mesoamerica eccentric flints appear to have been solely Maya products. On the other hand, had the truly remarkable Teotihuacan obsidian objects (see Rubin de la Borbolla, 1947) been discovered, say, at Benque Viejo, they very likely would be reported as "eccentrics."

As is true of the Piedras Negras eccentric flints, the quality of workmanship is very variable. Obsidian cores were frequently utilized. Their modification ranged from complete overall chipping to superficial notching, in which the original scars (from the striking off of flake-blades) and striking platform often remained. A great many other eccentrics were fashioned from thin and thick flakes, again through simple peripheral notching. Because of their usual simplicity and true eccentricity, these are very difficult to classify. Reference to cache illustrations will indicate how frequently carefully and hastily chipped obsidians were placed in the same offering.

The practice of offering small, notched obsidian flakes may have been a local ceremonial peculiarity. Their quantity is certainly outstanding. Unfortunately, the Pusilha material has been very incompletely reported on, despite the interest shown by Joyce and others. Obsidians such as these, however, evidently were not produced at sites like Uaxactun and Tikal, San Jose, and perhaps Benque Viejo. As it is, obsidian votive objects were very rare at San Jose, a few having appeared in a late (Period V) cache (Thompson, 1939, p. 188).

With regard to the Uaxactun eccentric obsidians, one is immediately struck by their limited shapes. Finely made tridents, exemplified only in flint at Piedras Negras, and notched cores and "core knives" complete the list. "Notched cores" are the equivalent of our "miscellaneous notched cores and flakes" (type 12 a and b), while "core knives" equate with "double-pointed blades." Eccentric obsidians were being deposited at Uaxactun as early as 8.18.0.0.0 (?) and 8.19.10.0.0. Our caches R–9–1 and R–9–2, containing obsidians, date somewhat later but within Early Classic times. These Piedras Negras caches include such shapes as the centipede, disc, serpentine, double-notched on one side, and double-pointed blade. Again, one asks whether the traits of producing and caching eccentrics, here of obsidian, at Piedras Negras were diffused from Uaxactun (or from the Central Peten in general). Quality, quantity and diversity suggest this not to have been the case.

Another feature worth comment is one incised obsidian flake, a number of sets of which were found in Late Classic Uaxactun and Tikal caches (see Kidder, *op. cit.*, pp. 21–24, Figs. 69–71; Berlin, 1951, Fig. 12; also Joyce, 1932, Pl. VIII). These did not occur at Piedras Negras but there is a chance that incised jadeite objects as well as shells, ceremonially functioned in much the same way as incised obsidians did elsewhere (see under Jadeite and Shell).

B. UNALTERED CACHED OBSIDIAN FLAKES AND CHIPS, 10 illustrated (Figs. 24 e, f, b'–d'; 26 j, x; 28 m; 29 b, c). Core-struck flakes as well as obsidian odds-and-ends appeared in caches. One or more were contained in *at least* the following: O–13–27, 37; O–16–1; J–1–2; K–5–1, 7. Four of these also yielded unworked flakes of flint.

COMMENT. A fine example of this trait appeared in a concentration at Caracol, British Honduras (Satterthwaite, verbal information). From below floor but concentrated around periphery of Altar 2 were quantities of obsidian flakes and chips. This same feature is seen in flint at Piedras Negras (see above).

C. CORES, 8 whole and fragmentary (Figs. 21 q; 22 q; 30 e; 37 f–j). Small polyhedral, elongate cores, greatly reduced by the throwing-off of prismatic blades (see below), appeared in Caches O–13–6, 16; J–1–2; R–11–3. Other examples, unassigned here, were very likely included in many of the Structure O–13 caches for which only catalogue listings exist.

COMMENT. Kidder (1947, p. 20) gives the occurrences of cached cores at other sites, including Uaxactun. These are rather rare at Piedras Negras in relation to the number of caches found, (see Table 5) and, in no case, I believe, were they accompanied by prismatic blades. The inclusion of a fragmentary specimen, as in Cache R–11–3, is of interest. Kidder (*ibid.*) comments that "The ceremonial use of cores was not restricted to the making of eccentric forms, for many examples with no secondary   working have been found in caches." The Piedras Negras specimens might then be considered potential but unrealized eccentric obsidians.

D. FLAKE-BLADES, 24   (Figs. 21 h, a¹; 24 a–d, i, n, e¹; 25 l, m, r–t, a¹; 27 c, d; 28 l; 29 f; 30 c; four

[3, O–13–10; 1, J–6–5] not shown). Examples of cached complete blades are rare. Edges of many fragments are use-nicked. Therefore, not all blades were specially made for immediate depositing. The longest specimen (Fig. 24 a, Cache O–13–27), 10.6 cm., tapers to a very sharp point; two others of this lancet type come from Cache J–6–5. These show no signs of use. The following caches contained flake-blades: O–13–4, 7, 10, 27, 30, 36, 37, 47, 50, 51, 54; O–7–1; J–6–5; K–5–8; R–11–3.

COMMENT.   Kidder, in his Uaxactun report (1947, pp. 20–21), has given a thoroughgoing discussion of the ceremonial use of the flake-blade for the whole of Mesoamerica. No cases of blades in burials were recorded at Piedras Negras.

GENERAL COMMENT AND COMPARISON OF CEREMONIAL CHIPPED STONE OBJECTS

Evidently the site did not share in the broad distribution of large bifacially flaked laurel-leaf blades of obsidian (Kidder, 1947, pp. 24–25). Nor as previously noted, did it share the incised obsidian flakes common to Tikal and Uaxactun, although certain jadeites and shells, unique to Piedras Negras, may have served as substitutes.

Among the Piedras Negras obsidians there are a number of shapes which recur in flint and others which interestingly do not. The lack of duplication in certain cases may reflect technical difficulties imposed by the fragility of obsidian and by basic core and flake size and degree of linearity. The scorpion, for instance, appears in both flint and obsidian, as do the centipede, anthropomorph, a general serpentine shape, unserrated crescent, disc, and small double-pointed blades, both plain and centrally notched. Outstanding flint shapes not represented in obsidian are the serrated crescent, double crescent, trident-crescent, trident, ring, and cross. Some of these were too intricate for execution in obsidian. Certain flint forms, it will be remembered, depended on an initial, natural pit. But others technically could have been readily made in obsidian judging by the   superlative workmanship evident in tiny objects like the "S-shaped and "monolithic ax" eccentrics. Large, thick flint flakes, of course, allowed a wider shape expression than linear obsidian cores. These physical factors, then, must be considered when attempting estimates of the significance of eccentric objects. For example, the absence, say, of a double-crescent in a cache of obsidians is probably due to the artisan's inability to fashion such an object with the raw obsidian available, though he was fully capable of doing so in flint.

To illustrate shape duplication in these media, Table 3 summarizes the incidence of similar shapes in both obsidian and flint within the same cache. In the light of the number of eccentric producing caches, instances of shape duplication are rare. The trait is heavily represented in Cache O–13–10 which yielded one flint and one obsidian scorpion, two flint and three obsidian discs, two flint and three obsidian double-pointed blades, two flint and three obsidian centrally notched blades, and one flint and one obsidian serpentine eccentric, yet lacked both anthropomorphs and centipedes, the latter a prevalent form in both media. Although unusual, this peculiarity of duplication must also affect consideration of function and significance.

These problems, perplexing as they admittedly are, still allow an oblique treatment of possibilities. In discussing eccentric flints, certain associations were hesitantly offered for shapes like the centipede, scorpion, double crescent, and, perhaps absurdly, the trident-crescent. Occurrences of these and other

Table 3—CACHED DUPLICATIONS OF ECCENTRIC FLINT AND OBSIDIAN FORMS

FORMS	LOCAL DISTRIBUTION (CACHES)
Scorpion	O–13–6, 7, 10
Centipede	O–13–1*, 37*, 44, 47*; K–5–1*; R–9–2 (*obsidian, "probably related")
Anthropomorph	K–5–6
Disc	O–13–10
Double-pointed blade	O–13–10
Blade, central opposed side notches	O–13–10, 54; J –1–2
Serpentine	O–13–1, 10
Crescent	O–13–10, 16

eccentric forms at often distant centers, and in certain cases separated by time as well, would seem to preclude execution by whim alone. It is unlikely that eccentrics in such definite shapes would have been made devoid of meaning and associations for their makers. Just as a glyph at Piedras Negras had the same meaning for a priest at Copan, so the centipede form presumably had a similar significance within a cache at Pusilha, Benque Viejo, Naranjo, Tikal, and Piedras Negras. It is almost axiomatic that the Maya loathed unfilled space in sculptural designs and other gaps. But it is improbable, from what is now known of their profound symbolism, that they cluttered space with meaningless content. And it is equally improbable that the hierarchy would have offered eccentrically made objects had not the various forms had widespread or at least local significance. Yet, while it is possible to derive associations for certain distinct forms, these constitute only a fraction of those that are presently known. To attempt to do so for the plethora of the truly eccentric objects would surely be futile. As noted, not all flints and obsidians at Piedras Negras are well made; many are merely flakes that have been notched to produce a variety of taxonomic headaches. Are these, then, to be treated with the same emphasis, say, as the trident and scorpion? The fact that superlative pieces occur with seemingly poor ones within the same cache surely precludes any euphoric scheme of development.

What one can never for certain know is whether eccentric objects were initially made for use in priestly ceremonies and then later cached, or whether production was followed immediately by their burial as votive objects. Pronged circular objects in the hands of priests, previously cited, suggest that eccentrics need not have been produced solely for deposition. Use-scarred obsidian flake-blades in caches point to prior use, albeit perhaps ceremonial. There are signs, then, of cache contents, at least in part, being functionally second-hand. But if primarily made for the votive occasion, one has to visualize a scene in which the hierarchy directs an artisan to flake a quantity of eccentric objects, some of flint, others of obsidian, one in this shape, two in that, and even three in another. Evidently there was no pattern to these specifications. Even if, as has been suggested here, these various forms were meaningful, the assemblage decided upon need not have had an interconnective significance. This impinges on the problem of cache function, which is treated in Part 3.

Of course, the whole problem of interpretation might be obviated by saying that eccentrics lack significance, that their quantity and shapes represented in a cache were matters of individual whim, without import or consistency—in short, a case of Maya vagary. And there is much to support this view provided that both the distribution of eccentrics and the symbolic predilections of the Maya are conveniently disregarded. But, perhaps, both views are partially correct. The individuals responsible for caches might have selected traditional pieces of definite import, and, for some obscure reason, filled out the offering with hastily fashioned objects of, at most, local significance. A final possibility would be that eccentrics reflected technical skill and merited votive burial on that basis only.

The many eccentric objects from Piedras Negras, while serving to extend and occasionally focus distributions in time and space, unfortunately, at least to my mind, bring this fascinating and almost standard problem no closer to solution. Forming as they do a single component of a still deeply obscure Classic Period complex, one cannot hope for an easy solution of their role. Towards this end, various features and problems have been mentioned. But all are clearly linked to that even more frustrating problem of caches, their contents, positions, and other details (see Part 3).

OBJECTS OF GROUND STONE

METATES AND MANOS

LARGE METATES

Legless, at least 16, whole and fragmentary (Fig. 39 a shows typical specimens). Presumably of local limestone. On the whole these are ponderous implements, deeply troughed from end to end, with heavily used ones showing steep lateral walls and fairly flat bottoms. These comprised the most frequent type at the site (Satterthwaite, 1933, pp. 16—17). All specimens, because of bulk and weight, were discarded.

Legged, 2 (Fig. 38 a, c). The complete specimen, 37.6 cm. in length, is basalt. Its grinding surface shows faint longitudinal dip. The surface groove running parallel to the edges has been largely obliterated by wear, although a relatively deep depression is located near one end. Underside is flat, somewhat irregular in thickness, with three legs comprising two truncated cones set across on corners from a beveled rectangular support. The second specimen (*c*) is comparable in many of these features. However it is made of a white-flecked fine green stone.

SMALL METATES

Two (Fig. 38 b, d). The first (*b*) is a quite soft brown sandstone. L 23.5 cm. Rectangular grinding surface with rounded corners, flat side to side, with moderate wear lengthwise. On underside, two truncated cones near one end and a beveled rectangular leg near other. A surface find in clearing camp road. Little can be said in regard to *d*. It apparently has been lost; it is illustrated here from a field photograph.

METATE (?) FRAGMENT

One (Fig. 42 d). Surface grooved near and parallel to edges. Underside has sheared off. Made of a green igneous stone. Presumably a fragment of a metate similar to that in Figure 38 c.

MANOS

Nine, fragmentary and whole (Figs. 39 b—f; 41 a—d). Length of intact specimens: 8.8, 15, 16.5, 17.5, 19.4 cm. Diabase, sandstone, crystalline limestone. Generally oval in cross section with varying degrees of flatness. Greatest thickness and width near center. Shapes for the most part suggest use on the large, troughed legless type of metate.

COMMENT. The number of metates recovered at Piedras Negras, while by no means great, still provide some basis for general remarks. The two types evidently employed here in the grinding of maize were, of course, the heavy troughed variety and the much smaller, flat-surfaced tripodal metate. The first, because of its clumsy size and weight must have been used in a manner somewhat different from that of the smaller, lighter, more easily transported metate. The standard, everyday, domestic metate at Piedras Negras unquestionably appears to have been this ponderous type. It is very probable that these were locally made, while certain of the tripodal implements were imported from igneous locales for the ceremonial grinding of maize. There is nothing to indicate that the two types did not coexist here. As for the sandstone specimen, I cannot say whether this material occurs in the predominantly limestone environs. Its size precludes daily household use and it too perhaps had some part in local ritual.

In contrast, the common metate at Uaxactun is of a type often referred to as "turtle-backed," that is, legless, roughly oval thin slabs with correspondingly shallow grinding grooves and convex undersides (see Kidder, 1947, p. 33). Similar specimens have been found at Benque Viejo

(Thompson, 1940, p. 27), San Jose (Thompson, 1939, p. 172), and Baking Pot (Ricketson, 1929, pp. 8–9). All these are Late Classic except for one from San Jose which is either late Pre-Classic or Early Classic in date (see Thompson, *op. cit.*, Table 13).

If relatively infrequent to the east, metates comparable to the common Piedras Negras type occur in fair numbers to the north, and have been particularly cited for sites lying in the area straddling the northern Peten, southern Campeche and Quintana Roo (Strömsvik, 1935; Ruppert and Denison, 1943, p. 96); also at Chichen Itza (Strömsvik, 1931). A few are reported for Chacchob (Pollock and Strömsvik, 1953, p. 92).

For the lowland sector, then, there seem to have been regional preferences in metates. The tripod type is exceedingly rare in the Peten—British Honduras area. Apart from those noted for Piedras Negras, only a few were encountered at Uaxactun (Kidder, *op. cit.*, p. 33; Ricketson and Ricketson, 1937, Pl. 64 b); none, I believe, have been recorded for either Benque Viejo, San Jose, or Baking Pot. Yet, in the southern part of the Colony, at Lubaantun, quantities of flat-surfaced, legged fragments were excavated (Joyce, 1926, p. 228). The effigy, tetrapodal metate is represented by one example at Copan (Longyear, 1952, p. 105) and might be considered evidence of southerly contact. But, interestingly, the tripodal metate does not seem to have been used by the Copanecos although they occupied a region not overly distant from Lubaantun. At Calakmul, a sandstone tripodal specimen was a surface find (Strömsvik, 1935, p. 123). Finally, Chichen Itza has produced many tripodal examples, but these are very distinctive, with their gross conical legs placed on, rather than back from, the periphery; the central leg is usually the largest, giving a characteristic slant to the grinding surface (Strömsvik, 1931). A simple, lava tripod was also discovered at this same site, and probably was imported (*ibid.*, p. 151). The tripodal, slanted flat-surfaced type has been discovered at Mayapan (for instance, Ruppert and A. L. Smith, 1954, Fig. 8 d); the common type, however, is said to be legless (Ruppert and A. L. Smith, 1953, p. 257).

With regard to temporal distribution, both metates and manos were curiously lacking in the Uaxactun Mamom deposits (Kidder, *op. cit.*, p. 35). However, a Uaxactun housemound, referable to Chicanel, or Late Formative (Pre-Classic) times, did produce a mano as well as a legless metate fragment (Wauchope, 1934, p. 168). Neither manos nor metates were found associated with Formative remains at Copan (Longyear, 1951, pp. 87–88). The presence there of comales has led to the postulation of metates and maize (*ibid.*). Longyear is likely correct in this but it should be noted that the comal has served for things other than the making of tortillas. For one, they evidently were used to roast cacao beans (Thompson, 1938, p. 597). Thompson actually seems doubtful about the Maya having eaten tortillas prior to the sixteenth century (1939, p. 126; also, *op. cit.*). A mano and a possible metate fragment did occur with Yohoa Monochrome sherds (Strong, Kidder II, and Paul, 1938, pp. 112, 114). At Yarumela, "Manos and metates were seen on the surface throughout the site, yet the twenty-five sections which were dug produced fragments of only four or five." (Canby, 1949, p. 270). Judging by Canby's summary (1951), they do not seem to have been a part of the early horizons. One "muller" is recorded for Playa de los Muertos (Strong, Kidder II, and Paul, *op. cit.*, p. 75). In the highlands, both metates and manos exist in Las Charcas and later Pre-Classic deposits (Shook, 1951 a, p. 97; 1948, p. 215) and fragments of legged metates appeared in Lothrop's excavations (1933, p. 28) in Chukumuk I and II.

These brief distributional notes affirm a widespread general use of the metate during Formative or Pre-Classic times, but still suggest that certain Maya groups, particularly in the Peten and southeastern region, may not have known it prior to the latter portion of this horizon. Engaging as it may be, the apparent lack of evidence for maize agriculture in the relatively early deposits of these regions perhaps does not warrant conclusive emphasis at this time. Maize replacing manioc (see Mason, 1938, p. 304; Kidder, 1940, p. 121) during the lowland Pre-Classic is a possibility verifiable by more problem oriented excavation as well as by publication of the nonceramic aspects of the sites investigated. For example, despite close ceramic tie-ins with the Peten during this horizon (Drucker, 1943; Thompson, 1953), Veracruz site reports are generally mute as regards the sequential positions of local metates and manos. Many more details must be known before we can begin to appreciate the economic basis of a transitional horizon so fundamental to later florescences. Apart from presence and absence, metates, if emphasized, might evidence a highland—lowland dichotomy via regional styles. It is not unreasonable to suppose that a community was accustomed to using the same metate type from generation to generation, even though great changes occurred in ceremonial paraphernalia—changes that were probably often remote to the greater part of any community. Surely one must ultimately turn to mundane metates and manos to answer the essential questions regarding the regional acceptance of maize and the cultural assemblages derived and dependent on its cultivation..

Shook (1951 a , p. 99) sees the Pacific and Atlantic lowlands as areas in which "the first steps from a nomadic existence to a sedentary one based on agriculture" occurred and from which, under population pressure, peoples pushed up into the highlands where a less fertile environment initiated industries whose products were traded to the lowlands in return for supplementary coastal food as well as cotton and salt. Remembering the spotty early signs of lowland (Atlantic) maize cultivation, one now can only ponder the significance of Shook's intriguing hypothesis.

SPECIALIZED GRINDSTONE

One (Fig. 42 b). Fragmentary basalt utensil featuring a depressed area at one end, and a flat grinding surface with raised edges. All upper surfaces slightly use-polished. Underside smoothly pecked. Fragment is legless. No traces of pigment.

SPECIALIZED GRINDING STONE

One (Fig. 40 f). Basalt with black crystalline inclusions. Cuboid. Maximum dimension 4.9 cm. Corners slightly rounded and surfaces smooth with very dull polish.

RUBBING STONES

Six (Figs. 40 k; 41 l—p). All pumice. L 6.7—11; T 2—7.2 cm. D of hemisphere 5.3; T 2.6 cm. The latter is the only one distinctly worked or worn.

COMMENT. These likely were carried from the highlands by the Usumacinta and collected for abrasive work; for example, stucco, or even in the tanning of leather. Such implements were rare at Uaxactun (see Kidder, 1947, p. 38).

POLISHING STONE

One (Fig. 41 f). Limestone, L 12; T 5.2 cm. Underside smooth except for slight breakage. Clearly used as a grinding or heavy polishing tool.

HAMMERSTONES

Subspherical, 3   (Fig. 40 c, d, j). Crystalline limestone. D 5.5, 6.5, 10.7 cm. Pecked and severely battered.

Elongate, 5   (Fig. 41 g—k). Limestone. L 11.5—18; T 1.4—7.7 cm. Considerable variation in cross-sections. Ends very much battered.

Discoidal, 3   (Fig. 40 a, b, e). D 8.3, 11, 16.3; T 2.7, 4.5, 6 cm. respectively. Limestone.

Others, 2   (Fig. 40 g, i). Cuboidal and hemispherical tools, heavily work-scarred.

COMMENT. Along with rubbing and polishing stones, these seemingly awkward implements were probably locally employed in the vast amount of construction that took place at Piedras Negras. At Uaxactun, the crumbling method was extensively used in masonry (Kidder, 1947, p. 37).

PECKING TOOL

One (Fig. 41 e). Limestone. Fragmentary. Remaining end fairly keen. Roughly surfaced.

PESTLE (?)

One (Fig. 42 a). Pink limestone. L 14; T 7.7. One side slightly faceted but surface otherwise round and fairly smooth. Butt and underside slightly fractured, pointing to at least occasional use as a hammer.

COMMENT. An implement closely resembling this was found at Xkichmook, Yucatan by E. H. Thompson (1898, Pl. XXV, c). Another, from Yucatan, is to be found in the Mercer Collection of the University Museum.

PROBLEMATICAL OBJECTS

Three (Fig. 40 h, l, n). These three unrelated objects have no apparent uses. The first is a large globular piece of pecked limestone with a short, possibly unbroken neck. That in l has been conically perforated and is fragmentary. The third object (n), made of a fine-grained green stone, is elongate and oval in cross-section.

WHETSTONES

Two (Figs. 40 m; 59 m). Dissimilar implements characterized by abraded grooved areas. The first specimen (L 5.8; W 3.9; Max T 1.9 cm.) is of smooth but unpolished green stone, very likely a water-worn pebble. Grinding has produced an end-to-end trough with maximum depth near center. This depression is very brown. While this tool may have served for the grinding of pigment, it more probably was used for sharpening wooden artifacts, perhaps wooden projectiles. The curvature of the groove precludes shaft-smoothing. The second whetstone, first thought to be of clay, is made of a fine-grained, pinkish stone, small and oval throughout, with one end notched through abrasion.

COMMENT. An object very much like that in Figure 40 m appeared at Uaxactun (Kidder, 1947, Fig. 78 a).

BARK-BEATER

One (Fig. 42 e). Tough limestone, broken. T 5; W 5.1 cm. Original length ca. 10 cm. Both sides corrugated: fourteen grooves on one surface, nineteen on other. Fragment is fully grooved. Round end.

COMMENT. On the Guatemalan side of the Usumacinta, across from the ruins of Yaxchilan, another bark-beater was found on the surface by the expedition. This implement (UM L—70—310) is corrugated on one side only. Opposite side is rough and apparently has sheared off. Roughly oval. Breakage has obscured hafting groove. L 9.5; W 7.3; T 2.8 cm. A third specimen from the Middle Usumacinta section has been described and illustrated by Satterthwaite (1943, p. 177, Fig. 1).

The Piedras Negras example is similar in all respects to those found at Uaxactun and elsewhere in the lowlands. Kidder has assembled much information on distributions and types (Kidder, Jennings, and Shook, 1946, p. 143; also Kidder, 1947, p. 38). These notes supplement Linné's earlier study (1934) of this interesting tool.

Exceptionally rare in the Maya area and actually in the whole of Mesoamerica is the bark-mallet, a monolithic implement archaeologically reported for the Bay Islands (Strong, 1935, p. 119, Pl. 16, 1, m), Quirigua (Lothrop, 1926, p. 99), Apatzingan (Kelley, 1947, pp. 133–34, Fig. 76, Pl. 19), and from the "Oaxaca and Vera Cruz regions" (Lothrop, *op. cit.*). One is contained in the Mexican collections of the Chicago Museum of Natural History (Cat. 95205); another, labeled as from Campeche, is in the Museum of the American Indian. One example comes from the site of Las Majadas near Kaminaljuyu (NM); it is Pre-Classic (E. M. Shook, verbal communication). Finally, two fragmentary bark-mallets were excavated at El Trapiche, El Salvador and are evidently late Pre-Classic in date (Coe, 1955, p. 20). The Lacandon, who occupy the general region of Piedras Negras, use a wooden bark-mallet in the ceremonial pounding of bark-cloth strips (Tozzer, 1907, p. 129, Pl. XIX, 4). Lothrop (*op. cit.*) also reports that other Mexican groups still use this type of implement.

BARREL-SHAPED STONES

Three (Figs. 39 g; 42 c; other not shown). L 13.5, 15.5, 16.1; T 7, 8.1, 8.8 cm. Limestone. Except for size, identical objects. Symmetrical with flat ends, almost perfectly round in cross-sections, with maximum thickness near middle. Smooth surfaces. None shows wear of any type. One was a surface find, another came from the base of Structure O–13, while the unillustrated piece cannot be assigned, having been shattered in the camp fire and the field number obliterated.

COMMENT. Apparently unique items. Conceivably these served as miniature altars for the sacrifice of small animals and birds. Occasional instances of bird remains in Piedras Negras caches as well as burials are noted on page 64 and in Part 3.

Much larger and permanently fixed column altars, calcined by fire, are frequent in Piedras Negras temples (Satterthwaite, 1937, p. 165 ff); these are somewhat tapered towards their bases and are not truly round in cross-section (Satterthwaite, 1936 b, Fig. 2, pp. 76–77). Another type of small altar is drum-shaped, portable and unburned. These portable altars are much wider than high (*ibid.*, p. 77). One of these was found on the floor of a vaulted building not classifiable as a temple (Satterthwaite, verbal information). Drum-shaped portable altars incidentally appear in Caches J–1–3, J–3–2, and J–3–3 (see Table 5). Column altars frequently had associated caches (see caches of Structure K–5 and R–9 in Part 3).

STONE VESSELS

One small fragment of a globular vessel of translucent calcite (not illustrated, in UM). Both sides smooth, outer side dully polished, with a thickness of .4 cm. Curvature, if from major body swell, suggests an original vessel diameter of about 25 cm. From Structure J–2, drain under Rooms 5 and 6 (field no. W–2–36). Field Catalogue lists a fragment of a second "stone vessel" (NM, not located) but material is not specified. From Structure V–1, probably on or above floor.

COMMENT. Satterthwaite (1943, p. 180) has had occasion to refer to the first specimen and suggests that it may evidence "late trade relations with the Gulf Coast region or farther afield." This of course refers to the Post-Classic Veracruz production of the handsome "Mexican onyx" or *tecali* cases (see discussion in Woodbury and Trik, 1953, pp. 242–43). Subsequent chemical tests by Mr. Albert Jehle (formerly of the Museum staff) have determined it to be calcite and not, as previously believed, marble or onyx. The piece is also too small for form reconstruction.

SPINDLE WHORLS

Five (Fig. 43 a—c; two [NM] not illustrated). Largest (*a*) is sandstone, others limestone. D 2.1—3.2; T .7—1.4 cm. Cylindrically bored to accommodate spindle. The largest specimen is subhemispherical, the others hemispherical. The only decoration occurs as a grooved edge on specimen *b*.

COMMENT. Two are from surface debris; Figure c and one NM example were surface finds on the camp road. All might be considered late in the occupancy of the site. This is consistent with the picture of rarity and lateness for stone spindle whorls elsewhere. Kidder (1947, p. 40) gives the distribution of these spinning implements. The majority of Uaxactun specimens (*ibid.*, Fig. 22) have incised simple decorations. Other whorls are described under Clay, p. 69.

DISCS

Three (Fig. 43 d—f). All limestone. D 2.1, 2.2, 2.6 cm. Figures e and f from Caches O—13—13 and O—13—17 respectively. Function of all unknown. Cache pieces may have been specially made for deposit and thus typologically "eccentric."

INCISED SPHERE

One (Fig. 43 u). Red limestone. D 2.4 cm. Incised small cross. On opposite side is a little protuberance with stucco adhering.

MINOR SCULPTURE

One (Fig. 43 g). Pumice. H 3.1; L 3.2; W 2.7 cm. A simply carved human head with depiction of browline, hair, nostrils, and mouth. From South Group, exact source unknown. Apparently unique.

GOUGES

Two (Fig. 44 a; possibly Fig. 44 b). First is of a green stone filled with lighter specks. L 3.9 cm. Bit edge depressed and sharp with diagnostic groove on one face. Poll rounded and use-scarred. Traces of a high polish occur on all surfaces. A second specimen, lacking bit end, may also be a gouge. Highly polished, veined, dark green stone. From Cache J—1—1.

COMMENT. Gouges seem to be exceptionally rare in the Maya area and Mesoamerica as a whole. Kidder (1942, p. 38) records two gouges rather similar to this one, made of a "very hard, dark green stone, possibly jadeite" which were found at Lake Flores in the Peten. Another was excavated at Tazumal (Tazumal Museum); the American Museum of Natural History possesses a second Salvadoran example. Two others, labeled as from Chiapas, occur in the collections of the Museum of the American Indian. Kidder (Kidder and Shook, 1952, p. 110) mentions still another from Chichicastenango. Zaculeu yielded a fragmentary gouge dateable as Early Post-Classic (Woodbury and Trik, 1953, p. 259). At least one other specimen is shown by Foshag, (1954, Fig. 5 e) who believes gouges to have been percussion instruments in jade working.

CELTS

Medium and large, 5 (Figs. 43 o –r; 44 f). The two largest and most intact celts (Fig. 43 o, p) are made of a dark green stone, probably diorite well polished, with polls and bits work-scarred. Largest: L 9, W 5.5, T 2.3 cm. Other: L 8.1, W 4.8, T 2.2 cm. Unfortunately, field numbers and thus proveniences are lacking for the NM examples. Another celt (Fig. 44 f) had a length of 4.4 cm., and is made of a hard , dark green stone with light green veining. Poll and sides squared. What remains of a convex bit is dull. Slightly polished. Celt fragment in Figure 43 r, from Cache K–5–2, is composed of an almost black stone with poorly polished, striated surfaces.   Squared sides and rounded bit. Remaining example (Fig. 43 q), gray-green stone, has a rounded battered poll and rounded sides. Faint traces of surface polish. Greatest width of all these implements on or near bit with maximum thickness near center.

Small, 2 (Fig. 44 c, d). L 3.2, 2.8 cm. Sides of first example, while flat, have rounded edges. Flat poll; work-scarred. Bit asymmetrically rounded and still quite sharp. Surfaces smooth and dully polished. Other celt is made of a fine green stone. Squared sides, convex poll, work-worn, and a dulled, symmetrically curved bit. Greatest width of each at bit end.

COMMENT.   Except for the noted cached celt fragment, these pecked and polished tools were recovered from superficial deposits. Various celtiform jadeites are described elsewhere in this section.

The material for the Piedras Negras celts must have been imported. Possibly they were imported in finished form. There is no evidence that these were hafted; hafting, however, is occasionally depicted in Classic sculpture. The crumbled butts actually suggest that these were used as chisels in conjunction with hammers. If so, they might have been utilized in the carving of monuments and other local sculptures As for the clearing of peripheral milpas, recent experimentation by Hester (1953) has shown that unaltered limestone flakes can very effectively be used to chop and girdle. Whether celts were so employed at Piedras Negras is problematic. It will be recalled that the collection includes a number of bifacially flaked choppers; crude flint flakes, such as described by Hester, may exist at the site but, if so, they would be too easily and understandably discarded.

The earliest recorded celts for the lowland Maya area occurred at Uaxactun in Pre-Classic sub-plaza deposits (Ricketson and Ricketson, 1937, Fig. 120, Pl. 62 a, 2). Lacking grooves, they conform to what is generally understood as a "celt," namely, an ungrooved axe. Whether these actually were hafted is something else again. Housemound excavations at Uaxactun yielded only one celt, dateable as Tepeu (Wauchope, 1934, p. 147, Pl. 4, b 13). Of the eleven celts excavated in Group A, one is Tzacol, the remainder Tepeu (Kidder, 1947, p. 38, Fig. 78). Edges are generally rounded with maximum width across bit end, but great variation in over-all length, from 4.7 to 17.3 cm. The Uaxactun excavations, then, suggest that the celt might have been preponderantly a Late Classic artifact. Size variation may reflect functional differences.

Turning to British Honduras, three rather large celt-like implements appeared in late San Jose contexts (Thompson, 1939, p. 174). Thompson (*ibid.*) has remarked on the absence at San Jose of the considerably smaller wedge-shaped celts found, for example, at Uaxactun (see Kidder, *op. cit.*, Fig. 78 k–m, q). Excavations by Thompson and   Ricketson at Benque Viejo and Baking Pot failed to turn up celts. Two large, elongate examples, one of them glyphically incised, came from Classic deposits in the Mountain Cow region (Thompson, 1931, pp. 27, 31, 303; Pls. XXXIII, XVII) . And at Kendal, a large celt, 21 cm. long, also inscribed with glyphs, was found in a mound together with several plain celts of polished green and pink stone "varying from 6 to 8 inches in length" (Price, 1897–99 , pp. 34–41; also Gann, 1918, pp. 91–92, Fig. 36, Pl. 16 c). The two incised specimens may have been imported from the 'Tabasco–Veracruz area as the glyphs evidently are of La Venta type (see Thompson, 1953, p. 451). A Pomona tomb, either Early or Late Classic, produced two other large celts, one of granite, the other jadeite (?) (Kidder and Ekholm, 1951, Fig. 5 c, d). Gann (*op. cit.*, pp. 99–100) mentions the inclusion of eight fairly large specimens in a Rio Hondo cache. For Lubaantun, Joyce (1926, p. 228) cites the paucity of small polished celts; his illustrated examples, though, appear to be on the small side and certainly wedge-shaped (*ibid.*, Pl. XXIV,

Fig. 2).

Information on the incidence and types of celts in the northern area is rather scant. Proskouriakoff (1952, p. 259; see also 1953, p. 283) states that at Mayapan: " Most common among other artifacts of imported stone were small polished celts of dark greenstone."

Two, illustrated by Thompson (1954, Fig. 3 j, k), are comparable in size to the largest of the Piedras Negras celts and have slightly flared sides near bits. Lothrop (1924, Pl. 10, i, j) shows two small wedge-shaped celts from Cozumel, while Charnay (1933, pp. 7–8) mentions a collection of some eighty, the bulk of which were found on the island; the figured pieces appear quite sizeable. Finally, a few examples, some seemingly large, are shown in one of Maler's plates, labeled as "Yucatan" (Maler, 1912, Fig. 2).

In the Guatemala highlands, celts occur as early as Las Charcas times (Shook, 1951 a, p. 97). A dark green celt comes from a Kaminaljuyu Esperanza Phase mound, and another from a possibly post-Esperanza deposit (Kidder, Jennings, and Shook, 1946, p. 142, Fig. 60). And at Cotio, greenstone celts were found with pottery corresponding to that of the Late Classic Amatle Phase of Kaminaljuyu (Shook, 1952, p. 183). Polished and unpolished celts appeared in all Zacualpa periods and ranged from small wedge-shaped· to large and more elongate in form; many were work-battered (Kidder, in Wauchope, 1948, pp. 13, 161–62, Fig. 77). Lothrop (1933, p. 27–28) reports a single surface find at Chukumuk and, at Chuitinamit nearby, polished celts are said to have been found in "some numbers" (ibid., p. 87). Three small ones occurred at Nebaj, one in a burial (A. L. Smith and Kidder, 1951, p. 51, Figs. 16, 84 g). Also illustrated (ibid., Fig. 84 f, g) are a celt from Cambote and three others from Chalchitan; the former site is said to be Pre-Classic. Relatively few celts, twelve in all, were recovered in the Zaculeu excavations; at least one of these pertains to the Atzan Phase (Early Classic) and Woodbury believes them to have been employed throughout the site's history (Woodbury and Trik, 1953, pp. 216–18). Fourteen complete and broken celts are reported for the Post-Classic site of Tajumulco (Dutton and Hobbs, 1943, p. 50 , Fig. 28) . Two, one longer than the other, both with rounded bits, were excavated at El Baul (Thompson, 1948, p. 40). Four are mentioned for San Agustin Acasaguastlan and these date as "probably Magdalena" (A. L. Smith and Kidder, 1943, p. 167, Fig. 36).

Celts have been reported for the following sites near the southern and eastern periphery. *Copan*: Small celts, ranging in length from 5 to 8 cm., are said to be fairly numerous in Pre-Classic through Late Classic deposits; sides seem to be flared toward the cutting edge (Longyear, 1952, pp. 105–06). *Yohoa sites*: Polished examples, some small and made of jadeite, were associated with Polychrome material at Aguacate, Aguatal, and Los Naranjos (Strong, Kidder II, and Paul, 1939, pp. 80, 111). *Ulua sites*: At Las Flores Bolsa, the butt end of a small celt of hard green stone was found together with Ulua Polychrome pottery (ibid., p. 45); also a small example in the Bichrome level at Santa Rita (ibid., p. 58). Popenoe (1934, p.69) notes the presence of celts at Playa de los Muertos. *El Rincon del Jicaque*: One complete and two broken specimens, all polished greenstone, come from this site, the main occupation of which occurred in very late times (Strömsvik and Longyear, 1946, pp. 50, 51). *Bay Islands*: Celts range from small wedge-shaped to long and relatively slender; the latter reportedly show more wear than the former (Strong, 1936, p. 68, Pls. 16, 17 j, k). Celts also occur on the mainland in the Guayamoreta Lagoon area (Stone, 1941, Fig. 41). *Tazumal*: One fragment of a dark greenstone celt (Boggs, in Longyear, 1944, p. 6.); others in Tazumal Museum. *El Trapiche*: A few celt fragments were found associated with Late Pre-Classic sherds (Coe, 1955).

This patently incomplete resumé of celts in the Maya area does little more than establish their time depth and persistence. The Formative or Pre-Classic distribution is notable: Las Charcas, Cambote, probably Zacualpa (Proto-Classic Balam Phase), Uaxactun, Copan, Santa Rita, Playa de los Muertos, and El Trapiche (El Salvador). Elsewhere in Mesoamerica, celts Pre-Classic in date have been discovered, at, among others, El Arbolillo I and II (Vaillant, 1935, p. 244), Zacatenco, Middle and Late (Vaillant, 1930, p. 168), El Tepalcate (Noguera, 1943, p. 40), and Cerro de las Mesas, Lower II (Drucker, 1943, pp. 13–14, 79).

The apparent universality of the celt in Mesoamerica is largely due to the fact that all groups eventually took on this implement at one time or another. Its use does seem to have grown with time. In the Peten—British Honduras area (assuming sampling to have been fairly adequate) it perhaps was not until Late Classic times that celts came to be functionally emphasized. Interestingly, celts and adzes are entirely absent in the lower Huastecan levels, occurring only in Post-Classic Periods V and VI (Ekholm, 1944, p. 490, Fig. 56 a—o; also see MacNeish, 1954); and, as mentioned in a prior section, obsidian flake-blades did not come into use there until the Late Classic. It is indeed puzzling why the lowland Maya (and their Huastecan cousins) should have accepted this tool in rather late times, having subsisted adequately for a long period with crude choppers. Was contact on a sub-ceremonial level so slight between highland and lowland Maya as to preclude the diffusion of the celt? Once adopted by the latter, did it initially occupy a non-utilitarian position as suggested by occasional finds of celts in burials and caches? And did it ultimately displace the bifacial chopper, assuming the latter to have had in part a cutting function?

PYRITE

PLAQUES

Solid discs, 2 (Fig. 43 h; 1 NM, not located). Illustrated fragment is from a thick but relatively small, beveled-edged disc. T 1.65 cm. Original diameter 5.8 cm. Surface, edge, and underside polished though not brilliantly. Fragment is unperforated. Faint bevel near edge of underside. From Cache J—6—5. The second specimen, only slightly broken on edge, was found with Burial 5 (for position, see Fig. 64, 19). Both surfaces polished (Field Catalogue). D of face 7.2 cm.; D of underside 7.6: T .8—1 cm. No data on whether or not perforated.

COMMENT. Solid plaques are certainly much rarer in Mesoamerica than mosaic plaques (see below). To the list of finds assembled by Vaillant (Merwin and Vaillant, 1932, p. 87, footnote 2), one might add those from two burials at Apatzingan, Michoacan (Kelly, 1947, p. 125, Fig. 73 c, Pl. 18, B); both are small (D 3.5, 7.2 cm.) and perforated and Kelly suggests that "one may have been attached to a shell-pyrites applique belt." Large numbers of such discs were included in certain Teotihuacan caches (Rubin de la Borbolla, 1947, Fig. 14); diameters are generally larger than most other examples, ranging as they do from 12 to 25 cm. And deposited in a late Period IV or V San Jose cache was a "mirror made of a single pyrite nodule" and, with it, a "flat disk of soft slate, presumably the back, pierced with two holes" (Thompson, 1939, pp. 176, 188, Pl. 26, b 3). The plaque had a diameter of about 6 cm. As to the manner in which these objects served, one can only point to the magnificent La Venta figurine on the breast of which adheres a tiny polished hematite disc (see Drucker, 1952, p. 154, Pl. 46).

Mosaic plaque, 1 (Fig. 42 f). Circular, consisting on discovery, of eighty-five polygonal thin (1—2 mm.) plates of surface-polished pyrite. D of face 24.4 cm. Set on a shale backing (present location unknown), light gray in color, and said (Field Catalogue) to have a thickness of about 4 to 5 cm. Edge of backing was beveled and the whole faintly convex. Evidently no means of suspension. Majority of mosaic elements, polished on exposed side only, are hexagonal. Found at foot of Skeleton B, Burial 5 (Fig. 64, 17).

COMMENT. For information on possible uses and distribution as well as manufacture of these extraordinary objects, the reader is referred to Kidder's detailed studies (Kidder, Jennings, and Shook, 1946, pp. 126—33; A. L. Smith and Kidder, 1951, pp. 44—50; see also Woodbury and Trik, 1953, pp. 232—39). In view of the relative scarcity of pyrite-incrusted plaques in the lowlands, the occurrence of one at Piedras Negras is of great interest. Its position within the burial would indicate that it was interred apart from any body. While the site undoubtedly could have afforded an artisan skilled in making these objects, the present piece and two isolated elements described below more likely were imported from the Guatemala highlands in finished form. Despite many richly stocked burials, no such objects appeared at Uaxactun (Kidder, 1947, p. 52).

Miscellaneous mosaic elements, 2 (Fig. 43 i, j). The intact piece (*i*) has a thickness of 5 mm.

Hexagonal, polished on one side only, beveled edges. Second is fragmentary and possesses ₐa double-beveled edge. Only one side is polished. This suggests a plaque with clear demarcation of pyrite parts. Both pieces encountered in general excavation.

FILLETS

Pair (Fig. 42 g; other [NM] not illustrated). Each composed of a series of rectangular and round pyrite pieces. Found together in Niche 1 of Burial 5 structure (Fig. 64, 21, 22); no remains of backing had survived. UM example has been restored according to *in situ* disposition of elements. It comprises four parallel bands, two of circular pieces and two of rectangular pieces, sixty-two in all. Longest band is 43 cm. Each element is polished on its exposed surface; 1–2 cm. thick. Not beveled. The NM specimen is almost identically composed. As discovered in the niche of Burial 5 their distribution indicates a pliable backing rather than one of wood or stone.

COMMENT. The function of these objects is purely speculative. Conceivably, they served as inlays in headbands, barely allowed by their lengths, or to encrust portions of a collar or belt. No Piedras Negras stela actually shows this particular ornamental alignment, but a number of personages wear bands of rectangular pieces across the chest and throughout their headdresses, notably those with "chin-straps."

OVAL OBJECTS

One (Fig. 43 k). L 1.9; T .15 cm. The polished surface has been deeply incised with an incomplete one-turn spiral. Obverse is unpolished. Possibly a reworked miscellaneous mosaic element. From drain of Structure J–2.

MISCELLANEOUS OBJECTS

Three (NM, not located). No description available. One each in Caches O–13–3, O–13–14 and O–13–15. That included in Cache O–13–14 is listed (Field Catalogue) as polished.

DENTAL INLAYS

Very small pyrite discs of perfect workmanship, polished on exposed surfaces, were used as inlays on prepared incisors. These appeared in Burial 2 and Burial 5 (Skeleton B). One such inlay is illustrated in Figure 69 a, third on lower right.

COMMENT. A complete listing of known pyrite dental inlays for the Maya area is given by Longyear (1952, Table 3). Their distribution includes Holmul, San Jose, Tzimin Kax, Copan, and Kaminaljuyu. For other areas, the reader is referred to Fastlicht and Romero (1951). Among the Maya, the custom of dental incrustation was exceptionally old, occurring as it does in the case of Burial E 8 at Uaxactun (Ricketson and Ricketson, 1937, pp. 143–44); unfortunately, the nature of the inlays is not known, but presumably they are of either jadeite or pyrite. Other Pre-Classic inlays have been recorded for Monte Negro and Monte Alban in Oaxaca (Fastlicht and Romero, *op. cit.*, Fig. 4, Cuad. 5).

HEMATITE

Worked, 3 (Fig. 43 l–n). The first specimen is a small disc (D l; T .2 cm.) with one perfectly flat, brilliant, glassy face slightly marred by pitting. The underside is dull. Edge beveled towards face. From Cache J–1–1. The other two, both part of Cache O–16–1, are broken and appear to be small parallel-sided plates with rounded ends. Both surfaces mirror-like. T .1 cm. Prior to deposition, these may have been mosaic elements.

Unworked, 3 (2 UM; NM, not located). A pair of small crystals of hematite was encountered in Cache J–1–1 along with the disc just described. The Field Catalogue lists a "nodule" of hematite in the surface debris of Structure O–7.

COMMENT. Instances of hematite are quite rare. Recent excavations have shown it to have been worked in Pre-Classic times, for a crystalline hematite plate formed part of the offerings placed in Tomb II, Structure E–III–3, Kaminaljuyu (Shook and Kidder, 1952, p. 116). Small pieces, possibly from mosaics, have been found in two Tzacol Uaxactun caches (Kidder, 1947, p. 52). At Caracol, thirty-eight such objects accompanied a cache below Altar 14 (in UM; Satterthwaite, verbal information). The archaeological distribution of hematite has been studied by Kidder (Kidder, Jennings, and Shook, 1946, p. 116).

JADEITE AND SIMILAR STONES

It must be emphasized that the minerals forming the objects here treated have in no case been submitted for expert identification. A variety of stones were fashioned into finely as well as poorly made objects at Piedras Negras. Brilliantly polished and well executed pieces are almost without exception jadeite, ranging in color from an emerald to a pallid green. Lesser grades of jadeite were employed along with pseudo-jades having in common hardness and greenness. The latter are frequently tremolitic and even micaeceous. Local lapidaries undoubtedly distinguished among these minerals, selecting from their importations the nodules of the finest jadeite for the fashioning of earplugs, bracelets, necklaces, and pendants. Poorer stones, as will be seen, were cut, smoothed, and incised for votive purposes. What was worn was carefully made, but what was cached was, for the most part, hastily made of the least precious stones. But de - spite technical and value distinctions, the Piedras Negras artisan may have generically viewed all hard and greenish stones as "jade." The object made reflected these distinctions—a possibility that has guided to a certain degree the following description of the collection.

Manufacturing techniques, object categories, object and mineral distributions, and the mineralogical context of jadeite for the Maya area have been treated at length by, among others, Kidder and Foshag (Kidder, Jennings, and Shook, 1946, pp. 104—24; Kidder, 1947, pp. 42—52; A. L. Smith and Kidder, 1951, pp. 32—43; Foshag, 1954).

INCISED CACHED OBJECTS.

The objects under this heading are all from caches (see Figure captions). A number were caught in the camp fire and thus cannot be assigned with certainty. There is fair evidence that the latter originated in Structure O—13 caches. These are relatively crude objects with little or no carved silhouette. Incised surface of each piece is smooth, occasionally flat, sometimes rounded, but never polished. Edges vary from rough to smooth. Incision varies from deep to almost imperceptible scratches.

Full figures, 7 (Figs. 45 g, i, l; 46 c, i, x, e'). Two clearly incised examples (Figs. 45 l; 46 e') portray standing human figures, front view, one with necklace and perhaps earplugs, and both arms flexed across chests. A number of the remaining pieces, crudely scratched, show seated individuals, either front or side views. Excision evident in Figure 45 i.

COMMENT. The standing flexed-arm specimens resemble certain Early Classic carved jades from Nebaj (A. L. Smith and Kidder, 1951, Figs. 2, 52 b—d). Comparable features are: arms flexed across chest, clenched hands, and less distinctly, the treatment of the nose and mouth. Similarities may also be found in a few of the cached ("Full Classic?") jade plaques of Copan (Longyear, 1952, Fig. 90). The pose itself, with arms awkwardly arranged as if to support a ceremonial bar, is likewise reminiscent of many monumental figures. Further correspondences are to be found in two Piedras Negras shell figures (Fig. 51 d—e).

Profile heads, 28 (Figs. 45 a—c, e, j, k; 46 a, b, e—h, k—n, p—v, y, b', c'). Majority of designs very faint. Some quite naturalistic, others seem very abstract. Figure 46 a is especially interesting, having been definitely made from a water-rolled nodule of evidently poor quality jadeite. At least three unsuccessful attempts were made to further divide this pebble (shown also in Fig. 50 q).

COMMENT. For the most part, these objects appear to have been very hastily made once the engraving surface was prepared. This of course confuses identification of these various heads. The majority are almost certainly of deities. One in particular, an open-jawed, long-nosed monster (for instance, Fig. 46 l, q, r) is repeated on certain Piedras Negras cached shell objects (see 51 i—k). Deities with up-turned noses are to be seen among these jades as well as ones with down-turned and projecting noses. A number of these depict what J. Eric S. Thompson (personal communication) has suggested to be conch shells (see Fig. 46 l, q, r, y, and less certainly e, n, t). Thompson (1950, p. 278) also writes that "the primary association of the conch is with water" and is secondarily "an attribute of gods of the underworld..."

Incised superficially worked bits of jade, deposited in caches, are a unique feature of Piedras Negras. Such objects are possibly counterparts of the incised obsidian flakes recovered in caches at Tikal and Uaxactun (see discussion under Eccentric Obsidians and General Comment below).

Plaited bands, 4 (Figs 45 h; 46 d, o, w). These may be either two bands wrapped simply upon one another as in Figure 45 h and 46 d, o, or complexly knotted as in 46 w.

COMMENT. The plaited design (rectilinear guilloche) found on these cache objects is substantially like that on incised obsidians from Tikal and Uaxactun caches. Thompson (in Kidder, 1947, p. 24) concluded that those on the latter symbolize the god Itzamna. In describing a more recent find of these obsidians, Berlin (1951, p. 45) observes that, when intact, the design comprises nine parallel elements—possibly a further suggestion of the Nine Lords of the Night. However, only one of the Piedras Negras jade examples (Fig. 46 w) approximates this feature of nine elements.

Although the mat pattern has been identified symbolically with Itzamna, there may exist a second but related possibility. The mat, of course, is one of the two principal elements of the month glyph Pop. Furthermore, Thompson (1950, p. 107) has extended the significance of "mat" to "jaguar mat," and, still further, to "authority" and "chief." And the jaguar is the patron of the month Pop. The apparent association of mat and jaguar is possibly reinforced in the case of the jaguar pendant from Piedras Negras (see below and Fig. 49 a), for the terminal glyph of its inscription is this very mat element. Alone, this glyph seems to lack calendrical meaning. There exist good grounds for relating Itzamna to the jaguar via rain or water. Thompson himself writes that the "most common wearer [of the water lily] is the jaguar god, the god of the interior of the earth..." (*ibid.*, p. 279). An incised peccary skull from Copan (Longyear, 1952, Fig. 107 o; Spinden, 1913, Fig. 210) contains a panel consisting of the essential element of the Cauac sign (rain) along with abbreviated mat designs. This same assemblage is to be seen twice in the Madrid Codex (101 c). Other water-jaguar associations have been presented by Thompson (1951, p. 36) and by Rands (1955, pp. 361–63). And Itzamna is a celestial rain being or beings. Conceivably, then, these particular cached jades, and obsidians incised with this design from other sites, signify rain as expressed by the plaited mat, an attribute of Itzamna and the jaguar. But one wonders, for the permutations of Maya symbols are so extensive that one is liable to push the meaning of this item far beyond its actual significance.

Essentially similar are the diagonally banded designs so common in Classic art. At Piedras Negras, these appear on the headdress and loincloth of the Stela 8 figure. Proskouriakoff (1950, p. 97) terms the design a "twisted band of mat motif," one which is of "great antiquity and duration." A second context is a "cross with mat design" (*ibid.*). This appears on the Stela 35 loincloth and on shoes at Naranjo (Stelae 13 and 24), on a ceremonial staff at Yaxchilan (Stela 11) and on clothing at Yaxchilan (Stela 8) and Bonampak (Stela 2). Mat ornaments worn on the chest have been noted for Tikal Stela 9 and Palenque, Temple of the Cross. At least structurally related to the last is the knot motif found in late contexts at Tuluum and Santa Rita. This knot closely resembles the incised design on the Piedras Negras jade in Figure 46 w.

From Piedras Negras caches to Palenque to Tuluum, these distributional and contextual facts suggest meaning but hardly provide answers. They are simply given to illustrate possible implications of the crude designs found on these Piedras Negras jades.

Unidentifiable designs, 8 (Figs. 44 q; 45 d, f; 46 j, z, a¹, d¹). Incised designs, some linear, others cursive. Design on one jade from Cache R–9–2 (NM) is too faint for illustration.

GENERAL COMMENT ON INCISED CACHED OBJECTS. The Tikal and Uaxactun obsidians, described by Kidder, Berlin, and Joyce, stem from caches associated with monuments whose dates range from 9.14.0.0.0 to about 9.16.0.0.0. In one instance (A. L. Smith, 1950, p. 34, Table 5), these obsidians have been used for cross-dating purposes. The Piedras Negras incised jadeites, a comparable trait, were being fashioned at an earlier date, surely prior to 9.12.5.0.0 (see Structure K–5 caches under Caches; also

Tables 4 and 5). At the moment, however, it would be foolish to speak of a western derivation for the Peten instances. In this regard, see Part 3, Distribution of Caches, Guatemala (lowlands, Tikal).

INCISED PLAQUES

Two (Fig. 45 v, w). Relatively large, thin pieces, unperforated, each with smooth incised surface. Each depicts a seated anthropomorphic individual. Figure *w* shows a very much stylized profile figure with a round-eyed, thick-lipped face turned to upper left of plaque. An arm is flexed across chest. Underside is smooth in places but largely rough. Saw marks evident on one edge (see illustration). From Cache O—13—51. Design on *v* is more difficult to make out. Apparently a figure seated cross-legged, body in front view, with one braceleted arm across stomach, the other flexed with clenched hand on chest. Head, in left profile, features a square eye and indications of a "long-nosed" god once again. Opposite surface is longitudinally divided by a septum and striated by regular saw marks (evident in Fig. 50 s). Squared edges. From Cache O—13—50.

COMMENT. Apart from Piedras Negras, unperforated jade plaques seem to occur only at Copan where they probably date as Late Classic (Longyear, 1952, pp. 107—08, Fig. 90). There is no reason to suppose that our specimens are any older than Late Classic. The Copan specimens also derive from caches. A close resemblance in execution, facial features, and perhaps even pose, may be noted between our Figure v and Longyear's Figure 90 d.

CARVED PENDANTS

The quantity and arrangement of biconical peripheral perforations to be seen on the majority of the following objects suggest that they might have been more suitable for sewn attachment to garments than for suspension from a cord as strictly pendants. These carvings totally lack the transverse or vertical perforations seen so commonly in jade work of the highlands. Their method of suspension alone relates them instead to other carvings from such lowland sites as Uaxactun (Kidder, 1947, Figs. 33 c; 34 b) and San Jose (Thompson, 1939, Fig. 94 a, b, d).

Human heads, 2 (Fig. 45 y, c¹). The first comes from Burial 10 (NM, not located) (see Fig. 67, 6) and is a carved face in front view, polished throughout, and biconically perforated back-to-side in four instances. A fifth perforation is said to occur at the base of the pendant and likely was used for suspendion of a secondary object, such as a tubular bead. Data from field photograph and Field Catalogue, as present whereabouts of object unknown. The other pendant (*c¹*) is a head in right profile, carved from fair quality jade, and, although burned in camp fire (Structure O—13 cache?), still retains the original high polish on its face. Ear and corner of mouth have been slightly drilled. Probably suspended face down. The underside is very rough.

COMMENT. It is puzzling why carved heads often are in right profile, like the one just described and the jaguar pendant (see below), when practically every head on cached incised jades (as well as shells) is facing left. The orientation of the latter is consistent with that of head variants and other glyphs in Maya epigraphy (curious exceptions are found on pages 22—24 of the Paris Codex).

Full figure, 1 (Fig. 47 e; NM, not located). Highly polished, good quality jade. L 7; W 2.7. Front view in shallow relief. A crouched individual, with loincloth, hands clenched on chest, earplugs, headdress, and horizontally grooved, tubular-drilled eyes. Perforated from top to back and from lower left (observer's) side to back. Latter perforation plugged with a prepared piece of jade. From Burial 5, Skeleton B, near jaw (Fig. 64 a). Its position on excavation indicated that it had been placed in the mouth (Mason, 1933, p. 55). This trait is discussed in Part 3 (Object in mouth of deceased).

Jaguar head, 1 (Figs. 47 f; 49 a). Found in Burial 5, partly under vertebrae of Skeleton B (Fig. 64, 12). L 8.2; T 1.5. A fine, low-relief carving in right profile. Quality of jade seems excellent and piece is highly polished throughout. Ear slightly broken. Biconically bored in at least three instances and perhaps as many as six, all back-to-side. Possibly worn sewn to a garment or headdress. Opposite surface is flat, also brilliantly polished, with two diagonal, parallel rows of incised glyphs.

COMMENT. This handsome effigy, undoubtedly the finest of jade recovered *in situ* at Piedras Negras, has been previously shown by Mason (1933, Pl. 11) and by Keleman (1943, Pl. 251 a), and both illustrated and studied from the standpoint of its inscription by Morley (1937–1938, pp. 173–74, Fig. 103). The latter assigned the piece a date of 9.15.0.0.0 with three interrogation points. The inscription, for the most part, is indecipherable, and dating largely depends on joint consideration of the four inscribed shell plaques from this same burial (see Fig. 53 a–d). Remarks have been made above on the terminal glyph of this inscription.

Mention should be made here of two other fine jade pendants, both inscribed and apparently Late Classic, that have been attributed to Piedras Negras on the basis of their inscriptions and lesser considderations. One superb head, beautifully carved in the round, was among the objects dredged from the Sacred Cenote of Chichen Itza (see Proskouriakoff, 1944; Keleman, 1943, 241 d; Morley, 1947, pp. 426–27, Pl. 91, e, f). Beyer (1945), in a stylistic analysis of a single glyph of an inscription on one side of a low-relief pendant of unknown provenience (also shown in Spinden, 1913, Fig. 195), very hesitantly pointed to Piedras Negras as its source.

One would certainly like to claim these excellent objects for the site. Unfortunately, no jade similar to that shown by Proskouriakoff was discovered in excavation. But as Proskouriakoff (*op. cit.*, p. 143) notes, its style is entirely consistent with certain elements shown on various Late Classic Piedras Negras stelae. Her calendrical argument is likewise impressive. As regards the Beyer example, Satterthwaite (1946) has pointed to a basic fault in Beyer's source drawing. Disregarding glyphs, the piece has various specific affinities to Late Classic highland jades, and even to one cached example from the Castillo intrastructure at Chichen Itza (Anonymous, 1937, p. 7).

While Piedras Negras, unlike a number of lowland sites, did yield a fairly impressive group of carved jades, it evidently neither imported nor locally produced the exceptionally beautiful carved plaques like these for example, from Nebaj. Most of the finer Piedras Negras objects have a single source, namely, Burial 5. Nevertheless, the apparent absence of carved, full-front depictions of seated figures, shown in the Nebaj collection, has some bearing on the postulated source of these superlative highland specimens. On the grounds of notable resemblances to sculptural content and ability at Bonampak and Piedras Negras (see Lintel 7), the Nebaj specimens have been attributed to a school that flourished in the Usumacinta region during Late Classic times (A. L. Smith and Kidder, 1951, pp. 5, 36 ; Kidder, 1947, pp. 51–52). Burial 5 was rich by lowland mortuary standards and Piedras Negras was a major ceremonial center in this Usumacinta region. But it did not produce jades in this style.

Pendant, square in section, 1 (Fig. 44 l). Green color of jade lost in ancient fire. L 6.4; W 1.5; T 1.1. Highly polished. Flared, double- banded end. Made from what was originally intended to be a banded, rectangular bead (as in Fig. 47 c, d; also Fig. 49 g) that broke during or prior to longitudinal boring for suspension. Or it might have been shattered in this fire prior to completion. The maker salvaged the piece by grinding down the broken end and perforating the opposite end with conical converging bores. This example of re-use does indicate that longitudinal perforation followed shaping and surface polishing. A surface find, Structure R–3.

MISCELLANEOUS SMALL OBJECTS

Flat figurines, 7 (Fig. 45 m–s). Made of full, smooth-surfaced poor quality "jade." Figures *m* and *n* basically similar, and being thin, roughly shaped bits of stone with facial features, neckline, and so forth incised on their surfaces with smooth but unincised undersides. Their full-front standing pose is shared by cruder examples in Figures *o* and *p*. The remaining objects are still simpler. All these are seated in left profile with little detail.

COMMENT. Analogous in many ways to certain silhouetted figures of shell from caches at this site (see Part 3, pp. 56, 57; Shell, for distribution). All lack field numbers (camp fire) but likely stem from Structure O–13 caches.

Human profile head, 1 (Fig. 45 a'). A better than average dark jadeite. L 2.3 cm. Carved in low relief, with left face of subject depicted. Carved side polished, but underside is smooth and unpolished. Cache O—13—4.

Problematical objects, pair   (Figs. 47 i; 49 d). Both from Burial 5 (Fig. 64, 19). Complementary. UM specimen composed of a hard white to light green stone, presumably jadeite. Grooved side is
polished while other side is smooth but striated and only faintly polished. L 2.7; T 1 cm. NM piece
(Fig. 47 i) not located, but comparable in size and details. Note shallow depression on each.

Disc, 1 (Fig. 45 f'). Light green stone. D 1.4 cm. Underside flat, upper surface slightly convex. An inlay? Debris of Structure R—10.

Hook-shaped objects, 2   (Fig. 45 t, u). L of each 2.8 cm. One is undecorated, but other has concentrically incised design near edge. First burned camp fire; second from Cache O—13—47.

COMMENT.   Essentially similar objects in shell and stone have been previously found at San Jose
and Hatzcap Ceel in what evidently are Late Classic caches (see Thompson, 1931, Pl. XXXI, 2, 5; 1939,
Fig. 29 c, 2—5). These are all unperforated. Were it not for their votive usage one might conclude that
they served as matched effigy canine teeth in masks of inlayed shell (as in Fig. 53 f) and stone. Thompson has noted their frequent cache association with the small figurines of stone and shell; these likewise
appear in Piedras Negras offerings but no such association has survived.

Perforated hook-shaped objects, particularly in jade, have been recorded in the highlands (see Woodbury and Trik, 1953, p. 257); it is doubtful that these are related to the lowland specimens, certainly not
functionally.

Conoidal objects, 1   (Fig. 45 g'). Unpolished, burned in camp fire. Underside slightly rounded
and unmarked.

Diagonally banded object, 1   (Fig. 45 x). Poor jade. L 2.5 cm. Probably represents band motif
(for discussion, see above under Incised Cached Objects). Camp fire.

Rectangular wedge, 1   (Fig. 44 k). Dark jadeite, dully polished. Tapered edge blunt. Found in
Burial 5 (Fig. 64 I).

Tabbed rectangular plaque, 1   (Fig. 49 j). Fair quality jadeite. L 2.2; T .3 cm. Surface on
which tab is grooved is unpolished but obverse is polished. Burial 5 (Fig. 64, 19).

Loaf-shaped object, 1   (Fig. 45 e'). Very tremolitic stone. L 2; W 1; T .7 cm. Somewhat
battered, otherwise smooth and barely polished, if at all. Some sort of substance adheres to illustrated
side. An inset? Cache J—1—1.

Celtiform object, 1   (Fig. 45 d'). Gray-green jadeite. L 2.5; T .7 cm. Bit end quite sharp.
Edge continuous except for butt. Traces of high polish and no evidence of use. Part of Cache R—9—1.

COMMENT.   Thompson (1950, p. 134) has pointed out that the axe ''is the symbol of Schellhas'
God B, a deity of the rains and storms.'' A hafted celt further forms the eye of the head variant for the
number six, whose patron is closely associated with vegetation and water (*ibid.*). Serviceable celts,
some of jade, appeared in Caches J—29—1, J—1—1, K—5—2, and K—5—6.

Spherical object, 1   (NM, not illustrated). Small, round, unbored, jadeite object, possibly a blank
for a bead, occurred with a few unworked and worked jade objects in Burial 5 (Fig. 64, 19).

Problematical object, 1   (UM, not located and not illustrated). On the basis of a field photograph,
this appears to be a fragment of a larger elongate object. About 4.5 cm. long. Highly polished jadeite.
Comprises a square-in-section shaft (broken), then a square collar, and a final segment (thinner than the
shaft) attached to collar. Object seems then to have been terminally cruciform. From Burial 10, Niche 1
(Fig. 67, 40).

Effigy stingray spine, 1   (Fig. 49 i). Light green jadeite. Fragmentary. L 3.3 cm. From Burial
5, Skeleton B, slightly north of right orbit (Fig. 64 c). Ovoid in section, longitudinal ridge along one surface, and oblique incisions along edges of opposite surface. Highly polished. A second, smaller fragment (UM, not illustrated), which fits the broken end of the first piece, was found in the right orbit. L 1
cm. As the second fragment is broken at both ends, the replica's original length exceeded 4.3 cm. but
was perhaps no more than 4.5 cm.

COMMENT. This remarkable object was probably worn in some fashion although no means of suspension are visible. Two other such jade replicas have been reported: one, from a La Venta tomb where it formed the central element in a necklace of perforated natural spines inset with crystalline hematite (Drucker, 1952, pp. 162–63, Pl. 54 d); the other, a squat, less naturalistic example among the offerings of a spectacular Cerro de las Mesas (Lower II) jade cache (Drucker, 1955, p. 63, Pl. 48 k). Stingray spines are more fully discussed in the section devoted to bone objects.

EARPLUGS

Matched pair (Fig. 47 g, h; g also shown in Fig. 49 b). Both mottled, highly polished cloudy green jadeite. Maximum width 5.4 and 5.5 cm. Square, flat face with rounded corners. Surfaces reflect slight cleavage unevenness. Very short stems relative to facial breadths. Central conical perforations with minute exits on faces. Found on either side of skull of Skeleton B, Burial 5 (Fig. 64, 5).

COMMENT. The UM example has been previously illustrated by Mason (1933, Pl. 11). Pair also mentioned in Kidder, Jennings, and Shook, 1946, p. 108. These were very likely manufactured from a single piece of stone. Few examples of this earplug type are known (ibid.). Detailed studies of earplug typology, manufacture, and distribution are to be found in the aforementioned source as well as in A. L. Smith and Kidder, 1951; Kidder, 1947; Drucker, 1955.

FILLET

Composed of 20 partially paired re-used small earplugs (?) (see Mason, 1933); found across the forehead and beneath the head of Skeleton B, Burial 5 (Fig. 64, 4). The greater part of these have been fashioned from a truly beautiful homogeneous, emerald green jadeite, thoroughly polished. The complete fillet is illustrated in Figure 48 a–t in their actual order. Figures e and f were central and most forward of the group. Note pairing. Many of these have been further shown in Figure 47 j–x. For coordination, see figure captions. No trace of adhesive was noted on any of these pieces.

A variety of quite distinct shapes are represented:

Flares, 12 (Fig. 48 a, c, e, f, h–l, o, p, t; some of these also shown in Fig. 47 j–o, r, s, w, x). Maximum width of face occurs in Figure 48 e: 2.3 cm. Considerable differences in size and execution. One pair (Fig. 48 e, f) has broad, slightly concave faces, round edges, short stems, and conical throats leading to faces. As mentioned, these rested directly on the smashed forehead of Skeleton B. In others (Fig. 48 a, c, h, l, etc.), throats are relatively wide, with squat indistinct necks. Horizontal conical bores are frequently found on these necks and originally may have been pinned for securing the flare in earplug assemblages. With re-use, these perforations perhaps could have served for threading the elements to their backing. Exceptions are those in Figure 48 e, f, k which lack secondary perforations. A lip perforation has been carefully fitted (on re-use?) with a conical jadeite plug (Fig. 47 o, arrow; also apparent in Fig. 48 t). The faces of a number of these flares have been radially grooved, possibly string-grooved in certain cases (Fig. 48 c, h, j, l).

Cup-shaped, 3 (Fig. 48 b, r, s; also shown in Fig. 47 t–v). Slightly flared sides with everted lips; broad, deep throat with a flat, centrally perforated bottom. Undersides either flat, as in Figure 48 s, or countersunk, as in 48 r. Apart from its minute basal perforation, one example (Fig. 48 r) has been bored in four other instances, one of which occurs on its lip. Figure 47 u is likely shown again in Figure 48 b; it was probably broken and partly lost in the time between field photography and laboratory drawing.

Dish-shaped, 3 (Fig. 48 m, n, q). Similar to the preceding form, and also with centrally perforated bottoms, but more flattened and everted.

Countersunk, pair (Fig. 48 d, g; also shown in Fig. 47 p, q). Matched pair. A single central conical bore. No secondary perforations. Ovoid faces. A second pair of similarly formed jades from Burial 5 is described below.

COMMENT. Eleven small flares, many of them paired, were discovered in a Kaminaljuyu Esperanza Phase tomb and may also have comprised a fillet (Kidder, Jennings, and Shook, 1948, p. 111). A Uaxactun Tepeu burial yielded evidence of a jade-studded headband (Kidder, 1947, p. 45). The basal portions of headdresses on Piedras Negras Stelae 8 and 9 are bordered with objects, presumably jadeite, resembling those just described. Small flares might have functioned as smaller than usual earplugs, perhaps of a child, but they were often used on garments and the like. Cup-shaped pieces appear rarely elsewhere. A Piedras Negras clay example is described in Part 3, p. 70. A pair of countersunk jades was recovered in a Magdalena tomb at Guaytan (A. L. Smith and Kidder, 1943, Fig. 54 c).   Other records of countersunk jades include a Mercado cache, Chichen Itza (Ruppert, 1943, Fig. 35, 3) and an Uxmal cache (Saenz, 1952, Fig. 5). On Yaxchilan Stela 10 they appear in a headband, necklace, and bracelets. The central element in the headband depicted on Stela 7 at Piedras Negras is countersunk, and others appear in headbands on La Mar Stelae 1 and 2, and on Yaxchilan Lintels 3 and 33. Late Classic highland jade work frequently shows figures with well defined countersunk earplugs (for instance, A. L. Smith and Kidder, 1951, Figs. 55 f; 59 a). A countersunk effect occasionally resulted from sharp, tubular drilling. Figures, though, on Early Classic jades were not infrequently depicted with earplugs in the form of either raised round or squarish elements with a central depression (the throat?) (*ibid.*, Fig. 52 c, d). Our Figure 47 e seems to agree with Early Classic highland jade carvings in this respect. What are perhaps other early traits in the collection have been previously noted in connection with the incised jade shown in Figure 46 e¹.

While the small flares in the Burial 5 fillet are shaped and perforated to allow mounting and pinning on earplug rods, there is some sculptural evidence that cups, dishes and countersunk jades were often employed in headdresses and other decorations and presumably secured by knotting and sewing. Despite negative evidence, we cannot, however, rule out the use of some sort of adhesive.

MISCELLANEOUS ORNAMENTS

Scalloped ornament, 1 (Fig. 49 e). Fragmentary. A light green jadeite with glassy polish on face. Scalloped edge, radially grooved face, and maximum point-to-point diameter of about 8 cm. Very wide throat. From chest of Skeleton B, Burial 5 (Fig. 64 D).

COMMENT. A figure on La Mar Stela 2 wears a large, widely perforated, scalloped ornament suspended from a necklace. To cover the possibility that this object is an outsized earplug (individuals on Piedras Negras stelae frequently wear enormous ear ornaments), one should note the occurrence of a pair of scalloped flares, also radially grooved, in an Early Classic tomb at Pomona, British Honduras. While smaller than the Piedras Negras specimen, they are nevertheless remarkably similar (Kidder and Ekholm, 1951, Fig. 4 i, j).

Small, flared, 2 (Figs. 44 i; 49 f). The first specimen is made of a dark mottled, highly polished jade with a smooth underside. Irregular face. From Cache O-13-54. The second (Fig. 49 f) comes from Burial 5 (Fig. 64, 1) and has a facial diameter of 2.1 cm. Shallow symmetrical depression on face with biconically perforated short neck.

Perforated ornament, 1 (Fig. 45 b¹). Irregularly edged (natural?) with highly polished flaring throat and face. Underside is rough. Cache O-13-4.

Countersunk elements, pair (Figs. 44 h; 47 y). First is polished gray-green jade, D 1.5 cm. Conical off-center bore. Both from Burial 5, near right knee of Skeleton B (Fig. 64 H). The NM example (Fig. 47 y) is almost identical.

Perforated oval ornaments, 4 (Figs. 44 j, m; 47 z; 48 k¹). Figure 44 m is polished gray-green jade, oval, with rounded edge and biconical central perforation, D 1.5 cm., and is from Burial 10 (Fig. 67, 9). Figure 44 j, with a D of 2.5 cm., is fire-blackened (ancient), highly polished throughout, conically perforated, from Burial 5 (Fig. 64,1). That in Figure 48 k¹, a small perforated adorno, has a flat, unpolished underside with scars of sawing; remainder of piece polished; from Burial 10 (Fig. 67, 32). Minutely perforated object in Figure 47 z known only from a field photograph (NM, not located) comes from Burial 5, Skeleton B.

Others, 3 (Fig. 44 n–p). Good quality jadeite. Small. Square-faced piece is well polished while irregularly-edged example is polished on underside only. All centrally perforated. Face of *o* slightly countersunk and radially grooved to corners. These adornos were discovered in Burial 10 (Fig. 67, 31, 33, 35 respectively).

CELTS

Three (Figs. 43 s, t; 44 e). Jadeite, variable in color. Negligeable polish. All three specimens badly broken. Two contained in Cache J–29–1 and one in Cache K–5–6.

COMMENT. The placing of celts in caches is an exceptionally rare trait. Cache 1 at Hatzcap Ceel contained a large, incised celt (Thompson, 1931, pp. 270–71). Possibly cached were another glyphically inscribed celt and a number of plain ones from Kendal (Price, 1897–99, pp. 339–41; also Gann, 1918, p. 91). Thompson (1953, p. 451) believes both these inscriptions to be in La Venta style. Various early reports by Gann on his excavations in British Honduras make occasional mention of celts, and often their contexts sound suspiciously votive.

Why celts should be selected for cache inclusion is a problem. The Hatzcap Ceel and Kendal examples were undoubtedly of great value, having been traded a considerable distance. Cache K–5–2 produced a fragmentary celt of non-jadeite stone. Thus all four cached Piedras Negras celts were broken prior to offering. One suspects that celts may have been something of a novelty during Classic times in the lowlands and were valued objects. The fact that three were of jadeite would compound their value. In discussing a small celt-like jade (see above), it was suggested that in Maya belief it might have possessed symbolic as well as intrinsic value. Jade, in itself, was of course an important water symbol throughout Mesoamerica.

BEADS

Quadrangular in section, decorated, a pair (Fig. 47 c, d; c also shown in Fig. 49 g). Banded long beads which probably were worn as bar pendants. Brilliantly polished, excellent cloudy green jadeite. UM bead (Fig. 47 c): L 10; W 2.9; T 1.4 cm. NM example is nearly identical. Slightly flared ends, cuffed with double bands. Ends have been radially grooved to corners and midpoint of each side. Biconically bored throughout for suspension. This fine pair was located in the thoracic area of Skeleton B, Burial 5 (Fig. 64 D).

COMMENT. UM piece previously shown by Mason (1933, Pl. 11). Beads of this type were among the material dredged from the Sacred Cenote at Chichen Itza (Kidder, Jennings, and Shook, 1946, p. 113).

Quadrangular in section, plain, 1 (Fig. 49 h). Highly polished rectangular bead, biconically bored. L 5.3; W 1.8; T 1.4 cm. Burial 5, under left hand bones of Skeleton B (Fig. 64 F).

Cylindrical, 7 (Figs. 47 d¹, e¹; 48 f¹; 49 l, left; 3 others lost). Polished fine jadeite. All from Burial 5. Great variation in size. Some slightly barrel-shaped. Majority biconically drilled but one (Fig. 49 l, left; also shown in Fig. 48 f¹, right) has a cylindrical bore. Largest specimen (Fig. 47 e¹) lay under right hand of Skeleton B (Fig. 64 G). All beads located in Fig. 64 A, D, E, G.

Subspherical. Practically all examples came from Burials 2, 5, and 10. (a) Burial 2 lot, 18 beads (8 UM, Fig. 48 g¹; 9 NM, not located). D of UM specimens .6– .75 cm. Dully polished, variable quality jadeite. All biconically perforated for suspension. From area of mouth or throat (Fig. 63 b, 1). (b) Burial 5 lot, at least 141 beads (Figs. 47 a, b, a¹–c¹; 48 v, a¹; 49 k, l; 64, 1, 11, B, D). D of UM specimens .7– 1.3 cm. As a rule, highly polished and made of excellent jade. Well shaped to quite irregular in outline. Generally with biconical perforations, but some feature conical and even cylindrical drillings (see Fig. 49 k, l). From areas of mouth, chest, pelvis, and periphery of Skeleton B (Fig. 64). (c) Burial 10 lot. Because of distinct differences in size, these were grouped on excavation according to size: *Class 1* comprises the smallest of the lot. 23 beads (10 UM, Fig. 48 c¹; 9 NM, Fig. 48 j¹; 4 not located). D .45– .7 cm. Poor jade, a few well polished. Biconically drilled. *Class 2,* 12 beads (6 UM, Fig. 48 b¹; 6 NM, Fig. 48 i¹). D .8–1 cm. Similar in material, finish, and bore to previous group. *Class 3,* 12 beads (7 UM, Fig. 48 y, z; 5 NM, Fig. 48 h¹). D 1.1–1.6 cm. Same as previous classes. One NM bead is aberrant. *Class 4,* 2 beads (1 UM, Fig. 48 x; 1 NM, Fig. 48 l¹). D 2.2 and 2.3 cm. Polished and biconically drilled. All Burial 10 beads are positioned by size in Figure 67.

Aberrant, 1 (Fig. 49 c). Small, well polished, fine quality jadeite bead, somewhat barrel-shaped, with one side flat and slightly grooved. Burial 5, Skeleton B, thoracic area (Fig. 64 D).

Oval, 1 (Fig. 44 g). Polished gray-green jadeite, oval in horizontal section, vertically round. Biconically drilled. Cache O—13—12.

COMMENT. Considering the quantity of Piedras Negras caches, it is odd that jadeite beads were so infrequently treated as cache items; Cache O—13—12 was unique in this respect. This is quite in contrast to Uaxactun (see Kidder, 1947, p. 51). From the evidence at hand, beads of shell never entered into caches at Piedras Negras.

MISCELLANEOUS WORKED OBJECTS

Halved, polished pebbles, 3 (Figs. 45 z and 48,d'; 48 e'; other not illustrated). One (Fig. 48 e') probably broken in half with roughness of fracture abraded but left unpolished. Other figured specimen was incompletely sawed from one side, then split. From Caches O—13—12 and O—13—4. A polished pebble was contained in Cache O—13—54, but whether sawed or not is uncertain.

COMMENT. Others similar to these, but unpolished, were found at Kaminaljuyu (Kidder, Jennings, and Shook, 1946, p. 120).

Slightly worked fragments (Fig. 50 a—g, k—p, r, t, w). For the most part these are found in caches and often accompany pieces of definite form. All show evidence of grinding. A few have been rather extensively altered. Far left piece in Fig. 50 t has a deeply sawed groove on underside. Poor quality stones. The following caches surely contained such objects: O—13—8, 17, 21, 35, 36, 37, 47, 48, 50; O—13—1; J—1—1; K—5—2; R—9—1, 2. 7 small pieces of worked and polished jadeite were located together in Burial 5 (Fig. 64, 19).

COMMENT. Evidently this was not a votive trait at Uaxactun. Slightly worked bits of shell also appear in Piedras Negras caches.

Others, 4 (Fig. 50 v; two not shown). All from Cache R—9—2. Illustrated specimens are roughly spherical, unpolished. Other two are nondescript pieces of shaped and smoothed gray-green jadeite.

UNWORKED BITS

Large to small pieces of unworked, generally poor quality jadeite and green stones (see Fig. 50 h—j, u, x). Material such as this accompanied Caches O—13—8, J—29 —1, K—5—8, and perhaps other Structure O—13 caches. Field Catalogue mentions for Burial 5 "small pieces of polished jadeite." These have not been located, and since they were polished, may be fragments of beads.

COMMENT. Small pieces of unworked jade were likewise cached at Uaxactun (Kidder, 1947, p. 51).

DENTAL INLAYS

Tiny circular pieces of finely polished, convexly-surfaced, emerald green jadeite decorated fifteen of Skeleton B's teeth (Fig. 69 a, all jadeite except for pyrite inlays on lateral lower incisors). A few teeth have lost their inlays. At least one incisor in Burial 2, besides being notched, is set with a jadeite disc (Fig. 69 b). Finally, one of the teeth of Skeleton A, Burial 3 (Fig. 63 c) is said to have been similarly decorated (Field Catalogue). One of the Burial 5 inlays was found loose. Its exposed surface is convex, its underside flat, and its edge is tapered toward the back surface. The subject of dental modification is discussed in Part 3.

COMMENT. Longyear (1952, pp. 49—50) has gathered much information on the practice among the Maya of inlaying teeth with jade and pyrite. A broader study of this remarkable trait , surely a manifestation of social gradation, is that by Fastlicht and Romero (1951). Fastlicht (1951) discusses in detail adhesive techniques and materials. The extension of inlaying to include the second pre-molar (Skeleton B, Burial 5) is, we believe, unique both within and beyond the Maya area.

GENERAL COMMENT ON OBJECTS OF JADE. Largely unspectacular, the collection's few high points provide some idea of the technical excellence achieved by presumably local lapidaries. The likelihood of production at or in the locale of Piedras Negras is, in part substantiated by the absence of trait-links in style and content with carved jades of other sites, both lowland and highland. Gem quality jadeite was brought in from the highlands. But one can only speculate on whether finished objects were exported in return. Judging by the jade remains encountered at the site, the Usumacinta valley during Late Classic times cannot be said with certainty to have been a focus for jade working and object trade. As noted, nothing was found in jade to verify the otherwise reasonable belief in the Usumacinta as the source of the magnificent carved plaques from Nebaj and other highland sites. Yet only ten burials were found of which only one was richly stocked, and its discovery was fortunate, for without it a good half of the collection, and the most sumptuous portion, would not have been realized. Actually, though, this half allows fewer generalizations and distinctions than that derived from caches and general excavation.

Turning to Uaxactun, to which this report is comparatively oriented, one immediately notes that its finer objects, wholly or in part jade, all stem from Early Classic graves and caches. Practically all the Piedras Negras jades came from sources safely dateable as Late Classic. Many more well stocked burials also appeared at Uaxactun. Thus, in many instances, one is quantitatively and temporally hampered in valid comparison.

Both collections abound in miscellaneous small objects and adornos. But resemblances in these are, at most, general. Both contain earplug flares and subhemispherical beads; in view of their near universality, this is somewhat meaningless. One important difference, however, is to be found in the unique trait at Piedras Negras of incising pieces of jade and depositing them in caches. This, as mentioned, sets the site apart from all others. But then, Uaxactun had incised obsidian flakes, a feature lacking at Piedras Negras. An even weaker link lies in the mutual offering of jade scraps and unworked bits. Jade dental inlays, a broadly distributed trait, also appear at the two sites. And Piedras Negras probably produced its best objects while Uaxactun was dependent on imports (see Kidder, 1947, p. 51).

Perhaps the closest link in jade between the two is that both share a generally indefinable style. With further discoveries, a stylistic, chronological breakdown in this category may emerge. Highland distinctions (A. L. Smith and Kidder, 1951) may aid in this. Among the jades probably fashioned at Piedras Negras are a few features which suggest earliness in accord with highland characteristics. Or they might be the result of lag. But if the Usumacinta, as some believe, developed various Late Classic diagnostics in jade, heirlooms and anachronisms become hopelessly confused.

As matters now stand, the jades treated here offer little in the way of solutions to the broad problems of Mesoamerican jadeworking. They do, however, widen distributions and, inevitably, the scope of generalization.

AMAZONITE

Sixty-six beads (Fig. 48 u, w; 7 NM, not illustrated). All encountered in Burial 5 (Fig. 64 I) scattered among jade beads associated with Skeleton B. White to robin's-egg blue. Dull surface. D of largest .9 cm; majority average .7 cm. Irregular in shape but all subhemispherical. Predominantly biconically bored.

COMMENT. This group of amazonite beads from a Late Classic burial augments the very limited archaeological incidence of this stone. Two lots of beads were discovered in a Late Classic Nebaj cache and tomb (A. L. Smith and Kidder, 1951, p. 43) and a pair of amazonite flares were also found at Nebaj. An Early Classic tomb at Zaculeu produced a group of amazonite beads (Woodbury and Trik, 1953, p. 252, Table 2). Foshag (1954, p. 23) records a perforated natural piece of amazonite in the highland Rossbach Collection.

CRYSTALLINE CALCITE

Two very small irregular pieces come from Cache K—5—2 (UM). A piece of "crystalline stone" is listed in the Field Catalogue for Cache J—29—1 (NM, not located). A fragment of a calcite vessel from Piedras Negras has been previously described (under Stone Vessels, p.38).

MICA

One small piece intermixed with quartz was included in Cache O—16—1.

COMMENT.   Sheet mica was placed in an Early Classic Zaculeu cache (Woodbury and Trik, 1953, p. 113), and mica formed part of a probable Cerro de las Mesas cache (Drucker, 1943 a, p. 10).

GENERAL COMMENT AND COMPARISON OF GROUND STONE OBJECTS

Three functional categories, which to some extent overlap, encompass the ground stone artifacts of Piedras Negras. Implements comprised metates and manos and various pounding, abrading, and cutting tools. These pertain to subsistence and construction. Building techniques and the tools they required have been summarized for Uaxactun by A. L. Smith (1950, pp. 69—70); in most respects his description applies equally to Piedras Negras. As to metates, some were locally made and domestic while others apparently were imported and perhaps reserved for ceremonial occasions.

Ornaments included jadeite and amazonite beads, jadeite fillets, pendants, earplugs and various other decorative objects of valued stones, as well as pyrite plaques and fillets. The raw materials and, in certain cases, most probably the finished product (for example, objects of amazonite and pyrite) were traded in from highland sources. Jadeite and lesser stones, once at hand, were locally cut, carved, perforated, and often engraved. The latter, the incised jades, constitute the third category, namely, objects made as votive offerings. But utilitarian as well as ceremonial objects often became cache items. Ornaments were both worn by the deceased on interment and placed in graves as mortuary offerings. No cases of ground stone implements, however, were noted in Piedras Negras burials.

The objects described in this Section well illustrate the extent to which the center depended on highland trade. For objects of materials other than limestone they were required to barter local products for raw materials and, perhaps not infrequently, for finished objects. The river itself, drawing on various highland sources, provided unusual opportunity for this trade. (see Summary and Conclusions). Jadeite was of great importance, followed by a variety of hard igneous stones in addition to pyrite and hematite, amazonite and possibly calcite. Subsequent drilling, pecking, abrading, and polishing transformed many of these materials into objects to serve and embellish both the common and exotic needs of local culture.

Variation and consistency, as one would expect, are evident in a comparison of Uaxactun and Piedras Negras ground stone artifacts. Recognizable are distinctions in metate forms, in the decoration of spindle whorls, and in the exclusive occurrences, at one or the other site, of gouges, earplugs made of two or more materials, pyrite beads and plaques, jade mosaic work, incised jades, and extra-fine jade carving. Points in common are the almost complete lack of minor stone sculpture, the general similarity of general utility tools, the use of back-to-side perforations, and the presence of grooved whetstones, spindle whorls, and celts. Both sites seem to have imported tripod metates.

The two collections are not the same. Underlying this trite conclusion are implications of cultural differences in the realms of tools and ornaments and votive aims, although a far stronger expression of localism is naturally to be found in sculpture and architecture. Differences in ground stone artifacts in part reflect differential access to trade and different hierarchal values. Differences in household metates, however, were, one suspects, the result of something more profound. We may someday recognize well-defined regional distributions which will have important bearing on both agricultural origins and the sources of the people who came to occupy sites like Uaxactun and Piedras Negras. Perhaps it will be such items as metates, celts, and choppers, which are least subject to whim and innovation, which will solve these problems.

OBJECTS OF SHELL

SPECIES REPRESENTED

ATLANTIC OCEAN

Arca occidentalis
Arca umbonata
Cardium muricatum
Livona pica
Vermicularia spirata

PACIFIC OCEAN

Crucibulum spinosa
Morum tuberculatum
Spondylus limbatus

PROVENIENCE UNCERTAIN

Conus sp.
Oliva sp.
Ostrea sp.
Strombus sp.

FRESH-WATER

Pachychilus indiorum
Pomacea flagellata
Pomacea ghiesbreghti
(also called *Ampullaria ghiesbreghti*)
Quadrula quadrata

LAND SNAILS

Euglandina decussata
Choanopoma radiosum

UNWORKED SHELLS

Arca occidentalis.   Caches O–13–9, O–13–11 (traces of cinnabar paint on interior), O–13–13.
Arca umbonata.   Cache O–13–13.
Cardium muricatum.   In a Structure O–13 cache (fire).
Choanopoma radiosum.   Cache K–5–5.
Crucibulum spinosa.   Cache O–13–12.
Euglandina decussata.   Cache K–5–5.
Quadrula quadrata.   Burial 5 (Fig. 64, 19)
Livona pica.   Cache O–13–4.
Ostrea sp.   Cache O–13–54.
Pomacea flagellata.   Cache O–13–27.
Pomacea ghiesbreghti.   Caches R–9–1 and R–11–6 and associated with Cache J–29–1.
Spondylus limbatus.   Burial 5 (Fig. 64, 3, 14, 19). Caches O–13–3, 4, 5, 6, 12, 15, 23, 54 and
        other unspecified Structure O–13 caches.
Vermicularia spirata. Cache O–13–4 and one from a Structure O–13 cache.
Fossil gastropod.   Cache J–1–1.

ORIGINAL FORM LARGELY PRESERVED

Note: In descriptions here of bivalve shell material there is always the risk of
confusion. "Valve" refers to one of the two portions that make up the articulated whole shell.

BIVALVES PERFORATED FOR SUSPENSION

Spondylus limbatus, 3 (Fig. 52 o, r; one [UM] not illustrated). Larger valve (*o*), stripped of
spines, has three holes near hinge and comes from Burial 5 (Fig. 64, 14). The other valve (not illustrated),
also with spines removed, underlay the head of Skeleton B, Burial 5 (Fig. 64, 3). The third specimen (*r*)
with two perforations near hinge, was found articulated with its unperforated mate in Cache O—13—4; it
contained objects of jadeite.

COMMENT. Numerous instances in burials of *Spondylus* valves with hinge perforations were found
at Uaxactun (Kidder, 1947, p. 62). This shell, as indicated by Kidder's survey (Kidder, Jennings, and
Shook, 1946, p. 147; see also Thompson, 1950, p. 275), was widely traded in Mesoamerica and figured importantly in mortuary and votive practices and frequently occurs as a container for small objects (see
Caches O—13—4 and O—13—54).

Ostrea sp., 1 (Fig. 52 a). Single hole near hinge. Cache O—13—54.

COMMENT. Large valves, to judge from Jaina-type figurines, were worn suspended from necklaces.

PERFORATED UNIVALVE

Pomacea ghiesbreghti, 1 (Fig. 52 q). Two large adjacent holes drilled on one side. From Cache
R—11—6 along with an unworked shell of the same genus. A prior description of this object (Satterthwaite,
1933, p. 18) notes that the desired products of drilling were the discs.

COMMENT. An identically treated univalve from Lubaantun is shown by Joyce (1926 , Pl. XXIV,
Fig. 4).

BIVALVES WITH CUT HINGES

Spondylus limbatus, whole (not illustrated, NM not located). Cache R—9—2. Field drawing indicates presence of both valves with hinges removed and present in the deposit.

CUT SHELL

INCISED CACHED OBJECTS

Anthropomorphic. (1) Large figurines, 3 (Fig. 51 c—e). H 3.4—4.1 cm. Encrusted surface of
c largely obscures incised details; yellowish (stained?) shell. From Cache K—5—8. The other two (*d,e*)
form a pair from Cache J—1—1 and are made of *Spondylus*. Full figure, front view, arms flexed on chest.
Right edge of *d* fits left edge of piece in Figure 51 s; (also from Cache J—1—1); cut was round-bottomed
and incomplete. Pose previously discussed in connection with incised jade cached objects (see under
Jadeite). (2) Small figurines, 7 (Figs. 51 f—h, o; 52, e—g). Figure 51 o is broken, having been burned
in camp fire. Height of others 1.8—2.5. Vesicular *Spondylus*. Limbs and shoulders filed from edges. Incising, gouging, and drilling used on majority to depict body divisions and facial features. Figure 52 g is
almost featureless but has general outline of others in this group. From Caches O—13—13 and O—13—23;
others lack field numbers but very likely come from other vaguely itemized Structure O—13 offerings.
(3) Profile head (Fig. 51 a). Cream-colored shell. L3.2 cm. Convex surface engraved and, as is the case
with other engraved shell objects, the incisions filled with red pigment. Illustrates a head, facing left,
with large nose, curved element at corner of mouth, and foliated head ornament. From Cache K—5—2. See
Thompson's discussion of this deity, a god "with foliated ornament projecting from forehead" (in Kidder,
1947, p. 23). (4) Dual (Fig. 51 b). Yellowish shell. W 2.9 cm. Concave surface incised. On left, a

head in left profile with a long nose. On right, with its back to head, a small figure, side view, with head looking up, and arm resting on bent leg. Cache K–5–8.

Irregularly shaped incised plaques, 8 (Fig. 51 i–n, p, s). All but *i*, *k*, and *p* are made from *Spondylus* shell. Surfaces of some have beautifully engraved profiles of deities. That of *n* is geometrically decorated; of *s*, concentrically. Finally, there is an oval piece (*p*) with indented sides, paralleled on concave surface by an incised line. From Caches O–13–7, O–13–37, K–5–5, and J–1–1 (see figure captions).

Discoidals, 11 (Figs. 51 t–v; 52 b¹; one not shown). D 1–1 and 1–4 cm. All *Spondylus*. Except for Figure 51 t (Cache O–13–23), each has been either incised or filed on one surface only. A tiny crossed square (not illustrated, UM) was partially burned in camp fire. Remainder are from Cache O–13–13. Plain discs are described below.

GENERAL COMMENT. A Copan cache (Maudslay, 1889–1902, text, p. 20, Pl. XXI) had within it a number of small red shell figurines almost identical to those shown in Figures 51 t–v and 52 e, f. These and others somewhat like them, from sites like Uaxactun, San Jose, and the Mountain Cow group, have been reviewed by Thompson (1939, pp. 191–92, Fig. 97). On the whole they appear to have been a Late Classic item.

The open-jawed, long-nosed monster deity with dots beneath his eye and a shell symbol on his forehead appears in Figure 51 i, j and possibly *m*. One recalls that he appears on certain cached jades (for example, Fig. 46 l, q, r). Notable is the scroll within the eye as well as dots beneath the eye. These various elements would seem to possess aquatic import (see Thompson, 1950, pp. 274–78). Mr. Thompson, who has seen drawings of a number of these shell pieces, has suggested that many are manifestations of the long-nosed god (personal communication). That in Figure 51 a "would pass as a long-nosed god on the strength of his forehead" (*ibid.*). The identification of Figure 51 l is problematical.

As is true of their jade counterparts, the essential interest of these curious objects is that they fashioned and placed in caches with perhaps the same intent that motivated the deposition of incised obsidian flakes at Tikal and Uaxactun (see discussions under Ceremonial Obsidian and Jadeite).

PLAIN CACHED OBJECTS

Discs, 4 (Fig. 52 i, c¹). *Spondylus*. D .9–1.8 cm. Figure c¹ from Cache O–13–13. Others probably from Structure O–13 caches with incomplete descriptions.

Irregular, 4 (Fig. 52 c, y, z, a¹). Three pieces of shaped *Spondylus* shell occurred in Cache O–13–4 and one in Cache O–13–54.

PENDANTS

Incised, 1 (Fig. 51 r). L 2.6; T .3 cm. Larger hole near upper border is conical while adjacent perforation is biconical. A slightly curved groove, on obverse, runs almost from side to side and intersects the larger perforation. Face smooth, with incised hand-like design. Provenience unknown (camp fire) but possibly a Structure O–13 cache.

Plain, 1 (Fig. 52 b). From Cache O–13–54, a piece of vesicular white shell with two oblique, convergent perforations which exit on underside. May have been used as a pendant.

Tinkler, 5 (Fig. 52 n, s, t). Made from *Morum tuberculatum* and *Oliva* shells, all very much altered by removal of spires and perforation. Four of the first genus accompanied Skeleton B, Burial 5 (Fig. 64 E) and one *Oliva* appeared in the debris surrounding Burial 1. Suspension holes both drilled and transversely sawed, located near altered tip of shell or along exit margin. In one instance, a tinkler was both drilled on the side and sawed near its top. Another shows two drilled perforations.

COMMENT. As Kidder has indicated (Kidder, Jennings, and Shook, 1946, pp. 148–49), these pendent decorative objects have a very wide distribution in the Americas in addition to being archaeologically frequent in Mesoamerica. They often appear on Maya monuments. For instance, the figure on Piedras Negras Stela 7 wears a fringe of these objects on his skirt (at least two were found at the hips of Skeleton B, Burial 5). Further representations may be found on Piedras Negras Stelae 9, 12, 13, 35, and on Lintels 2 and 4, and, elsewhere, on Seibal Stela 12, Naranjo Stelae 7 and 8, Tikal Stela 5, Yaxchilan Lintel 42, and on a number of the Copan monuments. Apart from skirt and belt fringes, tinklers were used to embellish jade bracelets (Piedras Negras Stela 12) and jade collars (Yaxchilan Lintel 42). Tinklers are often cross-hatched (see Piedras Negras Stelae 34, Motul de San Jose Stela 5, Bonampak Stelae 1 and and 2, Seibal Stela 12, Naranjo Stela 7, etc.). This device probably designated a particular, curiously crazed species, *Oliva porphyria* Linné (Boekelman 1935, pp. 268—69). Cross-hatching is also a symbol for black, which, of course, has connotations of darkness and death. The *Oliva* shell is believed by a number of students to constitute the sign for completion in the codices (Thompson, 1950, p. 138). Completion and death are conceptually not very far apart and one suspects that shells in burials have an interesting pertinency (Satterthwaite, verbal communication).

FACIAL (?) ORNAMENTS

Five (Fig. 55 q—t; one [NM, not located] not shown). Overall length of UM specimens (see figure captions) 2—4 cm. Figure *r*, drawn from a field photograph, is comparable in size. No information on a missing Burial 2 ornament. Each is composed of a shank and head and resembles a tiny elbow-pipe. While head is biconically bored, positions are variable. Each has a flared edge to head and its face is either peripherally plain, or carved in a petal design as in *s*, or square and notched as in *r*. Shanks usually taper without a break but one (*t*) is stepped. Traces of blue paint remain on *s*. Burials 2 and 5 each contained two of these objects. In Burial 2, one was discovered between the tibiae and the other among objects in the area of the mandible (Fig. 63 b, 1, 2). One was found on each side of the mandible of Skeleton B, Burial 5 (Fig. 64 A). These positions have been previously stated by Kidder (1947, p. 64).

COMMENT. Clearly related objects of shell have been reported for Uaxactun (Kidder, *op. cit.*, p. 64, Fig. 56; Ricketson and Ricketson, 1937, Fig. 132 c), Guaytan (A. L. Smith and Kidder, 1943, Fig. 54 b), and Bonaca in the Bay Islands (Strong, 1935, Pl. 15 h—m). Other examples in pottery, wood, and even copper are known for Mesoamerica (see Kidder, *op. cit.*, pp. 64—65; Ekholm, 1944, p. 467 for Mexican distribution; Longyear, 1952, p. 103 for Copan examples). The recently discovered, fabulously rich Palenque crypt burial yielded a pair of jadeite objects of this form which importantly were in the area of the skull— one below the craneal base, the other evidently attached to the left side of the face (Ruz, 1955, p. 100, Pl. XLII). They have been termed "probable nose-pendants."

It has been variously thought that these objects served as either labrets or flanged earplugs, or both. Kidder (*op. cit.*) has pointed out that the long shanks on many largely preclude use as labrets. I suppose that this applies to a number of the Piedras Negras examples. As regards the unmatched pair from Burial 5, jadeite earplugs were found in place and, therefore, these shanked objects must have been employed in some other fashion. This situation is cited by Kidder (*ibid.*), who suggests, perhaps rightly so, that they were inserted in the cheeks. His theory is partially supported by the Palenque finds. The presence of small oblique perforations among those from Piedras Negras is puzzling unless they were used in some manner to secure the pieces or to suspend tiny secondary ornaments. To my knowledge, Maya as well as Mesoamerican art as a whole is lacking in representations of this trait of inserting objects in the cheek. Palenque art and Maya Gulf Coast figurines, however, often emphasize forehead and what might be termed glabellar ornaments (to induce cross-eyedness?). Adhesion might have required the insertion of shanks below the skin. But ornamental pairing is improbable.

MISCELLANEOUS ORNAMENTS

Dentate, 13 (Fig. 52 p, x; two missing). *Spondylus*. L 2.8—3.4 cm. Tapered, with one end rounded, the other flat to concave. All from Burial 5 (Fig. 64 D).

COMMENT. Presumably decorative insets. A piece of shell cut to resemble a human incisor was found at Guaytan (A. L. Smith and Kidder, 1943, p. 169).

Perforated discs, 3 (Figs. 52 d'; 55 p; one [NM] not illustrated). The first has a diameter of .55 cm., and is very thin. Pearly shell. Discovered in surface debris of Structure J—12. The second specimen is nicely made with a countersunk face. White shell. D 1.2 cm. From Burial 2 (Fig. 63 b, 1). The third, from Cache J—29—1, has a diameter of 1.8 cm., a thickness of .2 cm., and features an incised circle on one face.

Countersunk disc, 1 (Fig. 51 w). White flaking shell. D 3.5 cm. Hollow-drilled circular depression. Unperforated. Structure K—5, surface of plaza.

SHELL-PLATED GARMENT

209 perforated pieces of cut *Spondylus* shell were found in the northeast corner of Burial 5 (see Fig. 64, 1 for arrangement of some). Four of these plates contained an engraved continuous inscription. In addition to minor objects of jade, 6 pieces of worked white shell (presumably conch) were located in the same area of the tomb. The arrangement of the many shell plates decidedly indicates that they were sewn to a garment of some kind, perhaps a short cloak.

Inscribed, 4 (Fig. 53 a–d). L 3.5–7.4; W 3.8–7.2 cm. Each conically drilled in two or more places for attachment. Text composed of 34 glyphs blocks. Incisions filled with accidentally deposited lime (against the orange of the shell).

COMMENT. These have been illustrated and studied by Morley (1937—1938, pp. 169–73, Fig. 102, Pl. 145, e–h), who assigned them a date of 9.15.0.0.0 ??? . He proposed that "the plain pieces [below] may have served as a border or background...for the four inscribed ones."

Plain, 205 Figs. 53 j–l; 54; those in NM not shown). All conically perforated. Bores quite consistently are from shell interior to exterior. Great variation in number, size, and to a certain extent position of bores. Largest plates in far left row in Figure 54 average about 7.4 cm. in length. On excavation these large rectangular plates were found lying in a series (see Fig. 64, 1). Most pieces are rectangular but among them occur triangles, trapezoids, and a few pieces with curved edges.

COMMENT. Similar shell plates, though not in this quantity, were part of the furnishings of an evidently Late Classic Comalcalco tomb (Blom and LaFarge, 1926, v. 1, p. 116, Fig. 98). These might also have been *Spondylus*.

White shell elements, 6 (Figs. 52 m; 53 e–i). Five conically bored while a small hook-shaped piece is unperforated.

COMMENT. On the basis of their forms, one wonders whether these pieces may not have composed a mask on the proposed garment, the two semilunar pieces forming the brows, the rectangles the eyes, and the triangular element the nose. If originally a second hook existed, the two perhaps formed the mouth volutes, a characteristic of certain Maya deities.

MISCELLANEOUS CUT SHELL OBJECTS

From various caches and burials as well as general excavations (some shown in Fig. 52 k, l, u–w, h', i'). All worked to varying degrees. Often appear to be scraps cut from objects of value. Some are simply perforated fragments, as in *u* and *i'*. There are also a number of long thin pieces of clam shell ground down along one side (as in *w*). Others include a thin, pearly rectangle (*v*) and cut conch columnella (not shown). Six small pieces of cut *Spondylus* come from Cache J—29—1. Cache O—13—43 yielded a semi-circle (D 3.7; T .25 cm.), flat, with a slight faceted, square-edged rim; its flat side beveled and centrally notched. No perforations (NM, not illustrated).

COMMENT. Cached odds-and-ends of shell recall the scraps of flint, obsidian, and jade so frequently a part of these votive offerings.

BEADS

Three lots (Burial 2, Fig. 52 f'; Burial 5, Figs. 52 e' and 53 m; Burial 10, Figs. 51 q and 52 g'). D .4–.9; T .1–.7 cm. Many tubular, others sub-hemispherical. Majority seem to have been cylindrically bored (see Figs. 51 q; 53 m). *Spondylus* is perhaps the most frequent shell. Some 110 such beads accompanied Skeleton B, Burial 5. See figure captions for locations within burials.

COMMENT. The technical and archaeological backgrounds of shell beads and their types are to be found in Kidder, Jennings, and Shook, 1946, pp. 150–51. Had more rich burials been found at Piedras

Negras, the diversity and quantity found at such centers as Uaxactun and Kaminaljuyu might have been equaled. Curiously, no shell beads are known at Piedras Negras from caches and in only one case was a jadeite bead found in a cache (Cache O—13—12, Fig. 44 g).

CORAL

The Field Catalogue mentions a piece of coral for Cache O—13—15; the unlabeled specimen in Fig. 52 d (NM) may be it. Another fragment (UM), burned in camp. fire, cannot be certainly assigned but probably belongs with the Structure O—13 group of caches. Finally, there is a fair-sized piece of branch coral (UM); exact provenience unknown.

COMMENT. Coral was a rare cache item. In this context, it has been noted at Uaxactun (Kidder, 1947, p. 66), Caracol (cache of Altar 14; Satterthwaite, verbal information), Hatzcap Ceel (Thompson, 1931, p. 273), and Mayapan (Shook, 1954, p. 98).

GENERAL COMMENT AND COMPARISON OF OBJECTS OF SHELL

As is evident from the above descriptions, the collection of shell and other marine material includes no clearly utilitarian object. All are either decorative (beads, plates, etc.) or fashioned as cache offerings (incised pieces, figurines, etc.). The absence of shell tools was a characteristic of Uaxactun and actually seems to be true of most other sites. A shell mound, in which shell tools might be expected, has yet to be thoroughly investigated in Mesoamerica.

There are a number of traits in shell common to Piedras Negras and Uaxactun; for example, beads, shanked ornaments, shell figurines, tinklers, perforated univalves, and trade contacts for securing material from both the Atlantic and Pacific coasts. Features appearing at Uaxactun, but not at Piedras Negras, include pearls, the variety of its shell adornos, and various specific items like carved pendants. Piedras Negras, unlike Uaxactun, produced perforated (and incised) shell plates, engraved pieces of shell in caches, and also caches containing unworked and perforated shells. These distinctions, though few, are likely real, but one cannot totally discount the effect of insufficient work at one or both sites.

The affiliations of Piedras Negras with other centers have been occasionally noted in the comments in this section. This is true for shanked facial (?) ornaments, the emphasis on *Spondylus*, perforated shell plates, the caching of coral, and, importantly, the small shell votive figurines. It is this last item that particularly distinguishes the collection as lowland Maya.

OBJECTS OF BONE

RASPERS

Four, fragmentary (Fig. 55 m—o; one [NM] not shown). Bones that have been transversely sawed in series to produce notched surfaces. Two and probably all specimens made of animal bone. Notches on that in *m* have been almost completely erased. No information on an unlocated NM specimen.

COMMENT. If these served as musical instruments, as seems likely, they greatly add to the limited list of such objects from Piedras Negras, for the site produced only three pottery drums, each identical apart from size (one shown by Satterthwaite, 1938 a, Fig. 1 a), a sherd of a fourth drum, and whistle figurines. But then, no site has been particularly generous in this respect, except, of course, Bonampak, whose magnificent murals depict trumpets, ankle-rattles, and drums of distinct types (see Ruppert, Thompson, and Proskouriakoff, 1955, especially p. 60).

Raspers have a meager distribution in the Maya area. Two broken ones were encountered at Uaxactun, one of which was fashioned from a human tibia (Ricketson and Ricketson, 1937, p. 206, Fig. 133). For Lubaantun, Joyce (1933, Fig. 2) illustrates a deer jawbone serrated along its lower margin, and further remarks (*ibid.*, p. xxvi) that "other bones, not jawbones, but corresponding to the Mexican type [i. e., as above], were also excavated at Lubaantun." One possible example in shell was a surface find at San Jose (Thompson 1939, pp. 181—82). Two bone raspers are reported for Quen Santo (Seler, 1901, pp. 152—58, Fig. 226). Another highland example, from Chipal (UM, Cat. NA—11530), comprises a small femur with deep transverse notches along one side of the shaft with distal end removed. Linné's distributional study (1934, pp. 204—07) indicates three other such objects from the Ulua region and Yucatan. Rasps have been lately discovered at Mayapan (Thompson, 1954, p. 79; Shook and Irving, 1955, p. 150, Fig. 6 m). Angel Fernandez (1941, p. 179) records one from Tulum. Probably entirely unrelated are the serrated deer tarsi excavated at Holmul (Merwin and Vaillant. 1932, Pl. 36, a).

A fine study of raspers, largely Mexican, was made many years ago by Seler (1898). Another is that of Castañeda and Mendoza (1933, pp. 562—67). Linné (*op. cit.*) gives much useful information on distribution, to which Kidder has added a number of subsequent finds (Kidder, Jennings, and Shook, 1946, p. 154). Other studies are those of Beyer (1934) and Driver (1953), the latter also covering ethnological occurrences. Whether *all* bones so treated were used as musical instruments is open to question. For example, Rubín de la Borbolla (1939, pp. 113—18) doubts that the quite numerous specimens from Tzintzuntzan are in fact instruments, because of inconsistent spacing of grooves. Actually, the Maya raspers seem generally regular in this respect. Nevertheless, groove spacing is an interesting point and one to keep in mind when dealing with these objects.

TUBULAR BONE OBJECTS

Carved and perforated, pair. Destroyed by camp fire. Satterthwaite (1934), quoting Dr. Mary Butler who excavated them, gives the following description of these tubes which accompanied Burial 6. "Two bone tubes about 13 cm. long, about 2.3 cm. in diameter, decorated in each case on the front with a wide band formed by two parallel lines enclosing a conventionalized snake head, shown in profile with simplicity and restraint. The backs were plain except for bands of rosettes encircling each end. The designs were carved in low relief. The serpent band in one case slanted from left to right, in the other from right to left, so that the two formed a complementary pair, probably worn on the breast. Three holes were bored in one tube in front of the snake head, arranged as at the points of a triangle; on the other tube, two of the corresponding holes were present, the third being begun but not carried through the bone. On these tubes were traces of red paint. They were found beside the skull, about 20 cm. away from it, and about on a line with the nose."

COMMENT. This pair perhaps resembled one illustrated by Kidder from Uaxactun (1947, Fig. 44). The drilled design on a San Jose bone tube is also suggestive (see Thompson, 1939, Pl. 29, 16).

Perforated, 1 (Fig. 55 i). L 2.2 cm. Thin-walled tube with a circular opening on one side. Could be a minature one-stop whistle.

Unperforated, 1 (Fig. 55 h). Fragmentary when found but repaired. L 5.6 cm. Terminal edges slightly beveled and apparently cut with a rather blunt instrument. Either a tubular bead, or again, a small whistle, but without stops.

PENDANTS

Double suspension; 1 (Fig. 55 g). A greatly modified vertebra, very likely human. Both the arched spine and a large portion of the body have been removed, the whole smoothed down with a fairly rough tool, and each prong (one missing) biconically drilled for suspension.

COMMENT. An identical ornament was discovered at Uaxactun (Kidder, 1947, Fig. 84 a).

Single suspension, 1 (Fig. 55 k). L 5.1 cm. Made from section of carnivore mandible. No teeth are in place. Biconically drilled. Balance is such that it must have been worn with dental border facing down. Ends beveled and scarred from initial sawing attempts. Cache O—16—1.

COMMENT. Holmul yielded a number of jaw sections with perforations similar to this one (Merwin and Vaillant, 1932, Pl. 36 b).

PERFORATORS

Awls, three (Fig. 55 a, j; one [NM] not located). First illustrated awl made from what was perhaps a deer metapodial. L 10.4 cm. A second example has a length of 6.8 cm. with a condyle forming butt. An "awl," listed for Burial 5, lacks data (Fig. 64 I).

Notched, 1 (Fig. 55 b). Transverse "V" notch at one end, tapered at other. Slight damage in area of notch confuses original condition. Evidently not a perforation and thus not a needle. Simple linear incision on one side.

CARVED PIN (?)

One (Fig. 57 i). Fragmentary. Present length, 6.9 cm. A delicately carved staff-like object surmounted by a human hand, a cuff below hand, and, on the shaft, two parallel spiralled bands, one of which is successively and tranversely notched. The hand itself, lacking its little finger, comprises an outstretched thumb with the index finger pointing up. The fingernails are minutely carved. The remaining two fingers are bent to the palm. The cuff is oval in cross-section, while the shaft is round. From surface debris of Structure J—11.

COMMENT. The shafts of two broken awl-like pieces from Uaxactun (Kidder, 1947, Fig. 41 d, f) are carved in a manner identical to one shaft of this specimen. Another, from a San Jose burial, is similarly decorated with this banded design (Thompson, 1939, Fig. 92 a). In both cases, however, the direction of spiraling is opposite to that on the Piedras Negras specimen.

Hands appear in Maya art quite frequently with many variations in position of fingers. A personage holding a staff surmounted by a hand occurs on the wall painting of Structure A–V at Uaxactun (A. L. Smith, 1950, Fig. 111). The staff-hand combination appears five times in the Dresden Codex, in four of which it is carried by some canine deity. In one instance, this being supports God B, and, in others, a jaguar and Gods A and E (Dresden 25 a, 26 a, 27 a, 28 a). And, in Dresden 31 b, God B himself carries this very same staff. A staff, essentially that shown in the Dresden, occurs once in the Madrid Codex (89 d) where it is carried by a black deity, who, although blindfolded, might be Schellhas' God M. The Codex Borgia shows a comparable staff (Spinden, 1913, Fig. 212). The hand also substitutes for the scorpion stinger in Madrid 44 b and 44 c, and, as such, grabs the tail of a deer in each case. In still another case (Madrid 39 b), the scorpion tail-hand substitutes for one deer's tail and also plunges a knife into a second deer. Thompson (1950, pp. 76–77), in discussing the day sign Manik, which itself comprises a clenched hand, demonstrates the association of God M, hunting, the scorpion, and the deer. The hand is also a symbol of completion. Perhaps also relevant are red imprints of hands occasionally found on and in structures at Kabah and Tulum, and on the Island of Cozumel. To the south, hands were noted by Maler at Lake Petha, not overly distant from Piedras Negras (1901, p. 30, Fig. 10). Hands are to be seen in Tikal *graffiti* (Berlin, 1951, Fig. 7); also red hands (*ibid.*, p. 38). Red hands appear on exotic fans in the Bonampak frescos (Room 3). Isolated jade hands have been discovered at Uaxactun (Kidder, *op. cit.*, p. 47, Fig. 34 a) and in the Ulua region (Keleman, 1943, Pl. 251, f) and also Nebaj (A. L. Smith and Kidder, 1951, p. 36, Figs. 55 e, f,; 58 c). The identical pose of the Piedras Negras hand appears in the Ulua piece and one of the Nebaj examples.

Much of this data may seem extraneous, but it is unlikely that such a carefully made piece was conceived of without some association in mind. The human hand alone clearly had symbolic import for the Maya (see Thompson, 1950, pp. 184–86). The duplication of pose (Piedras Negras, Nebaj, and the Ulua Valley) suggests something more than idle execution.

CARVED JAGUAR ULNA

Proximal portion of bone (Fig. 57 h). L 8.8 cm. Altered to represent a bird, on the head of which a kin sign has been carved, a not unusual feature in Maya art. The natural conformation of the bone has been used to great advantage. From Burial 5 (Fig. 64, 9).

ANTLER TOOLS

Four tips and one nearly complete specimen (Fig. 57 b–f). White-tailed deer (*Odoceileus* sp.). Some show terminal wear suggesting use in pressure flaking, indirect percussion, or perhaps coarse perforation. From general digging.

MISCELLANEOUS WORKED AND UNWORKED BONE OBJECTS

Shark teeth. Small specimen from Cache O–13–37 (Fig. 57 g). No evidence of use although it may possibly have once served as a simple cutting tool. Field Catalogue lists a questionable shark tooth from Burial 2 (Fig. 63 b, 3). One other (NM, not located) was found, according to a field photograph, in one of the Structure O–13 caches, but certain assignment is presently impossible.

COMMENT. An Early Classic Nebaj cache contained shark teeth (A. L. Smith and Kidder, 1951, Table 1) and, among other marine objects, shark teeth were found in Lower II Cerro de las Mesas caches (Drucker, 1943 a, pp. 12–13).

Fish remains. Two small teeth of an unidentified fish accompanied Cache J—29—1.

COMMENT. One San Jose IV cache yielded a few manatee bones, while the spines of a porcupine fish were included in a San Jose V cache (Thompson, 1939, pp. 185, 188). At Caracol, a swordfish beak (with a piece of coral) was discovered in one of the few votive offerings found at that site (Altar 14; Satterthwaite, verbal communication). And "dorsal spine bones of a small fish" were in a Hatzcap Ceel cache (Thompson, 1931, p. 274). Piedras Negras and British Honduras caches particularly abound in objects of marine origin (see under Shell and Caches).

Carnivore canines. One each in Burial 5 (Fig. 64 I) and Burial 10 (Fig. 67, 1).

COMMENT. Curiously, no perforated animal teeth were found despite their relative frequency at Uaxactun (burials and caches) and elsewhere (Kidder, 1947, p. 57; Kidder, Jennings, and Shook, 1946, p. 155).

Bird remains. Two birds, one small, the other comparatively large, had been placed in Cache J—29—1. Cache K—5—8 yielded the remains of a small bird, and a few other bird bones come from Cache J—1—1. Cache K—5—4 may also have contained a bird. Bird bones were found in the northeast corner of Burial 5 (Fig. 64, 1; see also 10) and bird claws appeared in Burial 10 (Fig. 67, 11).

COMMENT. Shook (1951, p. 240) records a quite early Pre-Classic Kaminaljuyu cache containing, in part, a "bird (?) skull," inside of which a large lot of jadeite objects was found. At the same site, an early Esperanza Phase cache evidenced bird bones (Berlin, 1952, p. 13). Early, Late, and Post-Classic Nebaj caches likewise produced bird remains (A. L. Smith and Kidder, 1951, Tables 1 and 2). Similarly, votive deposits at Zaculeu (Atzan and Late Qankyak Phases) occasionally contained bird bones, in one case a macaw skull and, in the other, quail remains (Woodbury and Trik, 1953, pp. 113, 115). Bird bones are mentioned for a Hatzcap Ceel cache (Thompson, 1931, p. 274); Wauchope (1948, pp. 35—36) believes that a supposed human cremation there is really that of a sacrificed bird. An owl and a finch were placed in a Chichen Itza offering (Morris, Charlot, and Morris, 1931, p. 186). Birds and bats were used as cache offerings at Palenque (Angel, 1943, p. 55). Bats may also have been cached at Uaxactun (see Ricketson and Ricketson, 1937, p. 55); a certain case appeared in a San Jose V offering, this being the skull of the ritually important leaf-nosed bat (Thompson, 1939, pp. 189—90). The practice of sacrificing birds (and bats) and subsequently depositing them as votive offerings evidently was established widely and persistently among the Maya. It has already been suggested that certain small, barrel-shaped stones found at Piedras Negras may have served in bird sacrifices (see under Ground Stone).

Others. A field photograph of the contents of Cache J—1—1 shows what appears to be a phalange, probably not human. "Phalanges" noted in deposit in Burial 5 (Fig. 64, 19). A nondescript long-bone fragment, distinguished only by an encircling groove, is shown here in Figure 55 l. Also, many of the Structure O—13 caches lack precise descriptions of contents. As will be noted in the itemized cache listing (Table 5), "bone" and "bone fragments" are referred to fairly frequently. These presumably pertain to fish, bird, and small animal remains, and even in some instances to stingray spines, items which are described below.

STINGRAY SPINES

Altered, at least 12 (two shown in Fig. 55 c, f). Modified spines appeared in Caches O—13—13, O—13—30, K—5—8, J—1—1 and J—29—1, as well as in certain unspecifiable Structure O—13 caches. A number of spines (in caches, O—13—30, K—5—8, J—1—1, J—29—1) show a longitudinal "V" groove (as in *f*) on the upper, that is, slightly convex surface. In no case was the flat underside worked. Although broken, the largest such spine is 13 cm. long. Other spines have been altered by longitudinal splitting (as in *c*). Fractures were smoothed and the new piece ground down on one end to a relatively dull point. Both UM examples of this type of modification occurred in Cache J—1—1. Still another spine, from Cache O—13—13, a proximal fragment, was notched on its curved base to produce five prongs. A field photograph of

Structure O—13 cache material shows two other modified spines. One fragmentary piece has a ground (?) constriction about two-thirds of the distance from its base. The other shows an incised dendriform pattern running the length of its flat underside.

COMMENT. One of the rare Uaxactun spines has been proximally ground to a fine point (Kidder, 1947, p. 59, Fig. 75); another worked spine is shown by Ricketson and Ricketson (1937, Fig. 134 a). Various spines were interpreted as awls at Holmul (Merwin and Vaillant, 1932, pp. 89, 90). I know of no other cases of the splitting, gouging, notching, and incising noted in the Piedras Negras collection.

Spines with hieroglyphic inscriptions, 10 fragments (Fig. 56). The group comprises four more or less complete spines. Apart from incision these are unmodified. The set is from Burial 5 and was found among unworked specimens near the right elbow of Skeleton B (Fig. 64, 10). These stingray spines are remarkable for the incised glyphs appearing on their upper (i. e. convex) surfaces. The four examples show that the inscriptions began above plain basal portions which may once have been inserted in some object. The majority of the glyphs are badly eroded. Judging from Fig. 56 a, at least 44 but probably not more than 48 glyphs were present in the possibly continuous text. Various familiar glyphic elements are visible: Imix, the hand as in Manik, the Ben-Ich superfix, possibly the "comb" affix, and so forth. No sure numerical coefficient is present; two horizontally placed dots, between crescentic fillers, appear with the third glyph from the present end of the spine in Fig. 56 b. It will be recalled that a second Burial 5 object, a jadeite pendant (Fig. 49 a), also contained a hieroglyphic text. The inscribed shell plaques in Fig. 53 a—d yielded still a third text, of 36 blocks, for this burial.

COMMENT. Only two examples of glyphically incised stingray spines are known, the set just described, and a single fragmentary spine found in a Holmul (III, Early Classic) burial (see Merwin and Vaillant, 1932, Pl. 36 e). These two cases are curiously separated by over 200 kilometers and considerable time (one, possibly two, centuries). The Piedras Negras finds indicate that minor texts could be of considerable length and that the inscriptions were of the same general calendrical nature as on the monuments. Were incised spines such as these to appear, say, in a Chicanel burial, a major problem in Mesoamerican archaeology would be brought closer to solution. Their perishability should be kept in mind when contemplating the apparent lack of lowland Pre-Classic texts.

Bone effigies of stingray spines, 13 whole, 5 fragmentary (typified by Fig. 55 d, e). One broken example (*e*), from Cache K—5—2, is relatively narrow with no attempt at simulating the sectional conformation of actual stingray spines; the bilateral rows of tiny sharp hooks found on authentic spines are here shown by series of finely incised, black-filled (evidently a pigment) oblique lines along both edges on both sides. The majority of the examples, as in *d*, were part of Cache K—5—8 where they accompanied a number of real unworked spines and one worked fragment. These are not only generally broader than the piece just described, but are incised on one face only. 4.5 cm. is about the average length of these objects, which seems to be slight compared with that of mature actual spines.

COMMENT. The distribution of bone replicas appears to be restricted to Piedras Negras and Sitio Conte, Panama (Lothrop, 1937, p. 201, Fig. 199). Mention has already been made of a jadeite stingray spine effigy from Piedras Negras (Fig. 49 i).

Unworked. Spines were deposited in Caches O—13—23, O—13—27, K—5—8, J—1—1 and J—6—1, and probably in O—13—8, O—13—9, and O—13—30. In the itemized listing of caches (Part 3 and Table 5) there are occasional references to "bone fragments," especially among the Structure O—13 group. Conceivably, some of these entries refer to stingray spines. Unworked spines also accompanied Burial 5 (Fig. 64, 10, 19) and Burial 2 (Fig. 63 b, 4). Both real and imitation spines appeared together in Cache K—5—8; and plain, incised, and one of jade in Burial 5. Because of fragmentation, the exact number represented in a cache or burial is difficult to determine.

COMMENT. The archaeological distribution of dorsal spines of the stingray has been given by Kidder in its ceremonial contexts (Kidder, Jennings, and Shook, 1946, p. 156). Subsequently, they have been discovered at Pomona, British Honduras, where nine unworked spines were recovered in an Early Classic tomb (Kidder and Ekholm, 1951, p. 129), and in a Miraflores Phase tomb at Kaminaljuyu (Shook and Kidder, 1952, p. 117). Spines were included in Tazumal burials (Tazumal Museum). They form part of the Mayapan collection, in at least one case having been cached (Proskouriakoff, 1954, p. 286; Shook and Irving, 1955, p. 144). The Pomona pieces are apparently the only ones to have been found in British Honduras despite the prevalence of marine objects in local caches. The Miraflores discovery extends the ceremonial use of spines back onto the Pre-Classic horizon—a practice that persisted until the Conquest, as evidenced by Landa's references to their use (Tozzer, 1941, p. 191). Also, the people responsible for the Mamom deposits of Uaxactun collected spines (Ricketson and Ricketson, 1937, p. 205). Further additions to Kidder's listing include Copan, where one rotted spine was encountered in a Late Classic stela cache and a few others in an entombed jar (Longyear, 1952, pp. 43, 51). A few appeared in structural fill at Nebaj and interestingly had been burned (A. L. Smith and Kidder, 1951, p. 57). Of importance throughout the Maya area as well as at La Venta and Cocle, it was perhaps at Piedras Negras that stingray spines received the greatest attention. As to their relative cache frequencies, among the many Uaxactun caches only two were found to contain spines and then, in very small amounts (A. L. Smith, 1950, Table 8).

In cases of burials, these objects frequently have been discovered in the pelvic area (see Kidder, Jennings, and Shook, *op. cit.*; A. L. Smith, *op. cit.*, p. 90), a position also occasionally shared by obsidian flake-blades. This would seem to be true for both Burials 2 and 5 at Piedras Negras. The position may be significant.

There is ample evidence, then, that the Maya considered the stingray spine worthy of votive deposition in addition to burial with apparently important individuals. According to Bishop Landa, spines were used by the Maya, at least in late Pre-Conquest times, "in cutting their flesh in the sacrifices of the devil and it was the duty of the priest to keep them, and so they had many of them" (Tozzer, *op. cit.*). This practice is not without modern parallel in the Americas, for the Siriono employ spines extensively in ceremonial bloodletting (Holmberg, 1950, pp. 83–84). Scenes of Maya bloodletting (lingual) are found on a number of Yaxchilan lintels and on Naranjo Stela 19 where a cord, usually barbed, is used. In the Madrid Codex (95 a) four personages, two of them God B, are shown piercing their ears, from which blood falls in a manner similar to that conventionally used in the codex for rain. The sacrificial instrument is not the spine, but rather a blade or flake perhaps of obsidian. However, in Madrid 96 b, God B pierces his tongue with a long, straight object paralleled on both sides by a series of dots; in view of the simplicity of the Piedras Negras bone replicas, this object may be the spine. A relationship between sacrificial blood and rain (God B) is not inappropriate, and, in the minds and even practices of the Maya, blood possibly entered into germination.

It is odd that the stingray, particularly its spine, should figure so little in Maya art. Even apart from Landa's observation, it is clear from caches and burials that it played an important part in ceremonialism. To cite the few cases I can find, the animal, with and without its dorsal spine, appears three times in the Chacmool murals at Chichen Itza, but always in marine scenes along with other aquatic forms (Morris, Charlot, and Morris, 1931, Pl. 139, 159). On Aguas Calientes Stela 1, a bowl is depicted holding a half-dozen thin, elongated, pointed objects, with bilaterally incised short diagonal lines (as in Fig. 55 e). The Madrid Codex shows similarly executed objects which have been identified in the past by Brinton, Tozzer, Allen, and others as feathers, maguey, etc. Stingray spines might be added to this list of interpretations. An enormous but very realistic replica of a spine is very likely depicted as a shaft-tip on Seibal Stela 1.

It is not inconceivable that the Maya employed large fresh spines as weapons. Lothrop suggests that the spines found in such profusion at Sitio Conte, Panama served as "spear or arrow points" (1937, pp. 97, 99). Ethnological cases of this occur in Australia as well as the Montaña region of South America; in the former case they are traded widely as fighting weapons (Sharp, 1952, p. 75) while various Montaña tribes employ them as fish-arrow barbs (Tschopik, 1952, p. 9). Bird (1943, p. 241) reports spines possibly prepared as dart points at the Coastal site of Quiani, Chile. That the Maya utilized them as weapons is evident in a statement by Follett (1932, pp. 389—90): "The use of the barbs of the sting-ray as arrow-points probably caused Herrera to say that the Guatemalans used poison on their arrows and spears." However, no source is cited for spines having been so used.

CUT HUMAN LONG-BONES

One of the two known examples is shown in Figure 57 a. This is the proximal portion of a human femur that had been transversely cut, and, when the cut was two-thirds complete, the bone was broken. Lot 21 under Burials gives further data on this specimen. A second example (UM, not located) was the head of probably a human femur, sawed through at the juncture of shaft and condylar mass. This was a surface find.

COMMENT. These very likely were cut to procure shafts which were subsequently split and made into implements like awls. Grave robbing and human sacrifice underlay this practice. Evidence for both is found elsewhere at Piedras Negras (see under Burials).

The trait of cutting up human long-bones is very well represented at Uaxactun where signs of it occur as early as Chicanel times. Ricketson (in Kidder, 1947, pp. 58—59) notes that all examples, when sexable, are male.

Both sites are very definitely related by the sharing of this interesting trait.

UNWORKED ANIMAL BONES

Small quantities of animal remains appeared wherever excavations were made. Some have been identified and these include deer, jaguar, opossum, peccary, and turtle. Other bones certainly appear to be from large and small birds, fish, and small mammals. Regretably, the entire collection has not been submitted for expert identification. When and if this is ever done, one presumably may expect a faunal listing generally comparable to that prepared for Uaxactun (see Kidder, 1947, p. 60). The dog evidently was the only domesticated animal at Uaxactun and it is assumed that this was true at Piedras Negras, although skeletal confirmation is presently lacking. On the basis of prior identifications and a superficial examination of the collection, the white-tailed deer appears to have had particular economic importance at the site. But the jaguar was predominant in ceremonial life as attested by sculpture and miscellaneous objects found at Piedras Negras. And, judging by the rather extraordinary votive and burial usages of spines, local religion in some odd way comprehended the stingray as well.

GENERAL COMMENT AND COMPARISON OF OBJECTS OF BONE

The Piedras Negras collection of bone objects fills only a small box. It is simply the excavated remains of a tiny residue that has survived a destructive climate. The objects are in part utilitarian and in part ceremonial and, as a whole, tell us little of function and significance. Apart from local sequential difficulties, there are too few of any type to indicate development of forms in time. In this instance, the value of recording their details is largely to be realized in the eventual recognition of existent regional emphases. Again, the quantity of material at hand must weaken any such conclusions.

As noted in the Introduction, this report is first of all oriented comparatively to Uaxactun, a site comparable in size, environment and extent of excavation to Piedras Negras. Side by side, one immediately notes the greater amount of worked and slightly modified bone at Uaxactun. This is true in practically all categories, and especially with respect to perforating tools, tubular objects, and transversely sawed long bones. Awls were poorly represented at Piedras Negras and needles were non-existent insofar as the site was investigated. Perforated animal teeth, seemingly common at Uaxactun, failed also to appear. On the other hand, stingray spines were not emphasized at Uaxactun to anywhere near the degree that they were at Piedras Negras. But, disregarding quantity, the two centers shared various general items like awls, tubes, sawed long bones, antler, and ceremonially deposited stingray spines. Specific trait sharing occurs in vertebral pendants and musical (?) rasps. On both levels of function, there is fair agreement. And, on both levels, there are signs of preference and variable emphasis.

I think that one can fairly conclude however, that there is nothing at Uaxactun in bone that would be out of place at Piedras Negras, and vice-versa. A knowledge of the Uaxactun bone objects and attention to distributions would surely suffice to pin down the Piedras Negras collection as lowland Maya, and probably Classic Period, were its origin unknown. The addition of the latter material helps in some ways to individualize lowland culture in terms other than ceramic and hierarchic, this despite highland affiliations in the case of rasps and stingray spines.

OBJECTS OF CLAY

SPINDLE WHORLS

Three (Fig. 59 g, h; other [NM] not shown). All plano-convex. The two illustrated specimens are sub-hemispherical with diameters of 2.5 and 2.7 cm., and bore widths of .5 and .7 cm. One is complete and made of buff colored clay with traces of orange slip. The other is fragmentary and made of unslipped pinkish clay. A third, not illustrated, is hemispherical, unslipped fine buff clay, D 2 and T 1 cm., site position unknown.

COMMENT. As noted in their figure captions, two of these whorls were encountered on or near the surface and thus are presumably late. Those of stone were also judged to be late. Specially formed spindle whorls at Uaxactun are "all from the latest above-floor debris" (Kidder, 1947, p. 68). Kidder (*ibid.*) writes that their "tardy appearance [there] ... is in line with what data we have on the introduction of formed spindle whorls throughout Mesoamerica." Also, they "are rarely found in the Guatemala Highland sites of any period. They appear to be relatively common however, on the south coast " (A. L. Smith and Kidder, 1951, p. 76). At Zacualpa all whorls belong to the Post-Classic occupation (Woodbury and Trik, 1953, p. 169). A general survey of spindle whorls and their distribution is contained in the Kaminaljuyu report (Kidder Jennings, and Shook, 1946, pp. 215–16).

Stone whorls have already been described under Ground Stone. Round objects, possibly whorls, have been made from potsherds (see below).

WORKED POTSHERDS

Perforated discs, 3 (Fig. 58 p–r). All three have been biconically reamed. D 3.2, 6, 6.4, with bore diameters of .5, .7, .9 respectively. Two cut from plain ware sherds, the other from an orange slipped sherd (r).

COMMENT. Potsherds, equivalently worked, have been recorded for many sites. For example, they appeared at Copan in deposits of all periods (Longyear, 1952, pp. 103–04) and were also quite common at Uaxactun (Kidder, 1947, p. 67) with a possible Pre-Classic incidence (see Ricketson and Ricketson, 1937, p. 219). These have generally been assumed to be spindle whorls. In view of the late appearance of formed whorls, artifactual evidence of early spinning ultimately depends on the identification of these perforated discs. While they very likely were so used, it does seem odd that people would have gone to so much trouble to chip and grind and perforate sherds as whorls when clay can be so quickly formed into a thin disc, then punched and fired.

Incompletely perforated disc, 1 (Fig. 59 b). A cut sherd of a black-on-light orange fine buff paste vessel. Nicely rounded edge with slightly off-center irregular depression on inner side. D 4.1 cm.

COMMENT. Might not such an object have functioned as a spindle bearing? Continued use as such would produce an exit; then pivoting would begin on the obverse, finally yielding a biconical perforation. What are felt to be sherd whorls are perhaps actually spindle platforms. In the absence of specially formed whorls of clay, ones of bone and wood were employed. According to Tozzer (1907), the Lacandon made whorls of these materials rather than altered potsherds. Other archaeological, incompletely perforated discs are shown in Ricketson and Ricketson, 1937, Pl. 78 b.

Unperforated discs, 8 (Fig. 58 s—x; two [UM and NM] not shown). D 2.6—6.1 cm. Three have been cut from polychrome sherds, the others from large coarse-surfaced sherds. Some rounded, others quite irregular in outline. One of the examples unillustrated was found in one fill of Structure K—5—3rd (early).

COMMENT. Function problematical. If perforated ones are whorls, then these are probably unfinished whorls (see Kidder, 1947, p. 68).

Unperforated, incised disc, 1 (Fig. 59 a). Max.D 5.3 cm. Exterior of roughly shaped sherd linearly incised. No apparent meaning to design. Interior surface undecorated. Possibly from an Orange 2 vessel.

Multiply drilled disc, 1 (Fig. 58 o). D 6.7. Evidently cut from a sherd of a heavily tempered buff paste olla. One side is rough while concave (inner side) is relatively smooth and decorated with nine conically drilled depressions, one central, the others surrounding it. Butler (1935, Pl. XIV, 3) has shown this piece and suggested it to be a "gaming disc." See also Satterthwaite, 1933, p. 16.

Pendant, 1 (Fig. 59 c; also shown in Butler, 1935, Pl. XIII, 12). D 3.5. Discoidal, cut from a red or dark orange sherd. Edge is grooved circumferentially. Biconical perforation near edge intersects groove which is particularly deep at that point. Both sides have been decorated with curious post-fire incised designs. The exterior may show a seated figure with hands outstretched to left.

COMMENT. Resemblance in intersection of groove and perforation occur in two Uaxactun undecorated cut sherd pendants (Kidder, 1947, Fig. 58 b, c).

SLAB

One (Fig. 58 y). Max.D 7.6. Irregular in outline, thin, flat, not a worked sherd. Reddish-brown tempered clay, with gritty unpolished surfaces. Shows no indications of use.

EARPLUGS

Earspools, 4 (Fig. 59 n—q). All broken. Figure n perhaps represents extreme in length. Figure p has greatest diameter of four (ca. 3.2 cm.). Walls are extremely thin. Minimum diameter of each spool falls near middle, with gradual flares to rims. Rims of n are gently scalloped while those of remainder are either broken or straight and rounded, as in q. The interior of the scalloped-edged piece alone has been decorated, here by rim-to-rim incisions. The exteriors of three have been delicately decorated by a combination of incision and champleve. All have been made of a fine untempered light brown clay. When not abraded, surfaces show a soft polish. That in p (design possibly glyphic) appears also in Butler, 1935, Pl. XIII, 4.

COMMENT. These are an ancient ornament in the lowlands, having been found without decoration, at Uaxactun in Mamom-Chicanel sub-plaza debris (Ricketson and Ricketson, 1937, Pl. 69, b). This class of earplug as a rule is round in section with concave walls. Those covered in Kidder's distributional study (Kidder, Jennings, and Shook, 1946, p. 215), from a broad area, are uniformly squat with width exceeding height. This ratio occurs in recently reported examples from Copan (Longyear, 1952, Fig. 82 a—c) and Zaculeu (Woodbury and Trik, 1953, p. 209). The relative dimensions of the Piedras Negras spools, thus appear quite unusual. Krieger (Newell and Krieger, 1949, p. 146) has indicated various typological and distributional factors relating to earspools. Earspools ("napkin-rings") figure very rarely, if at all, in Maya sculpture. A few possible cases are to be found on Piedras Negras Lintel 1 and Bonampak Altar 2 and Stela A (figure, far left). Additional ornamentation may have been achieved by inserting cloth and other materials in the spool itself.

Flare, 1 (Fig. 59 f; illustrated also in Butler, 1935, Pl. XIII, 6). D 3.3 cm. Cup-shaped, everted horizontal rim, base diagonally perforated prior to firing. Unslipped, made of red clay, but surface blackened.

COMMENT. A pottery duplication of a form fairly common in jade at Piedras Negras (see under Jadeite); the ones of jade, however, are very much smaller. Other clay replicas of shell and jade objects are described in this section (below).

BEADS

Spherical, 128 (UM specimens in Figs. 58 a; 59 i; NM specimens in Fig. 58 k, l). Burial 5 contained 124 of these beads (Fig. 58 a; also see Fig. 64, 8). One was found in Structure R–10 and two others, decoratively grooved, cannot be assigned. All cylindrically perforated by punching prior to firing. Made of buff, evidently unslipped, unpolished clay. Many overfired.

COMMENT. Surprisingly, clay beads did not appear at Uaxactun, San Jose, Copan, Nebaj, and other sites. If meant to be substitutes for jade beads, not a single one shows traces of the green paint or green stucco one might expect. A bead like this, but of stone, comes from Labna (E. H. Thompson, 1897, p. 12). In addition to clay beads, Burial 5 also yielded a few clay replicas of shells (see below).

Large beads (?), 6 (Fig. 58 f–i; two [UM] not shown). D 3.2–3.5. Considering their size and broad molded perforations, these may not be beads at all but rather hair ornaments. All surfaces unslipped and unburnished. Two (*f*, *g*) were located near the feet of Skeleton B, Burial 5 (Fig. 64, 15) among Skeleton C remains. Four others (represented in *h* and *i*) were discovered smashed in the rubble above the cover stones of Burial 1. This same rubble contained bone fragments, all human, that are described as Lot 18 (under Burials). Both groups of objects are nearly identical.

PENDANTS

Cylindrical, 1 (Fig. 59 e). L 4.7 cm. Transverse, biconical, pre-fire perforation near rounded and slightly battered end. Other end has an irregular flare and appears to be broken. Unslipped coarse reddish paste. In view of perforation probably not a reworked object.

Bar pendant, 1 (Fig. 59 d). L 5.3 cm. Two transverse suspension holes, near ends, off-center, with consequent protuberances. Solid body round in cross-section but ends are pinched. Unslipped dark paste.

Replicas of bivalve shells, 4 complete and fragmentary (Fig. 58 b–e). L 11–11.5 cm. All from Burial 5 (Fig. 64, 6, 7, D, I). Each doubly perforated near hinge, presumably for suspension. Edges irregularly scalloped by pinching. Light colored clay without noticeable temper. Neither slipped nor polished. Traces of red coloring evident, but Burial 5 was a "red paint" burial. One of these clay shells has been shown by Butler (1935, Pl. XIV, 2). Unique objects.

PROBLEMATICAL ORNAMENTS

Pair (Fig. 58 j; other [NM] not shown; also see Butler, 1935, Pl. XIV, 1). Both cylindrically bodied with flared cuff on one end. Other end was longitudinally bored about one-third the total length. Traces of stucco and blue paint are noticeable on the concave end of the UM piece. Both from Burial 5 (Fig. 64, 2, 20).

COMMENT. In regard to these objects, Dr. Butler (*ibid.*, p. 48) suggests that they might be "pottery imitations of the jade beads that project in threes from the ends of neckbars and sides and bottoms of amulet plaques." There seems to be some confusion as to whether or not they were perforated from end to end. Miss Proskouriakoff's drawing (Fig. 58 j) indicates that they were not. Without destroying the object, it is a point difficult to prove.

Blue paint also appears on a shanked shell ornament (see Fig. 55 s) and on a type of lidded cache jar

(e. g. Fig. 62 h). The color blue possesses various ritualistic associations (see Tozzer, 1941, p. 117, 159; also Part 3, Specialized Cache Vessels, p. 101).

MISCELLANEOUS MODELED OBJECTS

One object (Fig. 58 n; also Butler, 1935, Pl. XIII, 1) consists of two elements; a shallow "dish" and a small disc that originally sat in and adhered to it. The collection contains a small featureless clay sphere (Fig. 58 m). An oddly shaped, unslipped object is shown in Figure 59, 1 , composed of a broken ring , flat in section, .8—1 cm. wide, at the base of which is a small appliqued disc with a shaved surface; the ring sits on a stand of layered clay strips on a discoidal base (broken) with a slightly concave underside and a multiply nicked edge; present standing height 2.3 cm. Figure 59 k shows another curious piece—a tabbed perforated disc, unslipped, with one side depressed and rayed; other side flat with an appliqued vertical tab. Both these objects do not appear to have been broken from larger objects.

(Note: The clefted, oval specimen in Figure 59 m, originally thought to be of fine clay, is more likely sandstone and is described in the Ground Stone section under Whetstones).

Finally, in Figure 59 j, a fragmentary piece is shown: multiply perforated, it once was rectangular with a width of 2.9 and a thickness of 1 cm., irregular surface due to bulging of clay when punched wet; unslipped dark brown paste.

DOUBLE-CHAMBERED OBJECTS

Two (Fig. 60 f, g). The first, complete, is made of unslipped, light buff, tempered clay, worn and lime-encrusted. Both chambers are singly perforated on the same side. L 6.5; W 3.7; depth 2.5 cm. Finger modeled. Second example is fragmentary but has same physical characteristics as the first and may have been perforated similarly. However, it evidences greater separation of chambers than first. Orginal length ca. 8 and width 3.5 cm. Both were found together below or inside latest construction of Structure J—2.

COMMENT.   These have been included in this report inasmuch as they do not seem to be vessels, either normal or miniature (for examples of latter, see Butler, 1935, Pl. V, 4, 5). It is difficult to determine whether or n ot these fall into the category of "candalero," an artifact primarily localized to Teotihuacan and Copan (see discussion in Longyear, 1952, pp. 101—02). The Piedras Negras pieces interestingly lack the flat surfaces usually a feature of double-chambered "candaleros" (see also Kidder, Jennings, and Shook, 1946, p. 216). In contrast to the deep wells of "candaleros," the Piedras Negras objects are relatively shallow and rounded. But the puzzling little side vents are a point in common. The function of these double-chambered objects is indeed problematical. That they may be exceptionally old in the lowlands is shown by a Mamom "double- cup" from Uaxactun (Ricketson and Ricketson, 1937, Fig. 151 b).

GENERAL COMMENT AND COMPARISON OF OBJECTS OF CLAY

The present collection stems from general excavation and burials. Apart from containers, no items of clay are known from caches (but see Cache O—13—33). The decorative objects emphasize suspension. The presence of clay replicas of shells and perhaps of jade beads causes one to wonder how much of sculptural ornamentation may not also have been imitation. The utilitarian aspect of the collection relates entirely to weaving. Finally, there are a good many objects that cannot be functionally explained.

Uaxactun and Piedras Negras evidently shared specially formed spindle whorls, centrally perforated sherd discs, and pendants made from sherds showing a curiously similar method of perforation. No stamps, either flat or cylindrical, were recovered at Piedras Negras, but cylindrical ones (or beads resembling stamps?) are known for Uaxactun, even from pre-Tzacol times (Kidder, 1947, p. 69). The Piedras Negras collection is negligibly individualized by clay shell replicas, spherical beads, and large, finely made earspools.

PERISHABLE MATERIALS

Practically nothing of this nature has survived. One need only view the quantities of magnificent materials on the monuments of this site to appreciate how much has been lost to time and the perennial dampness of the Middle Usumacinta region.

COPAL

A few small pieces were found beneath the smoke-blackened sherds of the locally early Cache R–3–1. Copal may have been deposited in Cache O–13–25. A lump of questionable copal was found with a bowl on the floor of Structure J–12.

COMMENT. Further signs of the offering of copal might be found in the carbon-smudged column altars so distinctive of Piedras Negras (see Satterthwaite, 1936 b, pp. 76–77, Fig. 2; 1946 a). Elsewhere, the presence of copal in votive offerings has been noted for Nebaj ("copal [?] beads") (A. L. Smith and Kidder, 1951, p. 58); the cache is datable as Late Classic. Crude copal ("partly burnt ball") was contained in two lip-to-lip bowls in a Mayapan altar deposit as well as in another altar cache (P. E. Smith, 1955, pp. 111–12 , 119). Of course, copal was commonly offered in Post-Classic times, particularly in cenote rites.

TEXTILES

Understandably no actual textiles were discovered in the excavations. But Butler (1935, pp. 9–10, Pl. V, 7) notes rare lime imprints on Orange 2 cache vessels of "a loosely-woven plain cloth textile." Her illustrated example is here shown reconstructed in Figure 61 m. This vessel is sufficiently imprinted to suggest that it had been entirely wrapped when deposited. The Piedras Negras stelae and lintels, of course, often depict complexly patterned garments.

Part 3

CACHES AND BURIALS

CACHES

INTRODUCTION

In the preceding parts of this report we have been dealing with artifacts as such. Primary interests have been typology, detailed description, function, and local and distant distributions. Many of these individual specimens appear to have reached their final resting places by chance, but frequent mention has been made of "burials" and "caches." These latter sources are of an intentional nature; they are also hidden and usually involve a group of artifacts. These intentional deposits require further attention, the emphasis shifting from individual items to the deposit as a whole. Burials are treated in the next chapter.

Caches are responsible for a major portion of the collection treated in this report. Cache frequency and contents are most outstanding.

For the purposes of this report, the term *cache* (literally "a hiding place") refers to one or more objects found together, but apart from burials, whose grouping and situation point to intentional interment as an offering. The term is customarily used in Maya archaeology in conjunction with the term "votive" (e. g., see Thompson, 1931, Ch. III). The use of the latter term is of course imprecise; no implication of "vow" is intended. But the combined result, "votive cache," precludes confusion with the utilitarian storage caches found frequently in North American archaeology. Prior definitions (Ricketson and Ricketson, 1937, p. 139; Thompson, 1939, p. 184; A. L. Smith, 1950, p. 91) tend to stress the spatial factor, that is, the close grouping of objects apart from burials. Concern with function is implicit in the frequent use in reports of the words "votive," "dedicatory," "offertory," and in the expression "ceremonial deposit" or "offering."

The majority of Maya caches, including those from Piedras Negras, can be tagged and treated with no difficulty. But occasionally a subsurface deposit, intentionally placed, has appeared which was so situated and composed that its classification as either a burial or a cache has been necessarily arbitrary. If intentional deposits were exclusively one or the other, there would be little reason for arbitrariness. This can be illustrated by certain Uaxactun cases. A. L. Smith, 1950, p. 93) writes:

"Burials E21—E23 and A27 should possibly be classified as caches, for they appear to have been votive offerings although they contained human remains. Each consisted of a human skull inside two cache bowls... Three of the skulls were found with the upper two or three cervicals, indicating that they probably were not secondary burials but were the sacrificial victims whose heads had been cut off and placed below the temple floor as an offering."

Whether classified as burials or caches, these Uaxactun deposits were ceremonially and deliberately set and they did comprise offerings; because they share these characteristics, their classification is problematical. But would there be difficulty in assigning the skulls and cervicals as burials had they been found without containers? The factors of sacrifice and dedicatory interment remain regardless of the presence or absence of vessels.

The problem increases when one recalls various instances in which whole skeletons are so positioned as to indicate dedicatory sacrifice (e. g., San Jose; Thompson, 1939, p. 220). Eccentric flints are buried as an offering; skulls are similarly buried; and whole sacrificed individuals are interred with a dedicatory objective.

This apparent overlap or blending of caches and burials may result from inadequate terminology and definition on our part. Or it may reflect a blending of ceremonial concepts current among the lowland Classic Maya. But whatever probing is done will surely relate to both of these possibilities. At Piedras

Negras this problem is very real for there is at least one case of an intentional deposit which, at least in our minds, is "conceptually" confused (see Cache R—3—2).

A votive cache as the term is used here, involves the *offering* of "one or more objects." The cache may be either dedicatory or non-dedicatory, depending on its location. It is not associated with a burial although its contents may be partly or wholly human, or animal. The precise function of a cache presumably depends on whether it is dedicatory or not; whatever the function, this may partly condition the specific cache components.

As regards content in terms of objects, a cache may comprise a variety of things. Interestingly, Thompson (1939, p. 184) specifies that a cache contain "two or more utensils or ornaments;" a requirement like this would rule out of consideration a single vessel which originally contained perishable objects which have totally disintegrated. And there is no valid reason why a single pot, if originally empty, should not be considered a votive cache provided its situation meets our definition.

Cache components may be divided as follows:

POTTERY: Container vessel, votively specialized or non-specialized
          Special cover
          Second covering vessel (inverted)

ENTIRELY PERISHABLE OBJECTS (inferable only from complete emptiness of vessel)

PARTLY PERISHABLE OBJECTS: Animal skeletal material
                             Human skeletal material

IMPERISHABLE OBJECTS: Artifacts
                        Unworked materials

At Piedras Negras and elsewhere many different combinations of these components were found as caches. The listing is controversial in one respect, namely, the inclusion of human skeletal material. With good reason one might ask how much human material or how little must there be for the deposit to be classified as a cache? And must what there is of it be in a container? What diagnostic may be used in a borderline case (e. g., the Uaxactun skulls) to permit exclusive classification of the deposit?

If our estimation duplicates that of the Maya and severed human heads are thought of as *objects* suitable for votive use, in much the same way as an eccentric flint or a stingray spine was ritually suitable, then these deposits should be considered as caches. This of course impinges on the subject of human sacrifice which is treated in the chapter on Burials.

But it is our feeling that such sacrifices, at certain places and in certain times, did have a "cache objective." If the human remains were treated as simply objects with a certain symbolic value, one correlate of human interment was lacking, namely, careful interest in the deceased as a person. This principle cannot resolve every problem; undoubtedly cases will appear in which classification as a burial *or* as a cache will be impossible.

A major distinction can be made in votive caches between those deposited as dedicatory and as non-dedicatory offerings. Recognition depends on the deposit's position.   If evidence indicates placement with a monument, or during construction of an architectural feature planned to cover it, the cache is presumed to be involved with "dedication" of the monument or structure. Its position may be axial or non-axial. However, if the deposit was made through an existing surface, it may be interpreted as dedicatory or non-dedicatory, depending on such factors as method of concealment and actual stratigraphic relationship. A non-dedicatory cache is one that was made through an existing surface during the occupation of the surface, and it was made in terms of that occupation; a restored "patch" surface would be good evidence of a non-dedicatory cache (see Cache J—29—2). When a surface ceased to be used, a cache could have been set into it and a new structure placed over the old surface; this cache would then be considered dedicatory with respect to the new structure despite its intrusion into the old. In regard to dedicatory offerings, see Functions of Caches, under General Comment , p. 118.

Cache deposits at Piedras Negras were placed beneath the surfaces of temples and, less frequently, palace structures. Others occurred beneath plaza and ball-court floors. Dedicatory caches were found below column altars and outdoor table altars and before the buried bases of stelae. Non-dedicatory ("intrusive") motives are presumed for many of the non-axially placed Structure O—13 caches. One in Structure J—29 was definitely not dedicatory, but made during occupation (see Cache J—29—2). A more thorough analysis of cache phenomena, stemming from a broad comparative study of caches, is to be found at the end of this part of the report.

Cache numeration is as follows: caches have first been grouped according to the structure in or near which they were found and given the number of that structure, as, for instance, O—13 or J—1. A final number, like —10, as in Cache O—13—10, is entirely arbitrary and has no bearing on the actual or supposed sequence of caches within a structure. Nor do such phase-indicating structure designations as "K—5—1st, " "K—5—2nd," figure in cache numeration. The use of ordinals in architectural designations precludes confusion with cache numbers. The various methods used to date caches (in the Maya Long Count system) are described in the Appendix. Conclusions there have been utilized in the following pages and underlie much of Table 4.

Throughout the cache descriptions, mention is made of a "lime paste" coating partly and occasionally wholly, the interiors of many cache vessels (see Table 5 for its occurrences). An analysis and discussion of this paste occurs under Cache Contents in the General Comment following the individual descriptions of caches (p. 104). Caches have been described by structures in the following arbitrary order: O—13, O—7, O—16, J—1, J—3, J—6, J—29, K—5, R—3, R—9, R—11, and R—16 (see Table of Contents for page references).

THE PIEDRAS NEGRAS CACHES

STRUCTURE O—13

CACHE DATING. In all, 56 caches in 15 localities were discovered in and about this remarkable temple structure. It has received little mention in the literature, although a plan of it and related monuments is given by Morley (1937—1938, Pl. 204). Fronting the structure, on the plaza, were 6 stelae with texts reliably ranging from 9.16.15.0.0 (Stela 16) to 9.18.10.0.0 (Stela 14). These dates, however, are not necessarily indicative of local cache activity.

Major excavations were made in Structure O—13 by Mason, in 1931 and 1932, when all but one (Cache O—13—17) of this group of caches were recovered. These excavations showed that the temple involved an intricate series of both vertical and horizontal increments which were not then worked out in full detail. In subsequent years Cresson and Satterthwaite excavated a little further in strategic spots only. Proskouriakoff made accurate plans and sections and attempted to reconstruct the temple in its various known periods and phases. Unfortunately alternative sequences had to be allowed for. This work has not yet been published. The structural sequence used here may not be correct in every detail; it involves selections by Satterthwaite from among alternatives allowed by Proskouriakoff, but the scheme adopted can hardly mislead us significantly.

This complex consists of four vertically sequent buildings, with a postulated O—13—5th phase of the series, which further excavation supposedly would have revealed (see Appendix). The sequence concludes with Structure O—13—1st, which involved three important building phases, known as —C, —B, and —A, Structure O—13—1st—A being terminal. To anticipate, there is no evidence that the O—13 caches belong any earlier than Structure O—13—1st—C.

The dating of these various structures is a complicated matter and is dealt with in the Appendix of this report. For caches, the dating of O—13—1st—C is critical. O—13—1st—A seems secure at 9.17.15.0.0. Using an estimated building interval of 3 katuns, Satterthwaite concluded that O—13—1st—C may have been built at 9.12.0.0.0. A slightly revised interval yields 9.12.5.0.0, but the former estimate is used here.

The upper dating limit of the Structure O—13 caches is somewhat uncertain. If all these caches, stemming from O—13—1st, phase or phases unknown, were definitely dedicatory, none could date later than

9.17.16.0.0 which marks the construction of O—13—1st—A, the latest of the sequence. But, for reasons given below, many of the O—13 caches are believed to have been non-dedicatory, that is, intrusive. One approach would be to assume, perhaps validly, a cessation of votive practices with the conclusion of major ceremonial activities. Altar 3 carries the latest reliable date, 9.19.0.0.0. Building activity, with its cache feature, might have continued beyond this date but 10.0.0.0.0 seems reasonable as a round number date for the end of Piedras Negras Classic hierarchic activity (Satterthwaite, verbal communication). Certain late features, perhaps due to a reoccupation (see Introduction), need not be considered as evidence of this activity.

The two guess-dates, then, 9.12.0.0.0 ?? and 10.0.0.0.0 ??, are the lower and upper limits for the dating of the O—13 caches. The date 9.17.15.0.0 is definitely a more reasonable limit in the case of various caches. The date 9.12.0.0.0 ?? might seem too early for O—13—1st—C but it is unlikely that it is too early by more than two katuns, a constant allowance in the present system of estimated building intervals.

It seems unlikely that, once stairways were built, caches were placed beneath them; this also would seem true for intruded caches beneath standing walls. Various proveniences of caches (see list of locations below: Nos. 1, 3, 4, 6, and 11) were so situated that a dating no later than that of O—13—1st—A is probable. The respective caches may have been intrusively set during the occupation of O—13—1st—B or —C, or both, but they cannot antedate the construction of O—13—1st—C. The following caches, then, evidently date from 9.12.0.0.0 ?? to 9.17.15.0.0: Caches O—13—4, O—13—5, O—13—6, O—13—7, O—13—8, O—13—9, O—13—14, O—13—15, O—13—54, and O—13—55.

Location 9 (see below) is in a lateral extension of O—13—1st—A, at a level where there was nothing in earlier phases. The two caches from this source, O—13—20 and O—13—21, are thus no earlier than 9.17.15.0.0. They may be no later than this if we assume that they were the dedicatory offerings for the Phase A building activity. Of course they are not on the front-rear axis of the temple. One must also allow for intrusion during the occupation of O—13—1st—A. These two caches, then, are no earlier than the construction of O—13—1st—A and are assumed to be no later than the estimated date, 10.0.0.0.0.

Two caches, O—13—1 and O—13—56 (Locations 14 and 15), come from the plaza level. Cache O—13—1 was associated definitely with a plain table altar. There is good evidence that all East Group carved monuments are no earlier than about 9.16.0.0.0. But since the altar (Altar 5) is plain, it may have been earlier than any of the carved monuments of the group. On the other hand, the form of this altar relates to four carved and relatively late table altars. The best guess is that Cache O—13—1, dedicated to Altar 5, dates from the occupation of O—13—1st, phase unknown. If truly the dedicatory cache of Stela 18, Cache O—13—56 belongs at 9.17.5.0.0 ?; but, to be on the safe side, this cache is considered to belong to O—13—1st, phase unknown. The dating of 12 of the 54 caches found in the temple proper has already been discussed. Of the remaining 42 caches, we can only say that they were "in fill of Structure O—13—1st, phase unknown." In time they fall between 9.12.0.0.0 ?? and 10.0.0.0.0 ??. The upper limit is extreme because, lacking contrary evidence, we must allow that all 42 caches may have been intruded after the construction of O—13—1st—A. It is important to note, however, that an extraordinary number of monuments were erected in front of this same temple; they range in round-number dates from 9.16.0.0.0 to 9.19.0.0.0. It has already been presumed that cache activity locally ceased with the suspension of monument erection. The unprecedented cache deposition beneath the floors of the temple conceivably may have resulted from the ceremonial fervor evident in the rapid erection of monuments about the temples. Interestingly, though, excavations were completed, or nearly so, below the floors of three other temple structures (R—3, J—1, and K—5) without encountering any such quantity of caches.

In light of the time span of Structure O—13—1st, this stratigraphic vagueness is a pity but, naturally, it is now irreparable. The bulk of the caches seems to have been excavated by workmen who did not appreciate the potential value of precise positional data. At this time, structural terms and other identifications had not been standardized.

The building sequence with its firm and estimated dates and with its caches follows. This list summarizes the previous discussions in addition to much of that portion of the Appendix relevant to Structure O—13. This list is itself summarized in Table 4 (Sequence of Caches).

PERIODS AND PHASES	DATES	CACHES	
ABANDONMENT	10.0.0.0.0 ??		
		O−13−20,−21	
O−13−1st−A (latest)	9.17.15.0.0		All Others
O−13−1st−B	9.15.0.0.0 ??	O−13−4,−5,−6, −7,−8,−9,−14, −15,−54,−55	
O−13−1st−C	9.12.0.0.0 ??		
O−13−2nd	9.9.0.0.0 ??	No Caches Found	
O−13−3rd	9.6.0.0.0 ??	No Caches Found	
O−13−4th (earliest known)	9.3.0.0.0 ??	No Caches Found	
O−13−5th (postulated)	9.0.0.0.0 ??		

CACHE LOCATIONS

Inasmuch as the offerings to be described here are in an arbitrary, numerical order, a listing of specific proveniences, sequential positions, and caches follows. These are based on field notes, the Field Catalogue, and sometimes on inferences.

Location 1. Summit, under stairway about in center of fill. Probably no later than O−13−1st−A and no earlier than O−13−1st−C. Caches O−13−4 and O−13−54.

Location 2. Summit, beneath pyramid surface. O−13−1st, phase unknown. Caches O−13−2 and O−13−3.

Location 3. In rubble fill below rear wall at back of broad upper terrace. Probably no later than O−13−1st−A and no earlier than O−13−1st−C. Cache O−13−5.

Location 4. In front of entrance of lower front rooms, evidently in area of the platform stairway. Probably no later than O−13−1st−A and no earlier than O−13−1st−C. Caches O−13−6 through O−13−9.

Location 5. Beneath one of the doorways of the long front gallery. O−13−1st, phase unknown. Caches O−13−10 through O−13−12.

Location 6. Beneath east pier in the building's front gallery. Probably no later than O−13−1st−A and no earlier than O−13−1st−C. Cache O−13−55.

Location 7. Under floor of front gallery behind pier on right of building's left end doorway. O−13−1st, phase unknown. Cache O−13−17.

Location 8. Under floor of "room" of O−13−1st−A, beyond the west pier of buttress behind it; part of its floor may date back to O−13−1st−B or even to −C. O−13−1st, phase uncertain. Caches O−13−18 and O−13−19.

Location 9. Below the floor of the north end of the front gallery O−13−1st−A, but, if deposits intrusive, then later. Caches O−13−20 and O−13−21.

Location 10. Below floor of "central outer room." O−13−1st, phase unknown (catalogued provenience too vague). Cache O−13−13.

Location 11.   In vestibule beneath original or even secondary jamb of door to rear of temple. Probably no later than O—13—1st—A nor earlier than O—13—1st—C. Caches O—13—14 and O—13—15.

Location 12.   Under floor of the middle room, east half. O—13—1st, phase unknown. Cache O—13—12.

Location 13.   Under floor of rear room. O—13—1st, phase unknown. Caches O—13—23 through O—13—53.

Location 14.   Beneath Altar 5 (plain); axially located; altar typologically related to four carved table altars and perhaps to their late time span as well; suspected that Altar 5 belongs to O—13—1st but no basis for choosing between phases. Cache O—13—1.

Location 15.   Behind Altar 5, and perhaps originally from base of now fallen Stela 18 (9.17.5.0.0 [?]). Safest conclusion is that offering dates from time of O—13—1st, phase unknown. Cache O—13—56.

DESCRIPTION OF CACHES.   Most O—13 caches can be reliably reconstructed. Others are only partly known because of labeling and cataloguing deficiencies. Loss through time and the camp fire are also drawbacks. Occasionally an uncertain Field Catalogue reference has been used; the use of quotation marks sets it apart. All cache locations are given in relation to the preceding list of locations. Caches are summarized in Table 5 . Discussions of various cache components will be found in the General Comment near the end of this chapter (see Table of Contents).

CACHE O—13—1 (NM)

Location.   No. 14

Container.   Apparently none.

Contents.   6 eccentric flints (Fig. 4 a—f); 5 eccentric obsidians (Fig. 21 a—e)

CACHE O—13—2 (camp fire)

Location.   No. 2.

Container.   Orange 2 hemispherical bowl and sub-hemispherical lid (as in Fig. 61).

Contents.   2 eccentric flints; "obsidian fragments;" 3 "jadeites;" "bone fragments."

CACHE O—13— (camp fire)

Location.   No. 2.

Container.   Probably a small bowl.

Contents.   4 eccentric flints; 5 eccentric obsidians; 1 obsidian flake-blade; 1 jadeite figurine, 1 spherical piece of jadeite and 8 jadeite fragments; 6 shell figurines (presumably as in Figs. 51 f—h; 52 e—g) and a *Spondylus* "shell;" 3 "bone fragments;" 1 piece of pyrite.

CACHE O—13—4 (UM)

Location.   No. 1

Container.   Orange 2 bowl with flaring sides (Fig. 62 a) and a mate inverted over it as a cover.

Contents.   3 eccentric flints (Fig. 4 g—i); 2 eccentric obsidians and a flake-blade (Fig. 21 f—h); 1 polished and sawed jadeite pebble (Fig. 45 z; also Fig. 48 d'), 1 carved jadeite profile head (Fig. 45 a') and a polished, perforated piece of jadeite (Fig. 45 b'); 3 cut pieces of *Spondylus* (Fig. 52 y—a'), both valves of a *Spondylus*, one of which is perforated (Fig. 52 r), and 2 other shells, *Livona pica* and *Vermicularia spirata*. The whole articulated *Spondylus* shell evidently contained one or more of the jadeite objects.

CACHE O—13—5 (camp fire)

Location.   No. 3.

Container.   Present. No other information.

Contents.   4 "broken" eccentric flints; 10 eccentric obsidians; 1 jadeite bead and 2 pieces of jadeite; *Spondylus* valve and fragments, and various shell fragments; "piece of serpula worm."

CACHE O—13—6 (UM, NM)

Location.   No. 4.

Container.   Probably an Orange 2 hemispherical bowl (Fig. 61 q). Lime paste.

Contents.   6 eccentric flints (Fig. 4 j—o); 8 eccentric obsidians (Fig. 21 i—p), 1 obsidian core, and a flake (?) (Fig. 21 q, r); 5 incised jadeites (Fig. 46 d—g; one not located), both valves of a *Spondylus* and a fragment of a fresh water clam.

CACHE O—13—7 (UM)

Location. No. 4.

Container. Orange 2 hemispherical bowl (Fig. 61 p). Lime paste.

Contents. 7 eccentric flints (Fig. 5 a—g); 8 eccentric obsidians (Fig. 21 s—z) and 1 flake-blade (Fig. 21 a'); 1 faintly incised jadeite (Fig. 46 i); 1 incised cut shell (Fig. 51 j).

CACHE O—13—8 (UM, NM)

Location. No. 4.

Container. Orange 2 hemispherical bowl (Fig. 61, 1). Lime paste.

Contents. 7 eccentric flints (Fig. 5 h, i; others not located); 20 eccentric obsidians (Fig. 23 j; 19 not located); 7 unworked and slightly worked pieces of jadeite (Fig. 50 u) and 5 other "jadeites" not located; 2 "shells;" 1 stingray spine; "fragments of bone."

CACHE O—13—9 (UM, NM)

Location. No. 4.

Container. Probably an Orange 2 hemispherical bowl (Fig. 61 r) and sub-hemispherical lid not shown). Lime paste.

Contents. 2 eccentric flints (Fig. 5 j, k); 2 eccentric obsidians (not located); articulated bivalve shell (not located) and 2 *Arca occidentalis* shells; 1 stingray spine.

CACHE O—13—10 (UM, NM)

Location. No. 5.

Container. Presence (UM) of an Orange 2 sub-hemispherical lid suggests a hemispherical container similar to those in Figure 61. But the field number of a small flat-based, Orange 2 bowl (Fig. 62 f) indicates that it may also be associated with this cache; it seems too small to have contained all the objects in the offering.

Contents. 33 eccentric flints (Figs. 6, 7) and 4 unrelateable eccentric flint fragments (not illustrated); 28 eccentric obsidians (Figs. 22 a—n; 30 m; 31 c, m; 32 o, p; 33 n; 34 f; 35 j; 6 in NM not located), 3 fragmentary flake-blades (not located in UM and NM), and 1 obsidian flake (Fig. 22 o); 3 "jadeites" (NM, not located); 6 "worked shells" (NM, not located).

CACHE O—13—11 (UM, NM)

Location. No. 5.

Container. Orange 2 hemispherical bowl (disposition?) and sub-hemispherical lid (Fig. 61 k).

Contents. 5 eccentric flints (NM, not located); 4 eccentric obsidians (NM, 1 located, Fig. 23 k); 2 valves of bivalve, *Arca occidentalis* (Fig. 52 h).

CACHE O—13—12 (UM)

Location. No. 5.

Container. Pair of lip-to-lip Orange 2 bowls with flaring sides, flat bases (Fig. 62 c).

Contents. 1 jadeite bead (Fig. 44 g) and 1 sawed and polished jadeite pebble (Fig. 48, e'); 2 articulated *Spondylus* valves and a fragment of a second shell (*Crucibulum spinosa*). No information as to whether *Spondylus* contained one or more jadeite pieces.

CACHE O—13—13 (UM)

Location. No. 10.

Container. Probably an Orange 2 bowl with flaring straight sides, flat base (Fig. 62 b). Lime paste.

Contents. Limestone disc (Fig. 43 e), possibly morphological equivalent of eccentric obsidians (discs) seen in other caches; 9 eccentric obsidians (Fig. 23 a—i); 1 round shell piece (Fig. 52 c'), 7 incised shell discs (Figs. 51 u, v; 52 b'), 2 small shell figurines (Fig. 51 f, g), valve of a bivalve, *Arca umbonata*, with traces of red paint on interior; proximal portion of a stingray spine with end cut to produce five prongs (see under Stingray Spines, pp. 64 ff).

CACHE O–13–14 (camp fire)

Location. No. 11.

Container. None.

Contents. 9 eccentric obsidians; 2 pieces of shell; 1 "polished iron pyrite; " "animal bone fragments" and "stingray tails."

CACHE O–13–15 (NM ?)

Location. No. 11.

Container. Present. No information.

Contents. 1 eccentric obsidian; 2 pieces of jadeite; 1 piece of iron pyrite; *Spondylus* "shell" and a second shell and a fragment of coral.

CACHE O–13–16 (UM, NM ?)

Location. Uncertain. Either beneath east secondary jamb of doorway or beneath floor of rear room.

Container. No data.

Contents. 5 eccentric flints (Fig. 5 1–o; one other not located); 8 eccentric obsidians (Fig. 22 p, r; 8 not located) and 1 core (Fig. 22 q); 1 incised jadeite (Fig. 46 c) and 1 "worked jadeite."

CACHE O–13–17 (UM)

Location. No. 7. Bottom of bowl was 1 m. below sill level.

Container. Orange 2 hemispherical bowl (Fig. 61 t) and sub-hemispherical lid. Bowl was found broken into many sherds and had fallen to front and was lying almost on its side. Lime paste.

Contents. 1 eccentric flint (Fig. 8 a); 5 eccentric obsidians (Fig. 22 s–w); 1 limestone disc (Fig. 43 f; see limestone disc, Cache O–13–13); 1 incised jadeite (Fig. 46 b) and another incised jadeite with incompleted saw grooves on one side (Figs. 46 a; 50 q), and 3 slightly worked pieces of jadeite (Fig. 50 c).

CACHE O–13–18 (UM, NM ?)

Location. No. 8.

Container. A small Orange 2 bowl (Fig. 62 g) likely belongs to this deposit.

Contents. 2 eccentric flints (Fig. 8 b, c); 5 eccentric obsidians (Fig. 23 m, n; 3 not located); 1 "jadeite."

CACHE O –13–19 (UM, NM)

Location. No. 8.

Container. Under cache field number are two Orange 2 hemispherical bowl rim sherds and a few sherds of a typical sub-hemispherical lid (UM, as in Fig. 61).

Contents. 6 eccentric obsidians (Fig. 23,1 ; 5 not located); 4 broken eccentric flints (not located) and 4 "jadeites" (not located).

CACHE O–13–20 (NM)

Location. No. 9.

Container. No data.

Contents. 1 eccentric flint (not located); 2 eccentric obsidians (not located).

CACHE O –13–21 (UM, NM)

Location. No. 9.

Container. Orange 2 hemispherical bowl and sub-hemispherical lid (Fig. 61 g).

Contents. 9 pieces of slightly worked jadeite (Fig. 50 t); "bones" (not located); 3 "pieces of red stone" (not located).

CACHE O–13–22 (camp fire?)

Location. No. 12.

Container. Field Catalogue lists "two dishes, two lids."

Contents. 26 eccentric flints; 19 eccentric obsidians; 7 "jadeites."

CACHE O–13–23 (UM, NM)

Location. No. 13.

Container. No data.

Contents. 3 eccentric flints (Fig. 8 d–f); 3 eccentric obsidians (Fig. 23 o, p; other not located); articulated pair of *Spondylus* valves (1 UM; 1 NM), 3 fragments of *Spondylus* (UM), 1 small incised shell figurine (Fig. 51 h), and 1 incised shell disc (Fig. 51 t); 2 stingray spine fragments. (UM).

CACHE O–13–24 (UM, NM)

Location. No. 13.

Container. No data.

Contents. 7 eccentric flints (Fig. 8 g–l; one not located); 2 eccentric obsidians (Fig. 23 q; other not located).

CACHE O–13–25 (UM, NM)

Location. No. 13.

Container. Dark orange on light orange cylinder jar (Fig. 60 h).

Contents. 2 eccentric obsidians (Fig. 23 r; other not located).

CACHE O–13–26 (UM)

Location. No. 13.

Container. No data.

Contents. 6 eccentric flints and 1 flint flake (Fig. 8 m–s); 1 eccentric obsidian (not located).

CACHE O–13–27 (UM, NM)

Location. No. 13.

Container. Unslipped pear-shaped jar (as in Fig. 62 p) with a flat disc lid painted blue on its edge (UM).

Contents. Flint blade fragment (Fig. 9 b) and 6 flint flakes (Fig. 9 a); 1 whole and 3 fragmentary obsidian flake-blades (Fig. 24 a–d) and 2 obsidian flakes (Fig. 24 e, f); 1 incised jadeite (Fig. 46 j); 1 broken univalve, *Pomacea flagellata*; 1 fragmentary stingray spine gouged along one side (as in Fig. 55 f).

CACHE O–13–28 (UM, NM?)

Location. No. 13.

Container. Polychrome cylinder jar (Fig. 60 i). Contents definitely inside.

Contents. "Flints," presumably eccentric (NM?, not located); 3 eccentric obsidians (NM?, not located); 1 jar lid with blue painted rim (as in Fig. 62 o–q).

CACHE O–13–29 (UM, NM?)

Location. No. 13.

Container. "Pot with lid" (NM?, not located).

Contents. 2 flint flakes (UM); 1 eccentric obsidian (Fig. 24 g); small perforated bone tube (Fig. 55 i).

CACHE O–13–30 (UM)

Location. No. 13.

Container. No data.

Contents. 2 eccentric flints (Fig. 9 c, d) and 3 flint flakes (Fig. 9 e–g); 4 eccentric obsidians (Fig. 24 j–m) and 4 flake-blade fragments (Fig. 24 n); small piece of shell; fragmentary, longitudinally gouged stingray spine (as in Fig. 55 f).

CACHE O–13–31 (NM ?)

Location.   No. 13.

Container.   No data.

Contents.   3 "flint chips;" 2 eccentric obsidians; 2 "jadeites."

CACHE O–13–32 (UM, NM)

Location.   No. 13.

Container.   Pertinent sherds (UM) suggest an unslipped jar with a disc lid (as in Fig. 62 o–q).

Contents.   4 "flint chips" (NM, not located); 2 eccentric obsidians (NM, not located).

CACHE O–13–33 (UM)

Location.   No. 13.

Remarks.   A complete jar and disc lid (Fig. 62 p) contained nothing but a small pottery knob. Field Catalogue lists and UM has a second broken flat pot lid. And other totally different sherds, covered by the same field number, are in the UM. The extra disc lid may represent a cache disturbed during excavation or it may have formed part of the contents of the jar itself.

CACHE O–13–34 (UM)

Location.   No. 13 ; close to the rear wall and near the center.

Remarks.   Presumed cache consists of Miscellaneous Sculptured Stone 1, the location of which points to its having been placed, actually redeposited, below the floor as a cache. The object itself is half of a very small "portable altar" with a diameter of 25 cm. and a height of 13 cm. Originally its side had been inscribed with 7 or 8 glyph blocks, only 4 of which have survived. The stone has been studied by Morley (1937–1938, v. 3, pp. 105–107) who assigned it a date of 9.10.6.5.9. In this report, this is read to the current hotun (i. e. 9.10.10.0.0).

CACHE O–13–35 (UM, NM)

Location.   No. 13.

Container.   Probably an unslipped jar with disc lid, judging from sherds in UM with correct field number (see Fig. 62 o –q for examples).

Contents.   12 "flint chips" (NM, not located); 3 eccentric obsidians (NM, not located); 1 slightly worked piece of jadeite (Fig. 50 e).

CACHE O–13–36 (UM)

Location.   No. 13.

Container.   Unslipped jar with flaring rim (Fig. 62 t).

Contents.   1 eccentric flint and 1 flint flake (Fig. 9 h, i); 1 eccentric obsidian and a flake-blade fragment (Fig. 24 h, i); 1 slightly worked piece of jadeite (Fig. 50 g).

CACHE O–13–37 (UM)

Location.   No. 13.

Container.   No data.

Contents.   3 eccentric flints (Fig. 9 j–l) and 12 flint flakes; 13 eccentric obsidians (Fig. 24 o–a'), 3 obsidian flakes (Fig. 24 b'–d'), and 6 fragments of flake-blades (Fig. 24 e'); 4 slightly worked pieces of jadeite (Fig. 50 b); shark tooth (Fig. 57 g).

CACHE O–13–38 (NM)

Location.   No. 13.

Container.   No data.

Contents.   1 eccentric flint (Fig. 9 m) and 2 flint flakes (Fig. 9 n, o); 7 eccentric obsidians (not located).

CACHE O–13–39 (NM)

Location.   No. 13.

Container.   Field Catalogue notes presence of sherds (container ?).

Contents.   8 flint flakes (4 located); 6 eccentric obsidians (Fig. 25 a; others not located).

CACHE O—13—40 (NM)
Location. No. 13.
Container. Field Catalogue notes presence of sherds (container?).
Contents. 1 eccentric flint and 4 flint "chips" (not located); eccentric obsidians (not located).

CACHE O—13—41 (NM)
Location. No. 13.
Container. Unslipped jar with disc lid (Fig. 62 q).
Contents. 2 eccentric flints (Fig. 9 p, q) and 7 flint "chips" (Fig. 9 r, t; 2 not located); 2 eccentric obsidians (not located); 3 "poor jadeites" (not located).

CACHE O—13—42 (UM, NM)
Location. No. 13.
Container. Unslipped jar with disc lid (Fig. 62 o).
Contents. 1 eccentric flint (NM, not located); 2 eccentric obsidians (NM, not located).

CACHE O—13—43 (NM)
Location. No. 13.
Container. Field Catalogue notes presence of sherds (container?).
Contents. 8 eccentric flints (Fig. 9 u—w; 5 not located); 4 eccentric obsidians (Fig. 25 b; others not located); 5 "jadeites" (not located); 1 cut, semicircular piece of white shell (described under Miscellaneous Cut Shell Objects, p. 59).

CACHE O—13—44 (UM, NM)
Location. No. 13.
Container. Field Catalogue notes presence of sherds (container?) (NM).
Contents. 5 eccentric flints (Fig. 10 a—e); 5 eccentric obsidians (Fig. 25 e—i).

CACHE O—13—45 (UM, NM)
Location. No. 13.
Container. Orange 2 sub-hemispherical lid, D 20 cm., (UM) indicates hemispherical bowl (as in Fig. 61).
Contents. 7 eccentric obsidians (Fig. 25 c, d; others not located); 2 "jadeites" (not located); "fragments of bone" (not located).

CACHE O—13—46 (UM, NM)
Location. No. 13.
Container. Unslipped jar with blue painted rim (Fig. 62 i), fragmentary.
Contents. 7 pieces of flint, 3 or possibly 4 of which are crudely eccentric (Fig. 10 f—i); 2 eccentric obsidians (not located); "shell" (not located); "fragments of bone" (not located).

CACHE O—13—47 (UM, NM?)
Location. No. 13.
Container. Field Catalogue notes presence of sherds (container?).
Contents. 7 eccentric flints (Fig. 10 j—p) and 3 flint flakes (Fig. 10 q); 3 eccentric obsidians (Fig. 25 o—q) and three flake-blade fragments (Fig. 25 r—t); 1 incised hook-shaped jadeite object (Fig. 45 t), 1 incised jadeite (Fig. 46 k), a fragmentary piece of incised decomposed jadeite (Fig. 44 q), and 4 slightly worked jadeite pieces (Fig. 50 a).

CACHE O—13—48 (UM)
Location. No. 13.
Container. No data.
Contents. 2 eccentric flints (Fig. 10 r, s); 1 incised jadeite (Fig. 45 l) and 1 slightly worked jadeite piece (Fig. 50 f).

CACHE O–13–49 (NM)

Location. No. 13.

Container. Field Catalogue notes presence of sherds (container?).

Contents. 2 eccentric flints (Fig. 10 t; other not located); 4 flint "chips" (not located); 19 eccentric obsidians (not located); 2 "jadeites" (not located).

CACHE O–13–50 (UM)

Location. No. 13.

Container. No data.

Contents. 2 eccentric obsidians (Fig. 25 j, k), 1 crude possible eccentric (Fig. 25 n), and 2 flake-blade fragments (Fig. 50 l, m); 1 incised jadeite plaque with distinct saw marks on obverse (Figs. 45 v; 50 s).

CACHE O–13–51 (UM)

Location. No. 13.

Container. No data.

Contents. 2 eccentric flints (Fig. 10 u, v) and 3 flint flakes (Fig. 10 w; one not located); 6 eccentric obsidians (Fig. 25 u–z) and 1 flake-blade fragment (Fig. 25 a'); 1 incised jadeite plaque with definite saw marks along one underside (Fig. 45 w).

CACHE O–13–52 (NM)

Location. No. 13.

Container. Field Catalogue notes presence of sherds (container?).

Contents. 3 flint flakes and 5 eccentric obsidians (not located).

CACHE O–13–53 (NM)

Location. No. 13.

Container. No data.

Contents. 1 "flint chip" (not located); 3 eccentric obsidians (not located).

CACHE O–13–54 (UM, NM)

Location. No. 1.

Container. 2 Orange 2 hemispherical bowls (one shown in Fig. 61 s), apparently set so that one served as a cover, the lower bowl being smeared interiorly with lime paste and containing the cache objects.

Contents. 3 eccentric flints (Fig. 11 a–c) and a possibly related fragment (not illustrated); 5 eccentric obsidians (Fig. 26 a–e) and a flake-blade (not located); 1 jadeite flare (Fig. 44 i), 1 incised jadeite (Fig. 46 w), and 1 polished jadeite pebble (not located), all enclosed in an articulated *Spondylus* shell; 3 pieces of worked *Spondylus* (Fig. 52 b, c; other not located) and valve of a bivalve, *Ostrea* sp.

CACHE O–13–55 (UM, NM)

Location. No. 6.

Containers. 5 small flat-bottomed, straight-sided bowls, typified by that in Figure 62 e (4 NM; 1 UM).

Contents. Empty. No signs of lime paste.

Remarks. No data on whether or not bowls were nested.

CACHE O–13–56 (UM, NM)

Location. No. 15.

Remarks. 4 so-called choppers (Fig. 1 c, g–i) were evidently found close together. These were presumably cached in spite of their wholly utilitarian nature.

STRUCTURE O–7

CACHE DATING. Lack of inscriptions and diagnostic sherds does not allow any estimate of date.

The structure is known to have been probably used in very late (post-abandonment?) times, but this has no bearing on primary construction (Satterthwaite, 1954, pp. 28–40); in this regard the reader is referred to Cremation, under Burials, General Comment, p.132. Its cache or caches did however provide a remarkable obsidian (see Fig. 26 g). Only one other of these is known from the site (Fig. 36 d) and is probably from an O–13 cache. The cross-dating value of this situation is considered tenuous (see Chronological Value of Caches, under General Comment, p.106. As Satterthwaite has indicated (*ibid.*, p. 33), the positions of the cache items suggest at least two disturbed caches. These have been treated as "Cache O–7–1" for the sake of tabular convenience.

DESCRIPTION OF CACHE

CACHE O–7–1 (UM, NM)
Location.   In debris of northerly step (Positions 2 and 3, Satterthwaite, *ibid.*).
Remarks.   Presence of caches known from 3 eccentric obsidians in one position (Fig. 26 f, g; other not located) and a fourth (not located) from nearby. No evidence of containers.

STRUCTURE O–16

CACHE DATING.   The column altar and thus the cache are probably contemporaries of this temple building. It was not vaulted and therefore could be early in the local sequence. 9.10.0.0.0 is a "guess-date" for the introduction of the vault here (see Appendix).

DESCRIPTION OF CACHE

CACHE O–16–1 (UM)
Location.   Below axial column altar in single temple room near rear wall.
Container.   Orange 2 hemispherical bowl and sub-hemispherical lid (Fig. 61 h).
Contents.   2 eccentric flints (Fig. 12 q, r); 2 eccentric obsidians and 1 obsidian flake (Fig. 26 h–j); 1 incised jadeite (Fig. 46 z) and 2 slightly worked pieces (Fig. 50 o, p); perforated section of carnivore mandible, a pendant (Fig. 55 k); bones of a small bird.
Remarks.   The obsidians evidently were placed in the bowl first, then jadeites, followed by the eccentric flints. The bird seems to have been the uppermost offering, but, with decay, its bones became intermixed with all other contents. See Cache K–5–8.

STRUCTURE J–1

CACHE DATING.   This basal platform , at the base of the Acropolis, is associated with a line of eight stelae (Stelae 1 through 8); one altar (Altar 1) sits on the plaza below J–1. All stelae were investigated but only two (Stelae 6 and 8) were found to have caches associated with their bases. Cists with definite masonry outlines occurred below all eight stelae; they clearly had no bearing on caches. The two stela caches are dated by the associated monuments, as is the cache of Altar 1. They are presumed to have been dedicatory offerings.

DESCRIPTION OF CACHES

CACHE J–1–1 (UM)
Location.   Beneath Altar 1 (9.13.0.0.0) in front of Structure J–1.
Container.   Orange 2 hemispherical bowl and sub-hemispherical lid (Fig. 61 d). Lime paste.
Contents.   1 eccentric flint (Fig. 12 s), 1 very small piece of worked flint, and 2 flint flakes; small fragmentary celt or gouge (Fig. 44 b); 1 loaf-shaped piece of jadeite (Fig. 45 e') and 6 slightly worked pieces of jadeite (Fig. 50 n); 2 small pieces of crystalline hematite and a hematite disc (Fig. 43 l); 2 shell figurines and 2 other cut but otherwise unworked *Spondylus*

pieces; 1 fossil gastropod; 2 fragments of an unidentifiable fresh water clam; 5 bird bones; 2 animal phalanges; 1 grooved stingray spine (Fig. 55 f), 2 split and sharpened stingray spine fragments (one shown in Fig. 55 c), and remains of at least 3 unworked stingray spines.

CACHE J–1–2 (UM, NM)

Location. In cist of (fallen) Stela 6 (9.12.15.0.0).

Container. Orange 2 hemispherical bowl and sub-hemispherical lid (Fig. 61 f).

Contents. 7 eccentric flints (Fig. 13 a–g); 14 crude eccentric obsidians and 1 flake (Fig. 26 k–y).

CACHE J–1–3 (UM)

Location. Before base of Stela 8 (9.14.15.0.0 [?]; 9.14.10.0.0 ± 2 katuns, Proskouriakoff style date).

Remarks. A cylindrical portable altar was found placed against the center of the front face of the stela base at the bottom of its cist. Situation described and altar illustrated by Satterthwaite (1936, p. 13, Pl. V, C). A comparable offering occurred in Cache J–3–2.

STRUCTURE J–3

DESCRIPTION OF CACHES

CACHE J–3–1 (UM,NM)

Location. Contents, if truly from a cache, were badly disturbed. They were found scattered on the basal platform in front of the main stairway, except one specimen which was found in stairway debris at about the level of the fourth terrace.

Container. No evidence, but one is unlikely in view of the offering's size.

Objects. Whole specimens and fragments amount to at least 9 large, bifacially chipped flint blades (Figs. 19 l–o; 20).

Remarks. The belief that these blades constitute a cache is contrary to a previous reference (see Satterthwaite, 1936, p. 13). Their superficial location may have been the result of uprooting and slumping from a summit position, as indicated by one specimen at the fourth terrace level. Nothing strictly comparable was found elsewhere, which suggests a single cache source before collapse.

CACHE J–3–2 (UM)

Remarks. A spiked incensario with a ring base and a perforated, knobbed cover (Fig. 60 e) was found just in front of the front edge of the base of Stela 9 (9.15.5.0.0) and protected by the rock support of the stela. The empty vessel was accompanied by a small drum-shaped stone (portable altar). Description and illustration of the situation and objects have been given by Satterthwaite (1936, p. 14; see also Strömsvik, 1942, pp. 85–86). See Cache J–1–3.

CACHE J–3–3 (NM)

Remarks. A slightly conoidal portable altar was found in the center of Stela 11 cist (9.15.0.0.0) near probable front wall, .50 m. below basal platform level (Satterthwaite, 1936, p. 13). See Caches J–3–2 and J–1–3 for similar offerings of portable altars.

STRUCTURE J–6

CACHE DATING. The location of 4 caches (J–6–2 through J–6–5) provides no certain clue as to dating. However, they probably do not postdate 9.17.15.0.0, the date of Structure J–6–1st. One of these caches (J–6–5) yielded sherds of Dark-on-light Orange cylinder jars, a ceramic type quite certainly Late

Classic and late rather than early (see Butler, 1935, p. 8; Cresson, n. d.). Very likely all 4 caches were contemporaneous (see Cache Locations, Structure R —11). Cache J—6—1 is considered to belong to 9.17. 15.0.0 or earlier.

DESCRIPTION OF CACHES

CACHE J—6—1 (UM and camp fire)

Location. Below floor under Throne 1 (9.17.15.0.0). "Presumably it was cached in connection with the erection of the throne, but it may appertain to the earlier Structure J—6—2 nd or "Old Room 1" (Satterthwaite, 1935, p. 43).

Container. Unslipped jar, constricted neck, recurved body, and a flat disc cover which had broken and fallen inside (Fig. 62 s).

Contents. 1 or 2 "flint chips;" 2 "odd-shaped concretions;" 2 small red shells (*Spondylus* ?), one of them perforated and similar to those in Burial 5 (see Fig. 54) and a piece of a thin, pink shell; "small lump of a white chalky substance, coal black on one surface;" 4 stingray spine fragments. All specimens destroyed by camp fire.

CACHE J—6—2 (NM)

Location. 1 m. northeast and .50 m. northwest of northeasterly corner of stairway, under floor, and on pure rock fill of Court 1. With Caches J—6—3 through J—6—5.

Container. Fragmentary unslipped jar (as in Fig. 62 r). Not located.

Contents. 13 eccentric flints (Fig. 13 h—t).

CACHE J—6—3 (NM)

Location. See Cache J—6—2.

Container. Unslipped small jar (as in Fig. 62 r) covered by a much larger Dark-on-light Orange flat-bottomed bowl with flaring sides (NM, not located).

Contents. 4 eccentric flints (Fig. 14 a—d).

CACHE J—6—4 (UM)

Location. See Cache J—6—2.

Container. Small jar, thin walled, unslipped, orange paste (Fig. 62 r).

Contents. 3 eccentric flints (Fig. 14 e—g).

CACHE J—6—5 (UM)

Location. See Cache J—6—2.

Container. Sherds yield 2 incomplete Dark-on-light Orange cylinder jars (as in Fig. 60 h). Whether contents were in one or were distributed is not clear.

Contents. 3 whole and 1 fragmentary eccentric flints (Fig. 14 j—m); 2 eccentric obsidians (Fig. 27 a, b) and 3 flake-blades (Fig. 27 c, d; other not shown); 1 fragment of a beveled-edge pyrite disc (Fig. 43 h).

STRUCTURE J—29

CACHE DATING. This temple structure consists of four recognizeable building phases, labeled —D, the earliest, through —A (Satterthwaite, 1936 a, Pl. 5). Two caches were encountered. Cache J—29—1 appeared below the base of a column altar set in a ventilated niche at the ear of the room. The second cache, J—29—2, was found below but slightly protruding above a floor known as Floor 3.

This second cache, was patently intrusive, a hole having penetrated not only Floor 3 (which connects with Phase D), but Floor 2 b (which connects with Phase B), and Floor 2 a (which originally must have turned-up to construction of either Phase B or Phase A). The excavated hole for the cache was found plugged with concrete and plaster; its surface was flush with the surface of Floor 2 a, indicating that the cache was intruded during the use of Floor 2 a and not later. No sign of a turn-up was found for this floor and thus it might have conceivably related to Phase A rather than the earlier Phase B.

The altar cache, J—29—1, is securely tied to the niche and therefore to the sill in front of the niche and presumably to Floor 3 rather than any floor following it. It seems most probable, then, that Cache J—29—1 was dedicated at the time of building Structure J—29—D, which had Floor 3 as its room surface. Its dedicatory character is indicated by its placement below the altar and by the altar's axial position. Cache J—29—2, however, was made intrusively after the building cf J—29—B *or* after the building of J—29—A, near the right end of the room, about midway between the front and rear limits. The intrusion of many such caches would have produced the situation encountered at Str. O—13, that is, many non-axial caches at scattered sub-floor positions.

Structure J—29—A has been supposed (see Appendix) to mark the first attempt, known to have been successful, to utilize the corbelled roof at Piedras Negras. On the basis of comparisons with Structures K—5—1st—B and O—12, J—29—A has been "guess-dated" at 9.10.0.0.0. Thus Cache J—29—2 can belong in time no earlier than the date of J—29—B's construction; but it might also have been made at any time during the occupation of J—29—A. Field records suggest that the first conclusion is the more probable. The dating of phases other than —A is possible only on the basis of estimated building intervals, counting from the "guess-date" for —A. There is no reason to believe that any great amount of time was involved in the whole sequence (Satterthwaite, verbal communication); for one, only minor superpositioning occurred, a situation quite unlike that seen in such structures as K—5 and C—13. Perhaps one, perhaps two or three katuns at most, would have sufficed for the four phases. Cresson's J—29 ceramic analysis (Cresson n. d.) illustrates the presence, in every phase, of sherds attributable to Late Classic (Tepeu) times; Phase D contained one sherd of Polychrome B, a type intermediate in the Acropolis series, the bottom stratum of which contains Tepeu elements.

DESCRIPTION OF CACHES

CACHE J—29—1 (NM)

Location. Below column altar in niche of rear of room, Structure J—29—D.

Container. Orange 2 hemispherical bowl and sub-hemispherical lid (Fig. 61 n).

Contents. 2 eccentric flints (Fig. 14 h, i); 23 crude eccentric obsidians (Fig. 27 e—a^1); 2 fragmentary jadeite celts (Fig. 43 s, t) and 2 unworked bits of jadeite (Fig. 50 x); small piece of crystalline stone (not located); perforated and incised shell disc (not located; described under Miscellaneous Ornaments, p. 58) and six pieces of unworked shell (not located); large lump of "iron conglomerate" (not located; omitted from text); 1 grooved stingray spine (as in Fig. 55 f); bones of two birds, one relatively large, the other small (not located); 2 very small teeth, "probably fish" (not located); 7 snail shells, "possibly intrusive" (not located). In fill immediately beneath cache bowl was a univalve, *Pomacea ghiesbreghti.* Contents of bowl were found jumbled at bottom with no evidence of precedence in deposition.

CACHE J—29—2 (NM)

Remarks. An intrusive cache comprising a unique, large, lidded orange-slipped, fluted bowl with a painted black rim (interior and exterior) and a band of 15 conventionalized glyphs in black (Fig. 60 a). Vessel contained no traces of imperishable offerings. Traces of lime paste however appeared throughout the lower half of the interior. Bowl found under floor of room, near northeast end (as to phase of placement, see under Cache Dating, above).

STRUCTURE K—5

CACHE DATING. The architectural sequence of this temple, outlined by Satterthwaite (1939; 1940), disclosed a valuable sequence of caches. The "guess-dates" of the structures involved in this complex have been determined, for the most part, by estimating the length of an average building interval (see Appendix). Only one structure, K—5—1st—B, can be unquestionably tied to the Long Count. The results given in the Appendix are listed here in the form of a correlation of stratified structures, their dates (in my revision of Satterthwaite's scheme), and votive offerings. For reasons given under its description, Cache K—5—7 cannot be listed.

PERIODS AND PHASES	DATES	CACHES
K—5—1st—A (latest)	9.14.5.0.0 ??	No Caches Found
K—5—1st—B	9.12.5.0.0	K—5—3, K—5—5
K—5—1st—C	9.10.0.0.0 ??	K—5—1
K—5—2nd	9.8.0.0.0 ??	K—5—4, K—5—6
K—5—3rd	9.6.0.0.0 ??	K—5—2, K—5—8
K—5—4th (earliest known)	9.4.0.0.0 ??	Not Excavated

CACHE LOCATIONS. All caches were probably placed directly below column altars with the exceptions of Cache K—5—5, which was associated with Stela 39. These locations reasonably preclude intrusive deposition; hence, all the K—5 caches are considered to have been dedicatory. Stela 38 was thoroughly investigated but failed to yield a cache.

DESCRIPTION OF CACHES

CACHE K—5—1 (UM)
Location. Str. K—5—1st—C, probably below column altar in niche of building platform (Satterthwaite, 1939, p. 12, Fig. A). See Cache K—5—7.
Container. Orange 2 hemispherical bowl and sub-hemispherical lid (Fig. 61 j).
Contents. 7 eccentric flints (Fig. 15 a—g); 11 eccentric obsidians (Fig. 28 a—k), 1 obsidian flake-blade, and a flake (Fig. 28 l, m).

CACHE K—5—2 (UM,NM)
Location. Str. K—5—3rd, under column altar in center of room (Satterthwaite, 1939, Fig. C).
Container. Orange 2 hemispherical bowl and sub-hemispherical lid (Fig. 61 e). Lime paste.
Contents. 3 eccentric flints (Fig. 15 h—j) and 3 flint flakes (Fig. 15 k); 3 eccentric obsidians (Fig. 28 n; 2 in NM not located) and 9 "obsidian fragments" (NM, not located); fragmentary celt (Fig. 43 r); 1 incised jadeite (Fig. 46 p) and 4 slightly worked pieces of jadeite (Fig. 50 w); 2 bits of calcite; 1 shaped and incised piece of shell (Fig. 51, a) and 4 unidentifiable shell fragments, probably of land snails; 1 carved bone replica of a stingray spine (Fig. 55 e).

CACHE K—5—3 (camp fire)
Location. Str. K—5—1st—B, under floor of rear niche of room, and presumably beneath previously removed column altar (Satterthwaite, 1940, Fig. E).
Container. Field Catalogue notes presence of sherds (container?).
Contents. Eccentric flints; eccentric obsidians; shell.

CACHE K—5—4 (camp fire)
Location. Str. K—5—2nd, under column altar of final (building?) platform (Satterthwaite, 1939, Fig. B).
Container. Field Catalogue notes presence of sherds (container?).
Contents. 5 eccentric flints; 6 eccentric obsidians; 8 "jadeites;" 3 "pieces of bone."

CACHE K—5—5 (UM)
Location. Str. K—5—1st—B, presumably at base of fallen Stela 39 (9.12.5.0.0).
Container. Orange 2 hemispherical bowl and sub-hemispherical lid (Fig. 61 b).
Contents. 3 eccentric flints (Fig. 15 l—n); 3 eccentric obsidians (Fig. 28 o—q); 4 incised pieces of shell (Fig. 51 k—n), and 6 land snail shells (*Euglandina decussata* and *Choanopoma radiosum*).

Remarks.   Cache referred to by Kidder (1947, p. 27); his mention of "stela 29" is a misprint.

CACHE K—5—6 (NM)

Location.   Str. K—5—2nd, beneath column altar on pyramid top at head of stairway (Satterthwaite, 1939, Fig. B).

Container.   Orange 2 hemispherical bowl and sub-hemispherical lid (Fig. 61 a). Lime paste.

Contents.   3 eccentric flints (Fig. 16 a—c); 6 eccentric obsidians (Fig. 28 r—w); 6 incised pieces of jadeite (Fig. 45 a—g) and 1 fragmentary jadeite celt (Fig. 44 e).

CACHE K—5—7 (UM) —a doubtful cache

Location.   From in front of the supposed Lintel 7 position and in general location of Cache K—5—1 and K—5—3. There is a possibility that the objects found are remains of one or both of these structurally separated caches. The banded obsidian is identical to that in Cache K—5—1.

Container.   A single Orange 2 hemispherical bowl rim sherd might pertain to Cache K—5—1 or K—5—3.

Contents.   1 crude eccentric flint (not located); 1 eccentric obsidian and 2 flakes (Fig. 29 a—c).

CACHE K—5—8 (UM)

Location.   Str. K—5—3rd, beneath column altar in front of stairway leading to building platform (Satterthwaite, 1939, Fig. C). Extraction and opening of cache bowl shown by Satterthwaite (*ibid.*, Pl. II).

Container.   Orange 2 hemispherical bowl and sub-hemispherical lid (Fig. 61 c). Lime paste.

Contents.   4 eccentric flints (Fig. 15 o—r); 3 eccentric obsidians (Fig. 29 d, e, g) and 1 fragmentary obsidian flake-blade (Fig. 29 f); 4 incised pieces of jadeite (Fig. 46, l—o); 2 incised cut shell pieces (Fig. 51 b, c); 13 whole and 4 fragmentary bone replicas of stingray spines (typified in Fig. 55 d) and 15 whole and fragmentary true stingray spines, one of which is grooved along one side (as in Fig. 55 f); bones of a small unidentified bird; and a handful of small bits of jadeite, none of them shaped.

Remarks.   In filling the bowl with the objects, the incised jades and eccentric obsidians were placed first, followed by the eccentric flints and carved pieces of shell. The spines and bird bones were concentrated on one side of the container and evidently were placed last. See Cache O—16—1 for similar sequence of object placement, p. 89.

TERMINAL OFFERING

Before leaving the K—5 caches, a curious deposit should be mentioned. On the surface of Structure K—5—2nd, scattered in a small area around the column altar on the pyramid-stage were the sherds of two large, incomplete, open-base, vertical-flange censers (one shown in Proskouriakoff, 1946, no. 5). The question arises as to whether these remains represent a dedicatory cache in connection with the following Structure K—5—1st—C, or whether they indicate a terminal offering made to Structure K—5—2nd. They have not been considered dedicatory because large portions are missing in spite of careful clearing. Shortly before the burial of K—5—2nd, its priests may have sacrificed and destroyed two elaborate censers. For certain of the censer fragments to have been lost, some brief time must have elapsed between the sacrifice and the structure's abandonment to K—5—1st—C. This offering is interpreted as having been made in relation to K—5—2nd, not the succeeding structure. Thus it is not a cache (see Introduction to this chapter) but rather an example of ceremonial object-sacrifice at the moment of a structure's abandonment; suggestions of a "ritual of renewal" are strong.

This find illustrates a seemingly rare custom in the lowlands, or, perhaps better, a custom rarely detected there. Analogous cases are known from the highlands, particularly at Kaminaljuyu (see distributional study of caches, pp. 113—114). They surely complicate cache identification but perhaps yield worthwhile distinctions in this aspect of Maya ceremonialism.

It is suggested that the term "terminal offering" be applied to such deposits. The terminal offering constitutes a third type of intentional deposit, the others being caches and burials (see Introduction of this chapter, pp. 78–79.

STRUCTURE R–3

CACHE DATING.   Excavation disclosed a fourfold building sequence. Two caches were encountered: Cache R–3–1, deposited at the time of R–3–2nd's construction, and an earlier one, Cache R–3–2, lying below and associated with the deepest portion of the fill of R–3–4th.

Satterthwaite's scheme for dating the various buildings involved in the R–3 sequence seems consistent with the pottery found in the earliest strata (see Appendix). The building sequence in terms of estimated intervals of constructional activity may be summarized as follows:

PERIODS	DATES	CACHES
R–3–1st (latest)	9.6.0.0.0 (?)	No Caches Found
R–3–2nd	9.4.0.0.0 ??	R–3–1
R–3–3rd	9.2.0.0.0 ??	No Caches Found
R–3–4th (earliest)	9.0.0.0.0 ??	R–3–2

DESCRIPTION OF CACHES

CACHE R–3–1 (UM)

Location.   In fill under floor of Structure R–3–2nd, .60 m. below a point .50 m. forward of remnant of rear building wall, slightly southeast of front-rear axis.

Container.   Orange 2 flat-bottomed, flaring-sided bowl (Fig. 62 d).

Contents.   Empty. But among sherds of bowl were found small pieces of copal (see Perishable Materials, p. 74).   The container itself had been smoke-blackened. It seems clear that this was a dedicatory offering of burning copal.

CACHE R–3–2 (UM, NM)

Location.   In a slight bedrock depression, purposely excavated, below fill of Structure R–3–4th.

Container.   A pair of large, dark, mottled-ware tripod vessels with slightly incurving sides and softly convex bases. All feet had been removed prior to caching and were absent. One vessel (NM) was inverted over the other (UM, Fig. 60 b).

Contents.   Skeletal remains of an infant (described under Burials, Lot 16). Among bones were a tiny bit of polished jadeite (not located) and two pieces of unworked jadeite (Fig. 50 h; other lost in transit).

Remarks.   This deposit is one of those that, from one point of view, might be classified as a possible sacrificial burial and, from another, belongs in the category of dedicatory caches. The Introduction to this Part 3 treats at length this problem of borderline classification.

STRUCTURE R–4

CACHE DATING.   Masonry building (if any) was probably non-vaulted and, thus the cache might have been placed prior to 9.10.0.0.0, a "guess-date" for the introduction of the vault (see Appendix).

DESCRIPTION OF CACHE

    CACHE R–4–1 (camp fire)

      Location.   "Rear of structure."

      Container.   Field Catalogue notes presence of sherds (container?).

      Contents.   Eccentric flints; eccentric obsidians. Quantities unknown.

STRUCTURE R–5

CACHE DATING.   The floor under which this cache was found is in a vaulted structure but the cache itself might conceivably pertain to an earlier non-vaulted structure.

DESCRIPTION OF CACHE

    CACHE R–5–1 (UM)

      Location.   Buried immediately under floor behind northeast doorway.

      Contents.   In this location, fragment of a large, painted stucco, human head were found (Satterthwaite, 1933 a, Pl. I).

      Remarks.   This presumed offering recalls a similar one at Palenque (see Angel Fernandez, 1943). See also isolated eccentric obsidian in Fig. 34 x, which suggests presence of a more typical cache in this structure.

STRUCTURE R–9

CACHE DATING.   One of the three caches (Cache R–9–1) found in this complex structure probably was made after 9.8.15.0.0 (Satterthwaite, 1944, p. 16). All three however were axially placed in relation to a mound that ultimately featured a non-vaulted building; the vault evidently had its first successful use at the site at a "guess-dated" 9.10.0.0.0 (see Appendix). Therefore, Cache R–9–1, while it appears to fall later that 9.8.15.0.0, would have to be placed prior to 9.10.0.0.0. The other two caches can only be said to predate 9.10.0.0.0—always on the basis of the involved assumptions. Table 4 illustrates these probabilities.

DESCRIPTION OF CACHES

    CACHE R–9–1 (UM)

      Location.   Under column altar No. 1 on court, Position 19 (Satterthwaite, *ibid.*, p. 18, Fig. 9). Axial.

      Container.   An inverted Orange 2 grooved-edged, sub-hemispherical lid, interiorly coated with lime paste (Fig. 61 u). However, examination of other sherds from the immediate area indicates a second such lid, again with traces of lime paste. Perhaps the two lids were employed as separate containers or oddly combined lip-to-lip.

      Contents.   14 eccentric flints (Fig. 17), 3 flint flakes; 3 whole and 1 fragmentary eccentric obsidians (Fig. 29 h–k); 1 small celt-shaped jadeite (Fig. 45 d') and 8 slightly worked pieces of jadeite (Fig. 50 r); 2 fragments of a fresh water bivalve; and, directly underneath container, 2 *Pomacea ghiesbreghti* shells. See Fig. 30 u, for an eccentric obsidian found in R–9 surface debris.

    CACHE R–9–2 (NM)

      Location.   In plaza floor behind column altar No. 1; on front-rear axis in front of lowest terrace step very close to Cache R–9–1 (Satterthwaite, 1944, pp. 16, 18, Fig. 9).

      Container.   Fragmentary Orange 2 hemispherical bowl and sub-hemispherical lid (as in Fig. 61).

      Contents.   7 eccentric flints (Fig. 16 d–j); 8 eccentric obsidians (not located, see Fig. 29 l–s);

4 incised jadeites (Fig. 45 h–k) and 5 worked jadeites, one of which has faint incisions (Fig. 50 v; 3 not located); both valves of a *Spondylus* and 2 cut *Spondylus* hinge fragments. No indication that jadeites were contained in the *Spondylus*.

CACHE R–9–3 (NM)

Location. Under column altar No. 3 on pyramid in front of lowest step of building platform (Satterthwaite, 1944, pp. 11, 18, Fig. 9).

Container. No container noted. Objects rested on a stone slab 40 cm. below column altar. Satterthwaite (*ibid.*) points out that it "seems unlikely, but possible, that a cache bowl had been present, broke, and most of the contents worked down out of sight between the rocks of the fill."

Contents. 3 eccentric obsidians (not located), one a centipede (as in Fig. 29 n), while the others were discs (as in Fig. 22 j). As noted, majority of original contents probably lost in the fill.

STRUCTURE R–11

CACHE DATING. The southerly playing field of this ball-court structure produced 5 caches (R–1 through R–11–5). These deposits included pottery reputed to be characteristic of the earlier portion of the site's Classic occupation (Butler, 1935; Satterthwaite, 1944 a, pp. 21–22). Cresson (n. d.) emphasizes Polychromes D and E (involved in these caches) as quantitatively minor but significant components of the lower three strata of the Acropolis. These strata are, however, probably not Early Classic in spite of containing, among others, forms typical of that period. For one, a Type Y mold-made figurine head (as in Butler, *op. cit.*, Pl. XIII, 28, 29; see also Satterthwaite, 1954, p. 71) was found embedded in the basal clay of the deepest Acropolis stratum; another appeared in the lowest fill of Structure K–5–3rd which additionally yielded sherds of at least Tepeu 1 types (see Appendix). Moreover, the Copador affiliation of the two Polychrome E bowls in Cache R–11–3, noted by Butler (*ibid.*, p. 7), again indicates Late Classic attribution as viewed from Copan itself (Longyear, 1952, p. 60 ff). As regards Caches R–11–6 and R–11–7, no estimates of date are possible beyond simply "Classic Period."

CACHE LOCATIONS. Although the playing field caches have been judged to be Late Classic, it would be well to consider the nature of these caches. Four are grouped quite close together but the fifth, Cache R–11–5 (Position 5 in Fig. 10 of Satterthwaite, 1944 a), was 5 or 6 m. distant. Any one or all of these caches could be dedicatory or non-dedicatory, and, if the latter, could have been intruded jointly or successively. There is no evidence to settle this point. Ceramically, certain of these caches appear to be Late Classic. In view of the location of all, we assume them all to be roughly contemporary and Late Classic. This concentration of caches is much like that encountered in the court of Structure J–6 (see Caches J–6–2 through J–6–5 , p. 91).

DESCRIPTION OF CACHES

CACHE R–11–1 (UM, NM)

Location. Sub-floor, southwest end of playing field (Satterthwaite, 1944 a, Fig. 10, position 1).

Container. Orange 2 hemispherical bowl (Fig. 61 m) and sub-hemispherical lid. The bowl retains clear textile imprints, as if it had been extensively wrapped prior to placement.

Contents. 4 eccentric obsidians (Fig. 30 a, b; 2 others not located).

CACHE R–11–2 (NM)

Location. See Cache R –11–1 (Satterthwaite, 1944 a, Fig. 10, position 2).

Container. One Polychrome D bowl inverted as a cover over a Polychrome C bowl.

Contents. None found.

CACHE R–11–3 (UM)

Location. See Cache R –11–1 (Satterthwaite, 1944 a, Fig. 10, position 3).

Container.   Two Polychrome E bowls (Fig. 60 c, d), probably lip-to-lip although exact relationship could not be determined because of their condition.

Contents.   Among the sherds were 1 obsidian flake-blade fragment, 1 sectional fragment of an obsidian core, and 1 obsidian flake (Fig. 30 c–e).

CACHE R–11–4 (NM)

Location.   See Cache R–11–1 (Satterthwaite, 1944 a, Fig. 10, position 4).

Container.   Two Orange 2 hemispherical bowls, one probably inverted over the other (as in Cache O–13–54, Fig. 61 s).

Contents.   None found.

CACHE R–11–5(NM)

Location.   See Cache R–11–1 (Satterthwaite, 1944 a, Fig. 10, position 5).

Container.   ''Orange-colored bowl.''

Contents.   None found.

CACHE R–11–6 (UM, NM)

Location.   Structure R–11–a, near northwest corner of summit (Satterthwaite, 1944 a, position 9). Evidently remains of a disturbed cache.

Container.   No data.

Contents.   Chunk of obsidian, abraded (Fig. 30 f); 2 univalves, *Pomacea ghiestbreghti*, one of them with 2 drill holes (Fig. 52 q); and possibly a curious pottery object (not described in text; see Butler, 1935, Pl. XIV, 4).

CACHE R–11–7 (UM)

Location.   Structure R–11–2, base of apron marker (''Stela 45''). Probably remains of a disturbed cache.

Container.   No data.

Contents.   3 eccentric flints (Fig. 18 a–c).

STRUCTURE R–16

CACHE DATING.   Temple structure non-vaulted and thus probably earlier than 9.10.0.0.0, a ''guess-date'' for the introduction of the vault (see Appendix).

DESCRIPTION OF CACHE

CACHE R–16–1 (NM)

Location.   Probably from beneath small stone column altar on temple floor.

Container.   Field Catalogue lists sherds for this locality; container probable.

Contents.   4 eccentric flints (Fig. 16 k–o); 3 eccentric obsidians (Fig. 30 g–i).

GENERAL COMMENT AND COMPARISON OF CACHE DATA

QUANTITY AND PROVENIENCE

Although we have not specifically done so, we might assume caches for such structures as J–11, O–15, U–3, J–4, and E–1 on the basis of isolated eccentrics found in their debris (see Figs. 18 d, g, h; 32 i; 33 g). Other single eccentric objects illustrated here may belong to caches already described or they may be remnants of undetected caches from these same structures.

A total of 94 caches was found; a few are doubtful and a regrettably large number are known only from Field Catalogue entries. Over half the offerings came from temple Structure O–13. Caches were discovered in various other investigated temples, for example, Structures K–5, R–3, R–9, J–3, and

J—29. Only one cache, J—6—1, was found during the course of actual palace excavation but whether or not it was placed at the time of the construction of the palace is a problem. A group of caches (J—6—2 through J—6—5) occurred in Court 1, an area between two of the Acropolis palaces. Structure O—13, particularly below the rear room, offers a remarkable example of concentrations of offerings. A third concentration appears in the playing field of Structure R—11. Votive offerings were encountered in platform structures O—7 and O—16.

Stela caches are evidently not the rule at Piedras Negras. In Morley's classification, there were 46 stelae at Piedras Negras and 5 table altars. Most of the stelae were fallen on discovery. Only about a third of these monuments were excavated (Satterthwaite, verbal information). Systematic investigation of stelae was made only in the West Group; there, only Altar 2 was not checked. Of the West Group stelae, 13 in all, only 4 (Stela 6, 8, 9 and 11) were associated with caches (J—1—2, J—1—3, J—3—2, and J—3—3 respectively). Stela 39 was also associated with a cache (K—5—5) but the nearby Stela 38 definitely lacked one. West Group Altar 1 produced a cache (J—1—1). In the East Group, plain table Altar 5 had a cache (O—13—1); another (O—13—56) may have belonged with Stela 18. But caches for Stelae 12 and 15 should have appeared if present; the same is true for Stela 24 in the South Group.

One offering (Cache R—11—7) appears to have been with a ball-court apron marker.

Column altars, a ritualistic accessory common in Piedras Negras temples, lacking to the east, but appearing at Bonampak to the south, were frequently found with cache deposits beneath them. Structures O—16, J—29, K—5, R—9, and R—16 had such offerings. Nevertheless, the fact that two of the R—9 column altars (Nos. 2 and 4; see Satterthwaite, 1944) lacked caches indicates that these small altars did not always have offerings below their bases.

While caches occurred beneath table altars and column altars, none of those found with stelae can be said to be truly "sub-stela." Stromsvik (1942, p. 67), for instance, writes: "The placing of ceremonial offerings under the bases of stelae was a common practice among the Old Empire [i. e. Classic Period] Maya. The objects were usually deposited in the earth at the bottom of the hole destined to receive the stela's butt." The Piedras Negras Stela caches, however, were frequently, if not always, just in front of the butt.

CACHE SEQUENCE (TABLE 4)

Any scheme of Piedras Negras cache chronology and sequence is bound to be largely tentative. Table 4 is just such a scheme and is based on data given in the Introduction to this report, the introduction to this part of the report, and the Appendix.

While architectural investigations produced many excellent signs of sequence and relationship to dated monuments, the layout of the site rarely allows extensive structural correlations. Then again we lack a comprehensive study of the Piedras Negras pottery that might yield broad intra-site relationships. With little other choice, we have been forced to apply absolute dates, some sound, others shaky, to a good proportion of the offerings. This has resulted in the overall sequence seen in Table 4.

There are a number of sure points in this scheme. There is little doubt that Cache R—3—2, followed by Cache R—3—1, is the earliest of those discovered, and that the caches of Structure O—13—1st—A are among, if not actually, the latest. The well stratified K—5 caches, as previously mentioned, date at and prior to 9.12.5.0.0 (Stela 39). The earliest of this series of caches probably are no older than 9.6.0.0.0, a date chosen for a number of reasons as best marking the local changeover (ceramic) from Early to Late Classic (see Appendix, Structure K—5). Caches found in various non-vaulted buildings presumably predate the appearance of the corbel vault at the site; this sets them before a reasonable "guess-date" of 9.10.0.0.0 (see Appendix). The majority of caches seem to belong unquestionably to lowland Late Classic times. Only Caches R—3—1 and R—3—2, both seemingly atypical, can be confidently placed in what has been judged to be the Early Classic Period. Caches K—5—2 and K—5—8 may be considered transitional in period.

Table 4–SEQUENCE OF CACHES

ASSOCIATED INSCRIPTIONS	ARCHITECTURAL GUESS-DATES	CACHES (except for O–7–1, J–3–1, R–5–1, R–21–6,–7)				
	10.0.0.0.0 ??					
		O–13–20,–21				
9.17.15.0.0						
9.15.5.0.0	9.15.0.0.0 ??	O–13–4 to –9,–14–15 –54,–55		J–3–2 J–3–3		
9.15.0.0.0			Other O–13 Caches	J–1–3	J–6 Caches	?
9.14.15.0.0						R–11–1 to R–11–5
9.13.0.0.0				J–1–1 J–1–2		
9.12.15.0.0						K–5–3,–5
9.12.5.0.0	9.12.0.0.0 ??					?
	9.10.0.0.0 ??	. . . . K–5–1				
		O–16–1 R–4–1 R–16–1 R–9–2,–3			R–9–1	J–29–2
9.8.15.0.0	9.8.0.0.0 ??	? ? ? ?			K–5–4,–6	J–29–1
	9.6.0.0.0 ??	- K–5–2,–8 - - - - - - -				
	9.4.0.0.0.0 ??	R–3–1				
	9.0.0.0.0 ??	R–3–2				

. . . GUESS-DATED VAULT INTRODUCTION

- - - GUESS-DATED EARLY CLASSIC-
LATE CLASSIC DIVISION

POSSIBLE RANGE   PROBLEMATIC RANGE   UNKNOWN RANGE

CONTENTS (TABLE 5)

Table 5 comprises a summary of cache contents. The list is complete, in the arbitrary cache number order.

1. SPECIALIZED CACHE VESSELS. The following material is believed to have been specially made for votive purposes. A thorough study of the Piedras Negras pottery might well change some assignments, but frequencies of certain types in caches and their apparent scarcities beyond caches do provide some basis for distinguishing between votively specialized and unspecialized vessels, whether or not they contain anything imperishable.

One immediately notes (see Table 5) the extent to which the Orange 2 hemispherical bowl and sub-hemispherical lid were used in Piedras Negras cache activity. A decidedly specialized ware, it has been aptly termed "Votive Orange Ware" by Butler (1935, pp. 9—10). Although, for convenience, I have referred to these bowls in cache listings as "hemispherical," this term is actually inexact, as reference to Figure 61 will show. Bases in fact may be flattened or rounded, and the degree of wall curvature is variable. Lids, though, are much the same throughout the collection, differing only in degree of convexity and in the length of the diameter relative to that of the bowl. Paste, slip texture, and color are fairly constant but occasional shifts in color and burnish have led Butler (*ibid.*, p. 10) to distinguish an Orange 2 a; this distinction, while physically meaningful, has not been made here.

The Orange 2 hemispherical bowl with lid was used almost throughout the entire known range of Piedras Negras cache deposition. The earliest estimated date for its use is 9.6.0.0.0 (Caches K—5—2 and K—5—8). It appears securely at 9.12.5.0.0 (Cache K—5—5), 9.12.15.0.0 (Cache J—1—2), and 9.13.0.0.0 (Cache J—1—1); and is believed to have been in frequent use subsequent to 9.12.0.0.0 (see O—13 caches, Table 5). Its form combined with ware seems particularly characteristic of Piedras Negras; it does not occur at Uaxactun (see R. E. Smith, 1955, pp. 95—99). In one instance, lip-to-lip pairing apparently was found (see caption of Fig. 61 s). A probable second case of this interesting trait occurred in Cache R—11—4.

A second Orange 2 type, of considerable frequency, is the flat-based bowl (see Fig. 62 a—f). Walls have either an obvious flare or are flat and obliquely set. The break between base and wall may be either sharp or rounded. Cache R—3—1, judged to be Early Classic and around 9.4.0.0.0, contained a bowl of this general type; the basal angle however is exceptionally sharp (see Fig. 62 d). Flat-based bowls with flaring (e. g., Fig. 62 a) to flat (e. g., Fig. 62 b, c, e, f) walls occurred frequently in Structure O—13 caches, actually far more frequently than is indicated in Table 5; the University Museum collection contains many specifically unassignable fragments of such bowls. There are two good cases of lip-to-lip pairing (Fig. 62 a, c).

The Orange 2 flat-based bowl occurs as a cache vessel elsewhere; it was also used for mortuary purposes. R. E. Smith (*ibid.*, pp. 96—97) has an excellent discussion of them. He notes that they are exclusively Early Classic at Uaxactun; nevertheless the famed polychrome vase, which shows a jaguar holding a pair of tied lip-to-lip bowls of this type, is Tepeu 1 in date (*ibid.*, Fig. 72 b). But these bowls are shown as buff colored on the vase, rather than orange. Unslipped vessels of this form were in use at Uaxactun in Tepeu 2 times (*ibid.*, pp. 98—99). While the two sites jointly share this bowl in early times, it would seem that it persisted longer at Piedras Negras.

A third numerically important cache vessel is the unslipped jar, pear- to barrel-shaped, with an unslipped, specially made, flat to slightly convex, round lid (Fig. 62 h—q). The sample yielded examples only from Structure O—13 caches. A collection of miscellaneous lids (again from Structure O—13) shows a range in diameter of 5.5 to 13.5 cm. Occasionally both jar rims and lid rims were covered with a light, fugitive blue matte paint. This use of blue paint in votive context brings to mind the blue-painted lumps of copal offered in cenote rites at Chichen Itza (Tozzer, 1941, Note 537; ritual uses of blue paint are described by Wauchope, 1948, p. 125). Certain Tzakol 3 Uaxactun vessels are comparable in form but the relationship is quite weak (see R. E. Smith, *ibid.*, p. 97). Other small jars, of different paste and without lids, appeared in J—6 caches (e. g. Fig. 62 r).

Table 5—CONTENT TABULATION OF CACHES

CACHE	CONTAINER	ECC. FLINTS	ECC. OBSIDIANS	JADE	SHELL	OTHER CONTENTS
O—13—1	...	X	X	...	...	....
O—13—2	A	X	?	X	...	Obsidian and bone fragments
O—13—3	P	X	X	X	X	Flake-blade, pyrite
O—13—4	BB	X	X	X	X	....
O—13—5	D	X	X	X	X	....
O—13—6	A	X	X	X	X	Obsidian core and flake, lime paste
O—13—7	A	X	X	X	X	Flake-blade, lime paste
O—13—8	A	X	X	X	X	Stingray spine, bone fragments, lime paste
O—13—9	A	X	X	...	X	Stingray spine, lime paste
O—13—10	A	X	X	X	X	Obsidian flake-blades and flake
O—13—11	A	X	X	...	X	....
O—13—12	BB	...	...	X	X	....
O—13—13	B	...	X	...	X	Limestone disc, altered stingray spine, lime paste
O—13—14	...	...	X	...	X	Pyrite, bone fragments, stingray spines
O—13—15	P	...	X	X	X	Pyrite, coral
O—13—16	?	X	X	X	...	Obsidian core
O—13—17	A	X	X	X	...	Limestone disc
O—13—18	D	X	X	X	...	....
O—13—19	A	X	X	X	...	....
O—13—20	?	X	X	...	...	....
O—13—21	A	...	...	X	...	Bones, fragments of red stone
O—13—22	DD	X	X	X	...	....
O—13—23	?	X	X	...	X	Stingray spines
O—13—24	?	X	X	...	...	....
O—13—25	D	...	X	...	...	....
O—13—26	?	X	X	...	...	Flint flake
O—13—27	C	...	...	X	X	Flint flakes and blade fragment, obsidian flake-blades and flakes, altered stingray spine
O—13—28	D	X	X	...	...	Pottery jar lid
O—13—29	P	...	X	...	...	Flint flakes, bone tube
O—13—30	?	X	X	...	X	Flint flakes, obsidian flake blades, altered stingray spine
O—13—31	?	...	X	X	...	Flint flakes
O—13—32	C	...	X	...	...	Flint flakes
O—13—33	C	...	...	...	...	Pottery "knob"
O—13—34	...	...	...	...	...	Miscellaneous Sculptured Stone 1
O—13—35	C	...	X	X	...	Flint flakes
O—13—36	D	X	X	X	...	Flint flake, obsidian flake-blade
O—13—37	?	X	X	X	...	Flint flakes, obsidian flake-blades and flakes, shark tooth
O—13—38	?	X	X	...	...	Flint flakes
O—13—39	?	...	X	...	...	Flint flakes
O—13—40	?	X	X	...	...	Flint flakes
O—13—41	C	X	X	X	...	Flint flakes
O—13—42	C	X	X	...	...	....
O—13—43	?	X	X	X	X	....
O—13—44	?	X	X	...	...	....
O—13—45	A	X	...	X	...	Bone fragments
O—13—46	C	X	X	...	X	Flint flakes, bone fragments
O—13—47	?	X	X	X	...	Flint flakes, flake-blades
O—13—48	?	X	...	X	...	....
O—13—49	?	X	X	X	...	Flint flakes
O—13—50	?	X	X	X	...	Flake-blades
O—13—51	?	X	X	X	...	Flint flakes, flake-blades
O—13—52	?	...	X	...	...	Flint flakes
O—13—53	?	...	X	...	...	Flint flake
O—13—54	AA	X	X	X	X	Flake-blade, lime paste
O—13—55	BBBB	...	...	...	...	....
O—13—56	...	...	...	...	...	Limestone "choppers"

CACHE	CON-TAIN-ER	ECC. FLINTS	ECC. OB-SIDIANS	JADE	SHELL	OTHER CONTENTS
O—7—1	...	X	X	...	...	....
O—16—1	A	X	X	X	...	Obsidian flake, worked hematite, mica, bone pendant, bird bones
J—1—1	A	X	...	X	X	Worked flint, flint flakes, celt, crystalline hematite, hematite disc, fossil, animal and bird bones, worked and unworked stingray spines
J—1—2	A	X	X	...	...	Obsidian flake
J—1—3	...	...	...	...	...	Portable altar
J—3—1	?	...	...	...	...	Large flint blades
J—3—2	...	...	...	...	...	Incensario, portable altar
J—3—3	...	...	...	...	...	Portable altar
J—6—1	D	...	...	...	X	Flint flakes, concretions, white lump, stingray spines
J—6—2	D	X	...	...	...	....
J—6—3	DD	X	...	...	...	....
J—6—4	D	X	...	...	...	....
J—6—5	DD	X	X	...	...	Flake-blades, pyrite disc
J—29—1	A	X	X	X	X	Crystalline stone, bird and fish bones
J—29—2	D	...	...	...	...	Lime paste
K—5—1	A	X	X	X	X	Obsidian flake and flake-blade
K—5—2	A	X	X	X	X	Flint flakes, celt, bits of calcite, stingray spine replica, lime paste
K—5—3	?	X	X	...	X	....
K—5—4	?	X	X	X	...	Bone fragments
K—5—5	A	X	X	...	X	....
K—5—6	A	X	X	X	...	Lime paste
K—5—7 ?	?	X	X	...	...	Obsidian flakes
K—5—8	A	X	X	X	X	Obsidian flake-blade, real and replica stingray spines, bird bones, lime paste
R—3—1	B	...	...	...	...	Copal
R—3—2	DD	...	...	X	...	Remains of an infant
R—4—1	?	X	X	...	...	....
R—5—1	...	...	...	...	...	Painted stucco head
R—9—1	AA	X	X	X	X	Flint flakes, lime paste
R—9—2	A	X	X	X	X	....
R—9—3	...	...	X	...	...	....
R—11—1	A	...	X	...	...	....
R—11—2	DD	...	...	...	...	....
R—11—3	DD	...	...	...	...	Obsidian flake-blade, flake, and core fragment
R—11—4	AA	...	...	...	...	....
R—11—5	P	...	...	...	...	....
R—11—6	?	...	...	...	X	Obsidian polisher
R—11—7	?	X	...	...	...	....
R—16—1	P	X	X	...	...	....

KEY TO CONTAINERS: A—Orange 2 hemispherical bowl and/or sub-hemispherical lid   B—Orange 2 flat-based bowl   C—unslipped jar with disc lid   D—other (see text)   P—present but no data

2. NON-SPECIALIZED CACHE VESSELS.   A number of the caches contained vessels which are believed to have been re-used for votive purposes. These caches are O—13—25 (Fig. 60 h), O—13—28 (Fig.
60 i), J—3—2 (Fig. 60 e), J—6—3, J—6—5, J—29—2 (Fig. 60 a), R—3—2 (Fig. 60 b), R—11—2, and R—11—3 (Fig. 60 c, d).
Caches containing probably or possibly non-specialized vessels are O—13—18 (Fig. 62 g), O—13—36 (Fig.
62 t), J—6—1 (Fig. 62 s), J—6—3 (small jar covered by non-specialized vessel), and J—6—4 (Fig. 62 r).

Cache R—3—2, the earliest of the series, consisted ceramically of two tripod bowls, set lip-to-lip, and
surely Early Classic; the feet of each one had been removed (Fig. 60 b).   Fine   polychrome vessels occurred in Cache R—11—2 and also in Cache R—11—3 (Fig. 60 c, d); lip-to-lip pairing may have occurred in
both   cases.   Cache J—6—3 involved an unslipped small jar (as in Fig. 62 r) covered by a larger and more
certainly re-used Dark-on-light Orange flat-bottomed bowl with flaring sides.   With the exception of the
Cache R—3—2 vessels, the non-specialized vessels appear stratigraphically and/or ceramically Late Classic.

The handsome lidded container in the intrusive Cache J—29—2 (Fig. 60 a) contained no imperishable
material beyond the strange lime coating noted in the introduction to this chapter (see also below).   The
glyphic border and fluted sides strongly suggest re-use as a cache container.   The lid was perhaps not
specifically made for the vessel but is simply a re-used bowl.   Other non-specialized vessels without no -
ticeable contents were found in Caches J—3—2, R—11—2, and R—11—3.   Contents comprising one or more
typical cache items (eccentrics, jade, etc.) occurred either in or about votively non-specialized vessels in
Caches O—13—25, O—13—28, J—6—3, and J—6—5; similarly, with vessels not certainly non-specialized, in
Caches O—13—18, O—13—36, J—6—2, and J—6—4.   Atypical votive objects accompanied non-specialized
vessels in Caches J—6—1, R—3—2, and R—11—3.   Lime paste was noted only in vessels of this category
in Cache J—29—2.

3. LIME PASTE.   This is a yellowish paste, finger-smoothed (imprints often visible), up to 5 mm.
thick.   An analysis, by Mr. A. Eric Parkinson, disclosed a composition of iron, aluminum, calcium, mag-
nesium, and carbon dioxide; presence of silica doubtful; no tests made for sodium or potassium; no organic matter; material judged to be a paste probably made of an impure dolomitic limestone with iron oxide
added as coloring matter.   Its use was evidently confined to Orange 2 bowls (see Table 5), both hemispherical and flat-based.   The single exception is the fluted bowl from Cache J—29—2 (Fig. 60 a); the presence
of paste suggests that the bowl did contain objects but of a perishable nature.   Usually the paste is confined to the lower half of the container but in one instance (in Cache O—13—7, Fig. 61 p) the entire interior
was smeared.   Details are given in the figure captions of Fig. 61.   It is evident that this trait, whatever
its purpose may have been, occurred in both dedicatory and intrusive caches.   Its use seems to have had
no relation to the presence or absence of imperishable cache items.   Oddly enough, an inverted Orange 2
sub-hemispherical lid (Fig. 61 u), used to hold offerings in Cache R—9—1, was extensively coated.   This
puzzling trait, smearing the interior of the cache container with a paste of lime, occurs early, certainly as
early as Caches K—5—2 and K—5—8.   The range (see Tables 4 and 5) is from 9.6.0.0.0 to probably the latest Structure O—13 cache deposits.   Had this feature occurred elsewhere it is surely distinctive enough to
warrant reporting.   I have been unable to find any mention of it.

4. OBJECTS (other than vessels).   In spite of the profusion and variety of objects found in caches,
offerings seem to have had a basic eccentric component to which jadeite and/or shell objects were added.
Seventy-three out of 94 caches contained eccentrics of either flint or obsidian.   Fifty-one of these 73 caches
contained both eccentric flints and eccentric obsidians.   Among the 94 caches, objects of jadeite (or stones
resembling it) appeared in 41 instances, and objects of shell in 30.   Jade and/or shell occurs in 52 caches.
38 caches consist of eccentric flints, eccentric obsidians, and objects of either shell or jadeite or both.
Fifty-three caches consist of eccentrics of flint and/or obsidian with objects of jade and/or shell.

It must be remembered that these simple statistics are based on a series of offerings of which many
cannot be wholly reconstructed.   These figures, minimal as they must be, surely serve to illustrate the
characteristic composition of Piedras Negras caches.   The pattern of eccentric flint and obsidian, jadeite
and shell, appears in Caches K—5—2 and K—5—8, which are contemporary and, from all evidence, early

(9.6.0.0.0??; see Table 4). It further appears in Caches R—9—1 and R—9—2, in other K—5 caches, and in seven of O—13. If we trust Table 4 in a general way, the pattern is obviously early and persistent. Early Classic Caches R—3—1 and R—3—2, perhaps significantly, bear little resemblance in composition to later caches. But the votive use of jadeite, or at least something resembling it (see Part 2), is to be seen in the first cache of the series, R—3—2, "guess-dated" at 9.0.0.0.0. Offerings of jadeite persisted but it is actually Caches K—5—2 and K—5—8 that first manifest a constituent pattern that thereafter was maintained, although frequently with component addition and subtraction.

While the number of caches set beneath monuments seems unexpectedly small (see above under Quantity and Provenience, p. 98), there are a few signs of temporal distinctions in contents of known stela deposits. Only two stela offerings, Caches K—5—5, and J—1—2, resemble the general run of architectural caches. It is difficult to say how table altars were votively regarded but one of two pertinent offerings (Cache O—13 —1) did contain eccentric flints and obsidians; the other altar cache (J—1—1) seems somewhat atypical because of the extreme variety of its contents, but it did contain one eccentric. One can at least conclude that eccentric objects (see Caches J—1—1, J—1—2, and K—5—5) were being offered in relation to monuments from 9.12.5.0.0 to 9.13.0.0.0 (Stelae 6 and 39 and Altar 1). This leads us to suspect that plain Altar 5 and the associated eccentric offerings (Cache O—13—1) belong, despite contrary reasoning (see Location 14 of Structure O—13, p. 84), within this period and, further, that the altar itself may relate to Structure O—13— 1st—C, assuming the building's "guess-date" to be approximately correct. But, because of their uncertainty, our suspicions are not reflected in Table 4.

In the period from 9.14.15.0.0 to 9.15.5.0.0 stela offerings (see Caches J—1—3, J—3—2, and J—3—3) appear to have been reduced to caching an incensario and various drum-shaped stones classified by Satterthwaite as "portable altars." Cache O—13—56, if truly a stela offering, illustrates still a further shift in monument cache items.

There is some evidence, then, that at Piedras Negras monument-associated offerings (all presumably dedicatory), while at one time indistinguishable from architectural offerings, became with time atypical in content. On the other hand, structure caches, when statistically viewed (as above), have a certain constancy from the time of Structure K—5—3rd on up to and possibly through the occupation of Structure O—13— 1st—A.

Shaky as Table 4 may be, the perspective it provides still permits consideration of a few important problems. For one, are there marked changes in form and technological details of cache contents? The eccentric crescent, the double crescent, and the trident crescent, all in flint, and probably the scorpion in obsidian, are to be seen in Cache K—5—8, which likely antedates the majority of the Piedras Negras offerings. All or nearly all of these forms occur in Caches R—9—1 and R—9—2, but perhaps more significantly, in Caches O—13—7, O—13—8, and O—13—10 (see Tables 1 and 2). The latter offerings are surely later than Cache K—5—8 and probably the two R—9 caches as well. The trait of incised designs on miscellaneous pieces of shell appears first in the series in Caches K—5—5 and J—1—1, belonging to 9.12.5.0.0 and 9.13.0.0.0 respectively. But, in this instance, we lack a surely later occurrence; the trait appears in Cache O—13—7 which in the present scheme could date as early as 9.12.0.0.0 (see Table 4). Incised miscellaneous pieces of pseudo-jadeite, however, have early occurrences in Caches K—5—2 and K—5—8, somewhat later in Caches K—5—6 and possibly R—9—2 and O—16—1, and they were found in nine O—13 caches. Unfortunately, none of these O—13 offerings can be confidently assigned phases of Structure O—13—1st. The chances, though, of all belonging exclusively to —C, or to —B, or to —A are slight; thus one or more of these particular caches could pertain to —A, the latest, with a date of 9.17.15.0.0. Stingray spines, another distinctive votive item (but a mortuary one as well), appear actually or in effigy in early (9.6.0. 0.0. ??) caches like K—5—2 and K—5—8, in the seemingly later caches J—1—1 and J—29—1, and in six other offerings, one or more of which are presumably late, that is, at or after 9.17.15.0.0.

If we forget the problems and question marks integral to Table 4, the collection manifests little in a way of evolutionary evidence. On the contrary, certain basic eccentric shapes, or rather the concepts behind them, were early established and long persisted. It might be argued that, in the light of form diversification in O—13 offerings, additions were made to the traditional votive components. But evidence that new forms actually grew out of old is slight at best.

The evidence for an expected technological improvement with time is equally ambiguous. The rough eccentric obsidians of Cache J—1—2 (9.12.15.0.0) and of all K—5 caches stand in contrast to the extraordinary, bifacially worked obsidians seen in many O—13 caches. But they are also to be contrasted with equally fine ones found in the Structure R—9 offerings—offerings that probably overlap in time with the later of the K—5 votive series. The O—13 obsidians are by no means consistently well made. And the fine eccentric flints seen in Caches R—9—1 and R—9—2 would seem to well antedate a cache like O—13—10 which produced flints comparable in finish.

If Table 4 is trusted, even in context of extreme reservation, we must then conclude that the Piedras Negras votive deposits, once instituted in a typical form, tended to retain that form. Items seen in early offerings were maintained; what seems to be change is really addition; aesthetic and technological improvement is sporadic and likely represents a gifted but passing artisan. Both the early Caches K—5—2 and K—5- 8 are typical offerings for they contain eccentric flints and obsidians, incised and carved jadeite and shell, and such miscellaneous items as stingray spines, lime paste and bird bones. These offerings jointly show flints of subsequently common forms in addition to other flints (and obsidians) apparently not standardized. These features together appear over and over again in local caches. Proliferation of unique forms is suspected as time passed, but many eccentrics were votive constants. It is really those caches associated with monuments that show the greatest change, principally after 9.13.0.0.0; but the sample is small.

CHRONOLOGICAL VALUE OF PIEDRAS NEGRAS CACHES (TABLE 6)

It has long been felt, or at least hoped (see Thompson, 1931, p. 336), that caches might eventually prove chronologically useful. In the preceding discussions we have noted the frequency of Piedras Negras caches and, furthermore, have concluded that these offerings were, generally speaking, static, with the implication of votive conservatism.

Table 6 illustrates the presence or absence distribution, among 22 caches, of 14 readily identifiable eccentric forms (in obsidian and/or flint); eccentrics are the most ubiquitous items in Piedras Negras caches, a minimum of 592 having been found. These caches were selected on the following bases: to be listed, a cache had to have two or more form-traits among the 14 employed; we must have good to complete knowledge of the cache's eccentric component. The most frequently represented trait (the scorpion) is listed to the left, with other forms listed to its right in order of decreasing frequency, The sample frequency of each form is given below the tabulation. The caches are listed in an arbitrary order without regard to temporal conclusions and probabilities (for these, see Table 4). The indication of presence (''X'') records simply that the form occurs in a particular cache.

Three or four of the most common tabulated eccentric traits appear in Caches O—13—1, O—13—4, O—13—7, O—13—10, K—5—1 and R—9—1. The most frequent form and the second most common one are found in six of the sample caches (O—13—1, O—13—7, O—13—10, J—1—2, J—6—3, K—5—1). Relatively rare trait sharing is indicated, for instance, by the double crescent in Caches O—13—7, O—13—47, K—5—8, and R—9—1 ; by the obsidian ''S'' in O—13—10, O—13—13, and R—9—2. The trident, the rarest of the tabulated eccentrics, appears in Caches O—13—10 and J—1—2. ''Heavy'' trait representation (six or more) is to be noted in O—13—1, O—13—6, O—13—10, K—5—1, R—9—1, and R—9—2.

Our major interest here is in the potential value of caches for cross-dating. Is cache contemporaneity (and thus the fills from which they come) indicated by the sharing of various traits known to be common? Table 4 would indicate ''no.'' This is emphasized by the fact that Caches K—5—8 and J—1—2, believed to be separated by almost 7 katuns, share both the scorpion and the plain crescent, both common eccentrics in the sample. Unless we disregard the most credible portions of Table 4, these two caches could hardly equate temporally on the basis of frequent traits held in common. The sharing of rare traits, in our proposi-

Table 6—PRESENCE OF ECCENTRIC FORMS IN CACHES

CACHES	scorpion	blade w/ central opposed side notches	trident-crescent	double-pointed blade	crescent	serrated crescent	centipede	serpentine	disc	double crescent	anthropomorph	blade w/ offset notches each side	"S"-shaped	trident	
O–13–1	X	X	X	X			X	X				X			7
O–13–4		X	X	X				X							4
O–13–6	X		X	X	X				X			X			6
O–13–7	X	X	X						X	X					5
O–13–10	X	X	X	X	X	X		X	X		X	X	X	X	12
O–13–13				X				X					X		3
O–13–17		X					X								2
O–13–30		X							X						2
O–13–37	X						X	X							3
O–13–47	X							X			X				3
O–13–51	X							X							2
O–13–54		X		X				X							3
J–1–2	X	X			X	X								X	5
J–6–3	X	X			X	X									4
J–29–1	X				X	X									3
K–5–1	X	X	X		X		X					X			6
K–5–5		X										X			2
K–5–6		X		X								X			3
K–5–8	X		X		X						X				4
R–9–1	X		X	X	X	X	X		X	X					8
R–9–2			X	X		X	X	X	X				X		7
R–16–1			X									X			2
	13	12	10	9	8	7	7	7	6	4	4	4	3	2	

KEY: scorpion, blade with central opposed side notches, trident-crescent, double-pointed blade, crescent, serrated crescent, centipede, serpentine, disc, double crescent, anthropomorph, blade with offset notches on each side, "S"—shaped, trident

tion of contemporaneity, has equally negative results. Nor do caches chronologically align simply on the basis of sharing many tabulated forms regardless of their individual frequencies in the sample. It is true however that rough alignment occurs, but only insofar as the pertinent caches appear to be Late Classic. Caches K—5—6 and K—5—8, both stratified and estimated to be two katuns apart in time (see Table 4), have no tabulated trait in common. Our conclusion is that Table 6, treated from these points of view, yields little evidence or hints of a temporally useful pattern in the eccentric component of caches. Table 6, when coupled with Table 4, does seem to confirm our prior conclusion that various votive components occur early and persist. Table 6 indicates, for example, that specific eccentrics (e. g. the scorpion and the centrally notched blade) were of importance in early times and continued to be important.

The span for what might be justifiably termed "typical" cache items is considerable—two centuries seems reasonable. During this span an early established pattern (eccentrics, jade and/or shell) was maintained. Tradition is certainly implied. We have specifically noted the persistence of specialized containers, lime paste, engraved jadeites, stingray spines, and, at this point, have emphasized the evident continuity of various eccentric forms. The factor of tradition in caches would seem to minimize a theoretically useful method of cross-dating—a method which, if proved valid, would have great internal value in view of the scattered excavations at the site. This is not to deny that exceptionally unique items produced for votive purposes (e. g. the "monolithic ax" in Figs. 26 g; 36 d) might be used to supplement tested methods of cross-dating, but their presence ought not to be considered as primary evidence of contemporaneity (see Cache O—7—1 , p. 89).

The writer is aware of the statistical superficiality of Table 6. "Probability," "chance occurrence," and "meaningfulness" are concepts entirely relevant to this important problem of cache seriation and cross-dating. Pattern exists in caches but its nature does not seem to be chronological. But further analysis is certainly not precluded by this conclusion. Ignorance of sophisticated statistical techniques is admitted here. However, the writer is confident that anyone statistically equipped to handle the problems just touched upon will be able to find in this report the required data.

In the next division of this chapter, a survey is made of caches beyond Piedras Negras. Once again the question of the chronological value of caches will be raised but in terms of intersite rather than intrasite applicability (see Table 7).

DISTRIBUTION OF CACHES

Votive caches have been recorded at many sites in Mesoamerica, but, apart from a survey of monument-associated deposits (Strömsvik, 1942), caches have received little comparative study. This is unfortunate, for votive caches appear most characteristic of various culture regions of Mesoamerica and help to set it off as a whole from other important New World areas. Speculation, for instance, on the derivation of cache practices at Piedras Negras naturally requires discussion of all known Maya caches and even those known from elsewhere in Mesoamerica, and indeed from all the New World. Distribution and function are basic interests, and, motivated by a contextual concern for the Piedras Negras material, we have brought together here a mass of information relating to the phenomena of caches.

1. GUATEMALA (lowlands). *Uaxactun:* 64 caches with one Late Developmental, (i. e., Late Pre-Classic), 49 Early Classic and 14 Late Classic. Three types of repositories termed "simple" (unlined hole), "cist" (definite outlines, occasionally walled), and "crypt" (walled with capstones) (A.L. Smith, 1950, pp. 91—93). Caches appeared in palace and temple sub-structures, platforms, court or plaza floors, and associated with monuments both plain and carved. One cache was in the wall of a room. The majority of caches were judged to be dedicatory but cases where a cache "was put through the floor of a building after its completion" were noted (*ibid.*, p. 93). Particularly during the Early Classic specialized containers were used but during Late Classic times "well-known or ceremonial types" were used (R. E. Smith, 1955, p. 95). Pottery was not discovered in stela caches (A. L. Smith, *op. cit.*). Contents included eccentrics,

incised obsidians and obsidian flakes, shell and jadeite, animal bones and such miscellanea as lignite, seeds, a snake, pearls, and coral. In only one instance, eccentric flints and obsidians, shell and jadeite occur together. Offerings of human heads, in lip-to-lip bowls, appeared in Early Classic. A. L. Smith (*ibid.*, p. 93) writes: "There seems to be no great period difference in cache objects except that the orange ware bowls with flaring sides and skull burials in the same sort of bowls occurred only in the Early Classic Period, and that animal caches ...were found only in the Late Classic Period." However, Kidder (1947, pp. 28—29) comments on the lack of eccentric material excepting incised obsidians in Tepeu caches; A. L. Smith's Table 8 (*op. cit.*) indicates Cache A 37 to be the sole Late Classic offering yielding an eccentric object. There can be no doubt that eccentric-producing caches at Uaxactun are almost consistently Early Classic, extending as far back as 8.18.0.0.0 (?). *Tikal*: Strömsvik (1942, p. 87) lists 5 caches, 4 of them from plain stelae (A 16, A 18, A 21, A 24), and one from Stela 5 (9.15.13.0.0). All evidently yielded eccentric flints and incised obsidians except the cache of Stela 5, which is said to have contained only incised obsidians. Morley (1937—1938, v. 1, p. 268) mentions A 17 and A 26 as having been excavated for caches by General Hay but evidently none were found. Kidder (1947, p. 22) mentions a cache from Stela 16 (9.14.0.0.0) containing incised obsidians (see caption of his Fig. 70), and still another from Stela 10 (see also Morley, *op. cit.*, p. 325) which reputedly was composed of still more incised obsidians. The date of Stela 10 is in doubt; Morley gives 9.3.13.0.0.(??) while Proskouriakoff style-dates it as 9.8.0.0.0 plus-or-minus 2 katuns. Two more caches, both in Group I, were discovered by Berlin (1951). One occurred curred there with Stela 21 (9.15.5.0.0) and consisted of eccentric flints, incised obsidians and a single "jade?" bead. The second offering appeared below the floor in front of Altar IX and comprised a small Tepeu pot containing a few jadeite objects, an obsidian flake-blade, and a flint blade. With the possible exception of the Stela 10 deposit, all Tikal caches found to date (1956) appear to be Late Classic. They occur either with monuments inscribed with Late Classic dates or with plain monuments dateable as Late Classic on the basis of the presence of incised obsidians. But the fact that incised obsidians are claimed for the cache of Stela 10 raises the question of their value in cross-dating. They have been so used by A. L. Smith (1950, pp. 34, 87, Table 5). It is also remarkable that no eccentric obsidian has been attributed to any of these caches. Joyce nevertheless illustrates a few eccentric obsidians as from Tikal (1932, Pls. I, 4 d, 8 d; III, 2 b) as well as various eccentric flints (*ibid.*, Pls. I, 2 a; III, 1 a, 2 c, 5 c, 6 c; VI, 2 a). These pieces presumably stem from the work of Jolly, Herron, and Robson who are believed to have removed the caches of at least Stelae 5 and 10 (see Morley, *op. cit.*, p. 268). If we assume that they "potted" no more than these two, we must assign the Joyce pieces to one or both of these stelae. But, as previously noted, incised obsidians reputedly were found beneath both. Did the production of eccentric obsidians and incised obsidians concur or even overlap? At the moment, we have no evidence that they did. One wonders whether the report of incised obsidians in the Stela 10 cache may be in error. This is evidently an early monument, the erection of which might have ante-dated production of incised obsidians. In the present sample, the caching of incised obsidians, for the noted Stela 10 case, occurred from 9.14.0.0.0 to about 9.16.0.0.0. *Holmul*: While no specific mention is made of a cache, there are indications; for example, "Buried into the structure of Building F were three ... pots Holmul V in date" (Merwin and Vaillant, 1932, p. 72). *Naranjo*: Two Late Classic stela caches of eccentric flints, with no mention of containers (Maler, 1908, pp. 97, 100—101). *Ucanal*: Possible stela cache of pottery (see Strömsvik, *op. cit.*, p. 91). *Quirigua*: 7 Late Classic monument-associated caches, some composed of rectangular, lidded pottery boxes with few if any contents, while others consisted of beautiful laurel-leaf flint blades, a flamboyant eccentric flint, worked and unworked jadeite, and an unworked quartz crystal (Strömsvik, *ibid.*, pp. 80—83). Also one structure cache of 24 unillustrated eccentric flints (see Kidder, 1947, p. 27; Morley, 1947 a, p. 45).

2. BRITISH HONDURAS. *Benque Viejo*: Caches evidently common, both with monuments and in structures. Contents preponderantly eccentric. Without containers? (Gann, 1918, pp. 96—98; 1925 a, pp. 53—54, 57; A. H. Anderson, personal communication). *Baking Pot*: Ricketson (1929, p. 5) encountered eccentric flints and a jade in rubble of Mound E and, on the mound top, a cache of "somewhat more than two quarts of small flint chips." A probable third cache consisted of a pottery bowl, a bowl made of a

skull cap, a second example of a worked skull bone which contained a "finely shaped obsidian drill" (*ibid* ., p. 14). *Caracol*: A few sub-altar caches, with or without containers, of objects like eccentric obsidians (generally re-used, notched cores), jadeite objects, hematite and possibly pyrite mosaic elements, and various objects of marine origin (Satterthwaite, verbal information; collection in UM). *Mountain Cow sites*: 10 structure deposits (Thompson, 1931) emphasizing pottery containers, tiny figurines of jadeite, slate, and shell, marine and jadeite items and a notable lack of eccentric offerings, although a single eccentric flint occurred in a burial. All caches are Holmul V in date. *San Jose*: 20 caches throughout all phases but only one in Period I (Thompson, 1939). All are associated with structures but with no evident systematic placement. Eccentric offerings apparently minimized, with relative frequency of marine objects, obsidian points, pyrite plaques; unusual objects of clay, some culinary, were cached; one late cache with copper bells; one burial with eccentric flint.　　　*Pusilha*: 3 stela caches, all Late Classic, without containers, consisted of tremendous quantities of eccentric flints and obsidians, cores and flake-blades, and a few jadeite objects (Joyce, Gann, Gruning, and Long, 1928, pp. 333–35); also two structure caches, one a "rough pottery jar" with eccentric flints and obsidians and a jadeite pendant, and with perforated shell objects enclosed in an articulated *Spondylus* shell (Gruning, 1930, p. 478). *Lubaantun*. A probable structure cache of two eccentric flints (Joyce, Cooper-Clark, and Thompson, 1927, p. 312) and two other structure caches composed solely of "spiral shells." *Others*: Gann excavated many concentrations of artifacts without signs of burials at such sites as Nohmul, Santa Rita, and various mounds in the Rio Hondo region (Gann and Gann, 1939, pp. 10–11, 14–15, 30, 38–45, 52; Gann, 1900, p. 679 ff; 1918); three from Santa Rita were likely late Post-Classic, while many of the others appear to be Late Classic, the latter occasionally occurring in stone-lined repositories. Price (1897–99, pp. 341–42) describes from Kendal a suggestive concentration of objects associated with a possible crude altar.

3. MEXICO. *Tzibanche*: Gann (1935, p. 162) uses "cache" to cover many jadeite objects found together in a chultun; one jade contains a Period-End date equivalent to 10.4.0.0.0. *El Palmar*: Stela cache (9.15.15.0.0) of eccentric flints, one flamboyant, obsidian cores and flakes (Thompson, 1936, p. 126; also Morley, 1947, Pl. 95 a, b, e). *Calakmul*: Stela cache (9.12.0.0.0, latest of three dates) consisting of a "small, crude pottery jar" (Strömsvik, 1942, p. 84). *Uxmal*: In fill of Adoratorio Central (Ruz, 1955 a, pp. 62–63; Saenz, 1952), a scattered cache of *tecalli* vessels, large quantities of jadeite objects, many beads of miscellaneous stones, and flint blades. Cache of Adoratorio de la Picota (Ruz, 1955 b, p. 11) comprised pottery vessels, one containing a few minor objects. *Chichen Itza*: In a masonry box set in a Mercado floor were five carved jadeite objects and many shell beads (Ruppert, 1943, pp. 256–57). At least three caches were found in connection with the reconstruction of Caracol. One was an olla containing remains of a pyrite mosaic plaque, a shell ornament, a stone button, fragments of a human skull bone, and bones of 41 shrews (Ruppert, 1935, pp. 85–86). Beneath a door sill was a clay effigy turtle within which were a jadeite bead and a few stone and shell beads (*ibid.*, pp. 219–20); and, also sub-floor, was a small cone-shaped jar containing a single shell bead (*ibid.*, p. 220). Six caches were encountered in the Temple of the Warriors (Morris, Charlot, and Morris, 1931, pp. 57, 186 ff). Two appeared beneath walls while others were located inside dais-like constructions. Pyrite mosaic plaques seem to have been favored. One dais cache had been anciently looted and resealed. Another cache was exceptionally rich, made up of a turquoise mosaic plaque, carved jadeites and 100 jadeite beads, vestiges of a textile, and bones of an owl and a finch, all contained in a lidded barrel-shaped, limestone jar. Morris (*ibid.*, p. 198) writes that "some sort of offering is to be expected in every temple in Chichen Itza. It would also seem that cylindrical stone urns were favorite receptacles for the more pretentious deposits." *Mayapan*: At least 20 caches have been reported (*Current Reports, Carnegie Institution of Washington, Department of Archaeology*, Nos. 1–28). The majority are said to have been dedicatory; a few were intrusive,. Deposits are found in temples, residences, colonnaded halls, and even associated with gateways. Offerings exclusively of pottery vessels are frequent; however, one must allow for perishable offerings. Contents, when present, are variable but include objects of jadeite, flint, and obsidian, such marine objects as shells, coral, an occasional stingray spine, and other miscellanea like copper and copal. Miss Proskouriakoff relates (verbal communication) that many

caches were evidently looted by the local population at the time of the site's collapse; cache locations often seem to have been exactly known. *Palenque*: Angel Fernandez (1943, p. 55) briefly mentions the discovery of 20 offerings in the Temple of the Cross and two others in the Temple of the Foliated Cross. He describes three from the Temple of the Sun. One cache was very likely intrusive and consisted of a stucco head; the others were "little cylindrical vessels with flat-covers ... containing little bones of birds and bats with fragments of jade and bones of anthropoid extremities." Various offerings have been reported by Ruz (1955) in connection with the famous crypt of the Temple of Inscriptions but all seem to have been mortuary. A structure cache of only pottery vessels has been described (Ruz, 1952, pp. 42–43). Eccentric objects have yet to be found at Palenque (Robert L. Rands, personal communication).

4. HONDURAS. *Copan*: 13 stela deposits, usually of plain-ware cache vessels with traces of perishable offerings, as well as charcoal, *Spondylus* shells, stalactites, bone fragments, occasional flint and obsidian objects, jadeite beads, and in one case, a stingray spine (Strömsvik, 1942; Longyear, 1952). Occasional caching of articulated *Spondylus* valves containing jadeite objects and cinnabar, even worked crystal (Gordon, 1896, p. 21; Longyear, *op. cit.*, Fig. 94 d, e). A structure cache of shell and jadeite (Longyear, *ibid.*, p. 19). A cache of 9 incised jadeite plaques occurred in a small mound near Copan village (Longyear, *ibid.*, pp. 19, 109). Gann (1925, p. 279) cites another cache composed of many *Spondylus* shells together with jadeite objects and Mercury. The Hieroglyphic Stairway had as its cache a flamboyant eccentric flint, an eccentric trident flint, a jadeite plaque, flint knives, shells, and cinnabar (Kidder, 1947, p. 27). Mound 4 yielded a pottery vessel containing shell, jadeite, and greenstone beads, small shell figurines, irregular pieces of carved pearl shell, and cinnabar (Maudslay, 1889–1902, text, p. 20). The red-painted remains of a jaguar, presumed to have been cached, come from this same mound (*ibid.*). Kidder (A. L. Smith and Kidder, 1943, p. 164) notes a Copan cache of "several hundred" large core-struck obsidian blades that are almost identical to the nine cached ones at Guaytan (see below).

COMMENT (TABLE 7). Piedras Negras shared many cache traits with other lowland Maya centers. Notable are the deposition of eccentric flints and obsidians, flint and obsidian flakes, obsidian cores and flake-blades, pyrite mosaic elements, objects of jadeite, stingray spines, worked and unworked *Spondylus* shells, articulated *Spondyli* with contents, and faunal remains. More generalized shared traits are dedicatory monument- and structure-associated caches, intrusive caches in buildings, the latter perhaps more numerous than can always be established. Piedras Negras made extensive use of specialized containers frequently with lids, a trait also to be seen at Quirigua, Copan, Mountain Cow, Uaxactun, Chichen Itza, and possibly at Palenque. Here, as elsewhere, cached vessels were occasionally found empty, having once contained solely perishables, if anything. Cache vessels were also placed lip-to-lip, the inverted upper one serving as a cover. But a number of Piedras Negras votive characteristics are interestingly either lacking or rare elsewhere: for example, the relatively high local frequency of the previously described pattern of flint, obsidian, jadeite, and shell; also the absence of specialized repositories beyond the "simple" type; the presence of bone effigy stingray spines and worked spines; the lining of containers with a lime paste; and the scarcity of caches with stelae.

Individualized in these respects, the site nonetheless, as noted, manifests too many cache relationships to be considered aberrant with respect to caches. Distinctive points may very well, though, indicate a Middle Usumacinta variant votive pattern, verifiable, of course, only by excavations elsewhere in that region. Diversity of contents and the high frequency of eccentric items are outstanding features of Piedras Negras offerings. How far these traits extend to the west is not known. Palenque deposits, as reported by Angel Fernandez and others, are in a number of ways quite unlike those of Piedras Negras; this is illustrated by the evident lack of eccentric objects at that site.

The preceding survey indicates that the lowland Maya made votive offerings from as early as the late Pre-Classic, through the Classic Period, and continued to do so as late as the occupation of Mayapan. The ubiquity and persistence of this feature is indeed remarkable. Lowland caches, irrespective of time and place, emphasized objects of flint and obsidian, of jadeite, and items, both worked and unworked, of

Table 7—DISTRIBUTION IN TIME OF SELECTED ECCENTRIC FLINT FORMS

FORMS	DATES	PROVENIENCES
Ring	late San Jose IV *	
	9.15.5.0.0	Tikal St. 21
	9.15.0.0.0 (?)	Pusilha St. E
	9.14.0.0.0	Tikal St. 16
Crescent, plain	San Jose IV *	
	9.15.0.0.0 (?)	Pusilha St. E
	9.13.0.0.0 (???)	Naranjo St. 15
	9.13.0.0.0	Piedras Negras Alt. 1
	9.12.15.0.0	Piedras Negras St. 6
	9.12.5.0.0, prior to	* *
Crescent, serrated	9.17.10.0.0	Naranjo St. 13
	9.12.15.0.0	Piedras Negras St. 6
Trident-crescent	late San Jose IV *	
	9.12.5.0.0, prior to	* *
	8.18.0.0.0	Uaxactun St. 4
Double crescent	late San Jose IV *	
	9.12.5.0.0, prior to	* *
Scorpion	10.1.0.0.0	Benque Viejo St. 1
	9.15.5.0.0	Tikal St. 21
	9.14.0.0.0	Tikal St. 16
Centipede	9.15.5.0.0	Tikal St. 21
	9.14.0.0.0	Tikal St. 16
	9.13.0.0.0 (???)	Naranjo St. 15
	9.12.5.0.0, prior to	* *
Anthropomorph	late San Jose IV *	
	9.12.5.0.0, prior to	* *
Disc	9.15.5.0.0	Tikal St. 21
	9.3.10.0.0	Uaxactun St. 22
Double-pointed blade	9.15.15.0.0	El Palmar St. 10
	9.13.0.0.0 (???)	Naranjo St. 15
	9.12.5.0.0, prior to	* *
	9.3.10.0.0	Uaxactun St. 22
	9.0.10.0.0	Uaxactun St. 26
Blade, central opposed side notches	9.15.0.0.0 (?)	Pusilha St. E
	9.13.0.0.0 (???)	Naranjo St. 15
	9.12.5.0.0	Piedras Negras St. 39
	9.12.5.0.0, prior to	* *

* In "11.16" correlation, dated about 10.0.0.0.0 (see Thompson, 1939, Table 17; also Kidder, 1947, p. 28)

* * Structures K—5—1st—C, K—5—2nd, and K—5—3rd (see Appendix)

marine origin. Once objects of copper began to appear in the lowlands they too entered into caches (e. g. at San Jose and Mayapan). The offering having been made, it was generally left untouched, perhaps in time forgotten, but in the Post-Classic Period caches were often later uncovered and rifled; tomb looting is also to be noted in the lowlands (see Ancient Deliberate Disturbance of Burials p. 133). At all times, caches were preponderantly set at the time of construction, but there are instances of deposits being introduced into a structure after its completion and during its occupation. Judging from the objects found in lowland Maya caches, almost anything traded-in or produced and collected locally was suitable for votive use. A certain regularity is to be observed in lowland Classic Period caches, as well as variables, the latter suggestive of regional and even site votive differentials.

The potential usefulness of cache items in cross-dating has been raised at several points in this report. Our general conclusion is that objects in Piedras Negras caches have no clear-cut value in local chronology. The question remains, however, of temporal consistency, from site to site, of cache material beyond the obvious fact that a majority of southern lowland caches are Classic Period in date.

Table 7 has been prepared to illustrate the time (and space) distributions of eccentric flint forms throughout the area occupied by the Classic lowland Maya. The data pertain to cache material found with dated monuments and with buildings, the dates of which can be reasonably expressed in Long Count terms. The table is essentially a summary of distributions of many of the eccentric forms described in Part 2.

A few assumptions automatically pervade Table 7. First, eccentric items are considered to have been made for immediate votive use; and, second, caches were neither redeposits nor were they intrusive to the associated monuments. The area covered by the qualifying caches ranges from Piedras Negras east to Benque Viejo, from El Palmar in the north to Pusilha in the south.

Table 7 indicates that no form is restricted to a single katun nor even to two katuns. In fact, each has a discouragingly long time spread. The ring, for instance, occurs over a span of 120 years, the double-pointed blade some 300 years (relatively unspecialized form?), the serrated crescent about 100 years, the centipede at least 60 years, and the scorpion (bulbar types; see Part 2, Eccentric Flints, Scorpions) 140 years. These long periods of use hardly indicate value for intersite cross-dating. But, as more caches are found that relate to the Long Count, frequency curves in terms of time may gradually emerge. These would permit plotting of eccentric flints from a cache of unknown date, yielding a fairly narrow period in which the items were probably produced.

On the other hand, impatience might lead one to assume that Table 7 is sufficient for dating purposes were it properly adjusted, particularly in the extremes of each time distribution. Thus, we might push the whole Piedras Negras K–5 sequence ahead in time on the grounds that Stelae 39 and 38 were re-used early early monuments. And we could either put San Jose IV back considerably in Maya time, or dismiss the "11.16" correlation. While a relative degree of distributional conistency might result, the factual cost would be high.

It is concluded here that eccentric flints cannot be presently used in cross-dating with any confidence. This also seems to be true of eccentric obsidians. Yet, with further discoveries of dated specimens, a technique might be developed similar to that employed by Proskouriakoff (1950) for monuments. Incised obsidians (Tikal and Uaxactun) appear to be the most valid items present for cross-dating, but, as mentioned above, the situation in regard to Tikal Stela 10 offers a degree of uncertainty. Thompson (1938, pp. 191–92) attempted to use generally cached small figurines of shell, jade, and slate in this manner., but found their time span to be so enormous that he concluded that their earliest appearance, at Uaxactun, could be due to the fact that their "cache... is almost certainly not contemporaneous with the date the stela bears."

5. GUATEMALA (highlands). *Kaminaljuyu*: Cached offerings occur in both Pre-Classic and Classic contexts. An extremely rich, intrusive, structure cache is described by Shook (1951, pp. 240–41). Early Sacatepequez in date, it comprises 3 plain basalt columns, a sculptured stela, and 2 pedestal sculptures, along with 70 pottery vessels and a "bird (?)" skull containing 290 jadeite beads and pendants, a possible La Venta-style jadeite pendant, and miscellaneous small jadeite beads and mosaic elements.

Traces of "ceremonial fires" were found in the pit which had been dug into a still older mound. Excavations in Mound D—111-3, of the Esperanza Phase or somewhat earlier, yielded five caches, three of which were composed simply of pottery vessels, while the remaining ones comprised obsidian flake-blades and various beads of jadeite and other stones, also bird bones, impressions of burned organic material, and containers and associated pottery (Berlin, 1952, pp. 11—14; Shook, 1950, p. 197). Certain of the caches likely were intrusive. The objective of the offerings exposed in the Esperanza Phase excavations of Kidder, Jennings, and Shook (1946) are obscured by complex successive construction and severe slumping. In Mound B, seven concentrations of artifacts are termed caches (*ibid.*, pp. 30 ff). The positions of most are superficial, resting as they do on the surfaces of buried structures. Possibly these burned deposits represent offerings made in connection with renewed building activity. All were composed of incense burners and other vessels, often fire-blackened, and smashed in a bed of ashes and charcoal. These latter deposits recall a terminal offering of censers in Structure K—5—2nd at Piedras Negras (see under Caches, Structure K—5). Two other caches were discovered in Mound A (*ibid.*, pp. 15, 23). One, a single vessel placed in the center of a platform and covered over by adobe, was very likely intrusive. The other was found in platform fill, possibly dedicatory, and consisted of two vessels containing 9 serpentine and limestone earplug flares, 13 unworked marine shells, a perforated jadeite figurine, and many stone beads along with miscellanea. Finally, an intrusive Amatle-Pamplona cache of small stone ornaments is described by Kidder (1949, pp. 11—12). *Nebaj:* 21 caches, 5 Early Classic, 9 Late Classic, and 7 Post-Classic (A. L. Smith and Kidder, 1951, pp. 29—31). Simple and cyst repositories with no chronological distinctions. Majority of caches had non-specialized vessels with such contents as jadeite beads, pendants, and fine jadeite plaques, shell beads and tinklers, amazonite beads, obsidian cores and one flake-blade, unworked rock crystal (Post-Classic), birds, etc. Majority of caches dedicatory, having been found well in fill, beneath stairways, and sub-plaza fronting the mounds. Reburial of disturbed tomb contents as a cache is a possibility noted by the writers in one case (*ibid.*, p. 31). Skull burials and headless burials were found at Nebaj; while functionally related to caches, in that they were dedicatory, these and others like them have been treated comparatively here under Burials. *Guaytan:* Two caches reported. One consisted of a lidded pottery box (identical to those from Quirigua) set beneath a tomb floor at or prior to the time of its construction; it contained a red-painted flint knife, obsidian cores and flake-blades, shells, lizard (?) bones, stingray spines, and various bits of stone. (A. L. Smith and Kidder, 1943, pp. 125, 145). This offering, if set in connection with tomb construction, violates our cache definition. The second cache poses another problem. It was made up of nine core-struck large obsidian blades, in a hole "dug into natural earth" (*ibid.*, pp. 163—64). Kidder suggests that these may be blanks that were buried in order "to keep the stone in good condition for chipping." He notes their strong similarity to the hundreds in a Copan cache (see above). This deposit would conform, if Kidder is right, to the utilitarian rather than votive type of cache. The fact that nine were found, however, has a definite votive implication. *Zaculeu:* In all, 19 caches were found and these occurred in all periods (Classic and Post-Classic) (Woodbury and Trik, 1953, Ch. VI). Majority of Atzan (Early Classic) caches had been "placed in structural fill during construction, with no specialized type of repository to contain them." In the later Qankyak (Early Post-Classic) and Xinabahul (Late Post-Classic) Phases a number of caches were placed in cists. Trik notes that while no direct grave associations are to be seen in the Atzan caches, "it is probable that some of these caches had been placed in connection with funeral ceremonies." But the later caches "appeared to be of purely ceremonial or dedicatory nature with no relation to graves." Atzan contents include jadeite earplug flares and beads, sheet mica, shell objects, river pebbles, bird skull, etc., all both in and associated with pottery vessels. A Chinaq (Late Classic) offering yielded vessels, a pyrite mosaic plaque, and a jadeite pendant. Qankyak caches yielded items like jadeite beads, a pyrite polygon, and quail bones. Various vessels, a mano and metate, and a dog skull comprised a Xinabahul cache. Plumbate jars were offered in both Qankyak and Xinabahul times. *Zacualpa:* Concentrations of pottery were discovered but generally seem to have been associated with burials (Wauchope, 1948, pp. 89—92). Mention is made of a "large cache of *camahuiles*," that is, schist figurines placed in a vessel (*ibid.*, p. 162; also 1949, Fig. 4). A structure "votive cache" of two superimposed vessels, dateable as Tohil Phase, (Early Post-Classic) is also cited (*op. cit.*, p. 74). Another cache was curiously found apart from structures and, cist-enclosed, comprised a vessel, a jadeite bead, and a mano (*ibid.*, p. 91). *El Baul*: A sub-plaza cache of 36 knives or spearheads of flint, 2 similar ones of obsidian, and a pair of trident-shaped eccentric flints (Thompson, 1948, p. 40). *Tajumulco*: Perhaps significantly no caches were located at this late site (Dutton and Hobbs, 1943).

COMMENT. These highland Maya sites have been excavated on a sufficient scale to yield presumably fair cache samples. The major negative characteristic of highland caches is the general lack of eccentrics. The one exception, at El Baul, is most perplexing.

As in the lowlands, jadeite objects are fairly frequent, a fact certainly due in part to their intrinsic value and, thus, votive appropriateness. Birds were cached at a number of highland sites (Kaminaljuyu, Zaculeu, and Nebaj; see under Objects of Bone in Part 2). Caches solely of pottery vessels (with perishable contents?) are another common trait. Obsidian flake-blades occur with some frequency. And lowland-highland links occur in both specialized cache vessels and non-specialized vessels votively used; also in pyrite mosaic plaques, worked and unworked shells (but curiously not *Spondylus*), obsidian flake-blades, jadeite beads and carvings, and birds. The significance of these connectives is, of course, speculative. But the abundance and patent richness of highland tomb material may well account in part for the general drabness of highland cached offerings. And, in view of highland susceptibility to Mexican influence over a long period of time, something of a votive pattern, as noted in the lowlands, failed to develop. But perhaps the most important feature of many highland caches is their evident dedicatory placement. This factor may be considered a valuable highland-lowland correlate. Some caches in both areas were intrusive, a fact which tells us little. But that the placement of a majority of offerings occurred in both areas at the time of construction is perhaps a major though still puzzling common trait. The possibility of a utilitarian cache at Guaytan has been noted.

6. REMAINDER OF MESOAMERICA. Elsewhere in Mesoamerica cached offerings have been found. But, due to a lack of complete reports on various important Mexican sites, assessment of cache practices on even a fairly broad basis is difficult at the moment. The following abstracts, however, indicate something of the time-space range of caches and their characteristics.

Monte Alban: Discoveries of both Pre-Classic and Classic Period caches (Monte Alban 1—IV) have been made (see Caso, 1938, pp. 10, 18, 38, 65—66, 68; 1939, pp. 173, 177, 179, 181; Caso and Bernal, 1952, pp. 9, 10; Batres, 1902, Pls. XX—XXII). Majority were sub-floor and seemingly dedicatory; one offering was intrusive (Caso, 1938, p. 66); and at least one stela had an offering (an anthropometric vessel) situated below its base. Pots were often cached with artifactual contents, and in a number of cases pottery vessels yielded large quantities of finely carved jades, figurines, shells, flint and obsidian knives, and even a pearl. Pre-Classic caches appear to have been simple, comprising pottery vessels and a clay temple model. A human cranium with proximate vertebrae and a knife comprised a Monte Alban III—b sub-floor offering. *Yagul*: Six structure caches comprised stone "offering boxes" containing ashes, small pottery vessels, obsidian blades, and, in one case, 30 jades of Mixtec type (Paddock, 1955, pp. 25—26, 29, 44, 47). *Teotihuacan*: Various sub-floor dedicatory offerings have been described for the Tlamimilolpa group by Linné (1942, pp. 121, 123, 141—44, 180). General absence of specialized repositories is noted as well as a lack of a definite system deposition. Pottery vessels were usually offered though occasionally contents of a simple nature were found. One cache actually was of a whale bone. Two extremely rich deposits, structure caches and presumably dedicatory, come from the buildings Quetzalcoatl Viejo and Nuevo (Rubín de la Borbolla, 1947). These included objects of jadeite and other stones, shell, and bone. Fine stone figurines and intricately chipped obsidian objects, comparable to the best of the Piedras Negras eccentric obsidians, come from these Classic Period deposits. *Tenochtitlan*: Batres' Calle de las Escalerillas excavations (1902 a) disclosed a number of really large concentrations of objects related to constructions and without mention of skeletal material. These generally seem to have been temporally and culturally mixed lots, involving pottery, stone figurines, carved jades, etc. *Tres Zapotes*: Two Upper Period caches have been described, one consisting of pottery vessels and figurines and a possibly associated lone human skull; the other, a deposit of pottery vessels that was surely set prior to the mound's construction (Drucker, 1943, pp. 107–08, 109). *Cerro de las Mesas*: At least four cached offerings of Lower II date (Drucker, 1943 a, pp. 8, 12,14). One was composed of only pottery vessels, while in another various vessels were found with such contents as marine shells, shell objects, jadeite objects, shark teeth, a "sand dollar", a fossil, etc. Apparently below the plaza level near a stairways's basal step was a cache of some eight hundred objects of jadeite (see also Drucker, 1955). At the site, facial portions alone and even whole human sacrificial skulls (*op. cit.*, pp. 23– 24) were placed in pots and interred as offerings. *La Venta*: Sterling (1943, p. 55) records a sub-altar cache of 99 jadeite beads and a single one of amethyst. A large exploratory trench also disclosed many artifactual deposits, frequently of jadeite and serpentine celts, and occasionally of pottery vessels lacking imperishable contents (Drucker, 1952, pp. 26–27, 31, 38, 39, 55, 64–65, 68– 70, 71, 72–73, 75–76, 77). Certain of these concentrations were found in rectangular stone repositories and strongly resembled burials but skeletal material was not encountered. Many fine objects were found under these conditions. The question of dedicatory as opposed to intrusive deposition is not always clear. Certain celt caches, however, are stated to have been made at the time of building (*ibid.*, p. 77).

Excavations of sites on the southeastern periphery of Mesoamerica have occasionally produced deposits under cache conditions. For example, Longyear (1944, pp. 40–42) encountered three such offerings at Los Llanitos in eastern El Salvador. One cache, intrusive with regard to an associated floor, consisted of various pottery vessels, a large stone slab, and much evidence of burning: "After the fire had burned in the cache, the interior of the mound must have been filled in with dirt and rubbish" (*ibid.*, p. 41). A second cache also occurred with a stone slab, below which were a few obsidian artifacts. Stone (1941, pp. 75–76) speaks of "cache mound" at Travesia, but, as she notes, these concentrations yielded signs of associated burials and cremations. Investigations in the Bay Islands of Honduras have shown occasional enormous non-architectural, superficial deposits of artifacts to which such terms as "cache," "offertory," and "shrine" have been applied (Strong, 1935). That such concentrations are not caches in the sense of Piedras Negras or Uaxactun caches is evident by Strong's explanation of them as "fundamentally shrines where devotees deposited offerings ... and these offertories also served as the final resting place for disarticulated or partially cremated remains of certain priests or nobles" (*ibid.*, p. 144).

7. SOUTH AMERICA. Below Mesoamerica instances of cached offerings appear to be very scarce. At Sitio Conte, Panama, many pits were discovered and designated as "caches" by Lothrop (1937, p. 43). These occasionally were located near burials but in no case in contact with them. Some were filled with sand, carbonized material, and sherds; others with nothing but pottery and remnants of burning, while still others consisted of stone objects such as ornaments and utensils, "all invariably calcined by heat." In Colombia, a Santa Marta site yielded nine "caches" of ceremonial objects grouped within the boundary ring of a circular construction (Mason, 1931, v. 1, pp. 97–98). Also pottery vessels, many containing beads and other objects, were found under stone discoidal markers. The latter offerings presumably were dedicatory and thus analogous in a way to Maya monumental offerings.

There is hardly anything in the Central Andes comparable to the Mesoamerican cached offerings (Alfred Kidder II, verbal communication). The term "cache" infrequently appears in reports and generally is used to characterize finds unrelated to burials but with some indications of having been purposefully interred. For instance, Strong (1954, p. 217), in a summary of recent work in the Nazca region, reports a "great cache of textile grave wrappings" lacking grave associations. At Aspero, a "cache" of pottery discs was found (Willey and Corbett, 1954, p. 80). Kroeber (1937, pp. 249–52) records, as a "cache or deposit," a parcel of weaving objects. For the Viru Valley, intrusive "small cache pits" containing pottery are recorded in an "Earth-Refuse Mound" with a Puerto Moorin or Early Gallinazo date (Collier, 1955, pp. 82–83); 4 carved mace-heads and a mano-shaped implement were likewise grouped apart from burials here (*ibid.*, pp. 83–85, 89). It is obvious from these few examples that in Andean archaeology the term is loosely employed for non-mortuary concentrations of artifacts without necessary connotation of the idea of "offerings." The Viru Valley mace-heads possibly represent dedicatory, structure offering, though the nature of the mound itself seems hardly appropriate.

COMMENT. Wary of negative evidence, one nevertheless cannot fail to perceive the practical absence of the familiar Mesoamerican trait of dedicatory caches. Votive offerings with monuments and intrusive deposits in structures are further traits of, at most, rare incidence below Mesoamerica. But the Santa Marta deposits are interestingly reminiscent of Mesoamerican votive caches. Further to the south, though, resemblances seem to disappear. That votive caches, as known in Mesoamerica, are not expectable features in Central Andean archaeology is an important areal differential, but one hardly to be thought of apart from ceremonial construction and erection of monuments. As noted, Mesoamerican caches were, by and large, associated with platform-building (in the widest sense of the term); such caches occur early on a Pre-Classic or Formative horizon. If, then, there is validity in suggestions of a north to south Formative spread of "platform mound" building (see Willey, 1955), the evident failure of certain votive traits to diffuse coincidentally is of interest.

8. EASTERN NORTH AMERICA. In Eastern United States archaeology, the term "cache" has received frequent but equivocal usage. In this case it has been defined as a "group of artifacts occurring alone or with a burial..." (Cole and Deuel, 1937, p. 277). The first sense of the term, as defined, pertains to a concentration of incomplete artifacts, most usually of flint, which were deposited to keep them "green" or fresh for future finishing (see Martin, Quimby, and Collier, 1949, p. 29). Instances of such caches are numerous, many having been recorded for Ohio and Wisconsin but occurring also as far south as Texas (see Dustin, 1942; Buckstaff, 1937; Brown, 1907; Bennett, 1945, p. 53; Newell and Krieger, 1949, pp. 176—78). Particularly noteworthy is the fact that very few of such caches have been associated with construction; they generally seem to be isolated features. Determination of function would perhaps largely depend on whether or not the cached objects were actually completed or not. In any case, storage and protection were the probable uses of these caches, which satisfy Webster's definition of the term itself.

The inclusion by Cole and Deuel of concentrated burial offerings under the term has evidently been made by others (see Baker and others, 1941, pp. 9—10; Cotter and Corbett, 1951, p. 9; Clements and Reed, 1939, p. 27; etc.). But the meaning has still further been extended, for one reads of an Early Woodland Caddoan mound yielding "cache pits" filled with animal bones, ash, and mussel shells (Orr, 1952, p. 242); and other similarly described sub-floor features appeared in the George C. Davis excavations in Texas (Newell and Krieger, *op. cit.*, pp. 233, 235). And a "large cache-deposit of unio shells, burned" was discovered in an Illinois camp-site (Bennett, *op. cit.*, p. 147).

COMMENT. While no claim in made for thoroughness, a searching of many Eastern reports showed no case of a deposit, whether or not described as a cache, that corresponded to the votive cache of Mesoamerica. It is worth noting here that the Eastern storage-protective cache, however, seems to be absent from Mesoamerica. The problem of Southeastern—Mesoamerican relations, whatever its substance, would appear to stop short of caches.

9. SOUTHWESTERN NORTH AMERICA. Writers, dealing with the Southwest, particularly with Anasazi remains, have occasionally employed "cache" for certain sub-floor features. For example, Morris (1939) notes many instances of "corrugated cache pots" set beneath floors in predominantly domestic structures in the La Plata District. These rarely contain anything artifactual. From descriptions it is difficult to make out whether all such jars were constantly available or rather were permanently sealed beneath the floors, this factor being one important determinant of function. Some, however, were clearly placed so that there was always access to their interiors (*ibid.*, p. 49). Also, several thousand pecking stones, without architectural associations, were found as a "cache" in a rock cavity (*ibid.*, p. 65). Sub-floor "cache pits" were discovered in the Whitewater District (Robert, 1939, pp. 123, 178—79), one with contents "suggestive of a medicine man's paraphernalia," the other comprising a large, jug shaped, sub-floor cavity presumably fashioned for storage. "Caches" of curious shaped natural formations were also

located and one "cache contained a number of shark teeth and another produced two teeth from one of the Pleistocene horses" (Roberts, 1940, p. 127). The circumstances of these latter finds seem not to be given. Finally, and perhaps more pertinent from the standpoint of Mesoamerica, Judd, (1954, p. 322 ff) describes "sacrificial deposits" at Pueblo Bonito conisting of bone, shell, turquoise beads, a cockle shell containing pendants and beads of shell and turquoise; also obsidian and flint arrowheads, and other objects of stone, shell, bone, and clay. These were suggestively located in a kiva wall, in a masonry box beneath a kiva floor, hidden among roofing timbers of a kiva, and set in kiva pilasters.

COMMENT. It is perhaps the Pueblo Bonito deposits, at least partly ceremonial in content and votive in intent, that show the closest resemblance in North America to the familiar caches of Piedras Negras and Mesoamerica in general. Other Southwestern "caches" are of the storage or protective type (see Bryan, 1950, pp. 29—30) recorded so frequently in Eastern archaeology and thus have little bearing on the dedicatory and intrusive ceremonial offerings of Mesoamerica.

FUNCTIONS OF CACHES

The preceding resumes indicates two types of intentional and hidden deposits. One is the utilitarian cache, for protection and storage; it occurs frequently in North American archaeology and evidently exists in the Central Andean area. Its possible occurrence in the Maya area has been noted in summarizing the Guaytan caches. It has not as yet been reported definitely from Mesoamerica, but continued work in house-mounds conceivably might prove its existence. The other type is the ceremonial offering, variously referred to in the literature as an "offertory deposit," "votive cache," "ofrenda," "escondite," etc. This cache type is concentrated in Mesoamerica; it occurs sporadically to the north and south as well. Since this report is on Piedras Negras, an obvious interest is the function of the "votive cache."

In the introduction to this chapter, the votive cache was noted as occurring in customary terms as either "dedicatory" or "non-dedicatory."   While explicitly functional, this division tells very little. A. L. Smith, in this regard, writes (1950, p. 93) that some Uaxactun caches "were certainly dedicatory, especially those deposited in the fill at the time of the construction of a building." He continues: "In some cases a cache was put through the floor of a building after its completion. This type was evidently not dedicatory." Chronology, then, rather than contents, aids in making this distinction. A further aid is axial placement, implying regard for the plan of the structure. If the deposit was placed in the fill during construction and on the front-rear axis, its identification as a "dedicatory cache" is considered definite.

But are offerings placed in the fill during construction always found to be centrally located? In the case of San Jose, Thompson (1938, p. 192) concluded that there "is no evidence of any systematic placement of caches in relation to buildings." How then do we tag an offering off the axis and lacking evidence of having been intruded after construction (e. g. see Cache B 2, San Jose)? In practice, what do we call a cache so situated? The fact that it is non-intrusive but non-axial may disqualify it from being classified as "dedicatory." The writer feels that this apparent impasse is the result of too superficially defined terms. Though a chronologically uncertain cache may be judged to be non-intrusive if it is axially situated, other surely non-intrusive offerings need not be considered "non-dedicatory" simply because they occur off the axis. It may be well here to review terminology and the processes by which caches came to be made, particularly with regard to the lowland Classic Maya.

A deposit of one or more objects is placed in the fill of a building during construction. It is an "offering," the true purpose of which is highly problematical to us. It is an offering whether or not it is placed on the main axis of the structure. The offering is called a "cache" because it is "hidden." By custom, the term "cache" has been associated with "votive," a word which, though inexact, provides a religious, possibly sacrificial connotation. The "votive cache," when set during construction, is often placed on the axis of the building. The votive cache is thus intentionally oriented to an important feature of the structure; presumably the Maya thought of the front-rear axis as important too. We term a votive cache, so positioned, a "dedicatory cache." But what do we mean by "dedicatory?" Site reports do not define it though they do specify or imply certain spatial and chronological requirements for its use. The writer feels that the requirement of alignment with the structure's main axis is a false one, if the term "dedicatory" is to have any meaning apart from "axially positioned, non-intrusive." This clumsy phrase is what is meant in practice by "dedicatory;" "dedicatory" has thereby come to be used in an entirely non-functional sense.

The term should, we feel, be applied to any offering cached during construction, whether it is on the axis or not; such an offering is presumed, from its stratigraphic position, to have been dedicated to the structure or whatever religious or lay objective the structure may have had. The dedicatory cache is analogous to our cornerstone deposit, but presumably without the latter's implication of future extraction. Such caches are believed to have been set under priestly direction. Whether setting the cache involved anything comparable to our dedication ceremony is not known. A dedicatory cache presumably served to sanctify the structure or to dedicate it to a particular deity. While we may attempt to restore some functional meaning to this customary word, "dedicatory," it must necessarily be imprecise because of our lack of knowledge of priestly intentions.

Monument-associated caches, also termed "dedicatory," were at the very least related to the "tun count." They do not differ noticeably from dedicatory caches associated with structures. And it is clear that stelae and altars (plain and carved) were frequently set without offerings. The reasons for this evident inconsistency are unknown. And, at Piedras Negras, dedicatory caches occur beneath some column altars but not beneath others.

Intrusive caches are to be distinguished temporally from dedicatory ones in that they were set through a surface, usually an interior floor, after construction and during the building's occupation. This temporal distinction presumably implies functional ones; but the term "intrusive" is not functional in the same sense that "dedicatory" is, or, rather, ought to be. Intrusive offerings may have served various ritual needs; for instance, commemoration, celebration, intensification, propitiation. In this regard, one thinks of the commemoration of katun and tun anniversaries (see Thompson, 1950, pp. 194—96), of special offerings to celebrate festivals in the 260-day ceremonial cycle, of burned offerings and sacrificial caches to bend the gods in agricultural matters, and of other occasions requiring offerings in the form of pots and varied contents, all set beneath the floors on which their hierarchal donors walked.

As regards cache contents, we wonder whether components were meaningful in part and jointly? Were departures, say, at Piedras Negras, from the constituent pattern (flint-obsidian-jadeite-shell) due to the nature of the particular ceremony, to the ability of a donor to have the objects made, or perhaps sometimes to personal whim? The occurrence of distinct eccentric forms in cache after cache at Piedras Negras and far beyond implies similar votive ends. Shell with its symbolic associations, jadeite with its, and even those of flint and obsidian (see Thompson, ibid., pp. 86—87) bring to mind a possible interplay of meanings within the offering which when taken together with their alterations, directly reflect the offering's purpose. These items can be measured, described, plotted in time and space, but, singly or regrouped, they offer only the barest, most frustrating clues as to their significance.

BURIALS

INTRODUCTION

Human skeletal material was encountered in a variety of situations. It was discovered in excavating for architecture, in test pitting, and twice while investigating depressions in base-surfaces (Burials 5 and 10). Human bones were concentrated in graves and in a single cache (R–3–2), and were also scattered in general debris.

The introduction to the preceding chapter was largely devoted to discussion of what is meant by the term "cache." Mention was made that a burial and a cache were by-and-large two separate intentional deposits but that there were rare instances in which burial and cache features tended to merge.

Although applied to the Uaxactun burials the following definition by A. L. Smith (1950, p. 88) seems equally applicable to the Piedras Negras data: "The term *burial* includes everything connected with an interment, i. e., grave, skeletal material, and associated objects. The term *grave* is used as a general heading for the various types of resting places prepared to receive the dead ..."

Unlike a cache with contents (essentially offerings) of partly or wholly human skeletal material, a burial implies attention to the deceased as a human being and not as a mere votive object. This attention may be expressed as an elaborate tomb with rich furnishings, or as a simple grave. It surely took the form of funeral rites; Landa wrote of fear, wailing, and fasts for the dead (Tozzer, 1941, p. 129).

As noted in the introduction to the chapter on caches, a burial presumed to have been dedicatory, and a dedicatory cache may have had identical ends for the Maya, but that objective is utterly obscure to us. In classification we can depend only on the physical evidence.

Ten burials were encountered at Piedras Negras. Yet, in this small sample, a number of different grave types are present. A. L. Smith (*ibid.*) has published a list of grave types for Uaxactun. The list given below represents a compromise between Uaxactun terms and already published Piedras Negras nomenclature.

Simple. An "unlined hole in the ground or inclusion of a body in fill during construction." Taken from A. L. Smith (*ibid.*). Represented by Burials 4, 6, 7, 8, and 9.

Covered burial cist. Employed by Satterthwaite (1954, p. 50) to designate graves of Burials 2 and 3 which show cover slabs supported by a single course, rough stone perimeter. This type corresponds best to Smith's "crypt" –a "more carefully walled grave with capstones, sometimes with plastered floor, [that] may or may not have been filled with earth."

Covered burial chamber. Satterthwaite (*ibid.*) distinguishes this from the preceding by its having a "greater vertical distance between the floor of the chamber and its cover." Represented by Burial 1. Again, the Uaxactun "crypt" has the closest resemblances.

Tomb. A comparatively large mortuary structure with definite walls that rise to a roof that may be either flat or vaulted; it is definitely larger than needed to lay out the body. To this general definition one may add that at Piedras Negras, in known tombs (i. e., Burials 5 and 10), niches were present; both tombs were below floors which were base-surfaces for nearby architectural units, one a temple, the other a palace. In these tombs there were no doorways, but in one (Burial 10) there were steps. "Tomb" here is roughly the equivalent of the Uaxactun "chamber a" type of grave: a "large, specially constructed mortuary chamber." The problem is to define a term to cover both Burials 5 and 10, which structurally

120

possess a number of features in common, and to further distinguish Burial 10 from Burial 1 ("covered burial chamber"). The choice of "tomb" by the writer is as arbitrary as its definition but, as here defined, it satisfies certain descriptive ends.

Human bones, occasionally encountered in digging, often showed no evidence of intentional burial. These odd pieces of skulls, long bones, etc., nevertheless show interesting features and are described in this part under Miscellaneous Human Skeletal Material. This section also covers description of skeletal material found in a cache (R—3—2) and a doubtful burial (see Remarks under Burial 1).

The larger part of the skeletal remains unfortunately were found in a miserable state, necessitating much repair. Only those from Burial 1 could be described as in "fair" condition. Observations and measurements, when feasible, have been given in the hope that someday there will be sufficient data for a revealing synthesis of Maya skeletal remains.

In the preceding portions of this report the reader will have encountered scattered references to objects from burials. When present, offerings have simply been listed here with their respective illustrations noted. However, detailed listings of burial offerings may be found by turning to the individual figure captions; these additionally provide page references to enable the reader to locate the text descriptions.

THE PIEDRAS NEGRAS BURIALS

BURIAL 1

Location. Structure V—1—1st, sub-floor (for details, see Satterthwaite, 1954, p. 50).

Period. Late Classic, "some time after Structure V—1—1st—B was built, and before abandonment." Evidence is given in detail by Satterthwaite (*ibid.*, pp. 50, 54—55).

Grave. A covered burial chamber, 2 m. long, somewhat irregular in shape (Fig. 63 a). One side wall was corbeled, while the other three were vertical. The chamber was spanned by cover slabs, all of which were in place with the exception of one that had partly fallen. No evidence of a prepared floor was found. NE—SW axis. Details are given by Satterthwaite (*ibid.*, p. 50, Figs. 25, 34).

Age, sex. About 40, female.

Position. Though disturbed, body originally seems to have been extended on side with head approximately to NE. Primary but disturbed.

Furniture. None found.

Skeletal material. Skull has been badly smashed and, on repair, large portions were found to be missing (Fig. 68 a, a'). Endocranial suture closure complete for metopic and sagittal. The coronal suture, represented by bregmatic portion only, is likewise closed. What remains of lambdoid is patent. Mastoids small. Temporal lines distinct but not pronounced. Supraorbital ridges absent. Superior borders of orbits quite sharp. Nuchal lines present but seem weakly developed. Frontal bone transversely rounded with distinct recession giving the whole vault an unnaturally high-domed appearance. Occipital fragments appear flatter than in normal skulls. There is no doubt that the skull was artificially deformed. A small oval perforation is located 15 mm. posterior to bregma along the sagittal suture. It is probably the result of differential weathering rather than a parietal foramen. Conditions preclude most measurements. Approximate maximum length, 175 mm.; minimum frontal, 93 mm.; foramen magnum length, 35 mm.

The maxilla, lacking both posterior portions and associated teeth, retains a right Pm^1 and a right mutilated canine. Lateral incisor crypts are very shallow; those of central incisors are entirely absent with no evidence of breakage along border. Moderate alveolar prognathism. Mandible is missing right ramus, including gonial angle, and, on the left, the condyles. Present are right and left M^1, left Pm's and canine. Molars moderately abraded (dentine exposed on cusps). One lower incisor crypt is absent while remainder are very shallow. All teeth appear to be free of caries but all have tartar deposits. Mental protuberance is slight. Bigoniac diameter approximately 95.6 mm.; mandibular body length 87 mm.

Much of the remaining material was sufficiently intact to allow certain measurements. These were taken according to Hrdlička (1947).

Maximum length	Left	Right
Clavicles	134	133
Radii	225	...
Ulnae	...	224
Femora	386	...
Tibiae	331	...
Fibulae	...	310

Bicondylar length	Left	Right
Femora	383	...
Tibiae	326	...

Stature. 149.96 cm. (Pearson, 1899, Table VIII, F)

Also recovered were fragments of the pelvis, miscellaneous vertebrae, ribs, phalanges, and so forth. Edges of vertebral articular surfaces are lipped. Right acetabulum appears small.

Remarks.   The skeleton was covered by a thick mound of clay-like soil and some stone. The mound's formation, together with masonry data, strongly suggests that it was intentionally deposited and not the result of seepage into the chamber. At some time following interment, the grave appears to have been opened, its contents scattered (see Fig. 63 a), and any grave goods present were removed. The then disturbed burial was covered with soil and the cover slabs replaced. Further details of this situation have been given by Satterthwaite (*ibid*., pp. 50—51).

Human skeletal fragments were discovered below the floor level of Structure V—1—1st and above the cover stones of Burial 1, a vertical space of about 50 cm. (see Satterthwaite, *ibid*., p. 51: "Doubtful Burial"). These fragments have been treated as miscellaneous and are described under Lot 18 (below).

BURIAL 2

Location.   Structure V—1—1st, sub-floor (for details, see Satterthwaite, 1954, p. 51).

Period.   Same as that of Burial 1.

Grave.   A covered burial cist, irregular in shape, 1.75 m. long, with a maximum width of .45 m. (tapered) and a depth of .20 m. (Fig. 63 b). Three sides were formed by a single course of rough stones. The whole was roofed by cover stones. The skeleton rested on a floor of poor quality plaster. NE—SW axis.

Age, sex.   Apparently a child or very young adult. Sex?

Position.   Extended, arms at sides, with head approximately to NE. Primary.

Furniture.   The "richest" of the Structure V—1 burials. But as there are signs here of disturbance, possibly by a rodent, not too much emphasis should be placed on positions of all objects in this burial. Just below a jaw fragment were 17 jadeite beads (8 shown in Fig. 48 g'), 15 shell beads (6 shown in Fig. 52 f'), and 1 shanked shell ornament (Fig. 55 t). In the vicinity of the beads was a perforated countersunk shell disc (Fig. 55 p), and, between the tibiae, another shanked shell ornament similar to the first (NM, not located). A stingray spine (UM) occurred slightly west of the right hand bones together with a tooth of a shark (?) (NM , not located). Other non-skeletal material in this burial included dental inlays, discussed below. See Fig. 63 b, for exact location of all objects. Satterthwaite (*ibid*., pp. 52—53) also gives an inventory of objects.

Skeletal material.   Badly disintegrated. Right teeth and a few bone fragments were recoverable, and, except for one tooth, were sent to Guatemala. A few bones were located (NM) but were too badly shattered for observations. The UM specimen is a permanent incisor notched on both sides, and set with a now loose circular jadeite inlay (Fig. 69 b). In view of its size (D 3 mm; T 1 mm.), the inlay is a remarkable piece of work with its polished, rounded, exposed surface and tapered-to-back edge; the back is flat. Another tooth (NM, not located), probably also an upper incisor, was set with a pyrite disc. This was found in the region of what were the knees, a fact strongly pointing to rodent disturbance. Measurements of the skeleton *in situ* indicate a stature of roughly 145 cm., and a length of one arm, excluding hand bones, of about 40 cm.

BURIAL 3

Location.   Structure V–1–1st, sub-floor (for details, see Satterthwaite, 1954, pp. 53–54).

Period.   Same as Burials 1 and 2.

Grave.   A covered burial cist, "T"-shaped, containing two bodies (Fig. 63 c). The larger portion of the cist was about 1.95 m. long with a maximum width of .37 m. (tapered) and about .10 m. deep, the whole on a NE-SW axis. The smaller portion, set at a right angle and opening into the larger, was probably about .80 m. long and about .25 m. wide.

Age, sex.   Skeleton A (main portion) adult, and Skeleton B a child. Sex and age unknown. Satterthwaite writes: "Since this was a burial of an adult and child one imagines it was of a mother and child " (*ibid.*, p. 53). A small collection of bones exists (NM), but the majority of them are either too broken or non-diagnostic for reasonably accurate age and sex determinations.

Position.   That of the adult is uncertain, but head and thorax probably supine with lower half of body on right side, legs extended. Left arm was at side and also extended. Phalanges, other than those belonging to left hand, were found on both sides. Perhaps disturbed. Right arm, then, either extended along side, or placed across abdomen with hand on or near left elbow. Head to NE. The child lay on its back, arms at sides, its head and shoulders protruding into the main portion of the cist. Head approximately to NW. Lower ends of legs disturbed during excavation but accommodation must originally have been very close. There is no reason to believe that both are not primary burials.

Furniture.   None was found.

Skeletal material.   No worthwhile information. One of the adult's teeth had been set with a jadeite disc (NM, not located).

Remarks.   Despite seepage of dirt, the adult does not seem to have been intentionally covered at time of interment. However, all but the child's head (badly smashed) and shoulders were so covered.

BURIAL 4

Location.   Just under the floor and approximately in the center of the playing alley of the West Group Ball Court, Structure K–6–a and b (see Satterthwaite, 1944 a, p. 36).

Period.   Presumably Late Classic. Problems of structure dating are discussed by Satterthwaite (*ibid.*, pp. 37–38).

Grave.   Evidently a simple grave.

Age, sex.   About 35, male.

Position.   Badly disturbed by tree roots, since disappeared. Head oriented to NW. Primary.

Furniture.   None found.

Skeletal material.   Vault is represented by a few fragments (UM), only a couple of which could be repaired. One piece, centering on bregma, shows a post-coronal transverse depression likely associated with artificial deformation. Sagittal and coronal sutures, insofar as this bregmatic fragment represents them, are respectively almost closed and fully closed endocranially. A fragmentary occiput shows a strongly pronounced nucheal line. Both mastoids are relatively large. Lambdoid is open.

Portions of the mandible were recovered, one fragment containing M^1 and M^2. Also present were 9 M's, 7 Pm's, 3 C's, and 2 I's. All show slight wear and are on the whole larger than most in the Piedras

Negras collection. The two incisors have been mutilated (Fig. 69 d, e).

The grave also yielded shafts of both ulnae and humeri, and fragments of a rib and a phalange.

Remarks. In view of the location of this burial (approximately in center of axis of alley), it might be considered "dedicatory."

BURIAL 5

Location. The Acropolis, below floor of platform-terrace J—5, in front of stairway leading from latter to Structure J—8 (Fig. 65).

Period. Late Classic, possibly around, but probably no earlier than 9.15.0.0.0.

Grave. A large, rectangular tomb, corbel-vaulted on all four sides, with a NE-SW long axis (Fig. 65). Set against one end was a low bench running from wall to wall. A large niche, raised above the floor, occurred in each side wall near this bench. The floor was of earth and small stones on pure rock fill laid against protruding bedrock. If the floor was originally plastered, no satisfactory evidence of it could be found. The structure was in very poor condition on discovery, the whole vault having given. Collapse took place during the occupation of the center for there is good evidence that the resulting deep depression was leveled prior to the ultimate raising of the Structure J—5 platform. However, a depression in the final surface is what led to the discovery of the burial.

Age, sex. A triple burial. Principal interment was that of a male, about 45 years old (Skeleton B), accompanied by Skeleton C, a child (sex?), 9 to 10 years old; and Skeleton A, child (sex?) 7 to 8 years old.

Positions. Skeleton B was fully extended in center of chamber, arms at sides, with head to NE (Fig. 64). Head of Skeleton C was clearly to south and positions of certain incomplete long bones suggest extended, supine interment on a N—S axis, that is, diagonally below feet of Skeleton B. The arrangement of Skeleton A is somewhat doubtful but there are signs that it had been placed at a rough right angle to Skeleton B's abdomen. Dental remains strongly point to its head having rested on the pelvis (left side) of Skeleton B. Primary burials.

Furniture. The most elaborately equipped interment at Piedras Negras. Offerings comprised objects of clay, bone, shell, jadeite, amazonite, flint, and pyrite. For detailed listing, page references and identification as to locations, see Fig. 64. The bulk of this material was found on and about Skeleton B. But a concentration of offerings was discovered directly south of the skull of Skeleton C. The jade beads found on the left pelvis of Skeleton B, mixed as they are with the teeth of a child, may have formed a necklace belonging to Skeleton A or have been placed in its mouth. A jadeite pendant (Fig. 47 e) was found so close to the mouth of Skeleton B as to suggest that it had been placed inside his mouth after death. Many objects had been thinly covered by a red pigment.

Skeletal material. (a) Skeleton B. Though many pieces of the skull were recovered, restoration has proved impossible for one reason or another. The frontal bone, represented by a single fragment, is remarkably flat, pointing to frontal deformation at the least. Supraorbital ridges are laterally absent but present and strong medially. Glabella is prominent. Supraorbital foramina are very pronounced. An occipital fragment indicates complete closure of lambdoid suture. Its surface is very rugged. The sagittal suture, evident in one parietal piece, is also completely closed. Inferior portion of left temporal is large with heavy mastoid process. Exterior surfaces of many cranial fragments are covered with a thin layer, often impregnated, of red pigment.

Maxillae lacking but both halves of mandible were recovered. These are rather large; length of mandibular body approximately 100 mm. The dental border is completely destroyed. Muscle attachments seemingly well developed. 29 teeth were found and show extensive deposits of tartar. The upper central incisors are laterally notched and each set with a single jadeite disc (Fig. 69 a). At least 13 others, including one Pm^2, are tubularly drilled for inlays. The majority were of jadeite; and one medial and one lateral lower incisor contain pyrite inlay. See under Jadeite, (p. 52) and Pyrite (p. 43) for comparative remarks on inlaying.

Vault collapse had so thoroughly smashed the long bones that very little information is obtainable from them. Compared with those of Burial 1 (an adult female), these are large and rugged with heavy muscle attachments. Maximum lenght of left ulna, 258 mm. Other bones of Skeleton B include ribs, vertebrae (lipped edges), pelvis fragments, and many phalangeal and carpal bones. All seem large. Field plans indicate a stature somewhere in the vicinity of 150 cm.

(b) Skeleton C. Skull is irreparably broken and very few pieces were recoverable. Those present (UM) are very smooth surfaced. Sutures, poorly represented, are patent. An almost complete right maxilla, quite prognathic, lacks (postmortem) anterior teeth as far as Pm^2. M's have erupted with the exception of M^3, which is imminent. The palette is small. Although teeth are recent, there is already some slight wear. The mandible lacks the right ramus, left gonial angle and left ramus. Among the recovered loose teeth are shovel-shaped incisors. Left and right $Pm^{1\ \&\ 2}$ have not erupted. Buccal groove on right M^2, with eruption imminent, contains a small but very deep cavity. A deciduous root remains between unerupted Left Pm^1 and Pm^2. Mental protuberance slight. Length of mandibular body about 78 mm. Vertebrae are small with grooved margins. Long bones are too broken for measurements, but observably are small. None of this material evidences the red pigment so common elsewhere in the tomb.

(c) Skeleton A. Badly shattered. No skull fragments found. Skeleton presently consists of a small box of ribs, a few long-bone pieces, a number of very small vertebrae with radially grooved margins, and many unidentifiable fragments. On the whole these are smaller than those of Skeleton C. Found on the left pelvis of Skelton B were 12 mixed permanent and deciduous teeth. These can only belong to Skeleton A. Traces of red pigment noted on a few bone fragments.

Remarks. Two interesting features are present in this burial, namely, red paint and possible child sacrifice. The practice of spreading pigment over a burial is a very wide-spread trait. That the two children were killed and placed in the tomb cannot of course be verified but in this instance it seems likely. More will be said of this and red paint at a later point in this chapter (under Human Sacrifice and Red-Paint Burials).

BURIAL 6

Location. Small natural cave on hillside northeast of Structure O—13 (position marked on site map in Square L).

Period. ?

Grave. Simple. A pocket in the bedrock, possibly artificial, and covered by 25 to 30 cm. of cave earth.

Age, sex. Adult, male (?).

Position. Extended on back, arms at sides, head roughly to east. Primary.

Furniture. Two bone tubes with relief decoration were found about 20 cm. away from the skull and on a line with its nasal portion (tubes described on pp. 61—62). Probably also associated were two brown-ware sherds, one from the soil above the individual's legs, the other on bedrock in a depression near the entrance. Two stalactite fragments appeared; these do not occur naturally in the cave. Also some pieces tentatively identified at the time as armadillo scales, and various animal bones. The tubes are about the only objects that should be definitely assigned to the burial itself. All, however, were destroyed in the camp fire.

Skeletal material. Burned with the exception of certain noted pieces. Field notes mention that the skeleton lacked both right radius and ulna. Saved and now in the UM are a number of teeth and a section of a femoral shaft. Teeth are permanent and show little wear. One molar has a small occlusal cavity while another had been practically hollowed by decay. None are mutilated. A large elongate callus formation, probably the result of healing, appears on the shaft fragment. Sex is based on size of dentition and heavy structure of the bone specimen.

BURIAL 7

Location. Structure R—2, in the South Group, under earlier of two superimposed floors, beside and parallel to the northeasterly side of the lowest pyramid terrace, near northerly corner.

Period.   Considerably post-dates the beginning of building activity in the South Group area.   An early dating is unlikely.

Grave.   Simple, with head enclosed in a small crude cist composed of two lateral upright slabs covered by a single rectangular stone.   Remainder of body unprotected.   NE-SW axis.

Age, sex.   Adult male, about 35 (?).

Position.   Extended.   Head to SW.   Primary.

Furniture.   None.

Skeletal material.   Except for cist-protected skull, incomplete itself, the skeleton (UM) was found to be in very poor condition.   Vault consists of an incomplete right parietal which articulates with a large occipital fragment and the mastoid portion of the right temporal (Fig. 68 e).   Also present are the posterior portion of the right zygomatic and a few irreparable pieces which do not join.   Right lambdoid is open and contains a Wormian bone.   Mastoid is relatively (Burial 1) large.   A very pronounced nuchal line terminates close to this mastoid.   The vault, as now represented, is rugged and almost certainly deformed.   Mandible largely intact, lacking superior portions of both rami and dental border.   Length of mandibular body 93 mm.   Retains only the right Pm^2 and M^1.   These and five loose teeth are moderately worn with cusp pattern obliterated on M's.   Major long bones, none intact, exhibit prominent muscle attachments.   Stature, estimated from field plan, was in the vicinity of 158 cm.

BURIAL 8

Location.   Structure R–3, sub-floor, parallel and close to the wall of the first terrace, in the angle formed by the southeast retaining wall of the main stairway.

Period.   Could have occurred at any time during the period of local building activity.

Grave.   Simple.   NW-SE axis.

Age, sex.   Adult female (?), about 45.

Position.   Extended, supine, arms at side, head to NW.   Primary.

Furniture.   None.

Skeletal material.   A badly crushed frontal was largely repaired and joined with parts of both parietals (Fig. 68 b, b').   Occipital fragment could not be articulated.   Sagittal and coronal sutures fully closed. Nuchal lines and mastoids weakly developed.   The same is true of temporal lines and supraorbital ridges. An orbital fragment shows a sharp border.   Frontal bone is decidedly deformed, and since the remains of the occiput show a fairly vertical profile, deformation was probably fronto-occipital.   A transverse depression of the parietals in the area of the coronal suture is present, as it is in all observably deformed material from Piedras Negras.   Noted is a small endocranial tubercle on the frontal, approximately midway along and slightly to the right of the frontal sulcus, with a corresponding ectocranial depression; it may represent a healed wound.   Maxilla represented by a small piece.   Teeth not in place.   A relatively light mandibular fragment, corresponding to the right ramus and posterior portion of body, has a shallow, almost closed, M^3 crypt, with a considerable gap between it and the next anterior crypt (fracture point).   15 loose teeth were removed from the grave.   Three molars moderately worn; in one cusp pattern erased.   None mutilated. Long bones comprise a fragment from the shaft of each femur.   Also broken shafts from both ulnae, showing very sharp crests.   A few phalanges and the glenoid portion of a scapula complete the burial.

Found within the region of the burial, but not necessarily associated with it, were three animal long bone fragments, as yet unidentified.

BURIAL 9

Location.   Structure R–3, under earlier of two floors, near northeast corner.

Remarks.   Remains of a skull were encountered, but prior to uncovering the skeleton to which it belonged, excavations were halted by an unexpectedly early rainy season.   Remains left in place.   Apparently a simple grave , sub-floor.   It has been designated as Burial 9.

BURIAL 10

Location.   Below plaza floor, in front of Structure U–3, on projection of its axis.

Period.   Late Classic (based on form of plain tripod dish, Niche 2).

Grave.   A tomb type of structure with stepped ends and two niches in each side wall (Fig. 66).
The highest point of the subterranean structure was about 60 cm. below the general plaza surface. The
chamber floor probably was leveled, very soft bed-rock, and was about 2.35 m. below the plaza surface.
No evidence of corbel vaulting; a beam-and-mortar roof is presumed. A large portion of the floor had been
covered to a depth of 30 to 40 cm. with an intentional layer of white disintegrated limestone. Fires had
been built on this fill before it rose to full final height. This white earth also covered the niche floors.

Position.   Human skeletal material was found in Niches 1 and 2 (Fig. 67). In the former case a
few bones were pocketed, presumably by chance, in the debris which filled the niche. Niche 2 contained
however, a tripod dish, broken, behind which, face down, were a human calvarium, a mandible, and a long-
bone fragment; these were intentionally placed, presumably as offerings. Apart from one human molar, no
human remains were discovered on the chamber floor.

Furniture.   Many objects were found scattered in the white earth above the floor. These included
jadeite beads of various sizes, a carved jadeite pendant and perforated ornaments; also unworked shells,
shell beads, bird claws, and in Niche 3 a circular orderly pile of flint chips, a chipped flint implement,
and a flint blank. As mentioned, a tripod dish occurred in Niche 2 and may have originally contained the
human remains found near it. See Fig. 67 for itemized listing of objects and actual positions.

Skeletal remains.   The actual chamber floor yielded nothing more than a permanent human molar
and was probably a carnivore canine. We seem to be dealing with a tomb burial, but its principal occupant
was missing. With regard to the Niche 1 material, it is all very weathered and comprises the mastoid portion of a left temporal , pieces of a long bone, one terminal phalange, and a few other highly eroded, unidentifiable pieces. The material seems heavier than that of Niche 2. The position of the Niche 1 bones
suggests that they were not actually a part of the burial but rather were accidentally included in the debris
that filled the niche.

The Niche 2 cranial vault (Fig. 68 c, c') is small, brachycephalic, and apparently not deformed.
Diploe is exposed. The specimen (very incomplete) clearly was cut across the left parietal roughly to the
juncture of the coronal and assumed position of linea temporalis (arrow, Fig. 68 c'). The edge of the cut
is clean and continuous. Traces of similar cutting occur on the right parietal nearer the auditory meatus
and with a downward slant from back to front (arrow, Fig. 68 c'). In summary, the occipital bone seems to
have been torn off (uncut lambdoidal fragment still present), left parietal was cleanly cut, while inferior
part of right parietal was removed by both sawing and breaking. Operation may have been extended ante-
riorly as far as superior lateral borders of orbits. The base of the specimen was then removed. A fragmentary left   maxilla retains a deciduous M^1 and M^2. Teeth of mandible are present except for both canines
and left incisor. All deciduous with permanent Pm^1 in process of erupting. Length of mandibular body,
about 87 mm. The Niche 2 mutilated material, then, seems to be that of a child, about 8 years of age.
If the size of the first permanent molar is diagnostic, sex could be male.

Remarks.   Burial 10 is exceptionally confusing. It lacked a principal interment apart from a single
unabraded permanent molar. Extreme disintegration is unlikely. The mangled remains of a child, probably
offered in a now broken dish, and the carefully arranged mass of flint chips, the scattered positions of objects found on the floor, and evidence of fire are all features of this most perplexing burial. It is very
likely that the tomb was opened at one time or another and the remains of some important person were ex-
tracted to be reburied elsewhere. Prior to resealing the chamber, a layer of white limestone was spread
over the original floor and a fire of some sort built. If this actually did happen, motivations are indeed obscure. We may, perhaps, compare the white earth deposit with the earth heaped on the floor of Burial 1,
evidently a secondary operation there.

MISCELLANEOUS HUMAN SKELETAL MATERIAL

Isolated and odd small concentrations of human bones often appeared in the Piedras Negras excavations.
Human and animal remains would be found intermixed in test pits. An isolated jaw bone might appear while

clearing a court. And, in one instance, an infant skeleton or parts of it, occurred as a votive offering. Rather than disregard this material because it was recovered in situations not mortuary, it has here been divided into lots, as discovered, and described as fully as possible. The casual contents of many lots suggest a rather minimal "respect for the dead." Scattering may have been due to sacrifice as well as to robbing of graves. Successive building and repair conceivably involved occasional destruction of a sub-floor interment; then, rather than rebury the disturbed individual,the workmen tossed his bones aside or threw them into the structural fill. But these are speculations where evidence is lacking.

LOT 1. From third step or "plinth" in front of wall just beyond south corner of Structure J–2, cranial fragments of two individuals. One exhibits a deformed frontal (Fig. 68 d, d'). Occiput may also be deformed. Breakage occurred along the main sutures. Brachycephalic. A young adult male(?). The second individual is represented by a fragmentary left parietal, the anterior portion of which shows a slight but distinctive transverse concavity paralleling the coronal suture. This seems a feature resulting from frontal compression in deformation. A few broken adult long bones complete the lot.

LOT 2. From surface debris of Structure E–1, southeast side, a mutilated human incisor (Fig. 69 c) with both corners notched (filed) yielding a narrow lobe.

LOT 3. Provenience unknown. Cranial fragments. Only a small portion of these could be repaired, giving much of the occiput together with the posterior portion of both right and left parietals. Lambdoid patent. Also included are a largely complete mastoid process of the right temporal and a fragment of the right orbit and frontal. Apparently not deformed. A brachycephalic young adult or sub-adult female.

LOT 4. From surface debris, Structure J–2, a fragmentary mandible comprising right ramus and body as far as M^1 crypt. Teeth are lacking. Adult male (?).

LOT 5. From base of Structure K–5, upper strata, a fragmentary mandible comprising right ramus and body as far as central incisor crypts. Teeth have been lost. Adult.

LOT 6. From a cave (Survey Point 1869), test pit, 70 cm. below surface, a fragmentary mandible showing left ramus (lacking processes) and body as far as right canine. Large mental tubercle. Lacks teeth. Adult. Also a human phalange and the head of a humerus. Latter is certainly from a young person and does not belong with mandible.

LOT 7. Same locus as Lot 6 but at 80 cm. below surface, five cranial fragments. One, from the occiput, shows complete closure of lambdoid suture. This same piece contains an anomalous suture as well. Male (?), about 50 years. See Lot 8.

LOT 8. From general level of Lot 7, a mandibular fragment containing one right medial incisor and right Pm^1, and a portion of a right maxilla lacking dentition. M^1 crypt of latter fragment is pathological, probably abscessed. Also found were two molars, one of which has been hollowed by an interproximal cavity. Molars show moderate wear. This lot perhaps represents a mature male (?) and might actually belong to individual of Lot 7.

LOT 9. Same locus as Lots 6 through 8, about 65 cm. below surface, a mature left femur, shaft only. Also a distal portion of right humeral shaft, lacking condyles. Deltoid tuberosity very developed. Compared to those of Burial 1 (adult female) these are heavy and probably pertain to an adult male.

LOT 10. Same locus as Lots 6 through 9, surface or first level, a distal portion of a right humeral shaft lacking condylar ends. Also a shaft of a right radius lacking both ends. Radial tuberosity appears well developed. Very similar in construction to those of Lot 9. From an adult, probably male.

LOT 11. Same locus as Lots 6 through 10, 70 cm. below surface, a distal portion of a right humeral shaft lacking condyles. Rugged. Adult, possibly male.

LOT 12. "Surface," a fragment of a mandible containing right Pm^1 and C. Tartar on both. Former shows a small cervical cavity. Not mutilated.

LOT 13. From test pit between Structures R—11 and O—12, level 3, an almost complete frontal bone with parts of both orbits adhering. Possibly deformed. Supraorbital ridges and temporal lines are prominent. Minium frontal diameter 96.5 mm. Adult, male.

LOT 14. Same as Lot 13, a radius lacking both ends. Adult.

LOT 15. From base of Structure P—6, an occiput with part of left parietal. Bone is heavy. Nuchal attachments moderate. Probably a young adult male.

LOT 16. From Cache R—3—2, Structure R—3—4th (9.0.0.0.0??), vault fragments, portion of orbit, mental portion of mandible, a few long bones (humerus and femur), and rib fragments of an infant, 18 months to 2 years old. Teeth all deciduous, with milk canines in process of erupting. Other bones probably disintegrated. One wonders whether these bones represent all that were deposited. It would have been a seemingly tight fit to place an unmutilated infant of this estimated age between the lip-to-lip vessels (see Fig. 60 b) that contained it. In fact, it is doubtful that the infant could have been placed between them so that the rims met. If the infant was deposited whole (and not redeposited after decomposition), the bowl rims must have been separated; but, in time, they settled.

LOT 17. From concrete of floor of Structure R—3—3rd (9.2.0.0.0??), cranial fragments. Repair produced two incomplete parietals and an occiput. Present are mastoid processes; medium development. Frontal deformation indicated by slight trans-coronal concavity. The majority of these pieces are externally impregnated with some red substance strongly suggesting that they stem from an anciently disturbed burial. Adult, possibly male.

LOT 18. Structure V—1—1st, sub-floor and above cover stones of Burial 1. Lot mentioned in Satterthwaite, 1954, p. 51 as a "Doubtful Burial." Lot comprises the skeletal fragments of a possible secondary burial. The lot is surely later than the burial over which it lay, provided that Burial 1 was disturbed. The lot, on excavation, was rather scattered. A single fragment, centering on bregma, is all that remains of the vault. It features a transverse coronal depression (artificial deformation). No teeth were encountered, although a small gonial fragment was found. Also the mastoid portion of a left temporal. Long bones are represented by a fragment of a femoral shaft (rugged with prominent linea aspera) and a bit of a right humerus. Finally, a fragment of a scapula, a few phalanges, and vertebrae. Adult, probably male. In the immediate debris were the badly broken remains of four problematic clay ornaments (UM, two shown in Fig. 58 h, i), identical to those in the presumably earlier Burial 5.

LOT 19. From rock fill of floor section beneath lowest rounded stone of southern corner of Structure R—3, a femur lacking distal half. Its situation was such as to suggest that it was ceremonially interred. If so, one might consider it almost as a cache. Present location unknown but probably destroyed in camp fire.

LOT 20. From Structure O—7—1st—Cist Period, from earth removed from Cist 1 or 2, or from space between them, a moderate worn adult permanent molar and 3 fragments of burned human bone. Material evidently cremated. Situation described by Satterthwaite (1954, Structure O—7) and below (under Cremation).

LOT 21. From Structure J—5, among fallen stones of terrace wall, a section of a left adult femur, representing a quarter of the shaft, lesser trochanter, but lacking neck and head. Shaft has been cut medially to laterally a little more than half way through, then broken cleanly off (arrow, Fig. 57 a). See discussion, "Cut Human Long Bones," p. 67.

LOT 22. From lowest level of test pit, Court 1, Structure J—2, a mandibular fragment, right, composed of part of ramus and body as far as Pm^2. No teeth remain but loss was post-mortem as no crypt closure is evident. Possibly female. Also a broken, mature vertebral body.

GENERAL COMMENT AND COMPARISON OF BURIAL DATA

DATING

The question of relative dating for the most part either remains to be solved via ceramic studies or allows no orthodox solution. Burial 5 is Late Classic, surely no earlier than the presumably contemporaneous date of around 9.15.0.0.0 indicated on the four associated shell plaques (Fig. 53 a—d). Burial 10 is also Late Classic, but on the basis of an offered bowl. And Burials 1, 2, and 3, of Structure V—1—1st—A, cannot be earlier that the Late Classic sherds in the structure's fill. This structure and its burials are at the end of a considerable architectural sequence involving change in design if not function. The burials may be the latest of our whole series. Presence of rare and identical cuff-like ornaments (Fig. 58 f—i) in Burial 5 and above Burial 1 (see Lot 18) argues for placing the Structure V—1—1st—A burials late in the Late Classic at least. We have no real basis for dating Burials 4, 6, 7, 8, and 9.

FREQUENCY

Possibly the most outstanding feature of these burials is their *apparent* rarity. At Uaxactun, 116 burials were encountered (A. L. Smith, 1950, Ch. 7), 72 appeared at the relatively small site of San Jose (Thompson, 1939, Ch. VII), and many were recovered at Copan (Longyear, 1952, Ch. 3), to say nothing of their seeming frequency in highland sites.

But has our sampling which has resulted in only ten burials really been adequate? According to Satterthwaite (verbal information), several temple buildings were investigated on the axes with negative results: Structures O—13—1st, O—13—2nd, R—3—1st, 2nd, and 3rd, K—5—1st and 2nd, J—3 (final period) and J—4—1st. But three depressions were investigated which produced Burials 1, 5, and 10. Very little work was done below floors in palace structures. Loose fill and lack of personnel prevented extensive deep exploration. One suspects that had palaces and domiciliary structures been investigated for sub-floor conditions, the total of recovered burials might have been very much greater.

LOCATIONS

All but Burial 6 (a cave interment) were associated either with buildings or with courts and plazas. Three of the 10 burials (Burial 1, 2, and 3) occurred in the only investigated dwelling, Structure V—1. Three others (Burial 7, 8, and 9) were associated with temples. Burial 4 was beneath a ball court playing alley. Burials 5 and 10, as noted, were before a palace and a temple.

POSITIONS OF BODIES

Most bodies were placed in the graves in an extended position, supine, with arms at sides. The female in Burial 1 was evidently extended on her side. Orientation was not standard to cardinal points, but related to structural features. Burial 6 was necessarily on the long "axis" of the narrow cave; it could not have been extended otherwise.

OFFERINGS

Offerings accompanied Burials 2, 5, 6, and 10. Only in Burial 5 were there many elaborate offerings and personal ornaments. However, various fine objects may have been removed from Burial 10. Burial 1 also gives evidence of having been entered and it too may have been robbed (see below, Ancient Deliberate Disturbance of Burials). These three burials had the three most elaborate grave structures, in descending order. There were a modest number of personal ornaments in cist Burial 2, a still less elaborate grave structure. Two carved bone tubes accompanied Burial 6, a cave interment. No offerings accompanied the "simple" Burials 4, 7, 8, and, so far as we know, there were none with Burial 9. There is a suggestion, then, of a correlation between provision of offerings and personal ornaments and protective grave structures, particularly if we consider the cave, in Burial 6, a natural "tomb."

FEATURES OF TOMBS

Noteworthy are the niches, some containing offerings, in Burials 5 and 10. Niches are not a tomb feature at either Uaxactun, Kaminaljuyu, or Nebaj, but they seem to be relatively common among the Copan tombs (Longyear, 1952, p. 47, Figs. 8–12); also at Guaytan (A. L. Smith and Kidder, 1943, p. 130) and Palenque (Blom and LaFarge, 1926, v. 1, Fig. 145), as well as at Monte Alban (e. g., Caso, 1938, Tomb 104). Price (1897–99, p. 34) reports a wall niche in a Kendal tomb. Except for debris, most niches appear to have been empty. Longyear (*op. cit.*, p. 47) suggests that empty ones may have "contained, at the time of interment, some perishable material like incense." Vaulted burial structures (e. g., Burial 5) have a wide highland and lowland distribution (see A. L. Smith and Kidder, 1951, pp. 27–28). Simple benches, as in Burial 5, have been noted previously at Uaxactun and Guaytan (A. L. Smith, 1950, Fig. 121; A. L. Smith and Kidder, 1943). The steps at either end of Burial 10, apparently not functional, are probably a local invention.

HUMAN SACRIFICE

At Piedras Negras the excavated evidence for human sacrifice is none too secure. Burial 5, a multiple interment involving a principal and two possibly sacrificed children, is suggestive. A mutilated human skull in Burial 10 might also point to sacrifice. Cache R–3–2 contained the remains of an infant. And the material in Lot 19 may indicate sacrifice. The few cut human long bones from the site are also suggestive.

The best evidence of human sacrifice at Piedras Negras is to be found on Stela 11, which in part portrays a person bowed and on his back in death with his chest split open. This scene strongly recalls various depictions of sacrifice in Post-Classic Toltec Period art. But, in the Piedras Negras case, one sees, rising from the wound, a closed lily (?) and other elements possibly floral. Bound prisoners are to be found on other local sculptures. Decapitation was surely a part of Late Classic ceremony in the general region, as evidenced by the Bonampak murals. And at Bonampak there are also suggestions of heart extraction (see Ruppert, Thompson, and Proskouriakoff, 1955, p. 56).

Elsewhere in the Maya area, archaeological indications of human sacrifice do occur, but nonetheless are rather infrequent. Decapitation is to be detected in interments of skulls and in headless burials. It is often difficult to determine whether the skulls were the result of sacrificial severance (presence of atlas is diagnostic) or were reburied alone after having been removed from earlier burials. We are primarily interested here should the head be shown to have been primary. The discovery of an isolated skull with indications of decapitation brings up the possibility of its having been a temporary trophy which was carried, exhibited, and then buried.

Burials lacking heads have been encountered at Zacualpa, Balam Phase (Wauchope, 1948, p. 24); Uaxactun, Tzacol Phase (A. L. Smith, 1950, pp. 90, 91); Baking Pot (Ricketson, 1929, p. 10); and at Tayasal (Guthe, 1922, p. 318). Heads alone have occurred at Kaminaljuyu, Esperanza Phase (Kidder, Jennings, and Shook, 1946, p. 90); Nebaj, Early Classic (A. L. Smith and Kidder, 1953, pp. 27–29); Zacualpa, Balam Phase (Wauchope, *op. cit.*, p. 90); Zaculeu, Chinaq Phase (Woodbury and Trik, 1953, pp. 80–81); Uaxactun, Tzacol Phase (A. L. Smith, *op. cit.*); San Jose, Period III (Thompson, 1939, Burials A 5, A 6, and A 8); also in a mound near Rio Hondo headwaters (Gann, 1918, p. 87), at Santa Rita (*ibid.*, p. 78), and at Chichen Itza (Acosta, 1955, pp. 34, 38–39). Chukumuk (Period II) produced a multiple burial in which bodies were grouped apart from a mound of related skulls (Lothrop, 1933, pp. 24–26). The trait of skull burial intermittently continues as far as Sinaloa and southern Durango in Mesoamerica (Lister, 1955).

Sacrifice, without dismemberment, is presumed in those compound burials which have not resulted from successive interments and where one finds evidence of a ranking person and peripheral skeletons of lesser circumstances. These circumstances imply social stratification and include such factors as sex and age and the absence of associated grave goods. The ways in which victims were killed prior to burial are naturally speculative. Heart extraction is one possibility and, of course, may have preceded decapitation as well.

The inclusion in an important burial of one or more victims has been cited for the following sites: Kaminaljuyu, in both Miraflores and Esperanza Phases (Shook and Kidder, 1952, p. 64; Kidder, Jennings, and Shook, 1946, pp. 89–90); Nebaj, Early and Post-Classic Periods (A. L. Smith and Kidder, 1951, p. 28); and Zaculeu, Atzan and Xinabahul Phases (Woodbury and Trik, 1953, pp. 80–81). The trait, then, evidently was of long duration and primarily confined to the highland area, one exception being, of course, Piedras Negras. A variant is to be seen at San Jose, where a large proportion of burials were of children or infants (majority San Jose IV or V) which might suggest sacrifice, in some cases "dedicatory" (Thompson, 1939, pp. 219–20). Five to six individuals were found jammed before the famed Palenque crypt and these again suggest sacrifice (Ruz, 1955, pp. 84–86). Sure signs of immolation have yet to be found at Copan, Guaytan, Uaxactun, as well as the Mountain Cow sites. Compound burials, to be sure, occur, but evidently these were produced by successive additions of important individuals.

To my mind, these cases illustrate a sacrificial complex that formed part of Classic Period Maya ritual and, as such, involved traits like decapitation and immolation of adults as well as children. Decapitation was practiced in both lowlands and highlands, while the latter area saw a disproportionate emphasis on the burial of subordinates. It is impossible to assess to what extent heart extraction, hurling from high places, "arrow-sacrifice," etc. entered into these traits. Continued work on Pre-Classic remains may produce evidence of more sources and variations of human sacrifice, a feature probably present by the Miraflores Phase. A South American origin remains a possibility (see Lothrop, 1952, pp. 52–53; Kidder II, 1940, pp. 447–48), but further work, as noted, and further data and refinements in cross-dating might show the general trait to have been in Formative times common to both the Central Andes and Mesoamerica.

Mutilated human skulls, as in Burial 10, have appeared at Baking Pot (Ricketson, 1929, Pl. 15 c, e) and in a Uaxactun Chicanel burial (Ricketson and Ricketson, 1937, pp. 145–46). The latter example had been cut vertically through bregma and the facial portion removed, an operation quite different from that carried out on the Burial 10 specimen. That from Baking Pot was in the form of a cup, the calvarium having been cut circumferentially and flattened. Kidder (in Kidder, Jennings, and Shook, 1946, p. 154–55) provides excellent information on worked human bones in Mesoamerica.

CREMATION

Lot 20, originally comprising a burned human bone and a molar tooth, has been cited as evidence for local cremation. Satterthwaite (1954, pp. 29, 35) assigns this deposit along with related constructional features to a post-abandonment period (Structure O–7–1st–Cist Period). He writes: "We may conclude with considerable assurance that the Cist Period was a post-Classical one and, less surely, that it was a pre-Lacandon one. A single small burial mound does not amount to a reoccupation of the site, but it does tend to substantiate the view that the region was not depopulated at the end of the Classical or "Old Empire period." Other contiguous cists may have similarly served as repositories for cremated remains (*ibid.*, p. 26). It is also worth noting that cremation is here known from incompletely burned remains rather than ash.

As Wauchope has indicated (1945; 1948, pp. 32, 35–36, 86–87), cremations, when detected, have a late incidence throughout Mesoamerica. At Zacualpa, for instance, they occur in Yaqui context, this being a late post-Tohil plumbate period (*ibid.*); but at Zaculeu this custom existed at the end of the Qankyak Phase as well as in a phase equivalent to Yaqui (Woodbury and Trik, 1953, pp. 76—77). From the point of view of Piedras Negras it may be significant that Qankyak cremations involved incomplete burning while those of the terminal Xinabahul Phase resulted in a fine ash.

Elsewhere in the Maya area, human cremation has been noted at Post-Classic Mayapan (e. g., D. E. Thompson and J. E. S. Thompson, 1955, pp. 235—236), thus corroborating, at least in part, Landa's remarks (Tozzer, 1941, p. 278; see also Wauchope, 1945, p. 569). Other occurrences, the majority of which are evidently late, have been assembled by Wauchope, (1947, pp. 86—87). Noteworthy is his belief (*ibid.*, pp. 35—36) that ash, associated with Holmul V pottery at Hatzcap Ceel, originally thought by J. E. S. Thompson to be human, is likely of a sacrificially cremated bird.

The value of Lot 20 lies in the fact that it evidences what would seem to have been a Post-Classic and possibly highland intrusion that emphasized human cremation and the construction of mortuary features without Classic precedent.

ANCIENT DELIBERATE DISTURBANCE OF BURIALS

Both Burials 1 and 10 appear to have been re-entered for some purpose or other. In the first case, skeletal remains were disturbed, objects may have been stolen, earth was piled over what remained, and a burial (Lot 18) was made above the replaced cover slabs. More mysterious was Burial 10, which was broken into, its principal occupant presumably removed, grave furnishings scattered, white earth spread over the floor proper and in the niches, and a fire built within the actual tomb. We also suspect, as noted, that much of the "miscellaneous skeletal material" derives from aboriginally disturbed burials but whether or not disturbance was anything more than incidental to construction is impossible to say.

Robbery, vandalism, and cupidity come to mind when one is confronted with the odd happenings in Burials 1 and 10. There is every indication that disturbance was ancient and that it most likely took place in the Late Classic Period. Thompson (1942, pp. 27—28) recorded what appeared to be a purposely robbed burial at Benque Viejo. Tomb looting has been recognized at Mayapan (e. g., D. E. Thompson and J. E. S. Thompson, 1955, pp. 228—29). However, it is clear that deliberate looting in ancient times was, by-and-large, a rare lowland feature. Good evidence of accidental disturbance of earlier burials and removal of certain grave goods was encountered at Kaminaljuyu (Esperanza Phase) and Nebaj (Shook and Kidder, 1952, p. 121); and at Guaytan, tombs were successively reopened for inclusion of new corpses. But the trait of intentional re-entry for purposes of looting is best represented by the two magnificent Pre-Classic tombs encountered in Mound E—III—3, Kaminaljuyu (*ibid.*, pp. 121—22).

Disturbance of burials among the Maya was both accidental and, in certain cases, intentional. Deliberate re-entry, with its implication of memory or a record of burial position and perhaps contents, resulted in object looting and scattering, inclusion of a new corpse or removal of a corpse or skeleton, the spreading of earth and the building of fires (mollification?). Accidental re-entry, as far as our evidence goes, resulted in disturbance of remains and looting, but these acts were naturally after the fact of incidental re-entry during constructional activity. As Kidder has indicated (*ibid.*), this factor of ancient intentional grave robbing may not be too significant. It, nevertheless, does imply not only recollection of position and presumably contents but also that burials were not necessarily considered sacrosanct by the priests or by those in control.

OBJECT IN MOUTH OF DECEASED

Position would indicate that a finely carved jadeite pendant (Fig. 47 e) was placed in the mouth of Skeleton B, Burial 5. This practice was current in sixteenth century Yucatan and the Valley of Mexico, according to Landa, Sahagun, and Torquemada (Tozzer, 1941, p. 130; A. L. Smith, 1950, Fig. 117 a), but, in spite of these references, the trait appears very infrequently in Maya archaeology.

Two good instances, both with children, appeared at Uaxactun; one was dated as Post-Classic (A. L. Smith, *ibid.*, p. 90). Kaminaljuyu, Esperanza Phase, yielded four good to probable cases; the individuals were aged and male in two instances, middle aged male (?), and a young adult female (Kidder, Jennings, and Shook, 1946, pp. 92—93). Gann and Gann (1939, p. 5) recorded a probable example at Nohmul, which involved an exceptionally tall young adult male. Another instance is the famed one described by Blom (Blom, Grosjean, and Cummings, 1934) that was found in the Ulua region of Honduras. Ruz (1955, p. 100, no. 8) makes note that the personage in the Temple of Inscriptions tomb contained "inside the mouth" a jade bead; judged to be male, *in situ* measurements indicated a stature of about 173 cm. (Dávalos and Romero, in Ruz, *ibid.*, p. 110). There is one possible instance at Zaculeu (Woodbury and Trik, 1953, Fig. 44).

While no implication of a correlation between exceptional stature and this trait is intended, there is perhaps some suggestion of it at Palenque and Nohmul. In all cases here (the list is very likely incomplete) jade beads are present. Why this trait should appear so sporadically is a mystery. A great many Maya burials, in both lowlands and highlands, are known at present; the percentage of burials in which an object was placed in the mouth must be very small indeed.

RED PAINT BURIALS

Another noteworthy feature among the Piedras Negras burials was the occasional appearance of a brilliant red pigment (probably powdered hematite). In Burial 5 this was found adhering to the bones of Skeleton B as well as Skeleton A and furthermore covered many objects around these individuals. The material described under Lot 17 was also superficially impregnated with a red substance of some sort; its provenience is probably fairly early. That certain of the Maya painted themselves in this color is amply evident from the Bonampak murals. Maler (1901, pp. 58, 62, 63, etc.) observed that a number of Piedras Negras stelae had been polychromed and that traces of red were still to be seen on the naked areas of depicted individuals.

Obviously, "red-paint burials" involve a number of variables (see Peabody, 1927); pigmentation in primary burials might result from skin painting or from spreading a substance like cinnabar over the corpse. The ultimate effect is a red "painted" skeleton. As will be seen, this pigmentation occurs in other contexts, as in the painting of severed portions of the body, the painting of restricted areas of the body, the painting of the actual grave structure, the painting of interred animal remains, and the inclusion of lumps of coloring matter in a burial.

The Mesoamerican distributions of these traits are erratic, despite their breadth and time depth. For instance, among well known Maya sites, mortuary pigmentation has not been noted at Nebaj, Zacualpa, Zaculeu, the Mountain Cow sites, Baking Pot, and San Jose. Traces of red paint were noted in two Holmul burials (Merwin and Vaillant, 1932, p. 30) and rarely in Nohmul and Santa Rita interments (Gann and Gann, 1939, pp. 10, 20). Three such burials were found at Uaxactun, all Early Classic, all male, and from chamber tombs (A. L. Smith, 1950, p. 89); also a red-painted puma skull had been cached (*ibid.*, Table 8). Three tombs at Guaytan contained red-painted floors, and even benches, while a number of skeletal fragments in two of these tombs were pigmented; a skull found in a stone crypt "had traces of red paint" (A. L. Smith and Kidder, 1943, pp. 124—28). Blom states that the Comalcalco tomb had a floor of "highly polished red cement" (Blom and LaFarge, 1926, v. 1, p. 116). Still further, many of the shell ornaments and bone fragments had been covered with a red substance (*ibid.*). The richly ornamented person placed in the Palenque crypt showed signs of having been "wrapped in a red-painted shroud" (Ruz, 1955, p. 98). The principal occupant of the Miraflores Phase Tomb II, Structure E—111—3, Kaminaljuyu, had been "painted with brilliant red from head to toe, then elaborately clothed or wrapped..." (Shook and Kidder, 1953, p. 64). Esperanza Phase burials occasionally yielded signs of red paint: for instance, a red painted floor, red paint in surrounding fill, painted stingray spines, and a "*Spondylus* shell containing a jade head packed in cinnabar" (Kidder, Jennings, and Shook, 1946, pp. 48, 56, 70, 74). Strömsvik (1950, p. 28) records for Asuncion

Mita "Varios pedazos de cráneo humano, pintados de rojo y grabados." A jaguar skeleton, painted red, was found at Copan (Maudsley, 1889– 1902, text, p. 20). Both Piña (1948, pp. 7, 11) and Moedano (1946) agree on the frequency of red-painted burials on the island of Jaina.

Elsewhere in Mesoamerica, powdered hematite was discovered in Gualupita Burials 2, 9, and 11, although it was not encountered on the respective skeletons (Vaillant and Vaillant, 1934); two of these burials are likely of Gualupita I date (*ibid.*, p. 111). At El Arbolillo, Vaillant (1935, p. 183) recorded four cases of red-painted skeletons, all late Arbolillo I, and four others in which chunks of pigment were found, all Arbolillo II. Ticoman evidently produced cinnabar in burials (*ibid.*, p. 112), although I cannot locate an original reference. At Guasave, Ekholm (1942, p. 43) discovered two trophy skulls "coated with red ochre" in one burial and a third from another; other examples are on record for Western Mexico (see Lister, 1955, Table 193). La Venta yielded bundle burials, the skeletons of which were "coated with red cinnabar (?);" also a thick layer of cinnabar was found within a grave or cache (Drucker, 1952, pp. 23, 72–73, Fig. 23). Interments with red paint also appeared at Cerro de las Mesas (Drucker, 1943 a, Table 2). The only cases of painted interments that I have been able to find from the Huasteca are two from Las Flores (Period V) described by Faulhaber (1948, pp. 80, 88). Cases have appeared among the Chupicuaro burials; in one, various colors had been used to form a design on the grave floor (Estrada, 1949, p. 81). Finally, Moedano (1946, p. 233) mentions that red-paint burials have been discovered at both Tlatilco and Tula, and, that in Aztec III-IV times, blue pigment was so employed.

Gualupita, El Arbolillo, Ticoman, Tlatilco, Kaminaljuyu, and possibly La Venta attest to an early Mesoamerican association of death and redness; in this connection see Piña, 1955, p. 68. Red was applied postmortem to skin, clothing or wrapping, to grave surfaces, and even to ceremonially offered animals. Piedras Negras obviously was drawing on a long established, yet still sporadic trait.

Of course, red paint burials in the New World are hardly an exclusive Mesoamerican trait. In North America, they have been frequently found, particularly in Eastern archaeology (see Griffin, 1952, pp. 87, 91, 112, 229, 248, 263, 267; Peabody, 1927). Ford and Willey (1941, p. 332) have commented on the frequency of "bodies covered with red ochre" in Eastern Archaic interments and Orr (1946, p. 236) notes the presence of both green and red pigments in Spiro Mound burials.

They are to be found in South America as well. Random examples include a burial from the 3rd Period of Bird's Magellan sequence (Bird, 1938, Fig. 29) which had been smeared with ochre. The trait is well represented in burials of the Peruvian North Coast. Many of the Cupisnique interments were covered with a red pigment that was often restricted to the upper portion of the body (Larco, 1941; 1945, pp. 19, 24). Small pottery vessels containing red clays were encountered around bodies in Salinar burials (Larco, 1944, p. 19). And a number of quite early Viru Valley graves display partial smearing of bodies with red pigment (Strong and Evans, 1952, pp. 53, 57, 149, 152).

Despite its distribution in time and space for Mesoamerica, the comparative incidence of this practice is generally so slight that one hesitates to designate the area as focal. It is to be seen in early contexts in both North and South America. Viewed without regard to variations, "red paint burials," as such, might well be considered a Formative interconnective, on a level with certain early wide-spread traits assembled by Porter (1953). The possibility of an Old World origin ought not to be neglected. And the tracing throughout the Americas of certain obvious variations might prove rewarding.

One suspects that redness in death had a sympathetic value but one that could not always be expressed, due perhaps to the scarcity of appropriate pigments. With specific regard to the Maya, this feature and its variations seem to appear in burials that in other ways evidence richness and social importance. During Classic and even earlier times the use of red pigments in interments, and not unlikely in life as well, was possibly limited to individuals high in local social position. In death, it was surely an extravagant symbolic expression. An analysis of the Jaina graves (see Piña, 1948) reveals that, out of the 76 burials unearthed, 18 were painted, of which two were children, four adult females, and the remainder adult males. Three of the females were accompanied by objects of value indicative of importance; for instance, jadeite earplugs and the like. While there are suggestions of class prerogatives here one cannot forget the Copan jaguar and the Uaxactun puma, both painted red. The puzzlement of Mesoamerican red paint burials might well reflect many somewhat distinct provincial incentives. The factor of supply certainly had considerable bearing but probably does not wholly explain the absence of this obvious trait at so many clearly important Maya sites, both highland and lowland.

DENTAL FILING AND INLAYING

Another cultural peculiarity to be seen among human remains in the Piedras Negras burials is dental alteration, involving filing and inlaying and, occasionally, a combination of both. Modification of teeth appeared in Burial 2 (sex?), 3 (Sk. A, female?), 4 (male), 5 (Sk. B, male), as well as in Lot 2. Filing was confined to incisors and appears as single and bilateral corner notching with complementary pairing of the former to yield a "T"-shaped pattern associated with the Sun God. Filing may also be combined with incrustation (Fig. 69 a, b), the Piedras Negras examples being tiny convex-surfaced discs of jadeite and thin, flat, pyrite discs set in tubularly drilled depressions and secured by some form of cement. As noted before, Skeleton B, Burial 5, offers a remarkable example of dental decoration and is very likely unique in containing inlays through the second pre-molars, a total of 15 inlays (Fig. 69 a).

The customs of dental inlaying and filing were very widespread in the New World but their greatest concentration was in Mesoamerica (see Fastlicht and Romero, 1951). A number of Pre-Classic peoples (at El Arbolillo, Tlatilco, and Monte Negro) practiced either inlaying or filing or combined the two. However, the Maya do not seem to have known these practices until Early Classic times (Longyear, 1952, pp. 49–52). One case of enamel-removal is known from the Uaxactun Early Pre-Classic (Mamom) (Ricketson and Ricketson, 1937, p. 143), but I can find no source to show the practice of inlaying at that time, depite a reference to it (see Fastlicht and Romero, op. cit., p. 52). At Uaxactun, pyrite inlays first occur in the Early Classic and continue into the Late Classic, at which time jadeite inlays make their appearance (A. L. Smith, 1950, Ch. 7). Filed patterns include those represented at Piedras Negras. A study of adhesive materials has been made by Fastlicht (1951).

CRANIAL DEFORMATION

In describing the Piedras Negras skeletal material, mention was frequently made of weak to strong signs of intentional deformation of crania. While much of the material is badly shattered and incomplete, enough often remains to show that the frontal portions had been artificially compressed to give the forehead an unnatural but thoroughly Maya slope. There is little to no evidence either way for occipital and lambdoid flattening here. The principal diagnostic of local deformation is a transverse groove along the coronal suture, or close to it, suggestive of binding with a pad. Whether this was sufficient to produce the exceptionally flat, oblique frontal seen in Burial 8 and even in Burial 5, Skeleton B, is questionable. The application of a board in these instances is not improbable. But it must be emphasized that, although deformation of heads was practiced at Piedras Negras, the matter of how it was effected remains problematical.

Cranial deformities, like dental mutilations, have an extraordinary New World distribution (Neumann, 1941; Stewart, 1937; Davalos, 1946; Newman, 1947). Interest in ordering and typology, particularly for Mesoamerica, has only recently appeared, yet descriptive problems alone are deterrant to much general archaeological interest.

On the basis of Stewart's studies (1949; in Woodbury and Trik, 1953, pp. 296–97), two basic types of deformities are recognizable among Maya material, pseudo-circular and fronto-vertico-occipital, the latter occasionally paired with lambdoid flattening. The first involves a "flattened or transversely grooved frontal ... [which] sometimes is combined with a laterally and symmetrically compressed occiput." The use of a band is postulated. The second type is more extreme, for the occiput is flat and vertical, there is a flattened frontal, and compression results in lateral growth to the point where breadth exceeds length. But this terminology is very much confused when one encounters in archaeological reports references to the presence of "fronto-occipital deformation." Both types, recognized by Stewart, involve, of course, frontal and occipital alteration, though disproportionately. One suspects that much "fronto-occipital" flattening belongs to the pseudo-circular category, and somewhat hesitantly one might say that all Piedras Negras examples are of this same type.

The importance of identification lies in Stewart's conclusion as to the chronological value of deformation and its types, for there is evidence that the pseudo-circular type had a Classic incidence among the Maya with a general shift to fronto-vertico-occipital flattening during Post-Classic times (Stewart, *op. cit.*). The Zaculeu sequence of skeletal material is an important demonstration of these emphases. This aspect of culture change applies to a certain degree to Central Mexico as well. Elsewhere, Kroeber (1930, p. 71) has pointed to important differences in type frequencies for the Peruvian North Coast and to the bearing they might have on relative chronology; and Newman's study of Peruvian Central Coast deformities (1947, pp. 9—11) shows the reality of type changes and their chronological significance, although it is often difficult to appreciate these, due to the complex descriptive terms that reflect an equally complex variation of deformity. The trait of head deformation is treated by Porter (1953) as an important Pre-Classic (Tlatilco—Chavin connective.

Returning to the Maya, with whom we are primarily concerned here, it is hoped that the following distributional outline will serve as a context for appreciating the existence of the trait at Piedras Negras.

A. L. Smith (1950, p. 89, Table 6) has remarked on the prevalence of "fronto-occipital" deformation at Uaxactun, a type already current in Early Developmental (Mamom) times. Among the 20 examples in a condition to be observed, 18 were deformed, of which 10 were judged to be male, 5 female, and the remainder indeterminable; all were adult except for 3 children. Baking Pot produced much evidence of this practice. Here, interestingly enough, 5 of the 6 deformed crania, out of a total of 10, were sexed as female, while the 4 normal specimens were male (Ricketson, 1929). Thompson (1931, pp. 293, 321) reports two cases of "fronto-occipital" deformation in the Mountain Cow region of the Colony, and Hambly (1937) describes a number of occipitally flattened examples from San Jose, but pronounced frontal deformities failed to appear. Two skulls found near Nohmul and studied by A. J. E. Cave (in Gann and Gann, 1939, pp. 59—60) are evidently extreme examples of occipital flattening in which cephalic indices considerably exceed 100. Presumably these belong to Stewart's fronto-vertico-occipital type. Others from northern British Honduras include two recovered from near Santa Rita; in one, dimensions suggest deformation, while the other is excessively flat in both occipital and lambdoid regions (Gann, 1918, pp. 75, 78, Pl. 13, c). A frontally and occipitally altered cranium from Progreso, Yucatan is shown by Boas (1890). Other examples from Yucatan are to be seen in the Merida Museum; a number have been illustrated (Blom, Grosjean, and Cummins, 1934, Fig. 2; Rosado, 1945). Another specimen with a "remarkably flat and vertical" occiput was excavated by Stephens from a mound near Ticul (1843, v. 1, p. 281). One of the most thoroughly studied series is that from the Cenote of Sacrifice, Chichen Itza (Hooton, 1940). Of the 39 sufficiently intact for study, 35 were deformed frontally and/or occipitally. Of the 76 individuals all seemingly Late Classic, unearthed at Jaina (Piña, 1946), only 6 are noted as showing frontal and occipital deformation in one degree or another; all are adult and male except for two indeterminable cases. In contrast, there were 15 instances in which deformities are stated to have been absent; apart from a child and an adolescent individual, these are all adult, and, in a majority of cases, male as well (Piña, *ibid.*; also Moedano, 1946, p. 242, Fig. 10).

A Copan specimen has been typed by Stewart (in Dutton and Hobbs, 1943, App. 1) as "pseudo-circular," while Longyear (1940, pp. 151—52) notes in another specimen a "certain amount of lambdoid compression, but little or no frontal deformation ..." A well studied skull from the Ulua region "suggests fronto-occipital compression" (Blom, Grosjean, and Cummins, 1934, p. 19). References to skeletal evidence for deformation at Palenque are seemingly lacking, but the bas reliefs there surely attest to the practice. Chiapas has been most productive (*ibid.*; Davalos, 1946, lam. 87; Blom, 1954).

Eight cases of "fronto-occipital" compression were noted at Guaytan (A. L. Smith and Kidder, 1943); subsequently, Stewart (1949, p. 26) noted the pseudo-circular type among this material. Stewart (in A. L.

Smith and Kidder, 1951, App. B) distinguishes a number of distinct types of deformity in the skeletal material of Nebaj. Pseudo-circular deformation seems to have been particularly emphasized at Tajumulco (Stewart, in Dutton and Hobbs, 1943, App. 1; also Stewart, 1949, pp. 25–26). Mention has already been made of the Zaculeu sequence of types, pseudo-circular (Classic) replaced by fronto-vertico-occipital (Post-Classic) (Stewart, in Woodbury and Trik, 1953, p. 296). Frontal compression was favored during the Esperanza Phase of Kaminaljuyu (Stewart, 1947, pp. 196–97; 1949, p. 25). Finally, two unplaced pseudo-circularly deformed skulls from the Alta Vera Paz have been illustrated by Stewart (in Dutton and Hobbs, 1943, App. 1).

Bishop Landa, writing of conditions in Yucatan just prior to the Conquest, states that "four or five days" after birth, the mother placed the child "upon a little bed...with its face upwards" and its head was set "between two small boards, one on the back of the head and the other on the forehead, between which they compressed it tightly...until at the end of seven days the head remained flat and molded, as was the custom of all of them" (Tozzer, 1941, p. 125). At one point in his account, Landa mentions the "torment of flattening their forehead and heads" (*ibid.*, p. 129).

Landa's remarks would lead one to believe that at that time the practice was widespread, without class restriction, that it occurred early in infancy, and, indirectly, that the effects of artificial compression persisted throughout life. It is difficult to say whether the archaeological data entirely supports Landa in these respects. No mention, interestingly, is made of pad-binding. While the Uaxactun series surely is not representative of the population as a whole, it possibly bears out the implication of prevalence. On the other hand, the Jaina series evidences a greater incidence of normal over deformed material but, still, a large percentage of the Zaculeu crania were deformed (Stewart, in Woodbury and Trik, 1953, Table 11). At Chichen Itza, "All the skulls show clear traces of artificial deformation, with the exception of 4 in the group of younger children" (Hooton, 1940, p. 273). Regardless of these discrepancies, good evidence exists that cranial deformation was frequently practiced by at least the Maya hierarchic element from Early Classic times on, with possibly a gradual spread of the practice to lesser social elements. As noted, certain sites seem to have emphasized one type at the expense of another, while elsewhere a local population favored a number of types. For instance, among the peoples of Uaxactun there were many who preferred both a flattened forehead and occiput, while their Baking Pot contemporaries, not overly distant, apparently were content with only a deformed frontal.

MINOR MUTILATIONS

Scarification (see Thompson, 1946), if not practiced at Piedras Negras, was certainly known, if we may depend on the Stela 12 scene. Other minor mutilations evident in the sculptures were labial and earlobe perforations to allow the wearing of labrets and ear ornaments. Incidentally, no important figures portrayed on the Piedras Negras monuments wear beards, but a prisoner with one appears on Stela 12. This contrasts with Copan where beards are frequently shown.

PATHOLOGY

Clear-cut serious pathology appears to be absent in the Piedras Negras skeletal material. Dental caries are frequently seen and tartar accumulations suggest perhaps gum infections, for instance, pyorrhea. Caries and often extreme and early attrition were presumably dietary in origin. No case of ear exostosis (bony out-growth) were noted, but this is a feature quite common at Nebaj and Zaculeu. Pathology might possibly underlie the exposed diploe of the mutilated calvarium in Burial 10. A lesion appeared on a Burial 6 long bone.

ANTHROPOMETRY

This aspect of the burials is rather discouraging. Few measurements were possible and the ones taken provide little ground for interpretation. Such obvious conclusions as brachycephaly and short stature, apparent enough in the sculptures, are about as far as the data allow. Estimates of stature (4 samples) range from 145 cm. (female) to 158 cm. (male). At Zaculeu (Stewart, in Woodbury and Trik, 1953, pp. 299—300), average archaeological stature for males was 159.11 cm., and, for females, 147.56 cm. . Individuals over 159 cm. were found at Copan, which has led Longyear (1952, pp. 48—49) to postulate them as intrusive and the "bringers of Classic Maya ceremonial culture" to Copan. Stewart (*op. cit.*) has shown a significant decrease in stature during historic times in the highlands, as indicated by the Zaculeu archaeological series and by measurements carried out on living Guatemalan Indians in the vicinity. Finally, the effects of a hot, humid, lowland environment had perhaps an important effect on stature (Stewart, *ibid.*, p. 300); Newman, 1953), and this factor might be reflected in the few available hints that the Piedras Negras Maya belong very low in the stature scale of American Indians. In visualizing their buildings and platforms in use, the short stature of the users should be kept in mind.

Part 4

SUMMARY AND CONCLUSIONS

SUMMARY AND CONCLUSIONS

At a ceremonial center like Piedras Negras, maintenance of artifact production and the religious ends to which many products were put depended at all times on the efficiency of hunting and agricultural implements and techniques. The tools that allowed the hunting of game, the clearing of milpas, the grinding of corn, provided the economic basis for the fashioning of eccentric flints, the making of implements for building temples, and for trade contacts by which jadeite, obsidian, and other hieratic needs were acquired. In turn, uncertainties of subsistence made necessary and sustained an extraordinary religion that so long received the requisites for essential pomp and ritual. One suspects that lowland Classic Maya religion was remote from the common people in many aspects. The evident reciprocity of priest and farmer, however, provides a functional context for the objects and customs treated in the preceding sections. Class-positioned somewhere between the two were the traders, here implied in pyrite plaques, diverse raw materials, and idea diffusion. Judging from the militaristic theme in considerable Middle Usumacinta art, warriors were probably an important group at Piedras Negras. But their presence is none too securely shown in certain blades, perhaps in a burial or so, but little more. As for specialized artisans, one need only review the eccentric flints and obsidians to appreciate their proficiency. Presumably these specialists, perhaps initially derived from the farming level, acquired a social position equal to that of the traders, each so dependent upon the other. It was on these social levels and within these various relationships that the individual objects, burials, and caches functioned.

The fact that Piedras Negras, as a ceremonial center, seems to have lacked a Pre-Classic (Formative or Developmental) Period and that its Early Classic Period, while definitely present, is hard to appreciate without ceramic analysis of its expressions, provides little time-depth in which to detect change, whether it be in metates or burial customs. Obviously, some time-depth is to be noted in caches, but, as we have seen, they have yielded very few clear-cut shifts either in contents or in places and manners of deposit. The picture seems quite static and curiously not in accord with the site's architectural evolution. Such factors as artifact rarity (as contrasted with sherd frequency), the failure of the expedition to locate long-used and productive trash heaps, and occupational brevity, all contribute to this apparent conservatism.

Reference has often been made in this report to Uaxactun, an obvious point of comparison. Kidder (1947, p. 3) has proposed that "when data on more Maya sites and on other Mesoamerican groups become available, the artifacts of Uaxactun will take on greater meaning." Do, in fact, the Piedras Negras artifacts, including those from burials and caches, enhance the meaning of those of Uaxactun, and, of course, vice-versa? Many cases of divergence and duplication have appeared. Common sources, intersite trade, mutuality of ideas and ends, contemporaneity, differential emphases in ritual, local idiosyncrasies, frequency distinctions, and other conclusions have been drawn from a comparison of the two sites. To be sure, these are meaningful, but they are not entirely satisfying. Often the object itself is functionally or symbolically obscure, and, thus, intersite similarities, or lack of them, become that much harder to really appreciate. For instance, we find the same eccentric flint form at two quite distant sites. We can account for this particular distribution in any number of standard ways. Assuming diffusion from one site to the other, what actually was diffused? Surely more than form was diffused. We can measure and describe a particular object but its meaning, its function alone and with other eccentrics, evades us.

In comparing Uaxactun as well as other sites to Piedras Negras, the factor of unequal sampling has often limited conclusions stemming from frequency differences. The writer originally treated the fact that Piedras Negras produced only 10 burials and Uaxactun 116 as a remarkable difference between the two. But the "significance" of this difference tends to deflate when we consider such factors as the unequal lengths of their respective occupations, the heavy digging in palace structures at Uaxactun and greater excavation of house-mounds, the predominant interest in temples at Piedras Negras, etc.

One objective of all the preceding description has been to give substance, when possible, to Piedras Negras in terms of caches and burials and non-ceramic artifacts. Caches have greatly helped here. Quantity is outstanding; contents are presumed to be significant. The variety of eccentric forms, the presence of engraved pieces of shell, jadeite, and related stones, the importance of the stingray spine (e. g., worked and inscribed spines, bone and jadeite replicas), the use of lime paste coating on cache containers , and other traits, at least collectively, distinguish the site from all others. We suspect that the site is also individualized by an apparent paucity of graves in temples but, as noted above, this is difficult to demonstrate. On the other hand, many broadly distributed traits offset this individuality: grave types, red paint in graves, cranial and dental modifications, dedicatory and intrusive caches, the offering of eccentric objects, jadeite and so forth, the sacrifice of birds, human skeletal remains in caches, the ceremonial use of the stingray spine, as well as the presence of obsidian flake-blades, choppers, celts, various jadeite ornaments, pyrite mosaic work, shell and jadeite beads, bone awls, formed spindle whorls, perforated and plain sherd discs, miniature double-chambered vessels, and others.

Distinctions, to a certain extent, seem a matter of intensity rather than inventiveness. While sharing in a general sort of lowland uniformity, the artifacts, along with their specialized contexts, show certain characteristics in form and elaboration sufficiently unique as not to be confused in their entirety with those of other sites. Despite the participation of various centers in the erection of calendrical monuments, the building of temples, ball courts, and other structures, differences in specific content or emphasis surely characterized local ritual. And the fact that the Piedras Negras common metate is quite different from that of Uaxactun is perhaps as significant as are local ceremonial features, sweat-houses, column altars in temples, the prominence of caches, and the apparent rarity of burials in temple structures.

Trade was clearly an important element at the center. The river provided access to the highlands, a natural advantage denied many sites in the Peten. Artifactual evidence that Piedras Negras fully utilized this advantage is not easily determined. For example, without the mortuary offerings and personal effects of Burial 5 we would be left with a handful of jadeite objects, nothing of amazonite, and pyrite mosaic work would be represented by a few isolated fragments. The total yield, though, of jadeite far exceeds that of sites to the east (e. g., Uaxactun and Holmul), sites which have produced many more otherwise richer burials than Piedras Negras. Obsidian, also of highland origin, is exceptionally common here. The problem is whether a predilection for votive offerings demanded ready quantities of obsidian or whether the availability of obsidian permitted cache indulgence. The production of certain eccentric obsidians was, of course, dependent on the supply of exhausted cores which originally had yielded flake-blades.for frequent utilitarian use. Fine quality flints were presumably imported primarily for ceremonial and particularly votive ends. Shells relate the site to both the Atlantic and the Pacific. The Usumacinta derives from the highlands and terminates at the Gulf of Mexico. The highland Maya presumably functioned as middlemen in Pacific Coast—northern lowland shell trade. Yet, despite the river, only three Pacific genera were encountered at Piedras Negras. Only three appeared in the Uaxactun excavations. The Pacific *Spondylus* was most important at both centers but there seems to have been no great quantitative difference in imports of this ceremonial item. In fact, riverless Uaxactun appears to have been more vigorous than Piedras Negras in imports of Atlantic Ocean shells. Tripod metates and other non-limestone metates in general, as well as celts, arrived from the highlands in either finished or raw states. But, if the center's contact with the highlands was facilitated by the river, as one might assume, it is odd that there should be so few ex - amples, say, of celts, a tool long and commonly used by highland Maya. Again, this seeming discrepancy may be the result of inadequate sampling. Intensive house-mound excavations might have yielded evidence that celts were a rather ubiquitous local item.

Kidder (*ibid.*, p. 73) has written that the "Peten Maya seem, indeed, to have been a conservative lot." Conservatism, or at least a reluctance to change early established patterns, is probably best illustrated here by caches, which, as shown, seem to have changed little if at all from beginning to end. What may be a good architectural indication is the comparatively late introduction at Piedras Negras of the corbel-vaulted roof (Satterthwaite, 1938; see also Appendix). And regardless of real or potentially broad trade connections, the site fails to reveal anything momentous. Pertinent also is the geographic accessibility of lowland Classic sites among themselves. In spite of their proximity and many similarities, important changes in masonry techniques at Uaxactun (A. L. Smith, 1950) failed to affect Piedras Negras. But the trait of eccentrics evidently failed to diffuse from Piedras Negras, where it became fully developed, to Palenque. For some reason or other, Uaxactun's production of eccentric objects seems to have ceased at a time (see Kidder, *op. cit.*, pp. 28—29) when Piedras Negras artisans were making them in increasing quantities. Complex trait sharing in building design features between Tikal and Piedras Negras has been suggested as due to diffusion from east to west (Satterthwaite, 1941). Yet, changes in masonry techniques at Tikal (see Shook, 1951 b , pp. 29—30), more numerous than at Uaxactun, failed to influence Piedras Negras architects. This, however, may be related to differences in available local types of limestone. And one reads of a "Period of Uniformity" when certain calendrical differences were reconciled over a wide area; however, it did not last.

Conservatism, an apparently important factor in Piedras Negras ceremonialism, may have had much of what Kroeber (1948, p. 415 ff) terms "resistance to diffusion."

To conclude as optimistically as possible, the Piedras Negras collection, apart from containing many intrinsically fascinating and often aesthetically fine objects, is still another comparative source in any analysis of distribution and function of artifacts. It has added to our knowledge a number of significant lowland traits. It forms about all that is known of any site in the important Middle Usumacinta region apart from monuments, architecture, and ceramics. And, when the collection is compared with that from Uaxactun, various but often obscure discrepancies and identities emerge. In view of the nature of the site, much of the collection is ceremonial, yet it is only a small fraction of what once existed. But it often gives us provocative hints of what once took place in a complex trinity of farmers, priests, and time-bound gods. In this respect, we wonder whether study of monuments, murals, and painted pots can tell us much more than the pondering of a bowl smeared with a puzzling paste, filled with oddly shaped stones, stingray spines, and bits of shell and jade on which the heads of deities and other strange things were scratched. These objects were surely important to the remarkable men responsible for the more spectacular aspects of the total ritualistic complex.

APPENDIX

METHODS FOR DATING PIEDRAS NEGRAS CACHES

INTRODUCTION

Published data on local inscriptions suffice to show a minimum of three centuries of Piedras Negras Classic ceremonial functioning. This occupation is too obviously manifested to require comment here beyond noting its minimal span as indicated by Stela 30 (9.5.0.0.0) and Altar 3 (9.19.0.0.0). But the study of structural sequence and dating within and beyond these limits, while far from simple, is necessary if we are to realize in what ways associated caches may have developed. Architecture and ceramics are obviously beyond the scope of this report; yet, unavoidably, they must be considered, and thus the need of an appendix.

There are a number of approaches to local stratification and dating, few of which are sufficient in themselves. As regards caches, some are associated with dated monuments, others are tied vaguely to groups of dated monuments, and there are cases where dated monuments are related to structures yielding caches. Dates in the Maya Long Count system must be inferred from associations such as these. There is no reason to suppose that Piedras Negras monuments were moved or that their inscriptions do not record their dedicatory dates (Satterthwaite, verbal communication).

Some offerings were placed axially in relation to the front of a structure, a situation that reasonably points to existence, or planned existence, of the structure in some early or late period or phase, when the deposit was made. The fact that many buildings at Piedras Negras were unvaulted suggests a potential dating method according to the presence or absence of corbelling; it is necessary, however, to estimate the date when the site finally accepted this architectural trait. The pottery found in caches is also occasionally distinctive enough for sequential attribution. Ceramic analysis of the fill containing a cache is critical to temporal placement. Finally, some caches have been provisionally dated by Satterthwaite (in the form of memoranda) through a system of estimated building intervals, the lengths of which depend on the locus.

Rather than include in the chapter on caches the necessary but often very involved and detailed evidence and arguments behind the dating of every Piedras Negras cache not from beneath a dated monument, etc., all conclusions stemming from this appendix are given in the chronologic introduction to each structural group of caches. These conclusions, moreover are basic to much of Table 4.

DATING THROUGH PRESENCE OR ABSENCE OF VAULT

As previously mentioned, a few caches were found in buildings that showed no evidence of having been vaulted. Unlike Uaxactun, where the vault is a major Classic Period diagnostic present from the beginning of that period, the vault at Piedras Negras came into use only after a considerable period when thatch and probably beam-and-mortar roofs seem to have been used (Satterthwaite, 1938; in this regard, see also Andrews, 1943, p. 67 ff). Non-vaulted roofs occur on temple buildings which, like their substructures, show stylistic traits presumably derived from the Peten (Satterthwaite, 1941). An early example of the Tikal substructure style occurs in Structure K–5–3rd. Structure R–1 comprised a substructure of this style together with a building incorporating a roof-comb and a probable beam-and-mortar roof. Local architects clearly were aware of what was architecturally current to the east. It has been suggested (Proskouriakoff, 1950, p. 120) that the absence of the vault throughout the Early Classic Period might indicate that "this city ... originally [formed] part of a cultural area distinct from the rest of the Peten and [was] more closely allied to southern areas of

Mexico.'' The long failure of Piedras Negras to adopt such a major Classic trait as the corbelled roof might also be explained as resistance to this particular innovation, but the fact that corbelling requires considerably more labor and attention to structural dynamics might explain this resistance. This same architectural situation exists also at San Jose (Thompson, 1939, Table 3).

As to when corbelling was finally adopted at Piedras Negras, there are few leads, one of them of theoretical importance. Satterthwaite has generously provided the writer a memorandum on the chronological application at the site of the wall-span index, a ratio first used by Spinden (1912). Satterthwaite writes: "It is assumed that, *other things being equal*, a decreasing index means technological progress, hence chronological sequence.'' Ratios derived from only a single group of similar structures are compared; such groups are one-room temples, double-range free-standing palaces, etc. Among the site's vaulted one-room temples are three that are here vital:

Structure	Index
J–29–A	74
O–12	64
K–5–1st–B	63

It should be noted that such series of indices should not be used as time-markers without inquiring whether "other things,'' specified in the proposition, really are "equal.'' Structure J–29–A probably had a roof-comb, according to Satterthwaite, but its load was not carried even partially by its final phase vault. Structure K–5–1st–B also probably had a comb set to the rear in Tikal style. But here the load probably was carried in part by the front piers and vaulting. Thus the 11 percent difference in index between these two structures would be increased by any allowance for the extra load on vaulting.

J–29–A would appear to have a substantially higher index than those for the other two temples. This higher index is here interpreted as indicative of temporal precedence. Since there is no evidence that Structure O–12 had a roof-comb, the near duplicate indices of O–12 and K–5–1st–B could be re-evaluated to place O–12 between J–29–A and K–5–1st–B technologically and thus chronologically. K–5–1st–B can be rather securely attributed to 9.12.5.0.0, on the basis of the associated Stela 39, and also to the twice recorded date, 9.12.10.0.0 (Stela 38 and "Lintel'' 7).

Satterthwaite's memorandum concludes: ''I arrive at 9.10.0.0.0 as a guess-date for Structure J–29–A and the heaviest (and presumably earliest) vault at the site because it is at the mid-baktun point and thus obviously a guess; and yet it allows some time to elapse between the possibly first, second, and third vaulted temple constructions as suggested by the indices, with 9.12.5.0.0 for possibly the third   one, Structure K–5–1st–B.''

The belief that J–29–A represents the first successful use of corbelling around 9.10.0.0.0 at Piedras Negras is not inconsistent with the latest pottery from its fill (see Cresson, n. d.).

Caches believed to have been dedicated at the time of building a non-vaulted structure are therefore considered to be no later than 9.10.0.0.0 in the absence of more specific temporal evidence.

DATING BY ESTIMATES OF BUILDING INTERVALS

Dating of sequences in single mounds by estimates of intervals between the constructions has been undertaken by Satterthwaite on an entirely architectural basis (Satterthwaite, memorandum). Structures R–3, K–5, and O–13 were selected because, in addition to having incidentally yielded many important caches, each comprises a complex of stratified constructions, and each may be terminally fixed via associated inscriptions. In conversation, Satterthwaite has repeatedly underscored to the writer the necessary tentativeness of much of his approach and results. The resulting dates, for instance, are given two question marks to emphasize their speculativeness, although they are reached on the basis of identical assumptions. These assumptions are:

1. The dated time-span for the monument-building complex is taken as 9.5.0.0.0 (Stela 30) to 9.19.0.0.0 (Altar 3). A katun is added to the end, and 5 katuns are added to the beginning in order to obtain the whole of Baktun 9 as the theoretically assumed complete local Classic Period. This allows for two or three later monuments whose dates may have been lost; and for three building phases at Structure R–3 before 9.6.0.0.0 ??, taken as the date of the latest of the R–3 periods; and for a period of some length when stelae may have been small and plain. This early extension of the dated period, at 2 katuns per phase or period, is perhaps excessive rather than otherwise; if we shortened it, the guess-dates would come out a bit later.

2. Mere re-surfacings of structures are disregarded; numbered "periods" and lettered "phases" (see Satterthwaite, 1943 a, p. 25), formally recognized in the labeling system, are all assumed to have been of equal duration in a complex of sequent structures. This is, of course, a highly arbitrary assumption which, one hopes, results in guess-dates sometimes wrong in one direction, sometimes in the other. One *guesses* that a plus-and-minus allowance of 2 katuns ought to cover these errors, but there is no real check. Perhaps it should be more.

3. It is assumed not only that the occupation began at 9.0.0.0.0 but that it spread at once over the whole area which finally constituted the ceremonial groups (though not necessarily with ceremonial architecture at all spots at this time). This gives us a theoretically assumed date for the earliest construction at any spot, provided that it is on bedrock. (In the special case of Structure O–13, where the earliest known period is the top of a quite high pyramid, namely Structure O–13–4th, it is assumed that penetration at the base of the pyramid would show an earlier and low O–13–5th, analogous to situations at R–3 and K–5). Failure to allow for unprovable lags in building at specific spots would also tend to make the guess-dates a bit too early rather than too late.

As to the utility of the results, they are worse than nothing if taken literally. Possibly they may be useful in forming or checking hypotheses involving the site as a whole, or concerning temporal associations of architecture with pottery, caches, monuments, and other classes of objects.

Application of these assumptions, along with all available inscriptional checks, yields dates (in the Long Count system) for the sequent structures in each of the following loci: R–3, K–5, and O–13. As previously mentioned, though, these results are purposefully obtained without reference to associated pottery. But, to anticipate, a shift to ceramic emphasis requires adjustment in the length of certain building intervals. Adjusted dates have been finally chosen for cache dating.

To avoid losing sight of the various arguments, results for each mound are given and discussed separately.

STRUCTURE R–3 (see Satterthwaite, 1936)

PERIODS	DATES	REMARKS
R–3–1st (latest)	9.6.0.0.0 (?)	Stela 29 date, supported by early glyphic style of "Lintel" 11, and by the date of Stela 30, 9.5.0.0.0.0.
R–3–2nd	9.4.0.0.0 ??	
R–3–3rd	9.2.0.0.0 ??	
R–3–4th (earliest)	9.0.0.0.0 ??	Structure cannot be later than 9.5.-0.0.0, date of Stela 30.

Reasoning on the basis of these assumptions (including equality of intervals) and all associated dated monuments yields 2 katuns as the interval. Such a scheme, as mentioned, is arrived at independent of pottery. The question is, do associated ceramics bear out the time depth of the sequence and thus its building interval?

The very small collection of sherds from the fills of R–3–3rd and –4th was submitted to Mr. Robert E. Smith for identification. He very kindly examined it and found nothing later than Tzacol 3. This conclusion is supported by the two lip-to-lip cyclindrical tripod vessels of Cache R–3–2, from the deepest portion of the R–3–4th fill. At Uaxactun, Tzacol 3 pottery is best placed between 9.1.0.0.0 and the postulated transitional date, 9.8.0.0.0, and was definitely in use there at 9.3.10.0.0 (R. E. Smith, 1955, Ch. 7; A. L. Smith, 1950, Ch. 6).

A ceramic check on the dating of R–3–1st is thwarted by a lack of sherds surely positioned in its fill or masonry.

Satterthwaite's R–3 dating estimates are approximately in accord with the Uaxactun dating of the R–3 pottery. 9.0.0.0.0 for R–3–4th departs from the Uaxactun inception of Tzacol 3 by a mere katun; Satterthwaite's constant allowance of plus-or-minus 2 katuns well covers this difference.

STRUCTURE K–5 (see Satterthwaite 1939; 1940; 1954, p. 71)

PERIODS AND PHASES	DATES	REMARKS
K–5–1st–A (latest)	9.15.0.0.0 ??	
K–5–1st–B	9.12.5.0.0	Date of Stela 39; also tied to 9.12.10.0.0 on Stela 38 and to "Lintel" 7 (using current hotun marker).
K–5–1st–C	9.9.0.0.0 ??	
K–5–2nd	9.6.0.0.0 ??	
K–5–3rd	9.3.0.0.0 ??	
K–5–4th (presumably first)	9.0.0.0.0 ??	

Using this approach, the K–5 building interval was 3 katuns, in contrast to the 2-katun interval for R–3.

When the K–5 ceramic material is set against this scheme a number of severe discrepancies result, none of which are confidently soluble. Mr. Smith again was kind enough to examine a fair sample from the fill of Structure K–5–3rd. Without relating his specific identifications, it suffices to say that a good quantity of Tepeu 1 sherds was found in the sample, including many in true negative technique (Butler's "Polychrome A–1"). This sample furthermore produced sherds typed by Mr. Smith as Tepeu 2 and Tepeu 3. These identifications, in view of their provenience, raised the question of digging error, but Satterthwaite informs me that such was impossible in this particular deposit. As can be immediately appreciated, we are left with the task of accounting for the presence of not only Tepeu 1 pottery at 9.3.0.0.0 (plus-or-minus 2 katuns) but Tepeu 2 and 3 as well! If the identifications are correct, we have pottery, which elsewhere spans the whole Late Classic Period, occurring at Piedras Negras prior to 9.12.5.0.0 at the latest, this being the rather sure date (Stela 39) of K–5–1st–B. Yet Stela 39 has been additionally used to fix the important chronological line between Tepeu 1 and 2 (R. E. Smith, 1955, Table 4, p. 107).

The occurrence of Late Classic ceramics with K–5–3rd is corroborated by the existence of a few mold-made figurines—a trait evidently absent throughout the lowlands in Early Classic (Tzacol) times, but a significant feature during the period of Late Classic (Tepeu) ceramics (R. E. Smith, *ibid.*, pp. 5, 6).

In an attempt to reconcile these conflicting data, the writer suggests that K–5–3rd was constructed at a time when Tepeu 1 pottery surely was in vogue; but other ceramics co-existed which may be categorized as Tepeu 2 and 3 because of generalized resemblances to Uaxactun ceramics of these phases. Approaching this conflict somewhat differently, we also suggest that the presence in K–5–3rd fill of Tepeu 2 and 3 sherds may perhaps indicate an unanticipated early Usumacinta beginning of certain potteries which, because of lag or some other factor, appear chronologically distinct and sequent at Uaxactun. Smith's statement is accepted that Stela 39 is an important marker between Tepeu 1 and Tepeu 2; this shift has been recognized over a wide lowland area and ranges in time from 9.9.6.2.3 (Uaxactun) to 9.12.5.0.0 (Copan and Piedras Negras) (R. E. Smith, *ibid.*, p. 107). While we normally date a fill by the latest associated identifiable, non-intrusive sherds, we are forced in the case of K–5–3rd to consider Tepeu 1, rather than Tepeu 3, its valid ceramic date. This conclusion, a none too happy one, is maintained throughout this report.

Satterthwaite tentatively concluded (see above) that K–5–3rd was erected at 9.3.0.0.0 ??. While we may be sure that early Late Classic ceramic types (Tepeu 1) occurred at Piedras Negras prior to 9.12.5.0.0, can we extend them back to this date, or, with the full "plus-minus" allowance, to 9.5.0.0.0? Uaxactun reports (A. L. Smith, 1950; R. E. Smith, *op. cit.*) indicate, in this respect, that Tzacol 3 ceramics were definitely associated with a stela dated 9.3.10.0.0 and that Tepeu 1 was in existence at the time of setting Stela 6, the date of which (9.9.6.2.3 ??) is apparently very unreliable (Morley, 1937–1938, Vol. 1, pp. 203–08). A non-mean date of 9.8.0.0.0 was chosen to mark the Tzacol–Tepeu transition at Uaxactun. If Satterthwaite's "maximum" guess-date for K–5–3rd is correct, 9.8.0.0.0 must be incorrect for Piedras Negras, if not for Uaxactun. If we trust the evidence for K–5–3rd having been built in Tepeu 1 times and allow for no lag between the two sites, this discrepancy can only be reconciled by adjusting the K–5 estimated building interval, or the 9.8.0.0.0 estimate, or both.

As regards the K–5 stratigraphy, one can only assign the interval from 9.8.0.0.0 (Uaxactun transition estimate) to 9.12.5.0.0 (some 85 years) for the building of K–5–3rd, K–5–2nd, and K–5–1st–C; and surely by 9.12.10.0.0, but more likely 9.12.5.0.0, K–5–1st–B had been completed. The evolutionary details, the major innovations involved, and the volume of this building activity can be appreciated only by reference to Satterthwaite's publications on the complex (1939; 1940). This would seem a remarkably short time for building and occupation of these four constructions, the first three of which differ among themselves very greatly in temple design as well as height. Notable is the lack here and elsewhere at the site of evidence for an important burial motivating heavy building activity. Cases of this sort did occur at Uaxactun during its Early Classic Period (see A. L. Smith, *op. cit.*, Burials 20, 22, 29, 31) but not in connection with pyramid temples. Satterthwaite, in conversation, has stated his doubts that the time allowed by the Uaxactun estimated date, 9.8.0.0.0, is sufficient to have permitted all that was undertaken at this spot.

There is no actual reason—certainly none has been published—for not extending Tepeu 1 back to the mean date of 9.6.0.0.0 rather than 9.8.0.0.0 (a "hypothetical marker"; see R. E. Smith, *op. cit.*, p. 107). This possibility is confirmed by R. E. Smith (personal communication). This revised marker cannot possibly crowd Tzacol 3 as it is now known. Yet it does relax what is believed to be excessive temporal pressure in the case of the K–5 complex. 9.6.0.0.0 grants somewhat more than a century for what took place there. But the use of this date automatically requires revision of Satterthwaite's K–5 building estimates which notably place K–5–3rd at 9.3.0.0.0. This date would have to be altered to 9.6.0.0.0 if we are to allow for ceramic data—data intentionally neglected in the original scheme.

Applying 9.6.0.0.0 to K–5–3rd and 9.12.5.0.0 to K–5–1st–B results in a rounded interval of about 2 katuns, placing K–5–2nd at 9.8.0.0.0 and K–5–1st–C at 9.10.0.0.0. This revision, based first on stratigraphy and pottery, and secondly on a felt need that Tepeu 1 be set back 2 katuns, is perhaps on firmer ground than the original scheme based solely on architecture.

If K–5–3rd is placed at 9.6.0.0.0, we must reconsider the temporal assignment of K–5–4th, a low construction sitting on bedrock that is known only from what was seen of it beneath the K–5–3rd basal platform. K–5–4th was never penetrated and thus its sherd content is unknown. That it is the first in the K–5 sequence is definitely an assumption.

The original scheme called for placing K–5–4th at 9.0.0.0.0; but the consideration of ceramics indicates that 9.6.0.0.0 should be assigned as the date of K–5–3rd. The revised interval would place K–5–4th at 9.4.0.0.0. This is not inconsistent with Satterthwaite's third assumption (see above) which in no way precludes a *gradual* spread of *ceremonial* architecture over the site. We might then hypothesize that ceremonial construction began first in the South Group (e. g., the R buildings) due to the greater accessibility of the river, but that it eventually spread to the East and West groups. Some form of domiciliary occupation, simultaneous and at 9.0.0.0.0 ??, is supposed by this third assumption which would logically call for presence of a K—5—5th and a K—5—6th, still covered by a central and undetected structure of which the now known (but never penetrated or followed) K—5—4th was merely a frontal platform. This remains possible; but the assumption is one of convenience only, as an aid in reaching believable results.

While the R—3 dates proposed by Satterthwaite seem to hold true in the face of pottery, there apparently is need of a revised K—5 scheme. The following, then, is intended as a substitute for the list previously given of that sequence, and, for purposes of this report, these dates are alone applied. While change seems warranted, it is worth noting that we come out with about the same average interval between constructions.

PERIODS AND PHASES	DATES
K—5—1st—A (latest)	9.14.5.0.0 ??
K—5—1st—B	9.12.5.0.0
K—5—1st—C	9.10.0.0.0 ??
K—5—2nd	9.8.0.0.0 ??
K—5—3rd	9.6.0.0.0 ??
K—5—4th (earliest known)	9.4.0.0.0 ??

As noted above, we may assume two sequent structures earlier than K—5—4th which, on the basis of a 2—katun interval, carry the sequence back to 9.0.0.0.0 ??.

STRUCTURE O—13 (Satterthwaite, field data and MS in preparation)

PERIODS AND PHASES	DATES	REMARKS
O—13—1st—A (latest)	9.17.15.0.0	"Lintel" 3 (9.17.15.0.0) added to platform stairway at this date. Stela 15 (9.17.15.0.0) erected on pyramid stage at this date. "Lintel" 1 probably added during this phase. Stela 12 added at 9.18.5.0.0. "Lintel" 12 and Miscellaneous Sculptured Stone 16 fragments re-used as building stones (dedicatory dates, 9.5.0.0.0 ?? and 9.15.0.0.0 ?). Thus, O—13—1st—A seems reasonably dated.
O—13—1st—B	9.15.0.0.0 ??	Miscellaneous Sculptured Stone 16, a probable small stela, erected here at 9.15.0.0.0 ?. Agreement with estimated date coincidental?
O—13—1st—C	9.12.0.0.0 ??	"Lintel" 2, 9.11.15.0.0, dedicated in connection with building? To conform to estimated date, only a 5-tun adjustment is needed. Miscellaneous Sculptured Stone 1, fragmentary, cached either now or later (see Cache O—13—34 , p. 86).
O—13—2nd	9.9.0.0.0 ??	Miscellaneous Sculptured Stone 1 (9.10.10.0.0, current hotun of date on it) dedicated for use in this structure?
O—13—3rd	9.6.0.0.0 ??	"Lintel" 12 with date 9.5.0.0.0 ? dedicated here or elsewhere? Re-used later in O—13—1st—A.
O—13—4th	9.3.0.0.0 ??	
(O—13—5th)	9.0.0.0.0 ??	Structure postulated.

As may be seen in the above tabulation for Structure O—13, this scheme yields a 3-katun interval. The inclusion of a hypothetical O—13—5th has been justified in the third of Satterthwaite's three assumptions (see above).

Three monuments were surely re-used during the final "—1st" group of phases. Horizontal position indicates that Miscellaneous Sculptured Stone 16 must have come from masonry of a temple-widening extension of the final phase, while one of the halves of "Lintel" 12 was seen in position in a building wall of this phase. Plaster on Miscellaneous Sculptured Stone 16 (also to be seen on "Lintel" 2) points to its having been likewise re-used in masonry. These facts then quite securely show that a major rebuilding of the temple which comprises O—13—1st—A occurred after the dedicatory date of Miscellaneous Sculptured Stone 16, namely, 9.15.0.0.0. A 3-katun interval would indicate that this monument was dedicated in connection with O—13—1st—B.

The placement, however, of Miscellaneous Sculptured Stone 1 was in floor or fill of Phases —C, —B, or —A, presumably after breakage some time after its date (current hotun 9.10.0.0.0). The 3—katun intervals of the scheme allow the altar, which is portable, to have been dedicated for use in O—13—2nd, to have been broken and hence used as a cache item (so considered here though use as a fill stone is also conceivable) in the next period of construction, O—13—1st—C. Of course, the small fragment could have come from anywhere at the site, and/or breakage and re-use could have been at any later time. But the reasonableness of the suggested situation is one coincidence which tends to confirm the 3-katun average interval here. So far as definite mandatory controls are concerned, since the fragment may have been intruded as a cache, it proves only what is known from other sources; namely, that a temple was in existence at the O—13—1st level after 9.10.10.0.0.

Another coincidence in the architectural dating scheme is that only a 5-tun adjustment is needed to place "Lintel" 2 as a central addition on the steps of O—13—1st—C, which remained exposed thereafter, being flanked by "Lintels" 1 and 2 in Phase —A; there seems to be no doubt that they were panels and used to face masonry blocks on the stairway, though all had fallen at the time of excavation.

All O—13 caches are apparently contemporaneous with or later than O—13—1st—C (see p. 81). The dating then of O—13—1st—C is obviously critical. The scheme indicates that 9.12.0.0.0 ?? is its date, but "Lintel" 2, if truly dedicated in connection with this building, would provide 9.11.15.0.0 as its date of erection. Since only a 5-tun difference exists between these two dates, it would be best to disregard it and preserve the original scheme.

One might ask with justification, why invoke "gradual ceremonial expansion," so necessary to the revised K—5 scheme, in one case and not in the case of O—13? One reason is that the East Group (O—13, etc.) is lower and more easily accessible than the West Group (K—5, etc.) to the supposedly earliest South Group of ceremonial buildings (e. g., R—9). And in the case of O—13 we lack the ceramic contradiction so evident in K—5. Actually, the O—13 scheme cannot be ceramically justified because of the near lack of sherds in the earlier structures. What is known of the pottery of the O—13—1st phases does not violate their temporal position in the scheme (see Butler, 1935).

SUMMARY

Much of the information on dating contained in Part 3 and Table 4 is derived from the data just given. In the absence of a thorough, coherent analysis of Piedras Negras pottery, we must, in order to even roughly stratify caches, depend on direct and indirect associations with dated monuments, on the presence or absence of a vault in the structure in which the cache occurs, and finally on three schemes of building interval estimates, each one of which is as tentative as question marks, presumptions, and "working hypotheses" can make it. Working with architecture alone (and, of course, all available inscriptions), two schemes (R—3 and O—13) seem to show good to probable agreement with ceramics. But attention to pottery has caused us to revise the original K—5 scheme. The revised K—5 scheme is used for dating; the original R–3 and O–13 schemes are likewise used for dating.

The K–5 sequence has unexpectedly brought up the problem of where in time does the general lowland Early Classic end and the Late Classic begin. Obviously this was not a sudden stop and start but rather a transition. The K–5 ceramic and architectural sequence would seem to require a lowering of the Uaxactun estimate of date of transition (i. e., 9.8.0.0.0) to 9.6.0.0.0. This result appears in Table 4.

BIBLIOGRAPHY

BIBLIOGRAPHY

Acosta, J. R.
  1955   Exploraciones arqueologicas efectuadas en Chichen Itza, Yucatan: 1951. *Anales del Institu-to Nacional de Antropologia e Historia*, Vol. 4, Pt. 1, pp. 27–40. Mexico.

Andrews, E. W.
  1943   The archaeology of southwestern Campeche, *Carnegie Institution of Washington, Publication* 546, pp. 1–100. Washington.

Angel Fernandez, M.
  1941   El Templo Num. 5 de Tulum, Quintana Roo. In "Los Mayas Antiguos," pp. 157–80. Mexico.
  1943   New discoveries in the Temple of the Sun in Palenque. *Dyn.* Nos. 4–5, pp. 55–58. Mexico.

Anonymous
  1937   El Castillo, templo piramidal del dios Kukulcan. *Carnegie Institution of Washington, Supplementary Publication*, No. 32. Washington.

Aveleyra, L., and M. Maldonado K.
  1953   Association of artifacts with mammoth in the Valley of Mexico. *American Antiquity.* Vol. 18, No. 4, pp. 332–40. Salt Lake City.

Baker, F. C., and others
  1941   Contributions to the archaeology of the Illinois River Valley. *Transactions, American Philosophical Society*, n. s., Vol 32, Pt. 1. Philadelphia.

Batres, L.
  1902   *Exploraciones de Monte Alban.* Mexico.
  1902a   *Exploraciones arqueologicas en la Calle de las Escalerillas.* Mexico.

Bennett, J. W.
  1945   *Archaeological Explorations in Jo Daviess County, Illinois.* Chicago.

Berlin, H.
  1951   El Templo de las Inscripciones—VI—de Tikal. *Antropologia e Historia de Guatemala*, Vol. 3, No. 1, pp. 33–54. Guatemala.
  1952   Excavaciones en Kaminal Juyu: Monticulo D–III–13. *Ibid.*, Vol. 4, No. 1, pp. 3–18. Guatemala.

Beyer, H.
  1934   A musical instrument of the ancient Mexicans: The bone rattle. *Middle American Research Series, Tulane University*, No. 7, *Publication* 5. New Orleans.
  1945   An incised Maya inscription in the Metropolitan Museum of Art, New York. *Middle American Research Institute, Tulane University, Middle American Research Records*, Vol. 1, No. 7. New Orleans.

Bird, J.
   1938   Antiquity and migrations of the early inhabitants of Patagonia. *Geographical Review*, Vol. 28, No. 2, pp. 250–75. New York.
   1943   Excavations in Northern Chile. *American Museum of Natural History Anthropological Papers*, Vol. 38. Pt. 4. New York.

Blom, F.
   1950   A polychrome plate from Quintana Roo. *Carnegie Institution of Washington, Division of Historical Research, Notes on Middle American Archaeology and Ethnology*, No. 98. Cambridge.
   1954   Ossuaries, cremation and secondary burials among the Maya of Chiapas, Mexico. *Journal de la Societe de Americanistes de Paris*, n. s., Vol. 43, pp. 123–45. Paris.

Blom, F., and O. LaFarge
   1926   *Tribes and Temples*. New Orleans.

Blom, F., S. S. Grosjean, and H. Cummins
   1933   A Maya skull from the Uloa Valley, Republic of Honduras. *Middle American Research Series, Tulane University, Publication* 5, No. 1. New Orleans.

Boas, F.
   1890   Cranium from Yucatan. *Proceedings, American Antiquarian Society*, Vol. 4, Pt. 3, pp. 350–75. Worcester.

Boekelman, H. J.
   1935   Ethno-and archaeo-conchological notes on four Middle American Shells. *Maya Research, Tulane University*, Vol. 2, No. 3, pp. 257–77. New Orleans.

Brainerd, G.
   1941   Fine Orange pottery in Yucatan. *Revista Mexicana de Estudios Antropologicos*, Vol. 5, pp. 163–83. Mexico.
   1954   *The Maya Civilization*. Los Angeles.

Brew, J. O.
   1946   Archaeology of Alkali Ridge, Southeastern Utah. *Papers, Peabody Museum, Harvard University*, Vol. 21. Cambridge.

Brown, C. E.
   1907   The implement caches of the Wisconsin Indians. *The Wisconsin Archaeologist*, Vol. 6, No. 2. Milwaukee.

Bryan, K.
   1950   Flint Quarries—The sources of the tools and, at the same time, the factories of the American Indian. *Papers, Peabody Museum, Harvard University*, Vol. 17, No. 3. Cambridge.

Buckstaff, R. N.
   1937   A cache of Ohio chert discs. *The Wisconsin Archaeologist*, n. s., Vol. 17, pp. 45–50. Milwaukee.

Bushnell, G. H. S.
   1951   The archaeology of the Santa Elena Peninsula in South-West Ecuador. *Occasional Publications of the Cambridge University Museum of Archaeology and Ethnology*. Cambridge.

Butler, M.
  1935   Piedras Negras pottery. *University Museum, Piedras Negras Preliminary Papers*, No. 4.
          Philadelphia.

Canby, J. S.
  1949   *Excavations at Yarumela, Spanish Honduras.* Doctoral Dissertation, Harvard University.
  1951   Possible chronological implications of the long ceramic sequence recovered at Yarumela,
          Spanish Honduras. In "The Civilizations of Ancient America," *Selected Papers of the 29th
          International Congress of Americanists*, pp. 93–100. Chicago.

Caso, A.
  1938   Exploraciones en Oaxaca: Quinta y sexta temporadas 1936–1937. *Instituto Panamericano de
          Geografia e Historia*, Pub. No. 34. Tacubaya.
  1939   Resumen del informe de las exploraciones en Oaxaca, durante la 7^d y la 8ª temporadas 1937–
          1938 y 1938–1939. *Proceedings, 27th International Congress of Americanists*, Vol. 2, pp.
          159–87. Mexico.

Caso, A., and I. Bernal
  1952   *Urnas de Oaxaca.* Mexico.

Castañeda, D., and V. T. Mendoza
  1933   Los pequeños pecutores en las civilizaciones precortesianas. *Anales del Museo Nacional de
          Arqueologia, Historia y Etnologia*, Ser. 4, Vol. 8, pp. 449–577. Mexico.

Charnay, D.
  1933   *Viaje a Yucatan a fines de 1886.* Merida.

Clements, F. E., and A. Reed
  1939   "Eccentric" flints of Oklahoma. *American Antiquuty*, Vol. 5, No. 1, pp. 27–30. Menasha.

Coe, W. R.
  1955   Excavations in El Salvador. *University Museum Bulletin*, Vol. 19, No. 2, pp. 14–21. Phila-
          delphia.
  1955a   Early Man in the Maya area. *American Antiquity*, Vol. 20, No. 3, pp. 271–73. Salt Lake City.
  1957   A distinctive artifact common to Haiti and Central America. *Ibid.*, Vol. 22, No. 3, pp. 280–81.

Cole, F. C., and T. Deuel
  1937   *Rediscovering Illinois:Archaeological Explorations in and around Fulton County.* Chicago.

Collier, D.
  1955   Cultural chronology and change as reflected in the ceramics of the Viru Valley, Peru. *Fieldi-
          ana: Anthropology, Chicago Natural History Museum*, Vol 43. Chicago.

Collins, H.
  1953   Recent developments in the Dorset culture area. *American Antiquity*, Vol. 18, No. 3, Pt. 2,
          pp. 32–39. Salt Lake City.

Cotter, J. L., and J. M. Corbett
  1951   Archaeology of the Bynum Mounds, Mississippi. *Archaeological Research Series National
          Park Service, U. S. Department of the Interior* , No. 1. Washington.

Cresson, F. M., Jr.

    n. d.   Unpublished and incomplete MS studies of form and decoration of Piedras Negras ceramics. See Satterthwaite 1943a, Bibliography for details.

    1937   Foot forms of pottery vessels at Piedras Negras. *Publications, Philadelphia Anthropological Society*, Vol. 1, pp. 37–46. Philadelphia.

Dávalos, E.

    1946   Las deformaciones craneanas. In "Mexico Prehispanico," pp. 831–40. Mexico.

Dellinger, S. C.

    1954   A cache of batons from northeast Arkansas. In "Ten Years of the Tennessee Archaeologist," ed. T. M. N. Lewis and M. Kneberg, p. 86. Chattanooga.

Driver, H.

    1953   The spatial and temporal distribution of the musical rasp in the New World. *Anthropos*, Vol. 48, Nos. 3–4, pp. 578–92. Freiberg.

Drucker, P.

    1943   Ceramic sequences at Tres Zapotes, Vera Cruz, Mexico. *Smithsonian Institution, Bureau of American Ethnology, Bulletin 140*. Washington.

    1943a   Ceramic stratigraphy at Cerro de las Mesas, Vera Cruz. *Ibid., Bulletin 141*.

    1952   La Venta, Tabasco: A study of Olmec ceramics and art. *Ibid., Bulletin 153*.

    1955   The Cerro de las Mesas offering of jade and other materials. *Ibid., Bulletin 157, Anthropological Papers*, No. 44.

Dustin, F.

    1942   Caches of prehistoric artifacts discovered in Saginaw County, Michigan. *Papers, Michigan Academy of Science, Arts, and Letters*, Vol. 27, pp. 505–10. Ann Arbor.

Dutton, B., and H. Hobbs

    1943   Excavations at Tajumulco, Guatemala. *School of American Research, Monograph 9*. Santa Fe.

Ekholm, G.

    1942   Excavations at Guasave, Sinaloa. *American Museum of Natural History Anthropological Papers*, Vol. 38, Pt. 2. New York.

    1944   Excavations at Tampico and Panuco in the Huasteca, Mexico. *Ibid.*, Vol. 38, Pt. 5.

Ellis, H. H.

    1940   Flint-working techniques of the American Indian: An experimental study. *Ohio State Archaeological and Historical Society*. Columbus.

Estrada B., E.

    1949   Funeraria en Chupicuaro, Guanajuato. *Anales del Instituto Nacional de Antropologia e Historia*, Vol. 3, pp. 79–84. Mexico.

Fastlicht, S.

    1951   Contribucion al estudio del pegamento de las incrustaciones. In "Homenaje al Doctor Alfonso Caso," pp. 153–65. Mexico.

Fastlicht, S., and J. Romero

    1951   El arte de las mutilaciones dentarieas. *Enciclopedia Mexicana de Arte*, No. 14. Mexico.

Faulhaber de S., J.
    1948   Restos oseos de la Huasteca. *Revista Mexicana de Estudios Antropologicos*, Vol. 10, pp. 77–98. Mexico.

Follett, P. H. F.
    1932   War and weapons of the Maya. *Middle American Research Series, Tulane University*, No. 4. New Orleans.

Ford, J. A., and G. R. Willey
    1941   An interpretation of the prehistory of the eastern United States. *American Anthropologist*, Vol. 43, No. 3, pp. 325–63. Menasha.

Foshag, W. F.
    1954   Estudios mineralogicos sobre el jade de Guatemala. *Antropologia e Historia de Guatemala*, Vol. 6, No. 1, pp. 3–47. Guatemala.

Gamio, M.
    1922   *La poblacion del Valle de Teotihuacan.* Mexico.

Gann, T. W. F.
    1900   Mounds in northern Honduras. *Smithsonian Institution, Bureau of American Ethnology, 19th Annual Report*, Pt. 2, pp. 655–92. Washington.
    1918   The Maya Indians of southern Yucatan and northern British Honduras. *Ibid., Bulletin 64.* Washington.
    1925   Maya jades. *Proceedings, 27th International Congress of Americanists*, pp. 275–82. Goteburg.
    1925a   *Mystery Cities.* London.
    1930   Changes in the Maya censor from the earliest to the latest times. *Proceedings, 24th International Congress of Americanists*, pp. 51–4. Hamburg.
    1935   Tzibanche, Quintana Roo, Mexico. *Maya Research, Tulane University*, Vol 2, pp. 155–66. New Orleans.

Gann, T. W. F., and M. Gann
    1939   Archaeological investigations in the Corozal District of British Honduras. *Smithsonian Institution, Bureau of American Ethnology, Anthropological Papers*, No. 7. Washington.

Gebhard, P.
    1946   *Stone objects from prehistoric North America, with respect to distribution, type and significance.* Doctoral Dissertation, Harvard University.

Giddings, J. L., Jr.
    1951   The Denbigh Flint Complex. *American Antiquity*, Vol. 16, No. 3, pp. 193–203. Salt Lake City.
    1955   The Denbigh Flint Complex is not yet dated. *Ibid.*, Vol. 20, No. 4, pp. 375–76.

Gordon, G. B.
    1896   Prehistoric ruins of Copan, Honduras. *Memoirs, Peabody Museum, Harvard University*, Vol. 1, No. 1. Cambridge.

Griffin, J. B.
    1949   Meso-America and the Southeast: A commentary. In "The Florida Indian and his Neighbors," ed. J. W. Griffin, pp. 77–99. Winter Park.

Griffin, J. B., editor
    1952   *Archaeology of the Eastern United States.* Chicago.

Gruning, E. L.
    1930   Report on the British Museum Expedition to British Honduras, 1930. *Journal of the Royal Anthropological Institute,* Vol. 60, pp. 477–83. London.

Guthe, C. E.
    1922   Report on excavations at Tayasal. *Carnegie Institution of Washington, Year Book,* No. 20, pp. 364–68. Washington.

Haag, W. G., and C. H. Webb
    1953   Microblades at Poverty Point. *American Antiquity,* Vol. 18, No. 3, pp. 245–38. Salt Lake City.

Hambly, W.
    1937   Skeletal material from San Jose ruins in British Honduras. *Field Museum of Natural History, Anthropological Series, Publication* 380. Chicago.

Hester, J. A., Jr.
    1953   Agriculture, economy, and population densities of the Maya. *Carnegie Institution of Washington, Year Book,* No. 52, pp. 288–92. Washington.

Heye, G.
    1925   Eccentric chipped objects from British Honduras. *Museum of the American Indian, Heye Foundation, Indian Notes,* Vol. 2, No. 2, pp. 92–102. New York.

Holmberg, A. R.
    1950   Nomads of the long bow: The Siriono of Eastern Bolivia. *Smithsonian Institution, Institute of Social Anthropology, Publication* 10. Washington.

Hooton, E.
    1940   Skeletons from the Cenote of Sacrifice at Chichen Itza. In "The Maya and their Neighbors," pp. 272–80. New York.

Hrdlička, A.
    1947   *Practical Anthropometry.* Philadelphia.

Irving, W.
    1951   Archaeology in the Brooks Range of Alaska. *American Antiquity,* Vol. 17, No. 1, Pt. 1, p. 52. Salt Lake City.

Joyce, T. A.
    1926   Report on the investigations at Lubaantun, British Honduras. *Journal of the Royal Anthropological Institute,* Vol. 56, pp. 207–30. London.
    1927   *Maya and Mexican Art.* London.
    1932   The "eccentric flints" of Central America. *Journal of the Royal Anthropological Institute,* Vol. 62, pp. xvii–xxvi. London.
    1933   The pottery whistle figurines of Lubaantun. *Ibid.,* Vol. 63, pp. xv–xxv.

Joyce, T. A., J. C. Cooper-Clark, and J. E. Thompson
    1927   Report on the British Museum Expedition to British Honduras, 1927. *Ibid.,* Vol. 57, pp. 295–323.

Joyce T. A., E. L. Gruning, T. Gann, and R. C. E. Long
  1928   Report on the British Museum Expedition to British Honduras, 1928. *Ibid.*, Vol. 58, pp. 325—50.

Judd, N.
  1954   The material culture of Pueblo Bonito. *Smithsonian Miscellaneous Collection*, Vol. 124. Washington.

Keleman, P.
  1943   *Medieval American Art*. New York.

Kelly, I. T.
  1947   Excavations at Apatzingan, Michoacan. *Viking Fund Publications in Anthropology*, No. 7. New York.

Kidder, A. V.
  1940   Archaeological problems of the Highland Maya. In "The Maya and their Neighbors," pp. 117—25. New York.
  1942   Archaeological specimens from Yucatan and Guatemala. *Carnegie Institution of Washington, Division of Historical Research, Notes on Middle American Archaeology and Ethnology*, No. 9. Cambridge.
  1947   The artifacts of Uaxactun, Guatemala. *Carnegie Institution of Washington, Publication* 576. Washington.

Kidder, A. V., and G. F. Ekholm
  1951   Some archaeological specimens from Pomona, British Honduras. *Carnegie Institution of Washington, Division of Historical Research, Notes on Middle American Archaeology and Ethnology*, No. 102. Cambridge.

Kidder, A. V., J. D. Jennings, and E. M. Shook
  1946   Excavations at Kaminaljuyu, Guatemala. *Carnegie Institution of Washington, Publication* 561. Washington.

Kidder, A., II
  1940   South American penetrations in Middle America. In "The Maya and their Neighbors," pp. 441—59. New York.

Knuth, E.
  1954   The Palaeo-Eskimo culture of northeast Greenland elucidated by three sites. *American Antiquity*, Vol. 19, No. 4, pp. 367—81. Salt Lake City.

Kroeber, A. L.
  1930   Archaeological explorations in Peru: Part II, Northern Coast. *Field Museum of Natural History, Anthropological Memoirs*, Vol. 2, No. 2. Chicago.
  1937   Ibid: Part IV, Canete Valley. *Ibid.*, Vol. 2, No. 4.
  1948   *Anthropology*. New York.

Lane-Fox, A.
  1857   A flint implement brought from Honduras. *Proceedings, Society of Antiquarians, London*, Vol. 5, pp. 93—5. London.

Larco H., R.
  1941   *Los Cupisniques*. Lima.

1944   *Cultural Salinar: Sintesis Monografica.* Buenos Aires.

1945   *Los Cupisniques.* Buenos Aires.

Laughlin, W. S.
1951   Notes on an Aleutian core and blade industry. *American Antiquity,* Vol. 17, No. 1, pp. 52–55. Salt Lake City.

Laughlin, W. S., and G. H. Marsh
1954   The lamellar flake manufacturing site on Anangula Island in the Aleutians. *American Antiquity,* Vol. 20, No. 1, pp. 27–39. Salt Lake City.

Lehmann, W.
1910   Ergebnisse einer Forschungreise in Mittelamerika und Mexico, 1907–1909. *Zeitschrift fur Ethnologie,* Vol. 42, pp. 687–749. Berlin.

Lewis, T. M. N.
1947   The Duck River cache. *Tennessee Archaeologist,* Vol. 3, No. 4, pp. 54–7. Chattanooga.

Libbey, W. F.
1955   *Radiocarbon Dating, 2nd edition.* Chicago.

Linné, S.
1934   Archaeological researches at Teotihuacan, Mexico. *Ethnographical Museum, Sweden,* n. s., No. 1. Stockholm.
1942   Mexican highland cultures. *Ibid.,* No. 7.

Lister, R. H.
1955   The present status of the archaeology of western Mexico: A distributional study. *University of Colorado Studies, Series in Anthropology,* No. 5. Boulder.

Longyear, J. M., III
1940   A Maya Old Empire skeleton from Copan, Honduras. *American Journal of Physical Anthropology,* Vol. 27, pp. 151–54. Philadelphia.
1944   Archaeological investigations in El Salvador. *Memoirs, Peabody Museum, Harvard University,* Vol. 9, No. 2. Cambridge.
1951   A historical interpretation of Copan archaeology. In "The Civilizations of Ancient America," *Selected Papers of the 29th International Congress of Americanists,* pp. 86–92. Chicago.
1952   Copan ceramics: A study of southwestern Maya pottery. *Carnegie Institution of Washington, Publication* 597. Washington.

Lothrop, S. K.
1924   Tulum: An archaeological study of the East Coast of Yucatan. *Carnegie Institution of Washinton, Publication* 335. Washington.
1926   Pottery of Costa Rica and Nicaragua. *Contributions, Museum of the American Indian, Heye Foundation,* Vol. 8. New York.
1933   Atitlan: An archaeological study of the ancient remains at Lake Atitlan, Guatemala. *Carnegie Institution of Washington, Publication* 444. Washington.
1937   Cocle: An archaeological study of central Panama. *Memoirs, Peabody Museum, Harvard University,* Vol. 7. Cambridge.
1952   Metals from the Cenote of Sacrifice. *Ibid.,* Vol. 10, No. 2.

Luis F., J.
    1954   Snares and traps in Codex Madrid. *Carnegie Institution of Washington, Department of Archaeology, Notes on Middle American Archaeology and Ethnology*, No. 121. Cambridge.

MacNeish, R. S.
    1954   An early archaeological site near Panuco, Vera Cruz. *Transactions, American Philosophical Society*, n. s., Vol. 44, Pt. 5. Philadelphia.
    1954a   The Pointed Mountain site near Fort Laird, Northwest Territories, Canada. *American Antiquity*, Vol. 19, No. 3, pp. 234—53. Salt Lake City.

Maler, T.
    1901   Researches in the central portion of the Usamacinta Valley. *Memoirs, Peabody Museum, Harvard University*, Vol. 2, No. 1. Cambridge.
    1908   Explorations in the Department of Peten, Guatemala, and adjacent regions. *Ibid.*, Vol. 4, No. 2.
    1912   Lista de las ilustraciones para una proyectada publicacion, de Teoberto Maler, en el libro de recuerdos del Congreso de Americanistas. *Proceedings, 17th International Congress of Americanists*, added plates. Mexico.

Martin, P. S., G. I. Quimby, Jr., and D. Collier
    1947   *Indians before Columbus*. Chicago.

Mason, J. A.
    1931   Archaeology of Santa Marta, Colombia: The Tairona Culture. *Field Museum of Natural History, Anthropological Series*, Vol. 20, No. 1. Chicago.
    1933   Jade ornaments from Piedras Negras. *University Museum Bulletin*, Vol. 4, No. 2, pp. 51—6. Philadelphia.
    1935   Preserving America's finest sculptures. *National Geographic Magazine*, Vol. 68, No. 5, pp. 537—70. Washington.
    1938   Observations on the present status and problems of Middle American archaeology: Part 2. *American Antiquity*, Vol. 3, No. 4, pp. 300—17. Menasha.

Maudslay, A. P.
    1889—1902
            Archaeology. *Biologia Centrali-Americana*. London.

Merwin, R. E., and G. C. Vaillant
    1932   The ruins of Holmul, Guatemala. *Memoirs, Peabody Museum, Harvard University*, Vol. 3, No. 2. Cambridge.

Moedano K., H.
    1946   Jaina: Un cementario Maya. *Revista Mexicana de Estudios Antropologicos*, Vol. 8, Nos. 1—3, pp. 217—42. Mexico.

Morley, S. G.
    1937—1938
            The inscriptions of Peten. *Carnegie Institution of Washington, Publication* 437. Washington.
    1947   *The Ancient Maya. Stanford University Press*. Stanford.
    1947a   Guide Book to the ruins of Quirigua. *Carnegie Institution of Washington, Supplementary Publication*, No. 16. Washington.

Morris, E.

1939   Archaeological studies in the Là Plata District, Southwestern Colorado and Northwestern New Mexico. *Carnegie Institution of Washington, Publication* 519. Washington.

Morris E., J. Charlot, and A. A. Morris

1931   The Temple of the Warriors. *Ibid., Publication* 406.

Mullerried, F.

1928   Sobre los artefactos de piedra en la parte central y occidental del Peten, Guatemala ... *Revista Mexicana de Estudios Antropologicos*, Vol. 2, pp. 71–101. Mexico.

Murdoch, J.

1892   Ethnological results of the Point Barrow Expedition. *Smithsonian Institution, Bureau of American Ethnology, 9th Annual Report*, 1887–88. Washington.

Nelson, N. C.

1937   Notes on cultural relations between Asia and America. *American Antiquity*, Vol. 2, No. 4, pp. 267–72. Menasha.

Neumann, G. K.

1941   Types of artificial cranial deformation in the Eastern United States. *Southeastern Archaeological Conference, News Letter*, Vol. 2, No. 4, pp. 3–5. Lexington.

Newell, H. P., and A. D. Krieger

1949   The George C. Davis Site, Cherokee County, Texas. *Memoirs, Society of American Archaeologists*, No. 5. Menasha.

Newman, M. T.

1947   Indian skeletal material from the Central Coast of Peru. *Papers, Peabody Museum, Harvard University*, Vol. 27, No. 4. Cambridge.

1953   The application of ecological rules to the racial anthropology of the aboriginal New World. *American Anthropologist*, Vol. 55, No. 3, pp. 311–27. Menasha.

Noguera, E.

1935   Antecedentes y relaciones de la cultura teotihuacana. *El Mexico Antiguo*, Vol. 3, Nos. 5–8, pp. 3–90. Mexico.

1943   Excavaciones en El Tepalcate, Chimalhuacan, Mexico. *American Antiquity*, Vol. 9, No. 1, pp. 33–43. Menasha.

Orr, K. G.

1946   The archaeological situation at Spiro, Oklahoma: A preliminary report. *American Antiquity*, Vol. 2, No. 4, pp. 228–56. Menasha.

1952   Survey of Caddoan Area archaeology. In "Archaeology of the Eastern United States," ed. J. B. Griffin, pp. 239–55. Chicago.

Paddock, J.

1955   The first three seasons at Yagul. *Mexico City College, Mesoamerican Notes*, No. 4, pp. 25–48. Mexico.

Peabody, C.

1927   Red paint. *Journal de la Societe de Americanistes de Paris*, n. s., Vol. 19, pp. 207–44. Paris.

Piña C., R.

1948   Breve estudio sobre la funeraria de Jaina, Campeche. *Museo Arqueologia, Etnologia e Historia, Campeche*, No. 7. Campeche.

1955   *Las culturas preclasicas de la Cuenca de Mexico.* Mexico.

Pollock, H. E. D., and G. Stromsvik

1953   Chacchob, Yucatan. *Carnegie Institution of Washington, Department of Archaeology, Current Reports*, No. 6, Cambridge.

Popenoe, D. H.

1934   Some excavations at Playa de los Muertos, Ulua River, Honduras. *Maya Research*, Vol. 1, pp. 61—85. New York.

Porter, M. N.

1953   Tlatilco and the Pre-Classic cultures of the New World. *Viking Fund Publications in Anthropology*, No. 19, New York.

Price, W. H.

1897—1899

Excavations on Sittee River, British Honduras. *Proceedings, Society of Antiquarians, London*, n. s., Vol. 17, pp. 339—44. London.

Proskouriakoff, T.

1944   An inscription on a jade probably carved at Piedras Negras. *Carnegie Institution of Washington, Division of Historical Research ,Notes on Middle American Archaeology and Ethnology*, No. 47. Cambridge.

1946   An album of Maya architecture. *Carnegie Institution of Washington, Publication* 558. Washington.

1950   A study of Classic Maya sculpture. *Ibid., Publication* 593.

1952   Sculpture and artifacts of Mayapan. *Carnegie Institution of Washington, Year Book*, No. 51, pp. 256—59. Washington.

1953   Artifacts of Mayapan. *Ibid.*, No. 52, pp. 282—83.

Rainey, F. G.

1940   Archaeological investigation in Central Alaska. *American Antiquity*, Vol. 5, No.4, pp. 299—308. Menasha.

1953   The significance of recent archaeological discoveries in inland Alaska. *Ibid.*, Vol. 18, No. 3, Pt. 2, pp. 43—6. Salt Lake City.

Rands, R. L.

1952   *Some Evidence of Warfare in Classic Maya Art.* Doctoral Dissertation, Columbia University.

1953   The water-lily in Maya art: A complex of alleged Asiatic origin. *Smithsonian Institution, Bureau of American Ethnology, Anthropological Papers*, No. 34. Washington.

1955   Some manifestations of water in Mesoamerican art. *Ibid.*, No. 48.

Rice, R. G.

1909   Note on a flint in human shape found in the Thames. *Proceedings, Society of Antiquarians, London*, n. s., Vol. 22, pp. 359—360. London.

Ricketson, O. G.

1929   Excavations at Baking Pot, British Honduras. *Carnegie Institution of Washington, Contributions to American Archaeology*, No. 1. Washington.

Ricketson, O. G., and E. B. Ricketson
    1937   Uaxactun, Guatemala: Group E—1926—1931. *Carnegie Institution of Washington, Publication* 477. Washington.

Roberts, F. H. H., Jr.
    1939   Archaeological remains in the Whitewater District, Eastern Arizona: Part I, House Types. *Smithsonian Institution, Bureau of American Ethnology, Bulletin* 121. Washington.
    1940   *Ibid.*, Part II, Artifacts and Burials. *Ibid., Bulletin* 126.

Rosado O., W.
    1945   Tipo fisico y psiquico, organizacion social, religiosa y politica, economia, musica, literatura y medecina. In "Enciclopedia Yucatense," Vol. 2, pp. 53—307. Mexico.

Rouse, I.
    1941   Culture of the Ft. Liberte Region. *Yale University Publications in Anthropology*, No. 24, New Haven.

Rubín de la Borbolla, D.
    1939   Antropologia Tzintzuntzan-Ihuatzio. *Revista Mexicana de Estudios Antropologicos*, Vol. 3, pp. 99—121. Mexico.
    1947   Teotihuacan: Ofrendas de los Templos de Quetzalcoatl. *Anales del Instituto Nacional de Antropologia e Historia*, Vol. 3, pp. 61—72. Mexico.

Ruppert, K.
    1935   The Caracol at Chichen Itza, Yucatan, Mexico. *Carnegie Institution of Washington, Publication* 454. Washington.
    1943   The Mercado, Chichen Itza, Yucatan. *Ibid., Publication* 546, pp. 223—60.

Ruppert, K., and J. H. Denison
    1943   Archaeological reconnaisance in Campeche, Quintana Roo, and Peten. *Ibid., Publication* 543.

Ruppert, K., and A. L. Smith
    1953   Mayapan, Yucatan. *Carnegie Institution of Washington, Year Book*, No. 52, pp. 256—58. Washington.
    1954   Excavations in house mounds at Mayapan: III, *Carnegie Institution of Washington, Department of Archaeology, Current Reports*, No. 17. Cambridge.

Ruppert, K., J. E. S. Thompson, and T. Proskouriakoff
    1955   Bonampak, Chiapas, Mexico. *Carnegie Institution of Washington, Publication* 602. Washington.

Ruz L., A.
    1952   Exploraciones en Palenque: 1950. *Anales del Instituto Nacional de Antropologia e Historia*, Vol. 5, pp. 25—46. Mexico.
    1955   Exploraciones en Palenque: 1952. *Ibid.*, Vol. 6, Pt. 1, pp. 79—112.
    1955a   Uxmal: Temporada de trabajos 1951—1952. *Ibid.*, Vol. 6, Pt. 1, pp. 49—67.
    1955b   Uxmal—Kabah—Sayil: Temporada 1953. *Direccion de Monumentos Pre-Hispanicos, Instituto Nacional de Antropologia e Historia*. Mexico.

Saenz, C. A.
    1952   El adoratorio central, Palacio del Gobernador, Uxmal. *Tlatoani*, Vol. 1, Nos. 5—6, pp. 45—50. Mexico.

Satterthwaite, L.

1933   South Group Ball Court with preliminary note on the West Group Ball Court. *Piedras Negras Preliminary Papers*, No. 2. Philadelphia.

1933a   The Piedras Negras Expedition. *University Museum Bulletin*, Vol. 4, No. 5, pp. 121–26. Philadelphia.

1934   *Preliminary Notes on Piedras Negras Burials.* Unpublished MS.

1935   Palace Structures J–2 and J–6, with notes on Structure J–6–2nd and other buried structures in Court 1. *Piedras Negras Preliminary Papers, No. 3.* Philadelphia.

1936   A pyramid without temple ruins. *Ibid., No. 5.*

1936a   The sixth Piedras Negras Expedition. *University Museum Bulletin*, Vol. 6, No. 5, pp. 14–19. Philadelphia.

1936b   Notes on the work of the Fourth and Fifth University Museum Expeditions to Piedras Negras, Guatemala. *Maya Research*, Vol. 3, No. 1, pp. 74–93. New Orleans.

1937   Identification of Maya temple buildings at Piedras Negras. *Twenty-fifth Anniversary Studies, Philadelphia Anthropological Society*, pp. 161–177. Philadelphia.

1938   Evidence for a logical sequence of roof types on a Maya building at Piedras Negras. *Science*, Vol. 88, p. 504. Lancaster.

1938a   Maya dating by hieroglyph style. *American Anthropologist*, Vol. 40, No. 3, pp. 416–28. Menasha.

1939   Evolution of a Maya temple: Part 1. *University Museum Bulletin*, Vol. 7, No. 4, pp. 3–14. Philadelphia.

1940   Evolution of a Maya temple: Part 2. *Ibid.*, Vol. 8, Nos. 2–3, pp. 18–24.

1941   Some Central Peten Maya architectural traits at Piedras Negras. In "Los Mayas Antiguos," pp. 182–208. Mexico.

1943   Animal head feet and a bark beater in the Middle Usumacinta region. *Carnegie Institution of Washington, Division of Historical Research Notes on Middle American Archaeology and Ethnology*, No. 27. Cambridge.

1943a   Introduction. *Piedras Negras Archaeology: Architecture*, Pt. I, No. 1. Philadelphia.

1944   Structure R–9 (temple and associated constructions). *Ibid.*, Pt. II, No. 1.

1944a   Ball courts. *Ibid.*, Pt. IV.

1946   Review of Beyer, 1945. *American Antiquity*, Vol. 12, No. 2, p. 131. Menasha.

1946a   Incense at Piedras Negras. *University Museum Bulletin*, Vol. 11, No. 4, pp. 16–22. Philadelphia.

1954   Unclassified buildings and substructures. *Piedras Negras Archaeology: Architecture*, Pt. VI. Philadelphia.

1954a   Sculptured monuments from Caracol, British Honduras. *University Museum Bulletin*, Vol. 18, Nos. 1–2, pp. 2–45. Philadelphia.

Seler, E.

1898   Alt mexikanische Knochenrasseln. *Globus*, Vol. 74, No. 6, pp. 85–93. Berlin.

1901   *Die alten Ansiedelungen von Chacula im Distrikte Nenton des Departements Huehuetenango der Republik Guatemala.* Berlin.

1910   Die Tierbilder der mexicanischen und der Maya-Handschriften: Insekten und andere niedere Tiere. *Zeitschrift fur Ethnologie*, Vol. 42, pp. 242–87. Berlin.

Sharp, L.

1952   Steel axes for Stone Age Australians. In *Human Problems in Technological Change*, ed. E. H. Spicer, pp. 69–92. New York.

Shook, E. M.

1948   Guatemala highlands. *Carnegie Institution of Washington, Year Book*, No. 47, pp. 214–18. Washington.

1950   Guatemala. *Ibid.*, No. 49, pp. 197–98.

1951   Guatemala. *Ibid.*, No. 50, pp. 250–51.

1951a   The present status of research on the Pre-Classic horizons in Guatemala. In "The Civilizations of Ancient America," *Selected Papers of the 29th International Congress of Americanists*, pp. 93–100. Chicago.

1951b   Investigaciones arqueologicas en las ruinas de Tikal, Departmento de El Peten, Guatemala, *Anthropologia e Historia de Guatemala*, Vol. 3, No. 1, pp. 9–32. Guatemala.

1952   The ruins of Cotio, Department of Guatemala, Guatemala. *Carnegie Institution of Washington, Division of Historical Research, Notes on Middle American Archaeology and Ethnology*, No. 107. Cambridge.

1954   The Temple of Kukulcan at Mayapan. *Carnegie Institution of Washington, Department of Archaeology, Current Reports*, No. 20. Cambridge.

Shook, E. M., and W. N. Irving

1955   Colonnaded buildings at Mayapan. *Ibid.*, No. 22.

Shook, E. M., and A. V. Kidder

1952   Mound E–III–3, Kaminaljuyu, Guatemala. *Carnegie Institution of Washington, Publication* 596, No. 53. Washington.

Smith, A. L.

1934   Two recent ceramic finds at Uaxactun *Carnegie Institution of Washington, Publication* 436. No. 5. Washington.

1950   Uaxactun, Guatemala: Excavations of 1931–1937. *Ibid., Publication* 588.

Smith, A. L., and A. V. Kidder

1943   Explorations in the Montagua Valley, Guatemala. *Ibid., Publication* 546, No. 41.

1951   Excavations at Nebaj, Guatemala. *Ibid., Publication* 594.

Smith, P. E.

1955   Excavations in three ceremonial structures at Mayapan. *Carnegie Institution of Washington, Department of Archaeology, Current Reports*, No. 21. Cambridge.

Smith, R. E.

1940   Ceramics of the Peten. In "The Maya and their Neighbors," pp. 242–49. New York.

1955   Ceramic sequence at Uaxactun, Guatemala. *Middle American Research Institute, Tulane University, Publication* 20. New Orleans.

Solecki, R. S.

1951   Notes on two archaeological discoveries in northern Alaska. *American Antiquity*, Vol. 17, No. 1, pp. 55–7. Salt Lake City.

1955   Lamellar flakes versus blades, a reappraisal. *Ibid.*, Vol. 20, No. 4, pp. 393–94.

Stephens, J. L.

1843   *Incidents of Travel in Yucatan.* New York.

Stirling, M. W.

1943   Stone monuments of southern Mexico. *Smithsonian Institution, Bureau of American Ethnology, Bulletin* 138. Washington.

Stevens, E. T.

1870   *Flint Chips: A Guide to Prehistoric Archaeology.* London.

Steward, J.
  1947   American culture history in light of South America. *Southwestern Journal of Anthropology,* Vol. 3, No. 2, pp. 85–107. Albuquerque.

Stewart, J., et al
  1955   Irrigation civilizations: A comparative study. *Pan American Union, Social Science Monograph, 1,* Washington.

Stewart, T. D.
  1937   Different types of cranial deformity in the Pueblo area. *American Anthropologist.* Vol. 39, No. 1 pp. 169–71. Menasha.
  1947   Anthropometry of the Highland Maya. *Carnegie Institution of Washington, Year Book,* No. 46, pp. 195–97. Washington.
  1949   Notas sobre esqueletos humanos prehistoricos hallados en Guatemala. *Antropologia e Historia de Guatemala,* Vol. 1, No. 1, pp. 23–34. Guatemala.

Spinden, H.
  1913   A study of Maya art. *Memoirs, Peabady, Museum, Harvard University,* Vol. 6, Cambridge.

Stone, D. Z.
  1941   Archaeology of the north coast of Honduras. *Memoirs, Peabody Museum, Harvard University,* Vol. 9, No. 1. Cambridge.

Strömsvik, G.
  1931   Notes on the metates of Chichen Itza, Yucatan. *Carnegie Institution of Washington, Publication* 403, No. 4. Washington.
  1935   Notes on the metates from Calakmul, Campeche, and from the Mercado, Chichen Itza, Yucatan. *Ibid., Publication* 456, No. 16.
  1942   Substela caches and stela foundations at Copan and Quirigua. *Ibid., Publication* 528, No. 37.
  1950   Las ruinas de Asuncion Mita: Informe de su reconocimiento. *Antropologia e Historia de Guatemala,* Vol. 2, No. 1, pp. 23–29. Guatemala.

Strömsvik, G., and J. M. Longyear III
  1946   A reconnaisance of El Rincon del Jicaque, Honduras. *Carnegie Institution of Washington, Division Historical Research, Notes on Middle American Archaeology and Ethnology,* No. 68. Cambridge.

Strong, W. D.
  1935   Archaeological investigations in the Bay Islands, Spanish Honduras. *Smithsonian Miscellaneous Collection,* Vol. 92, No. 14. Washington.
  1954   Recent archaeological discoveries in south coastal Peru. *Transactions, New York Academy of Sciences, Series* II, Vol. 16, No. 4, pp. 215–18. New York.

Strong, W. D., and C. Evans Jr.
  1952   Cultural stratigraphy in the Viru Valley, Northern Peru: The Formative and Florescent epochs. *Columbia Studies in Archaeology and Ethnology,* Vol. 4. New York.

Strong, W. D., A. Kidder II, and A. J. D. Paul
  1938   Preliminary report on the Smithsonian Institution–Harvard University Expedition to northwestern Honduras, 1936. *Smithsonian Miscellaneous Collection,* Vol. 97, No. 1. Washington.

Tax, S., and others, Editors
    1953   *An Appraisal of Anthropology Today.* Chicago.

Thompson, D. E., and J. E. S. Thompson
    1955   A noble's residence and its dependencies at Mayapan. *Carnegie Institution of Washington , Department of Archaeology, Current Reports*, No. 25. Cambridge.

Thompson, E. H.
    1897   The chultunes of Labna. *Memoirs, Peabody Museum, Harvard University*, Vol. 1, No. 3. Cambridge.
    1898   Ruins of Xkichmook, Yucatan. *Field Museum of Natural History, Anthropological Series*, Vol.. 2, No. 2. Chicago.

Thompson, E. H., and J. E. S. Thompson
    1938   The High Priest's Grave, Chichen Itza, Yucatan, Mexico. *Ibid.*, Vol. 17, No. 2.

Thompson, J. E. S.
    1931   Archaeological investigations in the southern Cayo District, British Honduras. *Field Museum of Natural History, Anthropological Series*, Vol. 17, No. 3. Chicago.
    1936   An eccentric flint from Quintana Roo, Mexico. *Maya Research*, Vol. 3, pp. 316–18. New Orleans.
    1938   Sixteenth and Seventeenth Century reports on the Chol Maya. *American Anthropologist*, Vol. 40, No. 4, Pt. 1, pp. 584–604. Menasha.
    1939   Excavations at San Jose, British Honduras. *Carnegie Institution of Washington, Publication* 506. Washington.
    1940   Late ceramic horizons at Benque Viejo, British Honduras. *Ibid., Publication* 528, No. 35.
    1940a   Archaeological problems of the lowland Maya. In "The Maya and their Neighbors," pp. 126–38. New York.
    1944   The Dating of Seven Monuments at Piedras Negras. *Carnegie Institution of Washington, Division of Historical Research, Notes on Middle American Archaeology and Ethnology*, No. 39. Cambridge.
    1946   Tattooing and scarification among the Maya. *Ibid.*, No. 63.
    1948   An archaeological reconnaisance in the Cotzumahualpa region, Escuintla, Guatemala. *Carnegie Institution of Washington, Publication* 574, No. 44. Washington.
    1950   Maya hieroglyphic writing. *Ibid., Publication* 589.
    1951   Aquatic symbols common to various centers of the Classic Period in Meso-America. In "The Civilizations of Ancient America," *Selected Papers of the 29th International Congress of Americanists* , pp. 31–6. Chicago.
    1953   Relaciones entre Veracruz y la region Maya. *Revista Mexicana de Estudios Antropologicos* , Vol. 13, Nos. 2–3, pp. 447–54. Mexico.
    1954   A presumed residence of the nobility at Mayapan. *Carnegie Institution of Washington, Department of Archaeology, Current Reports*, No. 19. Cambridge.
    1954a   *The Rise and Fall of Maya Civilization.* Norman.

Tozzer, A. M.
    1907   A comparative study of the Mayas and Lacondones. *Archaeological Institute of America.* New York.
    1941   Landa's Relacion de las Cosas de Yucatan: A translation.   *Papers, Peabody Museum, Harvard University* , Vol. 18. Cambridge.

Tozzer, A. M., and G. M. Allen
    1910   Animal figures in the Maya codices. *Ibid.*, Vol. 4, No. 3.

Tschopik, H., Jr.
    1946   Some notes on rock shelter sites near Huancayo, Peru. *American Antiquity*, Vol. 12, No. 2, pp. 73–80. Menasha.
    1952   Indians of the Montaña. *American Museum of Natural History, Science Guide*, No. 135. New York.

Vaillant, G. C.
    1930   Excavations at Zacatenco. *American Museum of Natural History, Anthropological Papers*, Vol. 32, Pt. 1. New York.
    1935   Excavations at El Arbolillo. *Ibid.*, Vol. 35, Pt. 2.

Vaillant, S. B., and G. C. Vaillant
    1934   Excavations at Gualupita. *American Museum of Natural History, Anthropological Papers*, Vol. 35, Pt. 1. New York.

Wauchope, R.
    1934   Housemounds of Uaxactun, Guatemala. *Carnegie Institution of Washington, Publication* 436, No. 7. Washington.
    1941   Effigy head vessel supports from Zacualpa, Guatemala. In " Los Mayas Antiguos," pp. 211–32. Mexico.
    1945   Cremations at Zacualpa, Guatemala, *Proceedings of the 27th International Congress of Amercanists*, pp. 564–73. Mexico.
    1948   Excavations at Zacualpa. *Middle American Research Institute, Tulane University, Publication* 14. New Orleans.
    1949   1947 archaeological expedition. In "Extracts from Report to the President of Tulane University," *Middle American Research Institute, Tulane University, Miscellaneous Series*, No. 6, pp. 24–30. New Orleans.

Weiant, C. W.
    1943   An Introduction to the ceramics of Tres Zapotes, Vera Cruz, Mexico. *Smithsonian Institution, Bureau of American Ethnology, Bulletin* 139. Washington.

Willey, G. R.
    1955   The interrelated rise of the native cultures of Middle and South America. In "New Interpretations of Aboriginal American Culture History," *Publications, Anthropological Society of Washington*, pp. 28–45. Washington.
    1956   The structure of ancient Maya society: Evidence from the southern lowlands. *American Anthropologist*, Vol. 58, No. 5, pp. 777–82. Menasha.

Willey, G. R., and J. Corbett
    1954   Early Ancon and Early Supe Culture. *Columbia Studies in Archaeology and Ethnology*, Vol. 3. New York.

Willey, G. R., and P. Phillips
    1955   Method and theory in American archaeology II: Historical–Developmental interpretation. *American Anthropologist*, Vol. 57, No. 4, pp. 723–819. Menasha.

Witthoft, J.
    1952   A Paleo-Indian site in eastern Pennsylvania: An early hunting culture. *Proceedings, American Philosophical Society*, Vol. 96, No. 4, pp. 464–95. Philadelphia.

Woodbury, R. B., and A. S. Trik

    1953   *The Ruins of Zaculeu, Guatemala.* United Fruit Co., Boston.

Zamyatnin, S. N.

    1948   (Miniature flint sculptures in the Neolithic of Northeastern Europe). *Sovetskaya Arkheologiya,* Vol. 10, pp. 85–123. Moscow.

FIGURES

FIGURE 1

CHIPPED IMPLEMENTS, FLINT
All 1/2 scale

	DESCRIPTION	FIELD NO.	PROVENIENCE	DISPOSITION	REF. PAGE
a	Chopper	S—15—11	Burial 10, Niche 3	UM	11
b	,,	W—28—7	Str. K—5, surface	UM	11
c	,, (see g—i)	E—1—6	Cache O—13—56	UM	11
d	,,	W—8—53	Str. J—11 and J—12, between surface	UM	11
e	,,	W—4—10	Str. J—3, terrace floor (see Figs. 19,20)	NM	11
f	,,	S—11—5	Str. R—2, surface	NM	11
g	,,	E—1—6	Cache O—13—56	UM	11
h,i	Choppers	,,	,, ,,	NM	11
j	Chopper	W—29—70	West section, surface	UM	11
k	,,	E—1—191	Str. O—13, surface	NM	11
l	Blank (?)	S—15—12	Burial 10, Niche 3	UM	12
m	Chopper	W—3—12	Str. J—1, base of Stela 1	NM	11

Fig. 1

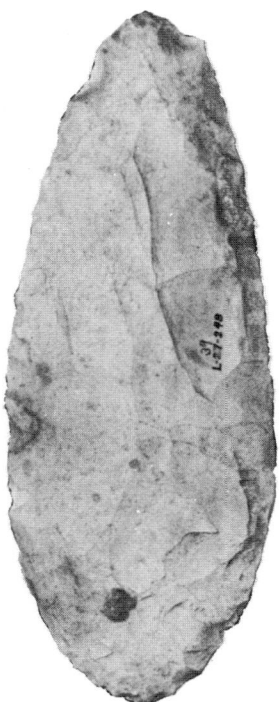

a

b

c

d

e

f

g

h

i

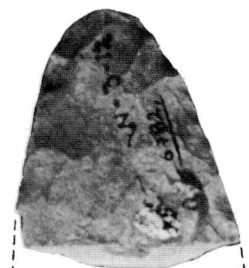

j

k

l

m

FIGURE 2

CHIPPED IMPLEMENTS, FLINT
All 1/2 scale

	DESCRIPTION	FIELD NO.	PROVENIENCE	DISPOSITION	REF. PAGE
a	Celtiform chopper	E—1—22	Str O—13, rear room	UM	11
b	Rectangular chopper	S—2—36	Str. R—3, platform floor, foot of stairway	UM	11
c	,, ,,	SE—10—4	Str. S—17, on floor	UM	11
d	,, ,,	S—22—3	Str. R—10, stela terrace debris	NM	11
e	,, ,,	S—21—48	Str. R—9, sub-surface, near stela terrace	NM	11
f	,, ,,	S—21—40	Str. R—9, in or on latest construction of Stela 25 buried platform	UM	11
g	Spherical hammerstone	S—1—42	Str. R—11—a, summit	UM	12
h	,, ,,	SE—11—4	Str. S—18, on floor	UM	12

a

b

Fig. 2

c

d

e

f

g

h

FIGURE 3

PROJECTILES AND KNIVES, FLINT
All 1/2 scale

	DESCRIPTION	FIELD NO.	PROVENIENCE	DISPOSITION	REF. PAGE
a	Knife or projectile point	SE—1—34	Str. V—1, east end, trench	NM	13
b	,, ,, ,, ,,	E—2—10	Str. P—7, southwest rear room	NM	13
c	,, ,, ,, ,,	W—5—155	Str. K—5—1st, surface or near surface	NM	13
d	,, ,, ,, ,,	W—5—49	Str. K—5, trench	NM	13
e	,, ,, ,, ,,	SE—10—3	Str. S—17, surface debris	NM	13
f	,, ,, ,, ,,	S—20—11	Str. Q—1 test pit	UM	13
g	,, ,, ,, ,,	W—5—207	Str. K—5—1st, surface	NM	13
h	Projectile point	W—12—28	Str. J—6—2nd, under floor	UM	12
i	,, ,,	W—5—121	Str. K—5, trench	UM	12
j	,, ,,	S—1—31	Str. R—11—a, debris	UM	12
k	,, ,,	W—5—50	Str. K—5, trench	UM	12
l	,, ,,	M—23—17	Milpa 1 km. from site	UM	12
m	,, ,,	S—22—46	Str. R—10, trench	UM	12
n	,, ,,	S—1—30	Str. R—11—a, debris	UM	12
o	Knife or projectile point	W—5—274	Str. K—5—1st, plaza surface	UM	13
p	Knife (?)	S—1—36	Str. R—11—a, debris	NM	13
q	Knife or projectile point	W—5—77	Str. K—5—1st, surface	NM	13
r	,, ,, ,, ,,	M—18—3	South section, surface	UM	13
s	Scraper	W—29—40	West Group, house mound, surface	UM	12
t	Polisher (?)	W—31—16	Str. J—11, surface debris	UM	12
u	Gouge (?)	S—20—5	Str. Q—1, test pit	UM	13
v	Knife	W—17—40c	Burial 5	NM	13

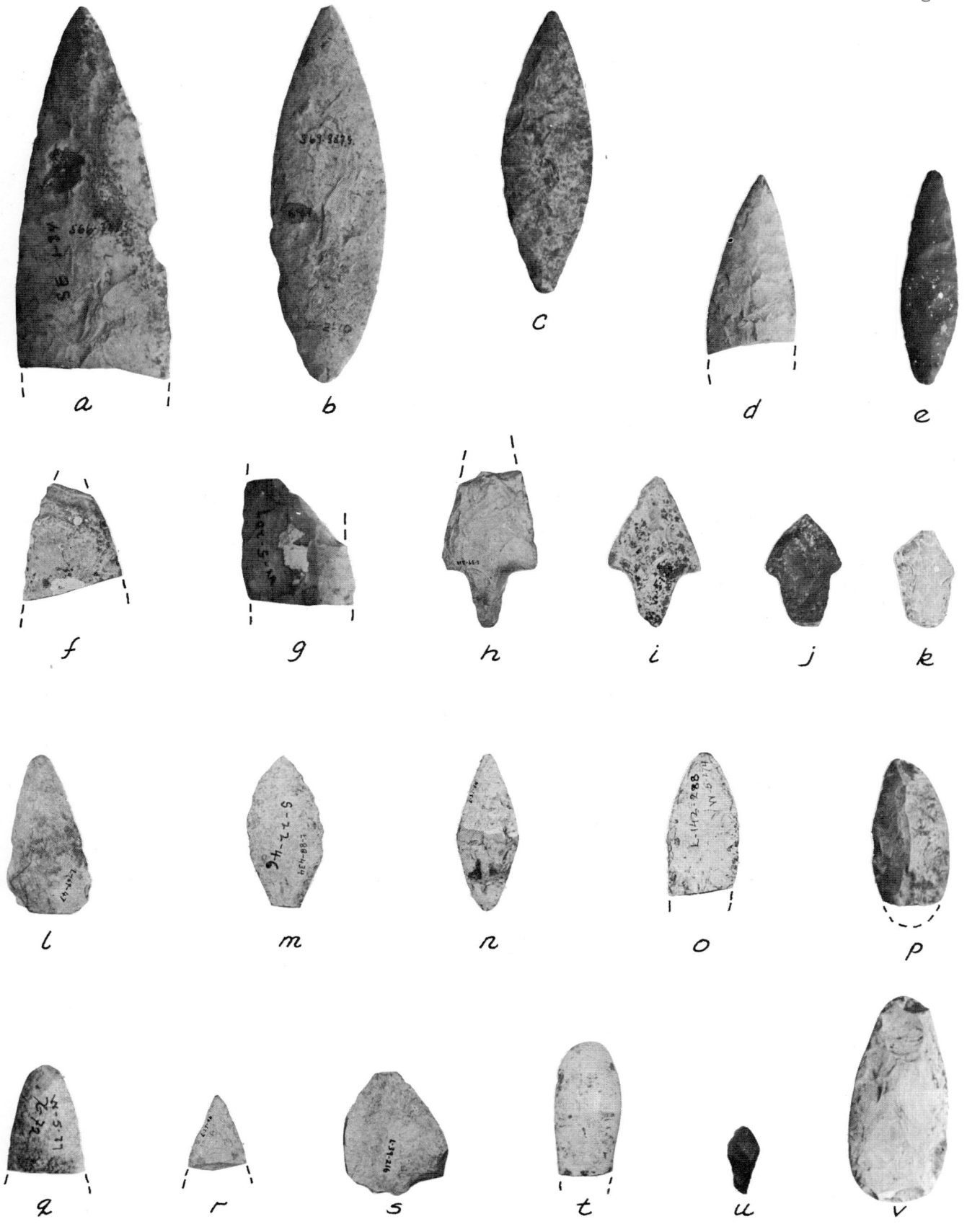

Fig. 3

FIGURE 4

CACHED FLINTS
All 1/2 scale

	DESCRIPTION		FIELD NO.	PROVENIENCE		DISPOSITION	REF. PAGE
a	Eccentric flint		E—1—4	Cache O—13—1		NM	18
b	,,	,,	,,	,,	,,	,,	20
c	,,	,,	,,	,,	,,	,,	21
d	,,	,,	,,	,,	,,	,,	21
e	,,	,,	,,	,,	,,	,,	18
f	,,	,,	,,	,,	,,	,,	20
g	,,	,,	E—1—11	Cache O—13—4		UM	20
h	,,	,,	,,	,,	,,	,,	18
i	,,	,,	,,	,,	,,	,,	21
j	,,	,,	E—1—122	Cache O—13—6		,,	17
k	,,	,,	,,	,,	,,	,,	17
l	,,	,,	,,	,,	,,	NM	18
m	,,	,,	,,	,,	,,	UM	19
n	,,	,,	,,	,,	,,	,,	18
o	,,	,,	,,	,,	,,	,,	20

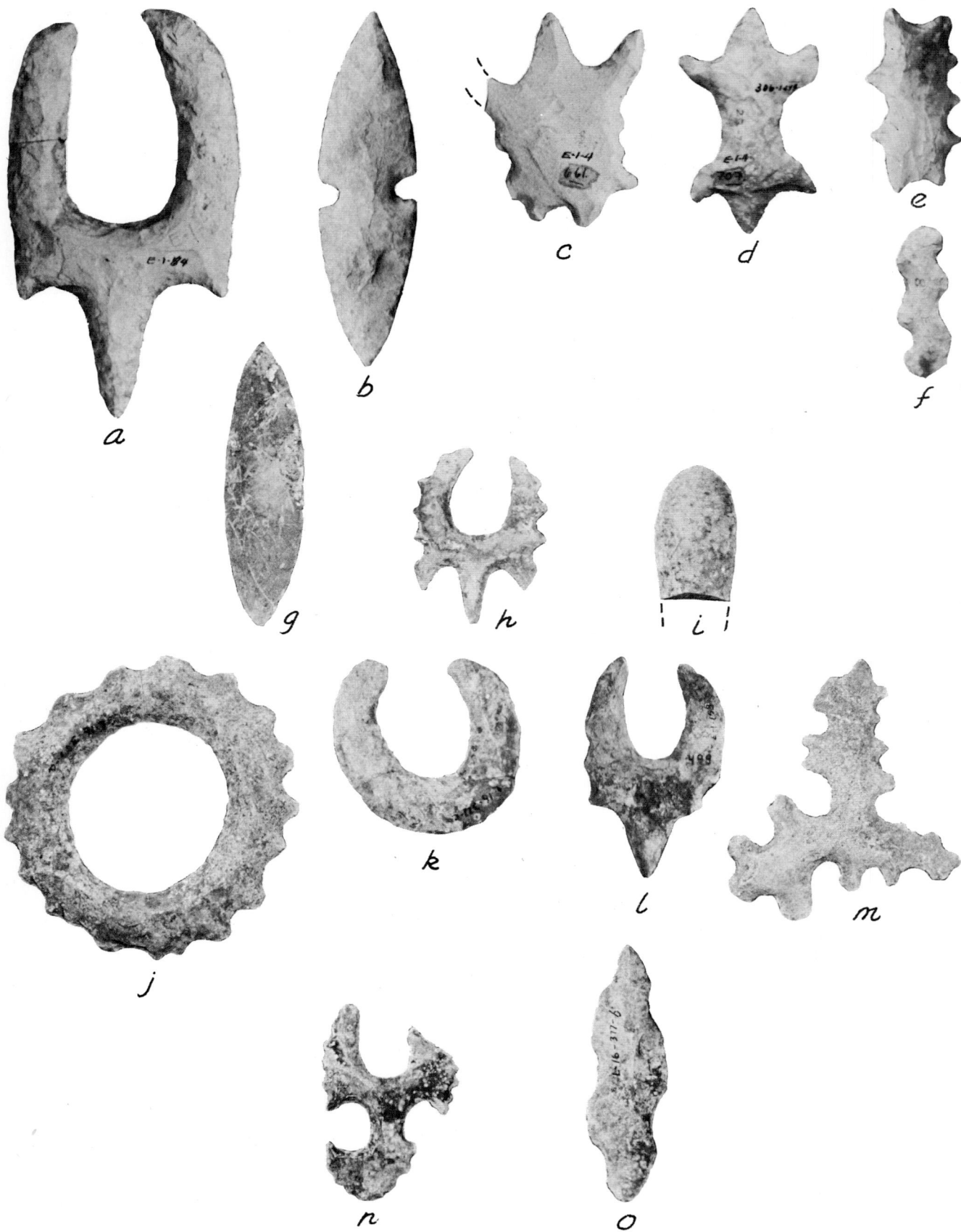

Fig. 4

FIGURE 5

CACHED FLINTS
All 1/2 scale

	DESCRIPTION		FIELD NO.	PROVENIENCE		DISPOSITION	REF. PAGE
a	Eccentric flint		E—1—119	Cache O—13—7		UM	21
b	,,	,,	,,	,,	,,	,,	21
c	,,	,,	,,	,,	,,	,,	18
d	,,	,,	,,	,,	,,	,,	21
e	,,	,,	,,	,,	,,	,,	18
f	,,	,,	,,	,,	,,	,,	18
g	,,	,,	,,	,,	,,	,,	21
h	,,	,,	E—1—120	Cache O—13—8		NM	21
i	,,	,,	,,	,,	,,	,,	18
j	,,	,,	E—1—121	Cache O—13—9		,,	18
k	,,	,,	,,	,,	,,	,,	21
l	,,	,,	E—1—153	Cache O—13—16		UM	21
m	,,	,,	,,	,,	,,	,,	18
n	,,	,,	,,	,,	,,	,,	20
o	,,	,,	,,	,,	,,	,,	17

Fig. 5

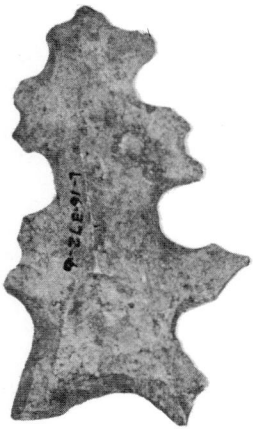

a

b

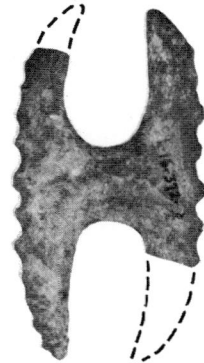

c

d

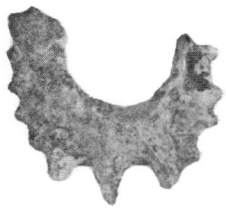

e

f

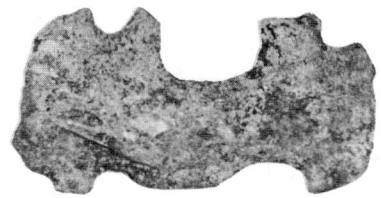

g

h

i

j

k

l

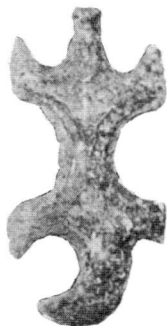

m

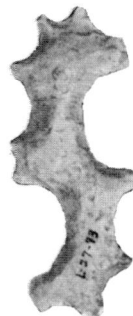

n

o

FIGURE 6

CACHED FLINTS
All 1/2 scale

	DESCRIPTION	FIELD NO.	PROVENIENCE		DISPOSITION	REF. PAGE
a	Eccentric flint	E–1–97	Cache O–13–10		UM	21
b	,, ,,	,,	,,	,,	,,	19
c	,, ,,	,,	,,	,,	NM	19
d	,, ,,	,,	,,	,,	UM	20
e	,, ,,	,,	,,	,,	NM	20
f	,, ,,	,,	,,	,,	,,	20
g	,, ,,	,,	,,	,,	UM	20
h	,, ,,	,,	,,	,,	,,	20
i	,, ,,	,,	,,	,,	NM	20
j	,, ,,	,,	,,	,,	UM	21
k	,, ,,	,,	,,	,,	NM	21
l	,, ,,	,,	,,	,,	UM	21
m	,, ,,	,,	,,	,,	,,	21
n	,, ,,	,,	,,	,,	,,	21

(Cache O–13–10 continued in Fig. 7)

Fig. 6

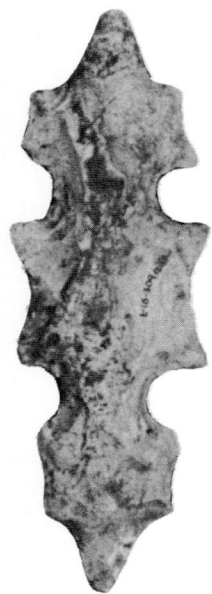

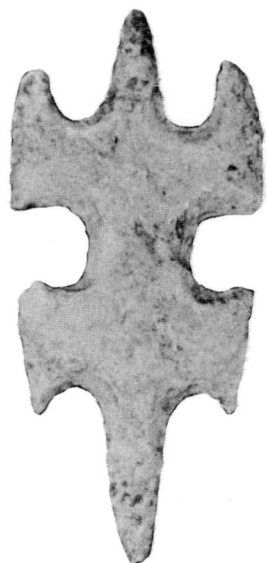

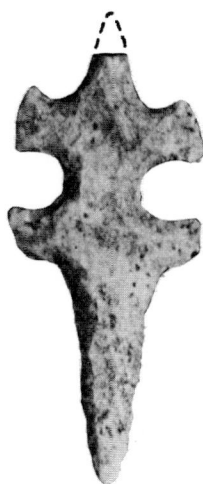

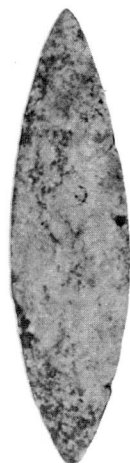

a

b

c

d

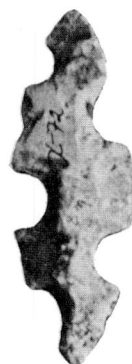

e

f

g

h

i

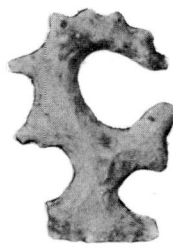

j

k

l

m

n

FIGURE 7

CACHED FLINTS (continued from Fig. 6)

All 1/2 scale

	DESCRIPTION	FIELD NO.	PROVENIENCE		DISPOSITION	REF. PAGE
a	Eccentric flint	E—1—97	Cache O—13—10		UM	18
b	,, ,,	,,	,, ,,		,,	18
c	,, ,,	,,	,, ,,		NM	18
d	,, ,,	,,	,, ,,		,,	18
e	,, ,,	,,	,, ,,		UM	18
f	,, ,,	,,	,, ,,		,,	18
g	,, ,,	,,	,, ,,		NM	18
h	,, ,,	,,	,, ,,		,,	18
i	,, ,,	,,	,, ,,		UM	18
j	,, ,,	,,	,, ,,		,,	18
k	,, ,,	,,	,, ,,		NM	18
l	,, ,,	,,	,, ,,		,,	18
m	,, ,,	,,	,, ,,		,,	17
n	,, ,,	,,	,, ,,		,,	21
o	,, ,,	,,	,, ,,		UM	19
p	,, ,,	,,	,, ,,		NM	19
q	,, ,,	,,	,, ,,		,,	21
r	,, ,,	,,	,, ,,		,, (not located, drawn from a field photo)	18
s	,, ,,	,,	,, ,,		NM	21

Fig. 7

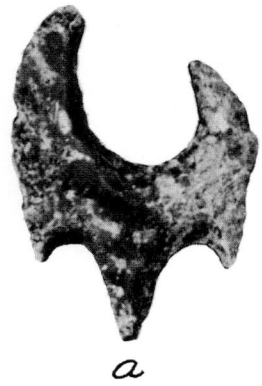

a

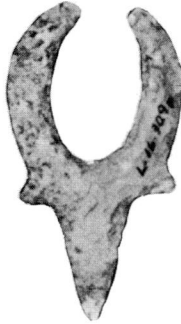

b

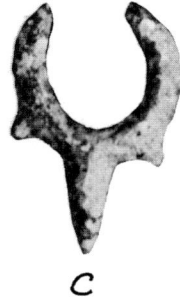

c

d

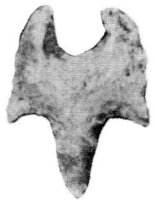

e

f

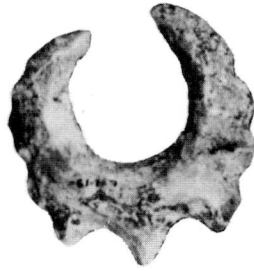

g

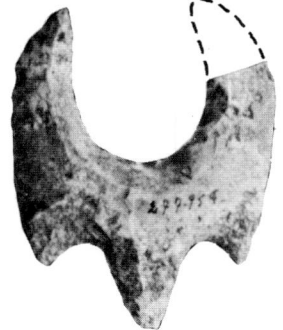

h

i

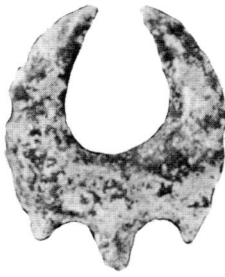

j

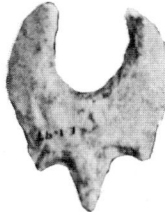

k

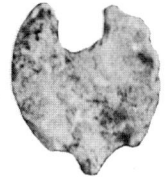

l

m

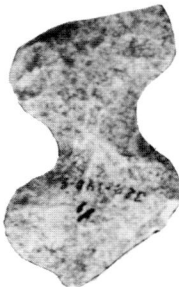

n

o

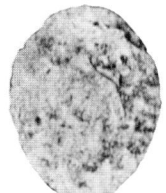

p

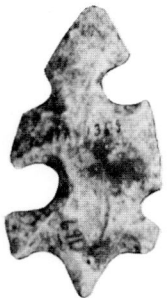

q

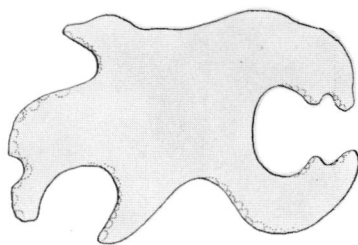

r

s

FIGURE 8

CACHED FLINTS
All 1/2 scale

	DESCRIPTION	FIELD NO.	PROVENIENCE	DISPOSITION	REF. PAGE
a	Eccentric flint	E—1—203	Cache O—13—17	UM	17
b	,, ,,	E—1—155	Cache O—13—18	,,	21
c	,, ,,	,,	,, ,,	NM	20
d	,, ,,	E—1—154	Cache O—13—23	,,	21
e	,, ,,	,,	,, ,,	UM	21
f	,, ,,	,,	,, ,,	NM	21
g	,, ,,	E—1—151	Cache O—13—24	,,	21
h	,, ,,	,,	,, ,,	UM	21
i	,, ,,	,,	,, ,,	,,	21
j	,, ,,	,,	,, ,,	NM	21
k	,, ,,	,,	,, ,,	,,	17
l	,, ,,	,,	,, ,,	,,	17
m	,, ,,	E—1—21	Cache O—13—26	UM	19
n	,, ,,	,,	,, ,,	,,	21
o	,, ,,	,,	,, ,,	,,	21
p	,, ,,	,,	,, ,,	,,	21
q	Flake	,,	,, ,,	,,	26
r	Eccentric flint	,,	,, ,,	,,	21
s	,, ,,	,,	,, ,,	,,	21

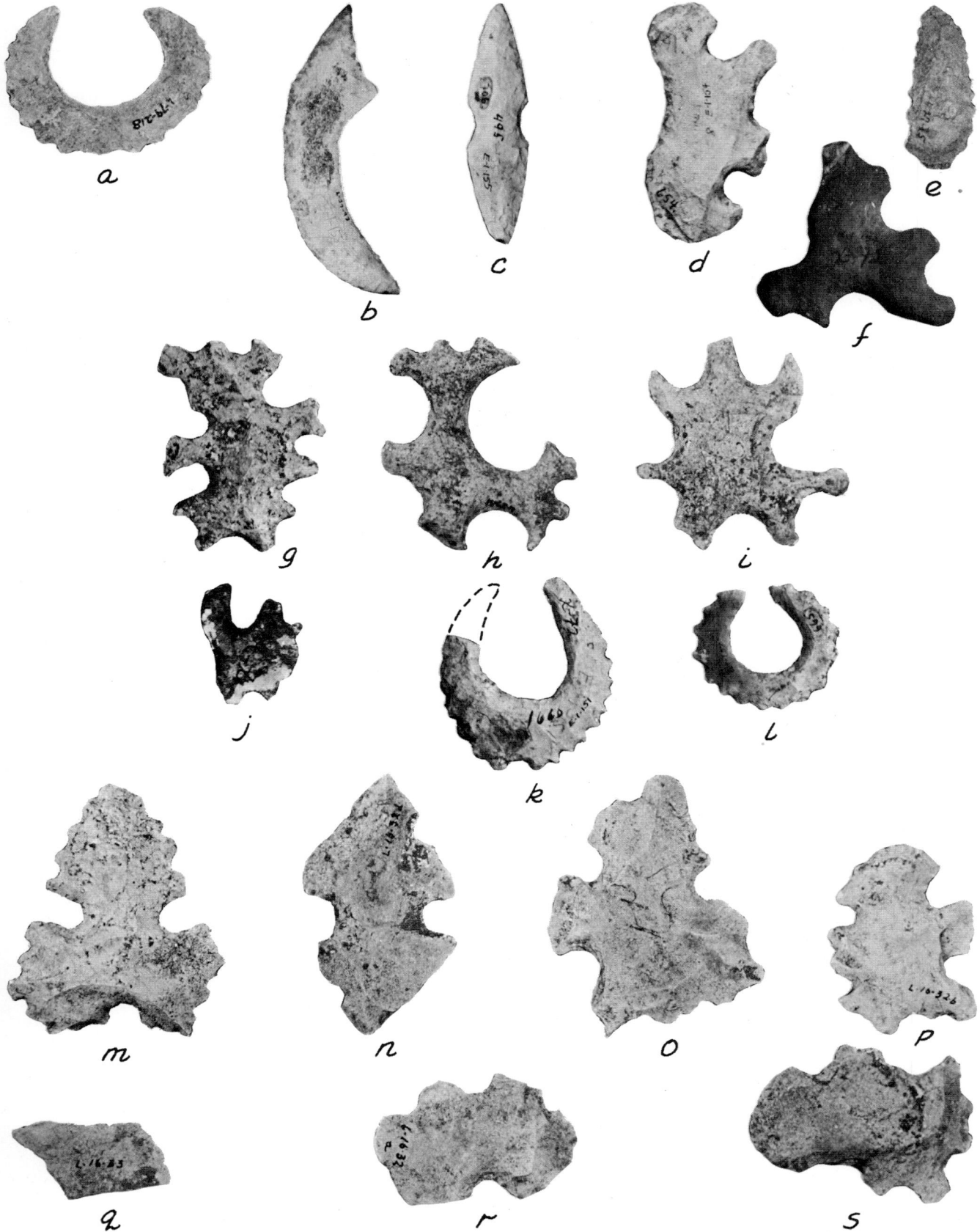

Fig. 8

FIGURE 9

CACHED FLINTS
All 1/2 scale

	DESCRIPTION	FIELD NO.	PROVENIENCE	DISPOSITION	REF. PAGE
a	Flakes	E−1−22	Cache O−13−27	UM	26
b	Blade fragment	,,	,, ,,	,,	20
c	Eccentric flint	E−1−32	Cache O−13−30	,,	21
d	,, ,,	,,	,, ,,	,,	20
e−g	Flakes	,,	,, ,,	,,	26
h	Eccentric flint	E−1−40	Cache O−13−36	,,	21
i	Flake	,,	,, ,,	,,	26
j	Eccentric flint	E−1−42	Cache O−13−37	,,	18
k	,, ,,	,,	,, ,,	,,	21
l	,, ,,	,,	,, ,,	,,	21
m	,, ,,	E−1−44	Cache O−13−38	NM	20
n, o	Flakes	,,	,, ,,	,,	26
p	Eccentric flint	E−1−48	Cache O−13−41	,,	21
q	,, ,,	,,	,, ,,	,,	21
r−t	Flakes	,,	,, ,,	,,	26
u	Eccentric flint	E−1−57	Cache O−13−43	,,	21
v	,, ,,	,,	,, ,,	,,	18
w	,, ,,	,,	,, ,,	,,	18

Fig. 9

a

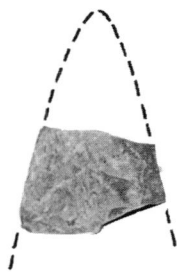

b

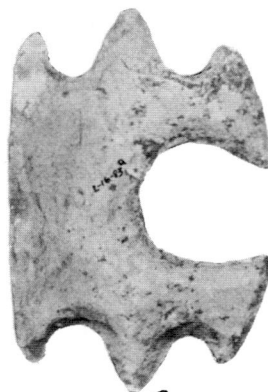

c

d

e

f

g

h

i

j

k

l

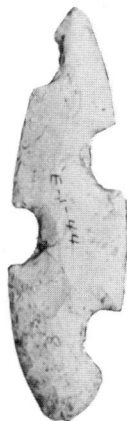

m

n

o

p

q

r

s

t

u

v

w

FIGURE 10

CACHED FLINTS
All 1/2 scale

	DESCRIPTION	FIELD NO.	PROVENIENCE	DISPOSITION	REF. PAGE
a	Eccentric flint	E—1—58	Cache O—13—44	UM	21
b	,, ,,	,,	,, ,,	,,	21
c	,, ,,	,,	,, ,,	,,	18
d	,, ,,	,,	,, ,,	,,	18
e	,, ,,	,,	,, ,,	,,	21
f—h	Eccentric flints	E—1—64	Cache O—13—46	NM	17
i	Flakes	,,	,, ,,	,,	26
j	Eccentric flint	E—1—83	Cache O—13—47	UM	21
k	,, ,,	,,	,, ,,	,,	18
l	,, ,,	,,	,, ,,	,,	18
m	,, ,,	,,	,, ,,	,,	19
n	,, ,,	,,	,, ,,	,,	18
o	,, ,,	,,	,, ,,	,,	21
p	,, ,,	,,	,, ,,	,,	19
q	Flakes	,,	,, ,,	,,	26
r	Eccentric flint	E—1—92	Cache O—13—48	,,	18
s	,, ,,	,,	,, ,,	,,	21
t	,, ,,	E—1—93	Cache O—13—49	NM	21
u	,, ,,	E—1—84	Cache O—13—51	UM	18
v	,, ,,	,,	,, ,,	,,	21
w	Flakes	,,	,, ,,	,,	26

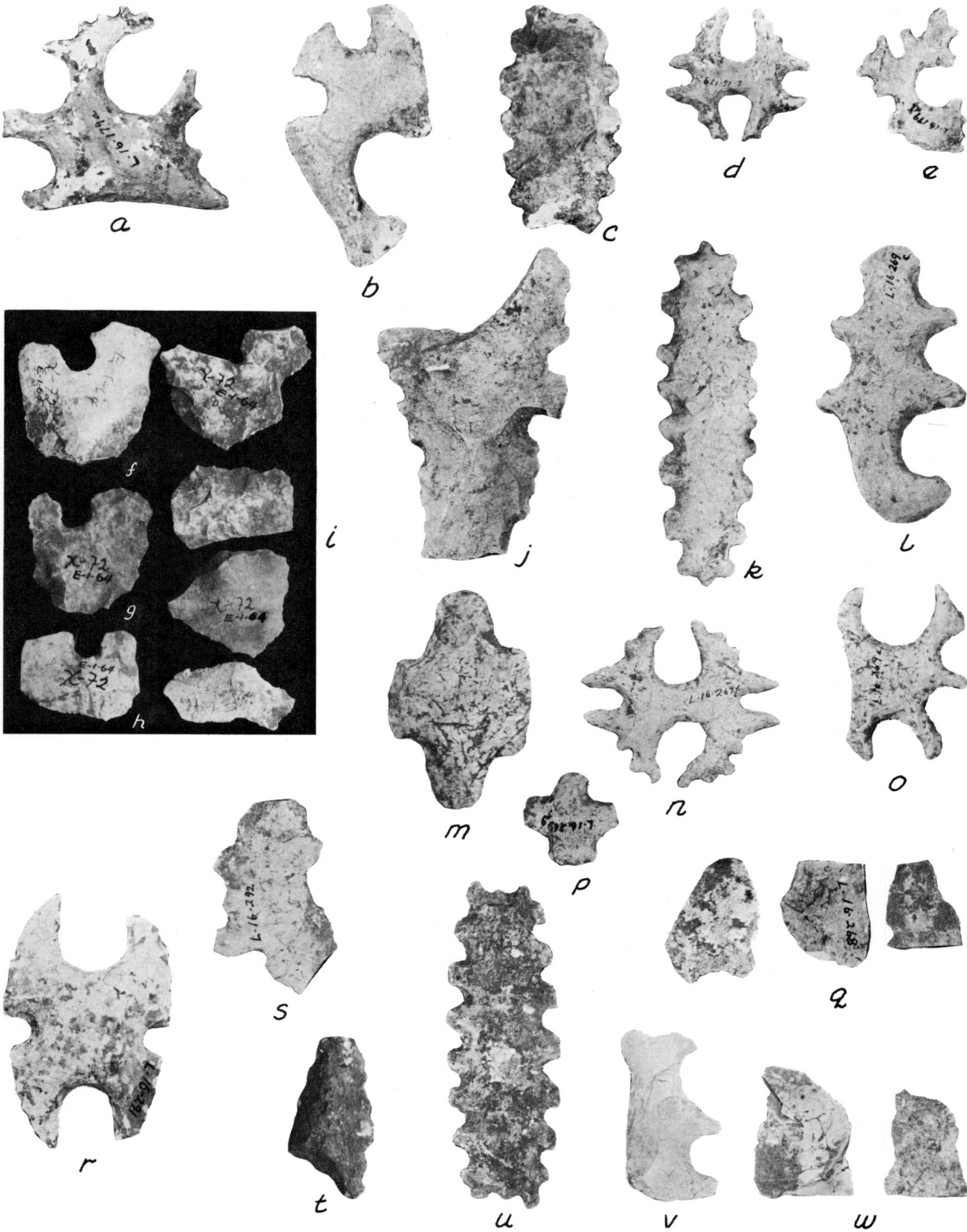

Fig. 10

FIGURE 11

CACHED FLINTS
All 1/2 scale

	DESCRIPTION	FIELD NO.	PROVENIENCE	DISPOSITION	REF. PAGE
a	Eccentric flint	E—1—10	Cache O—13—54	NM	18
b	,, ,,	,,	,, ,,	,,	20
c	,, ,,	,,	,, ,,	,,	21

The following objects lack field numbers but are believed to be from Str. O—13 caches. See Fig. 12, a —q

	DESCRIPTION	FIELD NO.	PROVENIENCE	DISPOSITION	REF. PAGE
d—i	Eccentric flints			,,	18
j—l	,, ,,			,,	17
m, n	,, ,,			,,	18
o	Eccentric flint			,,	19

Fig. 11

a

b

C

d

e

f

g

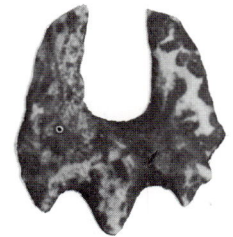

h

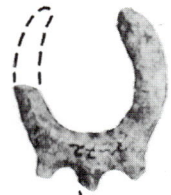

i

j

k

l

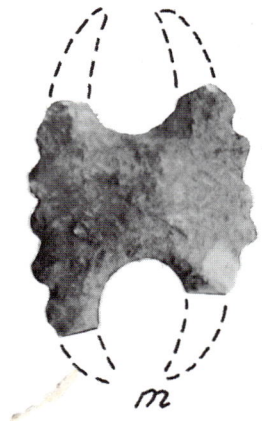

m

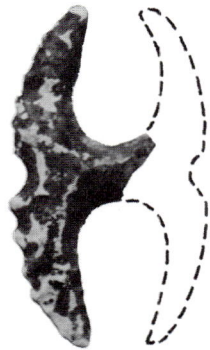

n

o

FIGURE 12

CACHED FLINTS
All 1/2 scale

	DESCRIPTION	FIELD NO.	PROVENIENCE	DISPOSITION	REF. PAGE
	The following objects lack field numbers but are believed to be from Str. O–13 caches. See Fig. 11, d–o				
a–c	Eccentric flints			NM	18
d	Eccentric flint			,,	19
e	,, ,,			,,	18
f	,, ,,			,,	21
g	,, ,,			,,	21
h	,, ,,			,,	21
i	,, ,,			,,	21
j	,, ,,			,,	21
k	,, ,,			,,	20
l	,, ,,			,,	20
m	,, ,,			,,	19
n–p	Eccentric flints			,,	21
q	Eccentric flint	W–40–13b	Cache O–16–1	UM	21
r	,, ,,	,,	,, ,,	,,	21
s	,, ,,	W–1–40	Cache J–1–1	,,	17

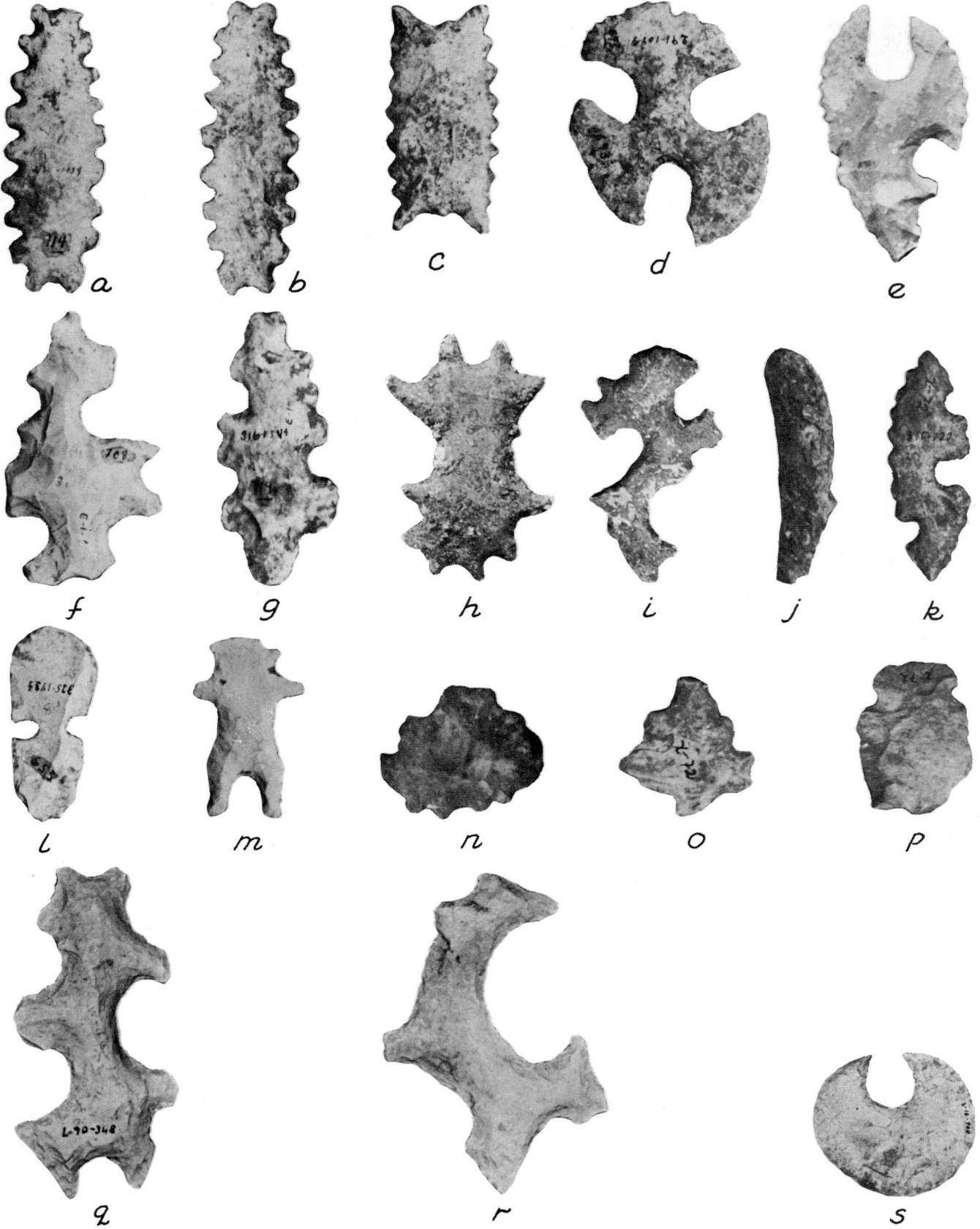

Fig. 12

a b c d e

f g h i j k

l m n o p

q r s

FIGURE 13

CACHED FLINTS

All 1/2 scale

	DESCRIPTION	FIELD NO.	PROVENIENCE	DISPOSITION	REF. PAGE
a	Eccentric flint	W—3—5	Cache J—1—2	NM	21
b	,, ,,	,,	,, ,,	,,	21
c, d	Eccentric flints	,,	,, ,,	,,	20
e—g	,, ,,	,,	,, ,,	,,	17
h	Eccentric flint	W—12—15b	Cache J—6—2	,,	21
i	,, ,,	,,	,, ,,	,,	19
j	,, ,,	,,	,, ,,	,,	19
k	,, ,,	,,	,, ,,	,,	21
l	,, ,,	,,	,, ,,	,,	21
m—o	Eccentric flints	,,	,, ,,	,,	17
p	Eccentric flint	,,	,, ,,	,,	21
q	,, ,,	,,	,, ,,	,,	21
r	,, ,,	,,	,, ,,	,,	21
s	,, ,,	,,	,, ,,	,,	21
t	,, ,,	,,	,, ,,	,,	19

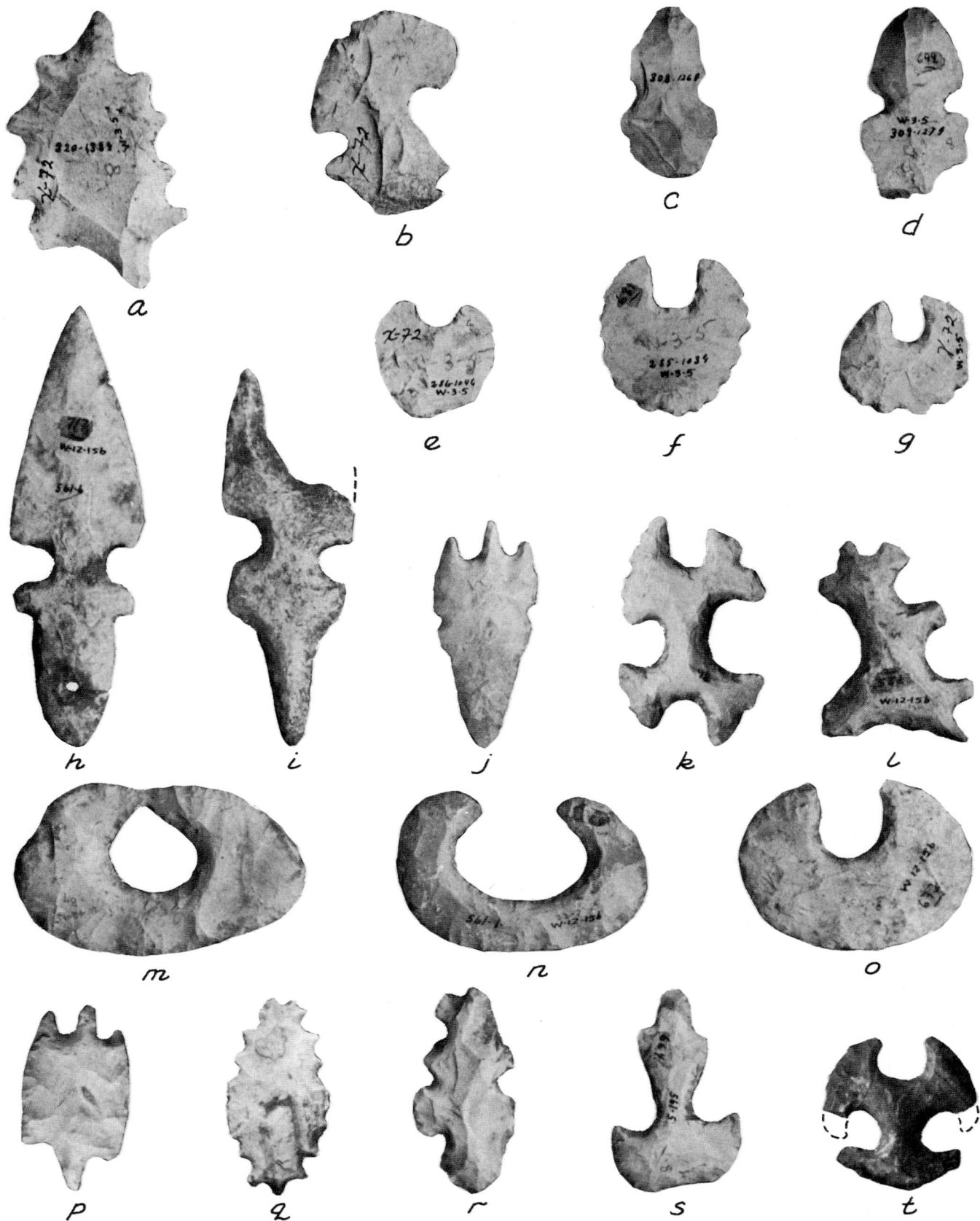

Fig. 13

a

b

c

d

e

f

g

h

i

j

k

l

m

n

o

p

q

r

s

t

FIGURE 14

CACHED FLINTS
All 1/2 scale

	DESCRIPTION	FIELD NO.	PROVENIENCE	DISPOSITION	REF. PAGE
a	Eccentric flint	W—12—16	Cache J—6—3	NM	20
b	,, ,,	,,	,, ,,	,,	21
c	,, ,,	,,	,, ,,	,,	17
d	,, ,,	,,	,, ,,	,,	17
e	,, ,,	W—12—17	Cache J—6—4	UM	21
f	,, ,,	,,	,, ,,	,,	20
g	,, ,,	,,	,, ,,	,,	21
h	,, ,,	NE—4—19	Cache J—29—1	NM	17
i	,, ,,	,,	,, ,,	,,	17
j	,, ,,	W—12—18	Cache J—6—5	UM	21
k	,, ,,	,,	,, ,,	,,	22
l, m	Eccentric flints	,,	,, ,,	,,	19

a

b

c

d

Fig. 14

e

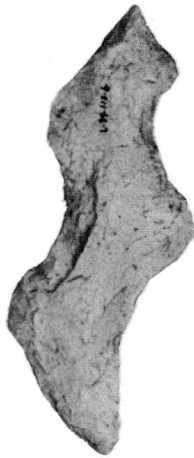

f

g

h

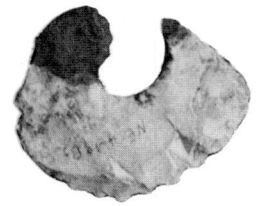

i

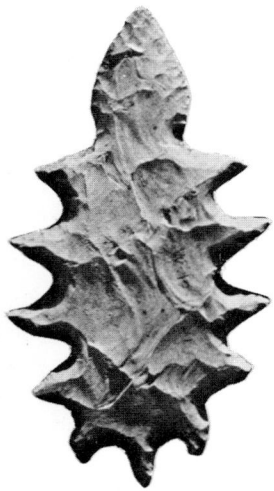

j

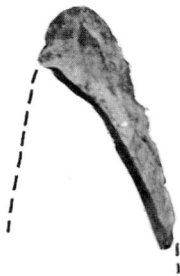

k

l

m

FIGURE 15

CACHED FLINTS
All 1/2 scale

	DESCRIPTION	FIELD NO.	PROVENIENCE	DISPOSITION	REF. PAGE
a	Eccentric flint	W—5—6	Cache K—5—1	UM	21
b	,, ,,	,,	,, ,,	,,	21
c	,, ,,	,,	,, ,,	,,	21
d	,, ,,	,,	,, ,,	,,	18
e	,, ,,	,,	,, ,,	,,	17
f	,, ,,	,,	,, ,,	,,	21
g	,, ,,	,,	,, ,,	,,	18
h	,, ,,	W—6—21	Cache K—5—2	,,	21
i	,, ,,	,,	,, ,,	NM	17
j	,, ,,	,,	,, ,,	,,	21
k	Flakes	,,	,, ,,	,,	26
l	Eccentric flint	W—5—145	Cache K—5—5	UM	21
m	,, ,,	,,	,, ,,	,,	21
n	,, ,,	,,	,, ,,	,,	20
o	,, ,,	W—5—275	Cache K—5—8	,,	19
p	,, ,,	,,	,, ,,	,,	18
q	,, ,,	,,	,, ,,	,,	18
r	,, ,,	,,	,, ,,	,,	17

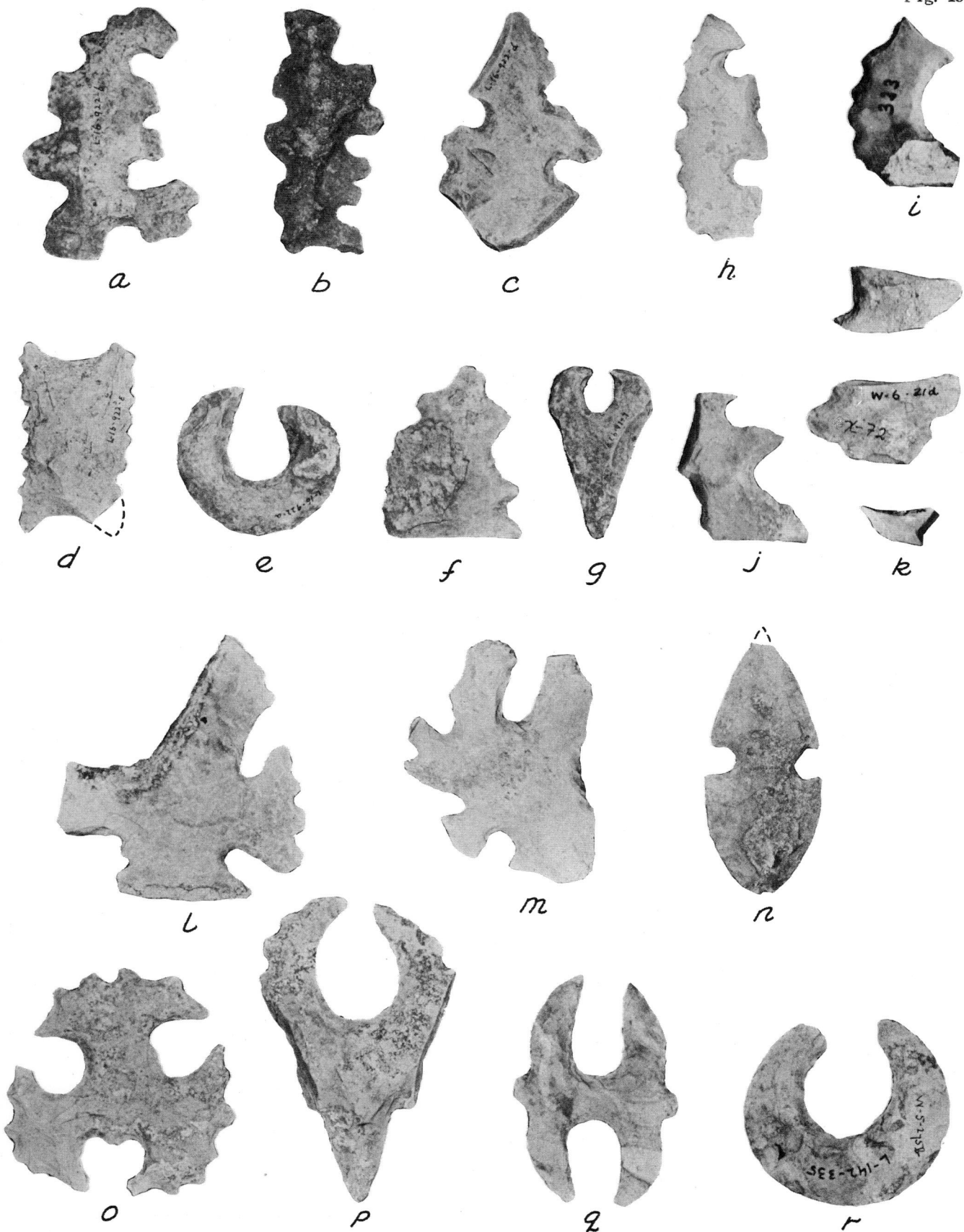

Fig. 15

FIGURE 16

CACHED FLINTS
All 1/2 scale

	DESCRIPTION	FIELD NO.	PROVENIENCE	DISPOSITION	REF. PAGE
a	Eccentric flint	W—5—183	Cache K—5—6	NM	19
b	,, ,,	,,	,, ,,	,,	20
c	,, ,,	,,	,, ,,	,,	20
d	,, ,,	S—21—27	Cache R—9—2	,,	18
e	,, ,,	,,	,, ,,	,,	21
f	,, ,,	,,	,, ,,	,,	18
g, h	Eccentric flints	,,	,, ,,	,,	19
i	Eccentric flint	,,	,, ,,	,,	19
j	,, ,,	,,	,, ,,	,,	17
k	,, ,,	S—18—2	Cache R—16—1	,,	18
l	,, ,,	,,	,, ,,	,,	21
m	,, ,,	,,	,, ,,	,,	20
n, o	Eccentric flint fragments	,,	,, ,,	,,	20, 21

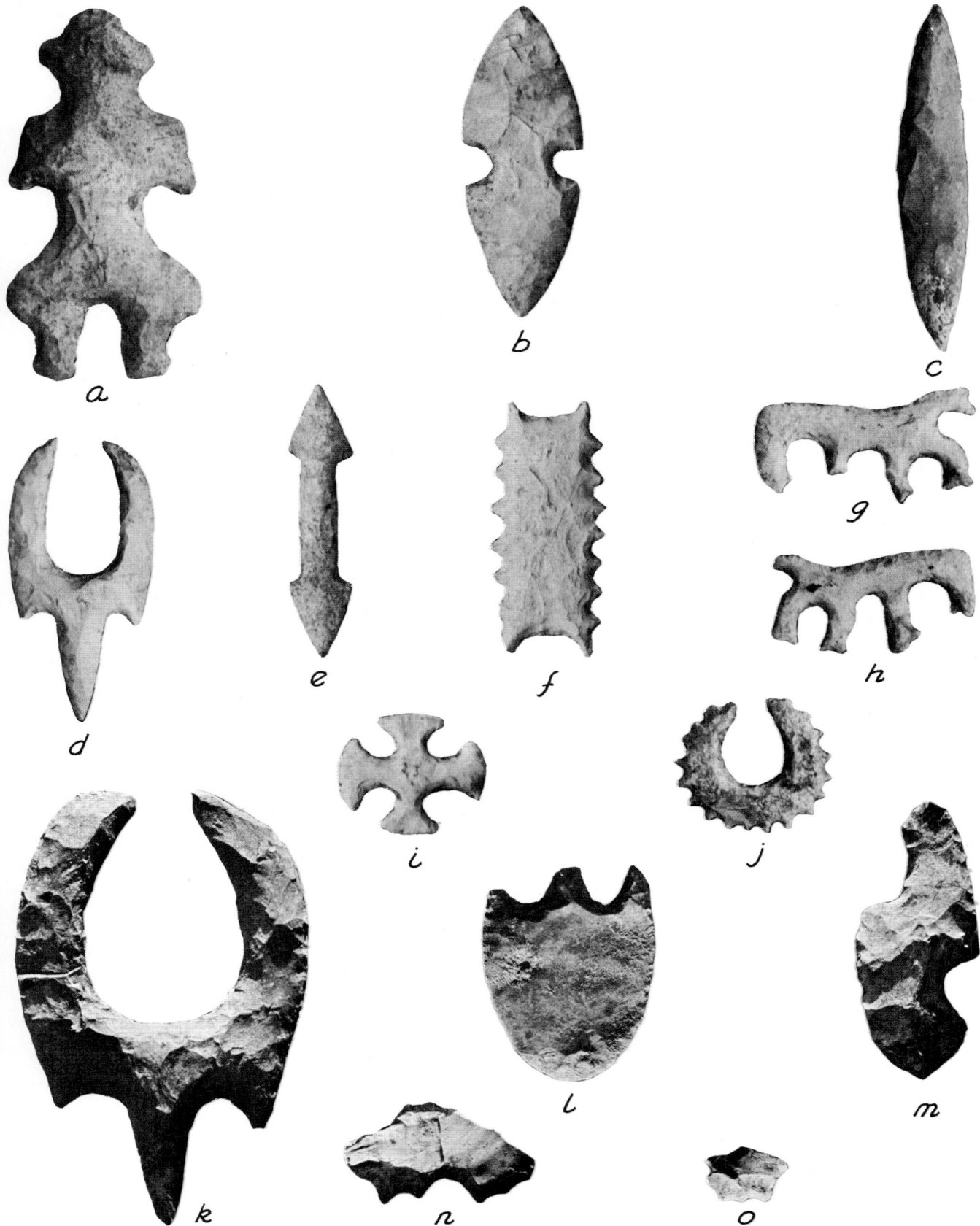

Fig. 16

FIGURE 17

CACHED FLINTS
All 1/2 scale

	DESCRIPTION	FIELD NO.	PROVENIENCE	DISPOSITION	REF. PAGE
a	Eccentric flint	S—21—20a	Cache R—9—1	UM	17
b	,, ,,	,,	,, ,,	,,	17
c	,, ,,	,,	,, ,,	,,	18
d	,, ,,	,,	,, ,,	,,	18
e, f	Eccentric flints	,,	,, ,,	,,	21
g	Eccentric flint	,,	,, ,,	,,	18
h	,, ,,	,,	,, ,,	,,	17
i	,, ,,	,,	,, ,,	,,	18
j, k	Eccentric flints	,,	,, ,,	,,	18
l	Eccentric flint	,,	,, ,,	,,	18
m, n	Eccentric flints	,,	,, ,,	,,	21

Fig. 17

a

b

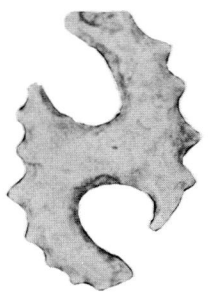

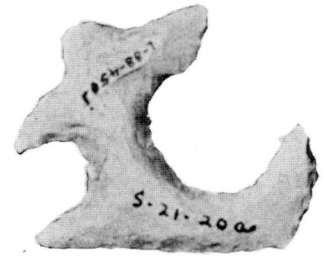

c

d

e

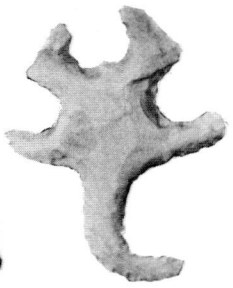

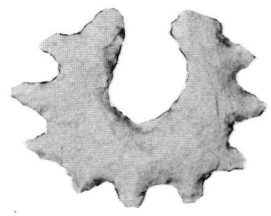

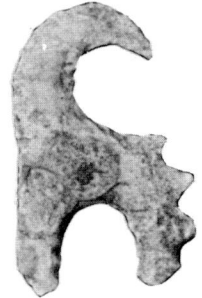

f

g

h

i

j

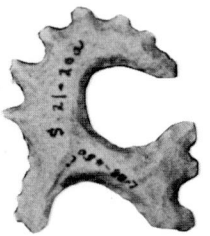

k

l

m

n

FIGURE 18

CACHED FLINTS

All 1/2 scale

	DESCRIPTION	FIELD NO.	PROVENIENCE	DISPOSITION	REF. PAGE
a	Eccentric flint	S—1—(50—51)	Cache R—11—7	UM	21
b	,, ,,	,,	,, ,,	,,	18
c	,, ,,	,,	,, ,,	,,	18
d	,, ,,	W—31—36	Str. J—11, surface debris	NM	21
e	,, ,,	W—12—104	Str. J—6, plaza. From one of the J—6 caches ?	UM	21
f	,, ,,	,,	See e	NM	21
g	,, ,,	W—39—1	Str. O—15, surface debris at foot of stairway	UM	21
h	,, ,,	S—25—15	Str. U—3	,,	17
i	,, ,,	E—7—144	Str. O—7	,,	21

The following objects lack field numbers, having been burned in the camp fire. They are believed to be from Str. O—13 caches. See also Fig. 19 a—k

	DESCRIPTION	FIELD NO.	PROVENIENCE	DISPOSITION	REF. PAGE
j	,, ,,			NM	18
k, 1	Eccentric flints			UM	18
m	Eccentric flint			NM	18
n	,, ,,			UM	20
o	,, ,,			NM	20
p	,, ,,			UM	20

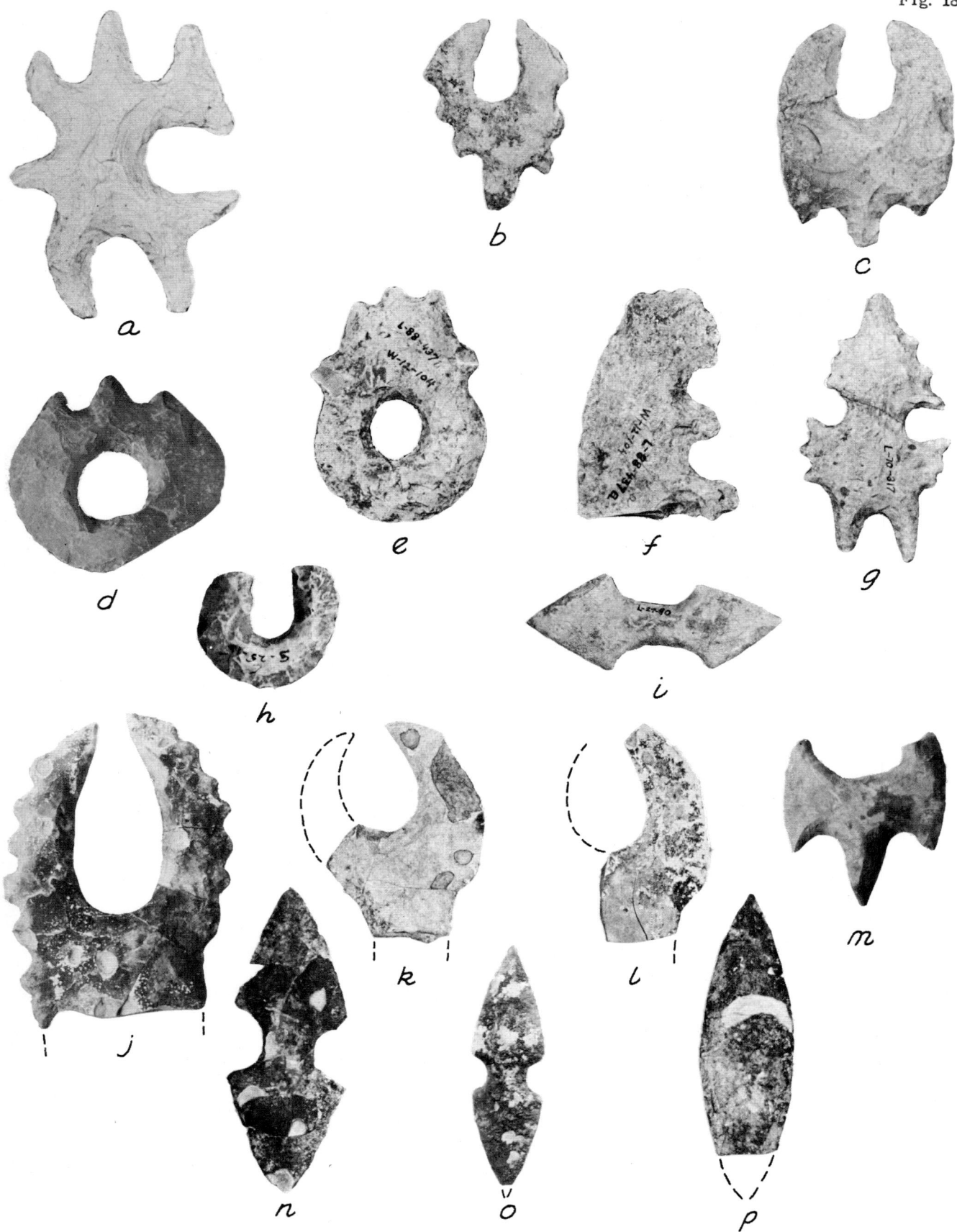

Fig. 18

FIGURE 19

CACHED FLINTS

All 1/2 scale

	DESCRIPTION	FIELD NO.	PROVENIENCE	DISPOSITION	REF. PAGE
		The following objects lack field numbers, having been burned in the camp fire. They very probably are from Str. O—13 caches. See also Fig. 18 j—p			
a	Eccentric flint			NM	20
b	,, ,,			,,	21
c	,, ,,			UM	18
d	,, ,,			NM	21
e	,, ,,			,,	21
f	,, ,,			UM	21
g	,, ,,			,,	21
h	,, ,,			NM	21
i, j	Eccentric flints			UM	21
k	,, ,,			,,	17
l	Large ceremonial blade	W—4—10	Cache J—3—1	,,	25
m	,, ,, ,,	,,	,, ,,	NM	25
n	,, ,, ,,	,,	,, ,,	UM	25
o	,, ,, ,,	,,	,, ,,	NM	25

(Cache J—3—1 continued in Fig. 20)

Fig. 19

FIGURE 20

CACHED FLINTS (continued from Fig. 19)
All 1/2 scale

	DESCRIPTION	FIELD NO.	PROVENIENCE	DISPOSITION	REF. PAGE
a, a'	Large ceremonial blade	W—4—10	Cache J—3—1	a in UM; a' in NM	25
b	Large ceremonial blade fragment	,,	,, ,,	UM	25
c	Large ceremonial blade fragment	,,	,, ,,	,,	25
d—h	Large ceremonial blade fragments	,,	,, ,,	NM	25

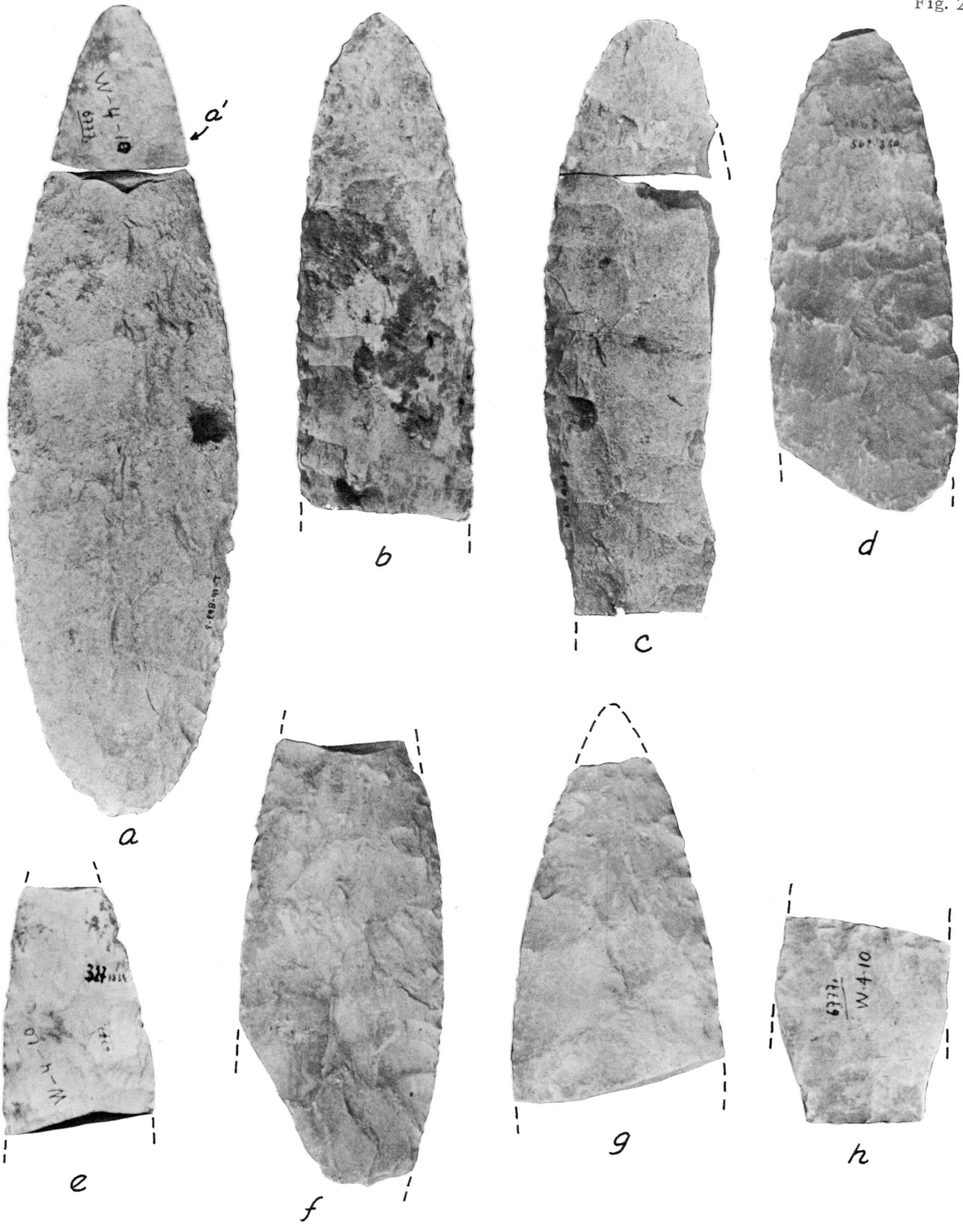

Fig. 20

FIGURE 21

CACHED OBSIDIANS
Natural size

	DESCRIPTION	FIELD NO.	PROVENIENCE	DISPOSITION	REF. PAGE
a	Eccentric obsidian	E–1–4	Cache O–13–1	NM (not located)	26
b	,, ,,	,,	,, ,,	,, (not located)	27
c	,, ,,	,,	,, ,,	,, (not located)	28
d	,, ,,	,,	,, ,,	,,	27
e	,, ,,	,,	,, ,,	,,	28
f	,, ,,	E–1–11	Cache O- 13–4	UM	28
g	,, ,,	,,	,, ,,	,,	28
h	Flake-blade	,,	,, ,,	,,	31
i	Eccentric obsidian	E–1–122	Cache O–13–6	,,	27
j	,, ,,	,,	,, ,,	,,	27
k	,, ,,	,,	,, ,,	,,	27
l	,, ,,	,,	,, ,,	,,	26
m	,, ,,	,,	,, ,,	,,	28
n	,, ,,	,,	,, ?,	,,	28
o	,, ,,	,,	,, ,,	,,	28
p	,, ,,	,,	,, ,,	,,	29
q	Core	,,	,, ,,	,,	30
r	Flake or eccentric	,,	,, ,,	,,	27
s	Eccentric obsidian	E–1–119	Cache O–13–7	,,	27
t	,, ,,	,,	,, ,,	,,	29
u	,, ,,	,,	,, ,,	,,	27
v	,, ,,	,,	,, ,,	,,	28
w	,, ,,	,,	,, ,,	,,	28
x	,, ,,	,,	,, ,,	,,	26
y	,, ,,	,,	,, ,,	,,	28
z	,, ,,	,,	,, ,,	,,	27
a¹	Flake-blade	,,	,, ,,	,,	31

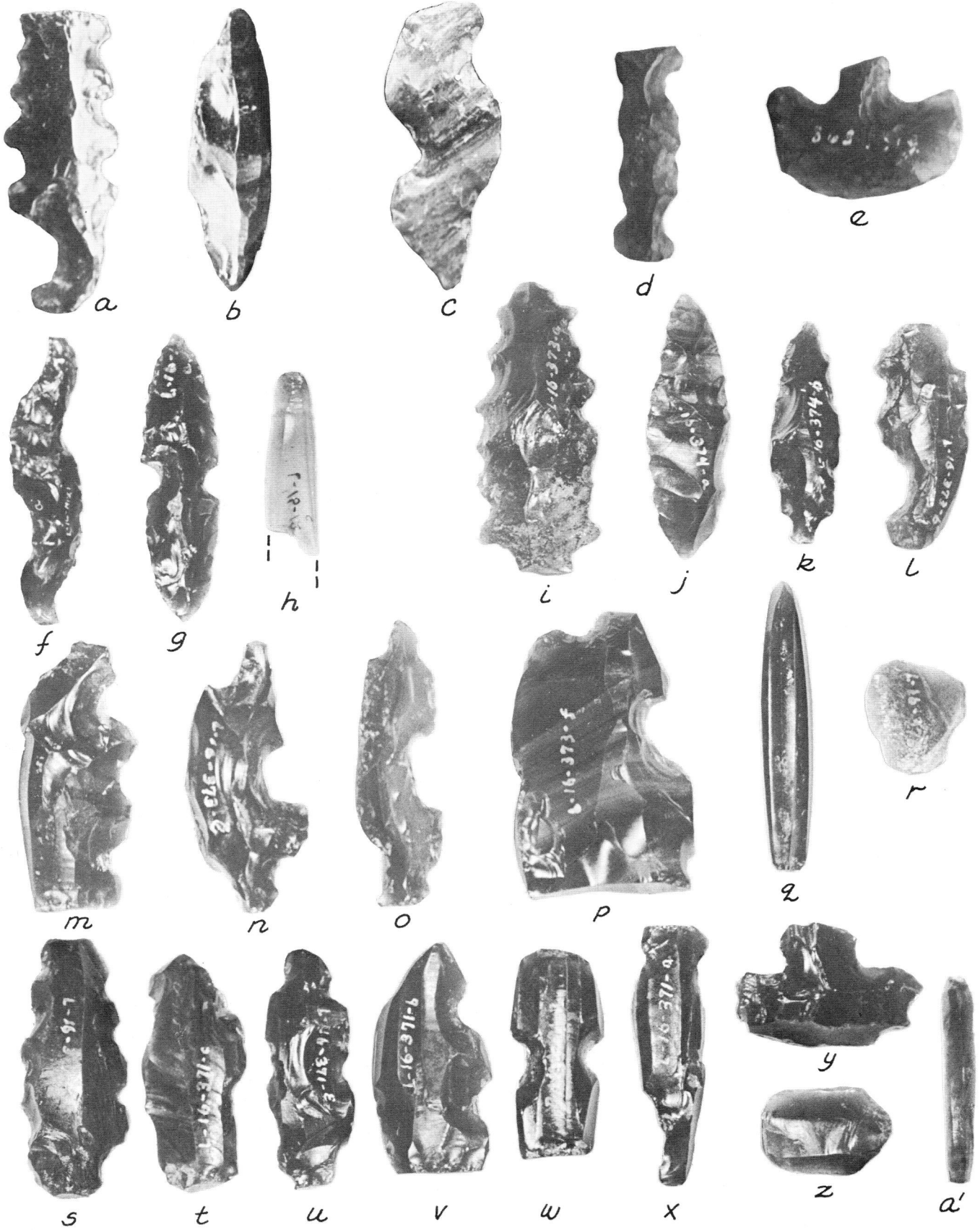

Fig. 21

FIGURE 22

CACHED OBSIDIANS

Natural size

	DESCRIPTION	FIELD NO.	PROVENIENCE	DISPOSITION	REF. PAGE
a	Eccentric obsidian	E—1—97	Cache O—13—10	UM	26
b	" "	"	" "	"	28
c, d	Eccentric obsidians	"	" "	"	28
e, f	" "	"	" "	"	27
g	Eccentric obsidian	"	" "	"	28
h, i	Eccentric obsidians	"	" "	"	28
j, k	" "	"	" "	"	27
l	Eccentric obsidian	"	" "	"	26
m	" "	"	" "	"	27
n	" "	"	" "	"	29
o	Flake	"	" "	"	29

Other Cache O—13—10 eccentric obsidians are shown in Figs. 30 m; 31 c, m; 32 o, p; 33 n; 34 f; 36 j

	DESCRIPTION	FIELD NO.	PROVENIENCE	DISPOSITION	REF. PAGE
p	Eccentric obsidian	E—1—153	Cache O—13—16	"	28
q	" "	"	" "	"	30
r	" "	"	" "	"	26
s	" "	E—1—204	Cache O—13—17	"	28
t	" "	"	" "	"	27
u	" "	"	" "	"	27
v	" "	"	" "	"	28
w	" "	"	" "	"	28

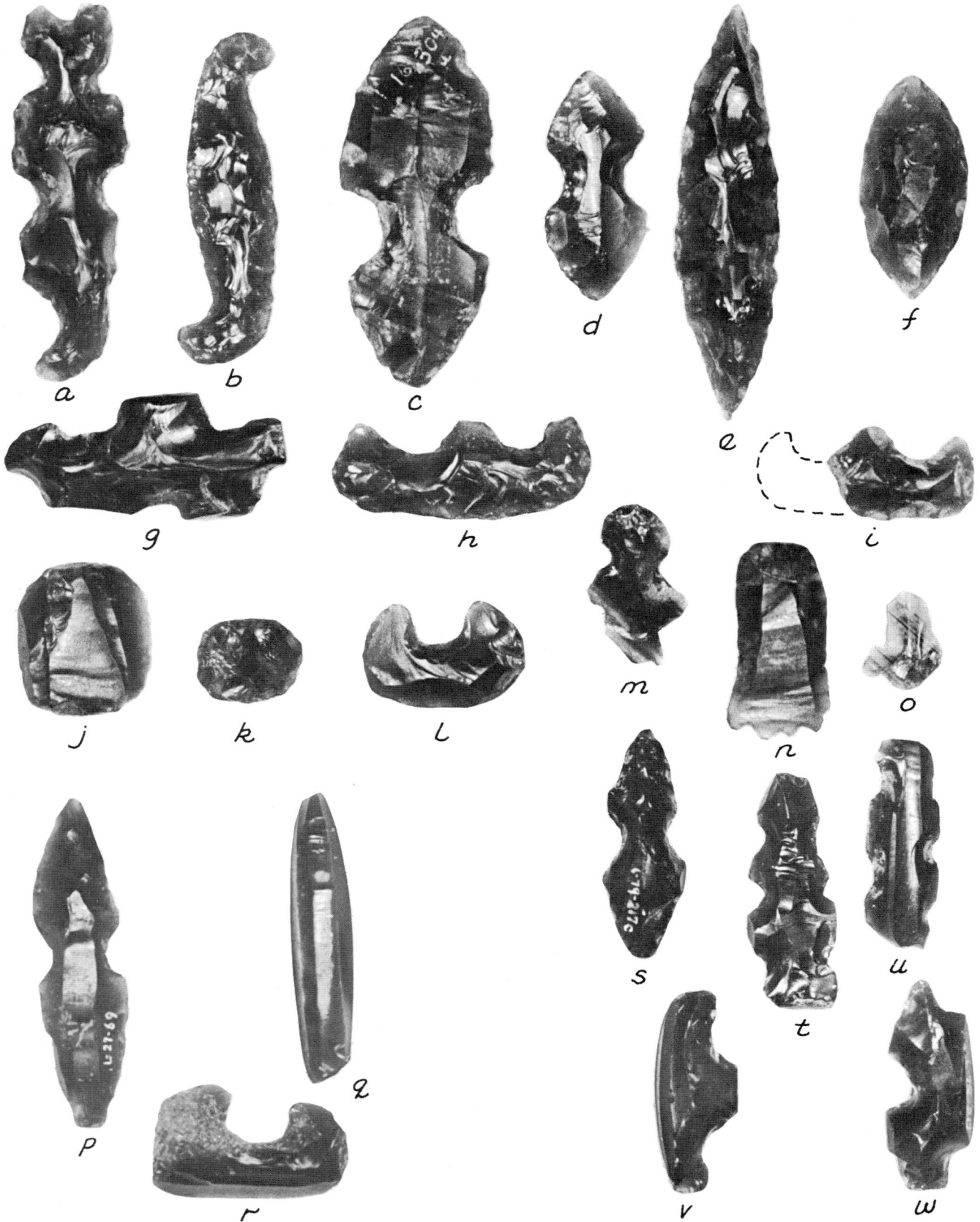

Fig. 22

FIGURE 23

CACHED OBSIDIANS

Natural size

	DESCRIPTION	FIELD NO.	PROVENIENCE	DISPOSITION	REF. PAGE
a	Eccentric obsidian	E-1-109	Cache O-13-13	UM	28
b-d	Eccentric obsidians	,,	,, ,,	,,	26
e	Eccentric obsidian	,,	,, ,,	,,	28
f	,, ,,	,,	,, ,,	,,	28
g	,, ,,	,,	,, ,,	,,	27
h	,, ,,	,,	,, ,,	,,	29
i	,, ,,	,,	,, ,,	,,	28
j	,, ,,	E-1-120	Cache O-13-8	NM	27
k	,, ,,	E-1-104	Cache O-13-11	,,	28
l	,, ,,	E-1-108	Cache O-13-19	,,	28
m	,, ,,	E-1-155	Cache O-13-18	UM	27
n	,, ,,	,,	,, ,,	,,	29
o	,, ,,	E-1-154	Cache O-13-23	,,	29
p	,, ,,	,,	,, ,,	,,	29
q	,, ,,	E-1-151	Cache O-13-24	,,	26
r	,, ,,	E-1-19	Cache O-13-25	NM	27

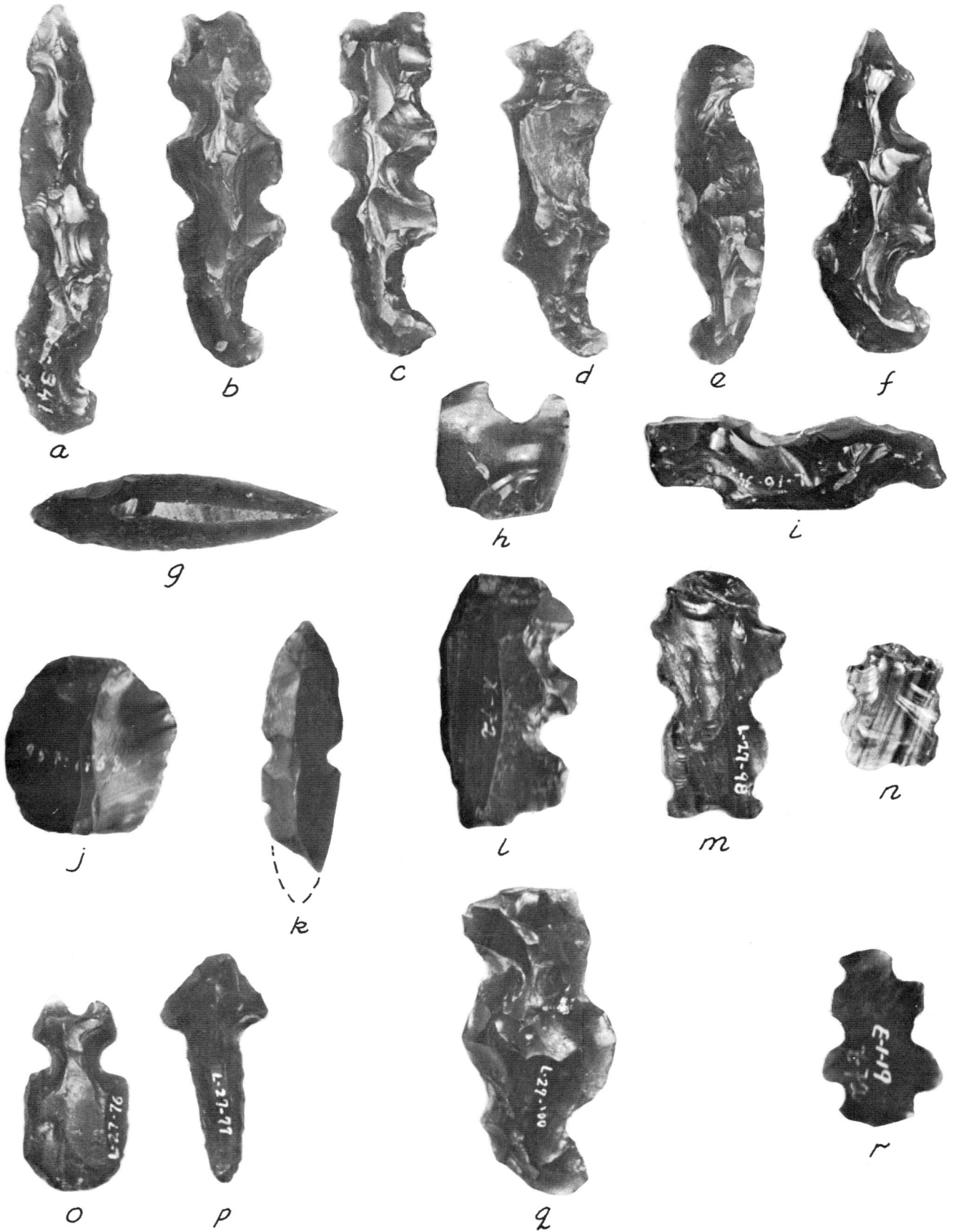

Fig. 23

FIGURE 24

CACHED OBSIDIANS
Natural size

	DESCRIPTION	FIELD NO.	PROVENIENCE	DISPOSITION	REF. PAGE
a—d	Flake-blades	E—1—22	Cache O—13—27	UM	31
e, f	Flakes	,,	,, ,,	,,	30
g	Eccentric obsidian	E—1—24	Cache O—13—29	,,	28
h	,, ,,	E—1—40	Cache O—13—36	,,	27
i	Flake-blade	,,	,, ,,	,,	31
j	Eccentric obsidian	E—1—32	Cache O—13—30	,,	28
k—m	Eccentric obsidians	,,	,, ,,	,,	27
n	Flake-blades	,,	,, ,,	,,	31
o, p	Eccentric obsidians	E—1—42	Cache O—13—37	,,	26
q	Eccentric obsidian	,,	,, ,,	,,	28
r	,, ,,	,,	,, ,,	,,	29
s	,, ,,	,,	,, ,,	,,	29
t	,, ,,	,,	,, ,,	,,	29
u	,, ,,	,,	,, ,,	,,	29
v	,, ,,	,,	,, ,,	,,	29
w	,, ,,	,,	,, ,,	,,	27
x—a'	Eccentric obsidians	,,	,, ,,	,,	29
b'—d'	Flakes	,,	,, ,,	,,	30
e'	Flake-blades	,,	,, ,,	,,	31

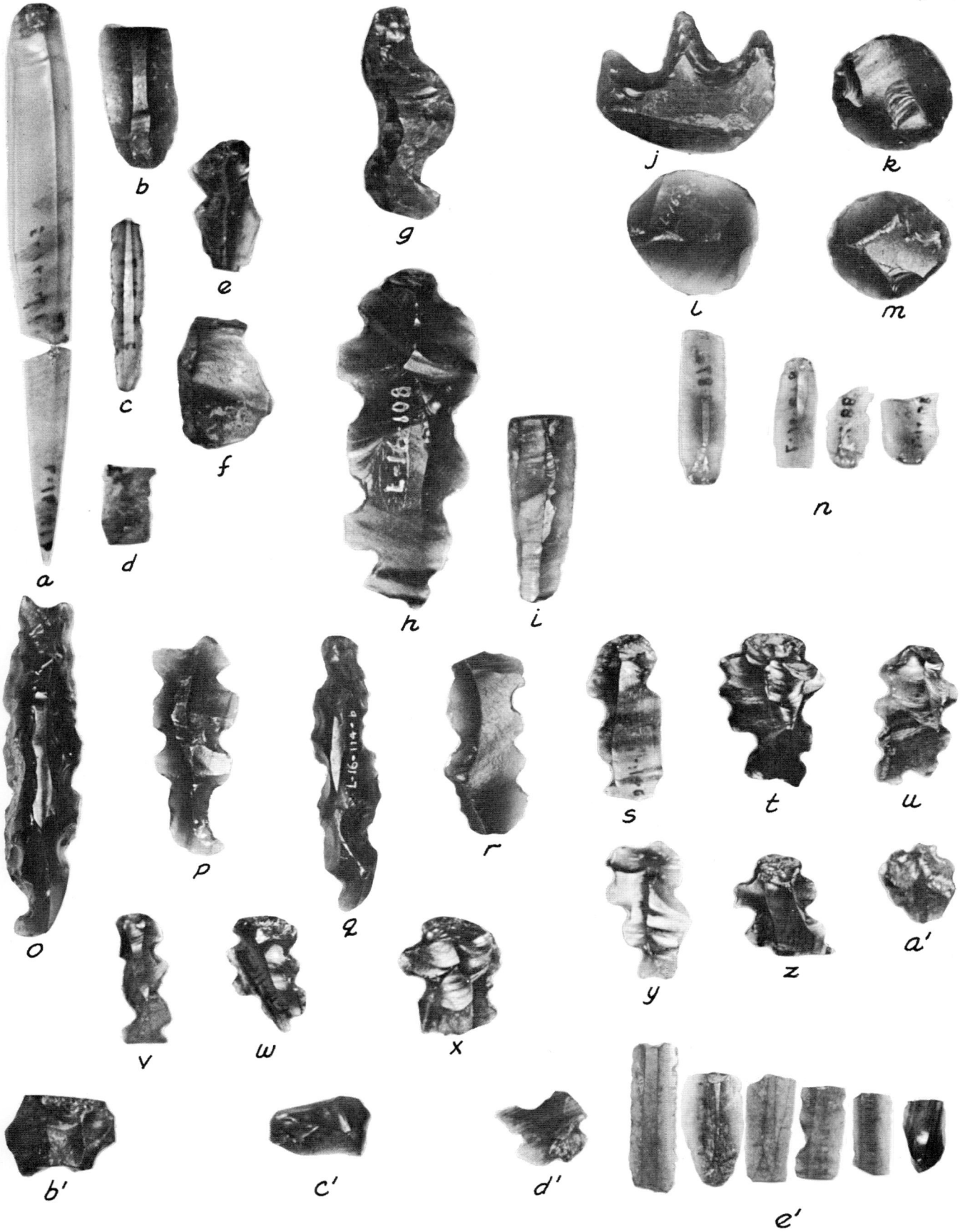

Fig. 24

FIGURE 25

CACHED OBSIDIANS
Natural size

	DESCRIPTION	FIELD NO.	PROVENIENCE	DISPOSITION	REF. PAGE
a	Eccentric obsidian	E—1—46	Cache O—13—39	NM	27
b	,, ,,	E—1—57	Cache O—13—43	,,	27
c	,, ,,	E—1—60	Cache O—13—45	,,	28
d	,, ,,	,,	,, ,,	,,	28
e	,, ,,	E—1—58	Cache O—13—44	UM	26
f	,, ,,	,,	,, ,,	,,	28
g	,, ,,	,,	,, ,,	,,	27
h	,, ,,	,,	,, ,,	,,	29
i	,, ,,	,,	,, ,,	,,	27
j	,, ,,	E—1—85	Cache O—13—50	,,	26
k	,, ,,	,,	,, ,,	,,	28
l, m	Flake-blades	,,	,, ,,	,,	31
n	Eccentric obsidian	,,	,, ,,	,,	29
o	,, ,,	E—1—83	Cache O—13—47	,,	29
p	,, ,,	,,	,, ,,	,,	27
q	,, ,,	,,	,, ,,	,,	29
r—t	Flake-blades	,,	,, ,,	,,	31
u	Eccentric obsidian	E—1—84	Cache O—13—51	,,	28
v, w	Eccentric obsidians	,,	,, ,,	,,	26
x, y	,, ,,	,,	,, ,,	,,	29
z	Eccentric obsidian	,,	,, ,,	,,	26
a'	Flake-blade	,,	,, ,,	,,	31

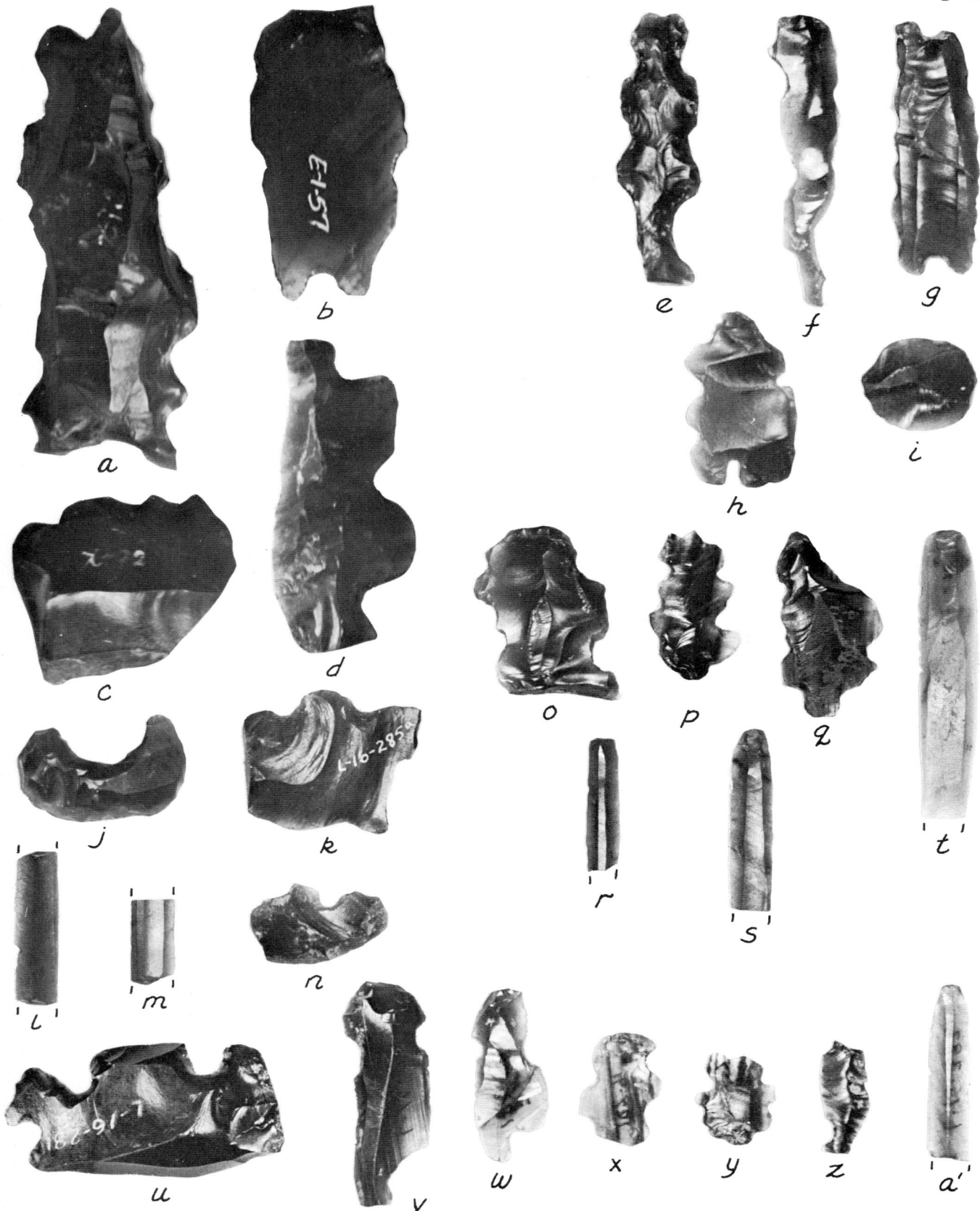

Fig. 25

a · b · c · d · e · f · g · h · i · j · k · l · m · n · o · p · q · r · s · t · u · v · w · x · y · z · a'

FIGURE 26

CACHED OBSIDIANS
Natural size

	DESCRIPTION		FIELD NO.	PROVENIENCE		DISPOSITION	REF. PAGE
a	Eccentric obsidian		E—1—10	Cache O—13—54		NM	28
b	,,	,,	,,	,,	,,	,,	28
c	,,	,,	,,	,,	,,	,,	28
d	,,	,,	,,	,,	,,	,,	28
e	,,	,,	,,	,,	,,	,, (not located ; from field photo)	28
f	,,	,,	E—7—3	Cache O—7—1		UM	28
g	,,	,,	,,	,,	,,	,,	27
h	,,	,,	W—40—13d	Cache O—16—1		,,	28
i	,,	,,	,,	,,	,,	,,	28
j	Flake		,,	,,	,,	,,	30
k	Eccentric obsidian		W—3—5	Cache J—1—2		NM	28
l	,,	,,	,,	,,	,,	,,	29
m	,,	,,	,,	,,	,,	,,	28
n	,,	,,	,,	,,	,,	,,	28
o	,,	,,	,,	,,	,,	,,	28
p	,,	,,	,,	,,	,,	,, (not located)	28
q	,,	,,	,,	,,	,,	,,	28
r	,,	,,	,,	,,	,,	,,	28
s	,,	,,	,,	,,	,,	,, (not located)	28
t	,,	,,	,,	,,	,,	,, (not located)	29
u	,,	,,	,,	,,	,,	,, (not located)	29
v	,,	,,	,,	,,	,,	,,	29
w	,,	,,	,,	,,	,,	,,	29
x	Flake		,,	,,	,,	,, (not located)	30
y	Eccentric obsidian		,,	,,	,,	,,	29

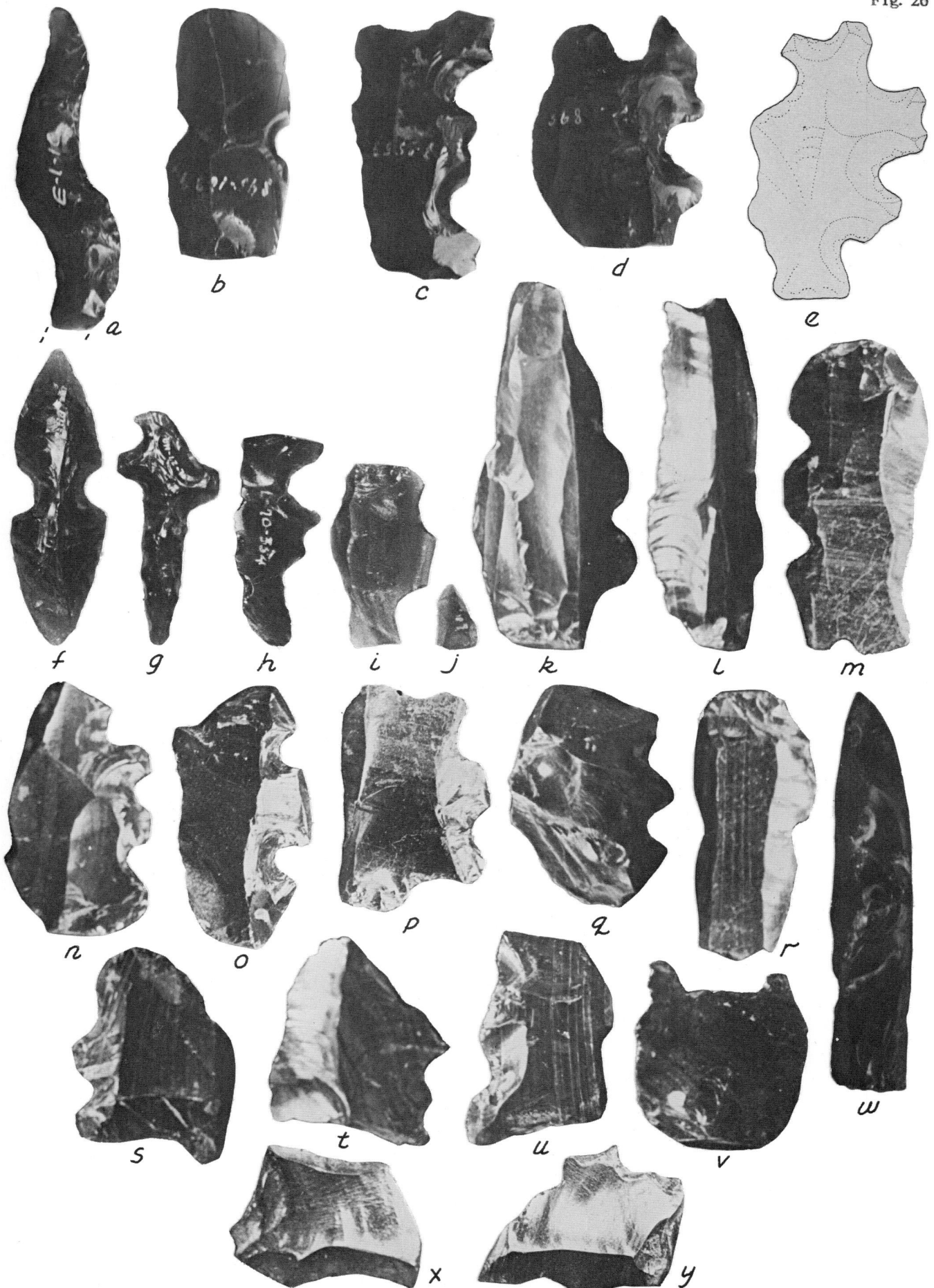

Fig. 26

FIGURE 27

CACHED OBSIDIANS
Natural size

	DESCRIPTION	FIELD NO.	PROVENIENCE	DISPOSITION	REF. PAGE
a	Eccentric obsidian	W—12—18	Cache J—6—5	UM	28
b	,, ,,	,,	,, ,,	,,	27
c d	Flake-blades	,,	,, ,,	,,	31
e—g	Eccentric obsidians	NE—4—19a	Cache J—29—1	NM	27
h—j	,, ,,	,,	,, ,,	,,	26
k	Eccentric obsidian	,,	,, ,,	,,	28
l	,, ,,	,,	,, ,,	,,	29
m	,, ,,	,,	,, ,,	,,	28
n—a'	Eccentric obsidians	,,	,, ,,	,,	29

Fig. 27

a   *b*   *c*   *d*

e   *f*   *g*   *h*   *i*   *j*   *k*

l   *m*   *n*   *o*   *P*   *q*

r   *s*   *t*   *u*   *v*   *w*

x   *y*   *z*   *a'*

FIGURE 28

CACHED OBSIDIANS
Natural size

	DESCRIPTION	FIELD NO.	PROVENIENCE		DISPOSITION	REF. PAGE
a	Eccentric obsidian	W—5—6	Cache K—5—1		UM	28
b	,, ,,	,,	,, ,,		,,	28
c—f	Eccentric obsidians	,,	,, ,,		,,	28
g	Eccentric obsidian	,,	,, ,,		,,	28
h	,, ,,	,,	,, ,,		,,	27
i	,, ,,	,,	,, ,,		,,	28
j	,, ,,	,,	,, ,,		,,	27
k	,, ,,	,,	,, ,,		,,	28
l	Flake-blade	,,	,, ,,		,,	31
m	Flake	,,	,, ,,		,,	31
n	Eccentric obsidian	W—6—21	Cache K—5—2		,,	28
o	,, ,,	W—5—145	Cache K—5—5		,,	27
p	,, ,,	,,	,, ,,		,,	28
q	,, ,,	,,	,, ,,		,,	26
r, s	Eccentric obsidians	W—5—183c	Cache K—5—6		NM	28
t	Eccentric obsidian	,,	,, ,,		,,	27
u	,, ,,	,,	,, ,,		,,	27
v	,, ,,	,,	,, ,,		,,	28
w	,, ,,	,,	,, ,,		,,	28

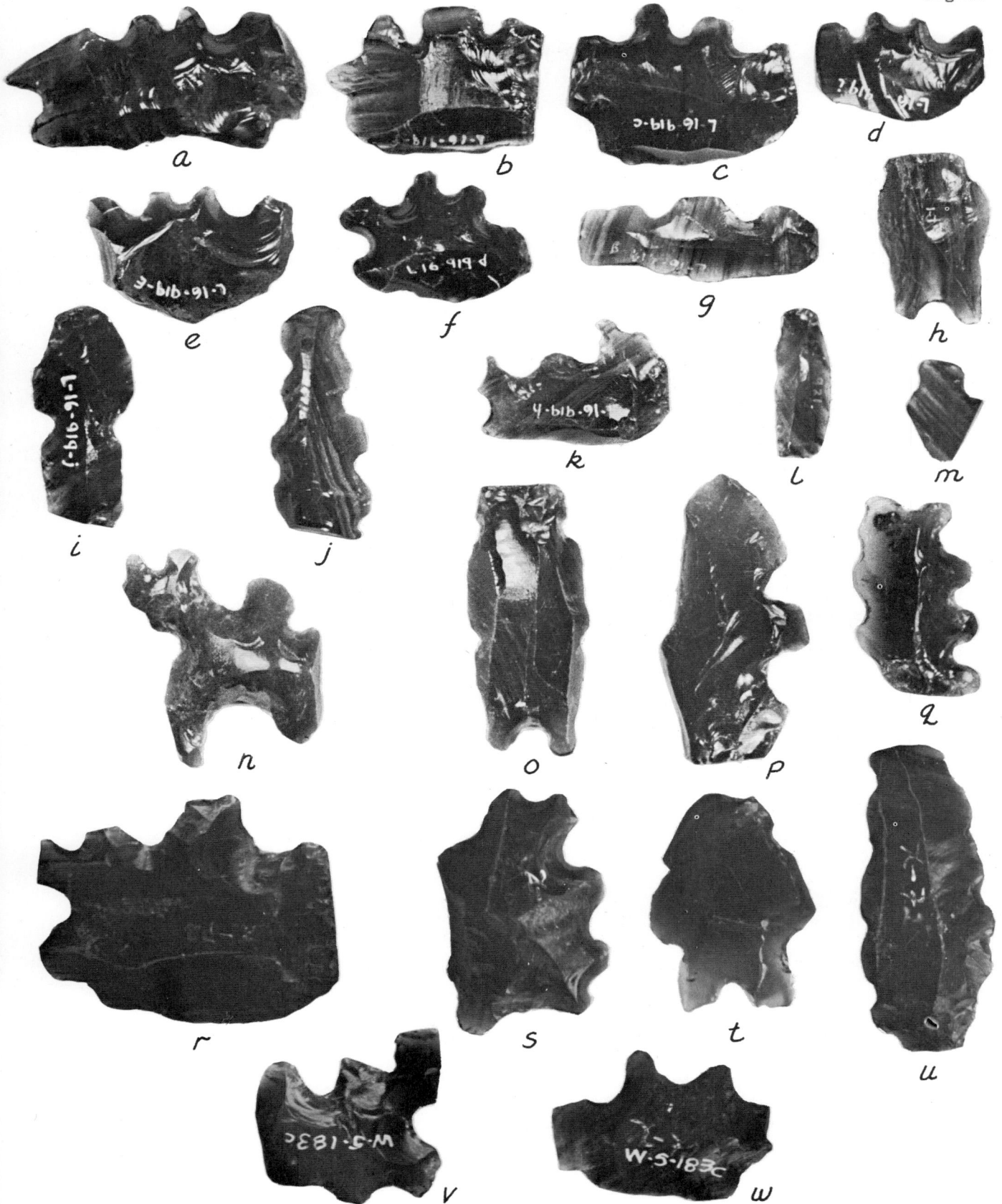

Fig. 28

FIGURE 29

CACHED OBSIDIANS

Natural size

	DESCRIPTION	FIELD NO.	PROVENIENCE		DISPOSITION		REF. PAGE
a	Eccentric obsidian	W—5—219	Cache K—5—7		UM		27
b, c	Flakes	,,	,,	,,	,,		30
d	Eccentric obsidian	W—5—275	Cache K—5—8		,,		26
e	,, ,,	,,	,,	,,	,,		28
f	Flake-blade	,,	,,	,,	,,		31
g	Eccentric obsidian	,,	,,	,,	,,		28
h—j	Eccentric obsidians	S—21—20b	Cache R—9—1		,,		27
k	Eccentric obsidian	,,	,,	,,	,,		27
l	,, ,,	S—21—27	Cache R—9—2		NM	(not located, from field photo)	28
m	,, ,,	,,	,,	,,	,,	,,	28
n	,, ,,	,,	,,	,,	,,	,,	27
o	,, ,,	,,	,,	,,	,,	,,	28
p	,, ,,	,,	,,	,,	,,	,,	28
q	,, ,,	,,	,,	,,	,,	,,	28
r—s	Eccentric obsidians	,,	,,	,,	,,	,,	27

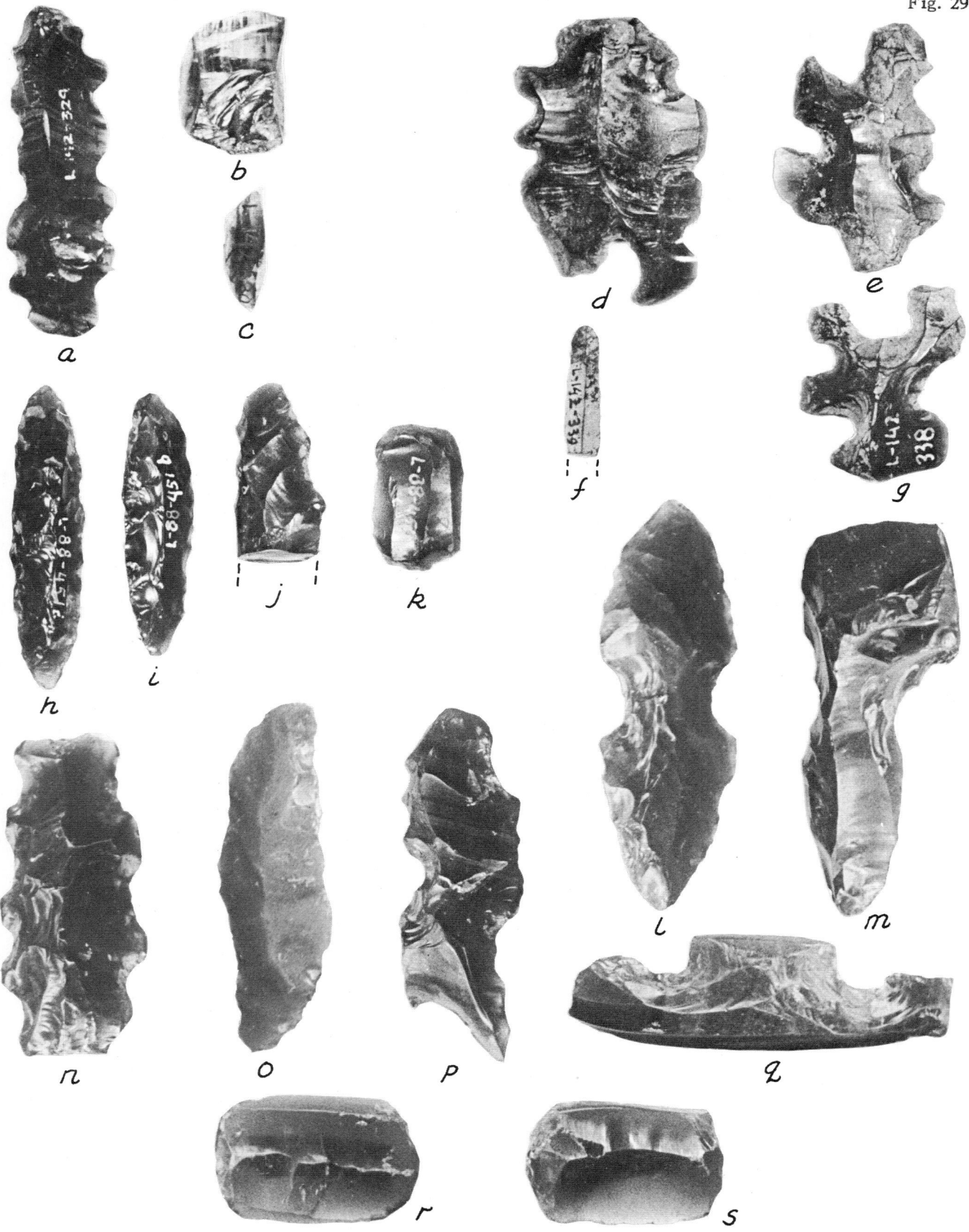

Fig. 29

FIGURE 30

CACHED OBSIDIANS
Natural size

	DESCRIPTION	FIELD NO.	PROVENIENCE	DISPOSITION	REF. PAGE
a	Eccentric obsidian	S—1—16	Cache R—11—1	UM	28
b	,, ,,	,,	,, ,,	,,	27
c	Flake-blade	S—1—19	Cache R—11—3	,,	31
d	Flake	,,	,, ,,	,,	29
e	Core fragment	,,	,, ,,	,,	30
f	Polisher	S—1—40	Cache R—11—6	,,	13
g	Eccentric obsidian	S—18—3a	Cache R—16—1	NM	28
h	,, ,,	,,	,, ,,	,,	27
i	,, ,,	,,	,, ,,	,,	26
j—1	Eccentric obsidians	Field numbers lacking. Probably from Str. O—13 caches		,,	27
m	Eccentric obsidian	E—1—97	Cache O—13—10 (See Fig. 22 a—o)	,,	27
n—q	Eccentric obsidians	See j—1		,,	28
r	Eccentric obsidian	,,		,,	27
s	,, ,,	,,		,,	28
t	,, ,,	,,		,,	27
u	,, ,,	S—21—28	Str. R—9, surface debris	,,	28
v, w	Eccentric obsidians	See j—1		,,	29

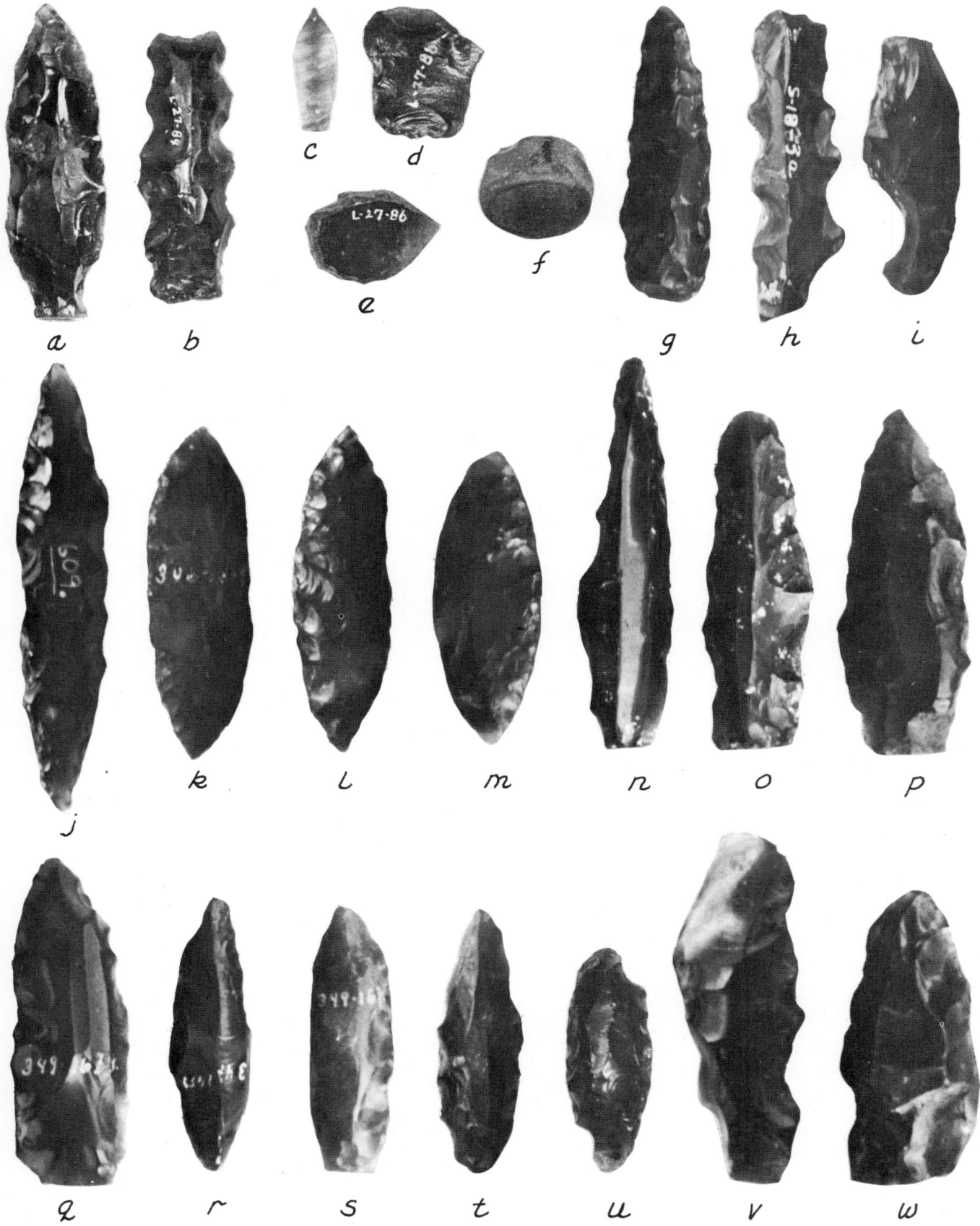

Fig. 30

a   b   c   d   e   f   g   h   i

j   k   l   m   n   o   p

q   r   s   t   u   v   w

FIGURE 31

CACHED OBSIDIANS
Natural size

	DESCRIPTION	FIELD NO.	PROVENIENCE	DISPOSITION	REF. PAGE
a, b	Eccentric obsidians	Field numbers lacking. Probably from Str. O—13— caches.		NM	28
c	Eccentric obsidian	E—1—97	Cache O—13—10 (see Fig. 22 a—o)	,,	28
d	,, ,,	See a, b		,,	28
e	,, ,,	,, ,,		,,	28
f—j	Eccentric obsidians	,, ,,		,,	28
k, 1	,, ,,	,, ,,		,,	28
m	Eccentric obsidian	E—1—97	Cache O—13—10 (see Fig. 22 a—o)	,,	28
n—r	Eccentric obsidians	See a, b		,,	28
s	Eccentric obsidian	,, ,,		UM	28
t—x	Eccentric obsidians	,, ,,		NM	27

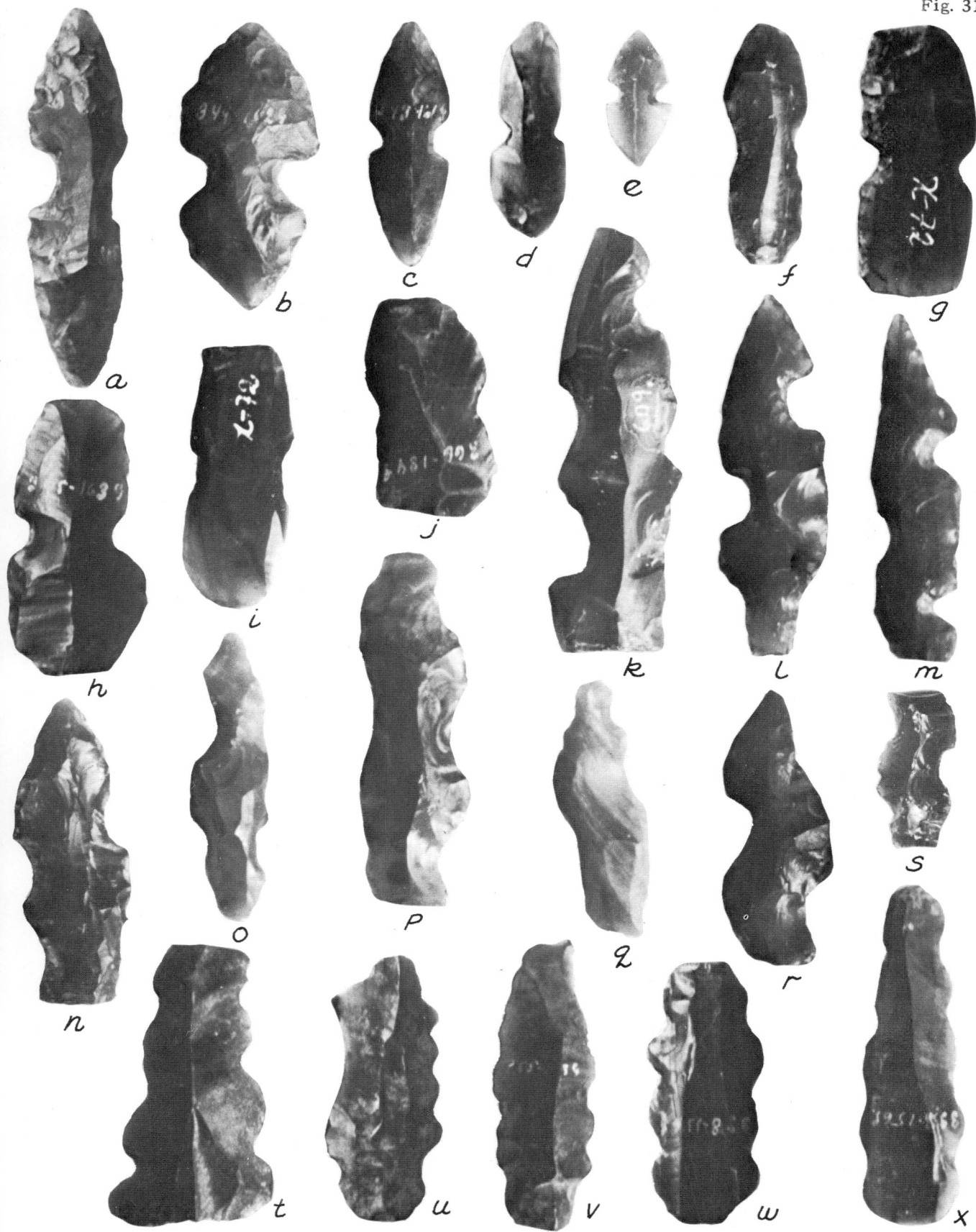

Fig. 31

FIGURE 32

CACHED OBSIDIANS
Natural size

	DESCRIPTION	FIELD NO.	PROVENIENCE	DISPOSITION	REF. PAGE
a—g	Eccentric obsidians	Field Numbers lacking. Probably from Str. O—13 caches		NM	27
h	Eccentric obsidian	See a—g		UM	27
i	” ”	W—16 —17	Str. J—4, floor debris	”	27
j—n	Eccentric obsidians	See a—g		NM	26
o, p	” ”	E—1—97	Cache O—13—10 (see Fig. 22 a—o)	”	28
q—s	” ”	See a—g		”	27
t	Eccentric obsidian	E—1—172	Str. O—13—, rear surface debris	”	29

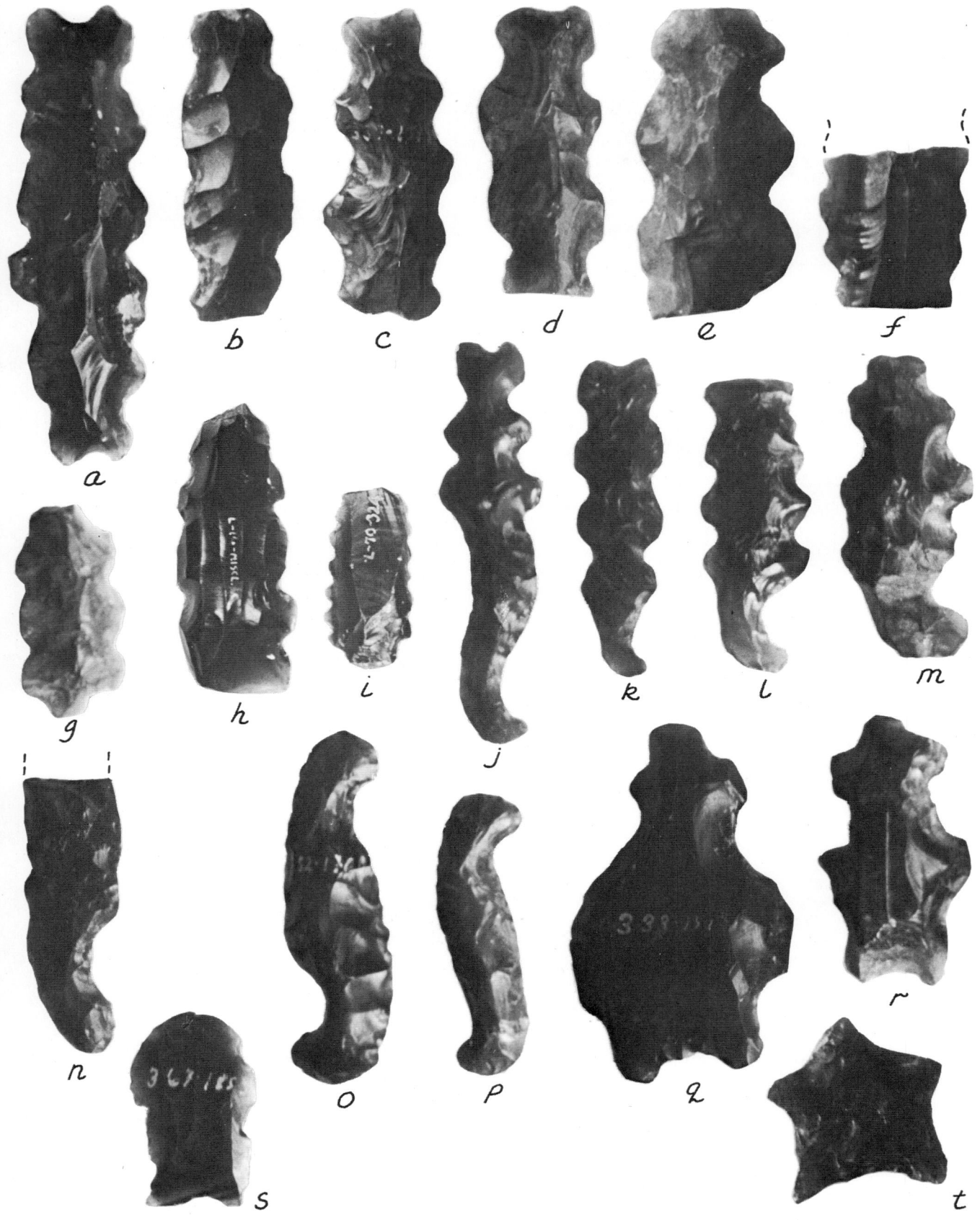

Fig. 32

FIGURE 33

CACHED OBSIDIANS
Natural size

	DESCRIPTION	FIELD NO.	PROVENIENCE	DISPOSITION	REF. PAGE
a—f	Eccentric obsidians	Field numbers lacking. Probably from Str. O—13 caches		NM	28
				UM	
g	Eccentric obsidian	NE—6—2	Str.　E—1, surface debris	UM	28
h—m	Eccentric obsidians	See a—f		NM	28
n	Eccentric obsidian (see Fig. 22 a—o)	E—1—97	Cache O—13—10	,,	26
o	Eccentric obsidian	See a—f		,,	26

Fig. 33

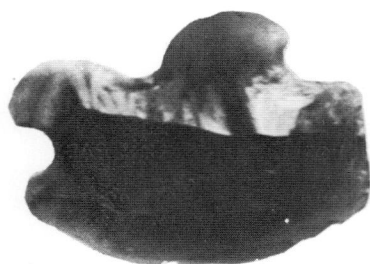

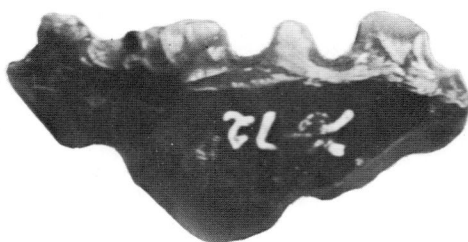

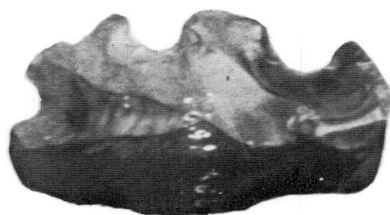

a

b

c

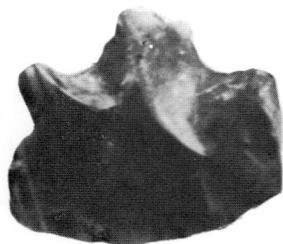

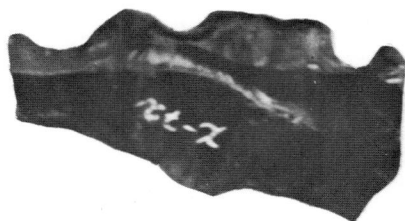

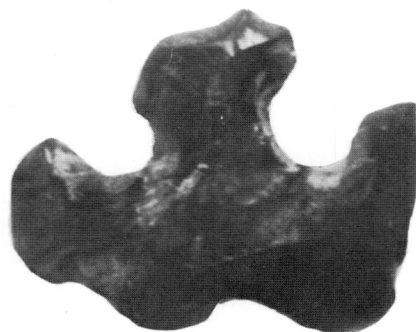

d

e

f

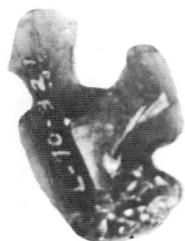

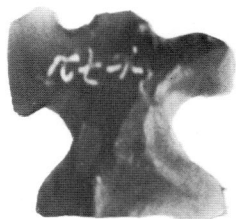

g

h

i

j

k

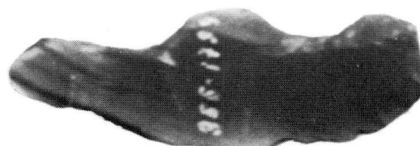

l

m

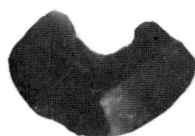

n

o

FIGURE 34

CACHED OBSIDIANS
Natural size

DESCRIPTION		FIELD NO.	PROVENIENCE	DISPOSITION	REF. PAGE
a—e	Eccentric obsidians	Field numbers lacking. Probably from Str. O—13 caches		NM	27
f	Eccentric obsidian	E—1—97	Cache O—13—10 (see Fig. 22 a—o)	,,	27
g	,, ,,	See a—e		UM	27
h	,, ,,	,, ,,		NM	27
i—j	Eccentric obsidians	,, ,,		,,	29
k	Eccentric obsidian	M—15—2	Surface	UM	29
l	,, ,,	See a—e		NM	29
m	,, ,,	,, ,,		UM	29
n	,, ,,	,, ,,		NM	34
o	,, ,,	,, ,,		,,	29
p	,, ,,	,, ,,		,,	27
q	,, ,,	,, ,,		UM	29
r—w	Eccentric obsidians	,, ,,		NM	29
x	Eccentric obsidian	S—16—3	Str. R—5, sub-floor near northeast doorway	UM	29
y—z	Eccentric obsidians	See a—e		NM	29
a'—d'	,, ,,	,, ,,		,,	29

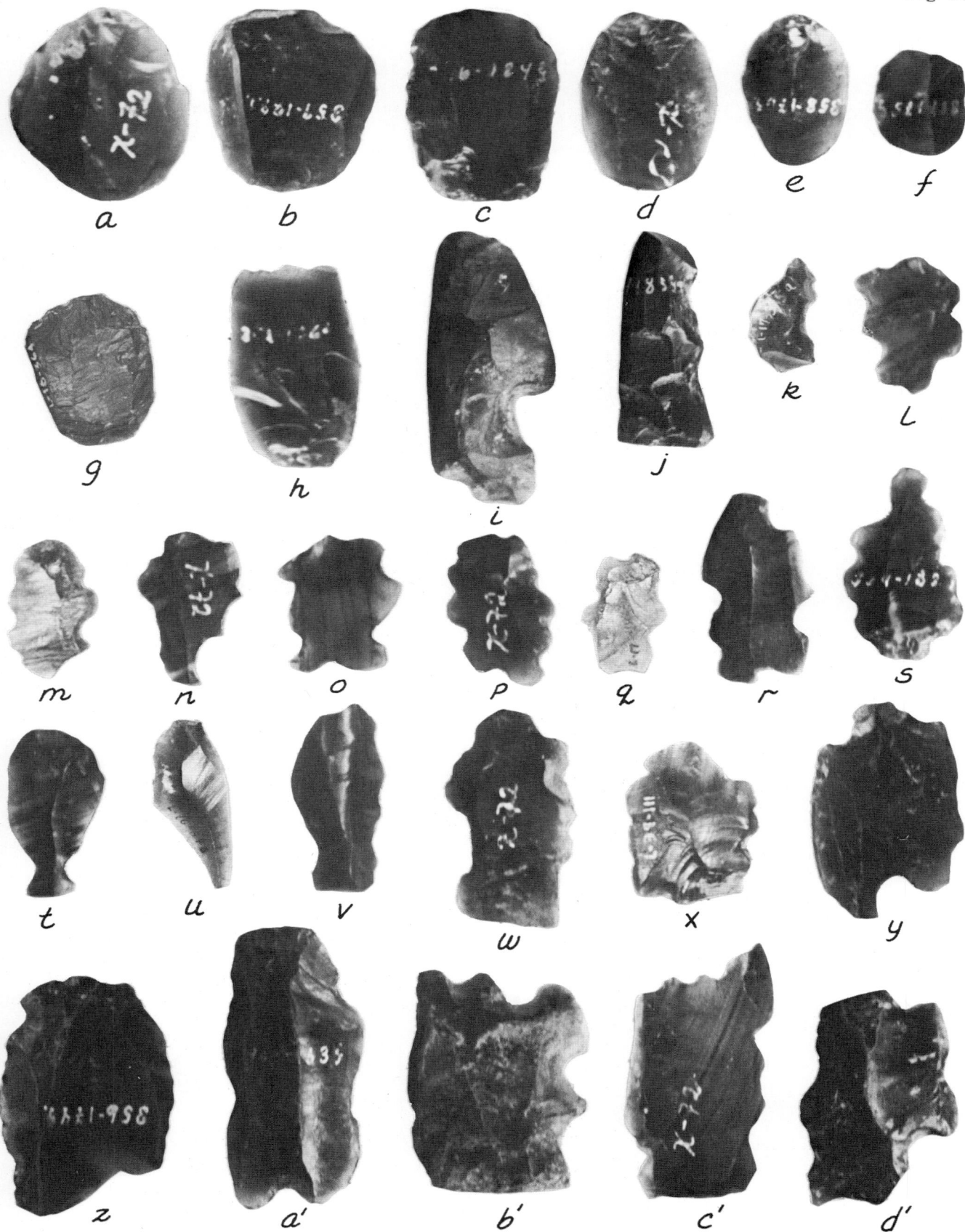

Fig. 34

FIGURE 35

CACHED OBSIDIANS
Natural size

	DESCRIPTION	FIELD NO.	PROVENIENCE	DISPOSITION	REF. PAGE
a—i	Eccentric obsidians	Field numbers lacking. Probably from Str. O—13 caches		NM	29
j	Eccentric obsidian (see Fig. 22 a—o)	E—1—97	Cache O—13—10	,,	29
		The following objects lack field numbers, having been burned in the camp fire. They are believed to be from Str. O—13 caches (see also Fig. 36)			
k	,, ,,			UM	27
l—n	Eccentric obsidians			,,	27
o	Eccentric obsidian			,,	29
p	,, ,,			,,	28
q	,, ,,			,,	27
r	,, ,,			,,	28
s, t	Eccentric obsidians			NM	28
u	Eccentric obsidian			,,	29
v	,, ,,			UM	29
w	,, ,,			,,	28

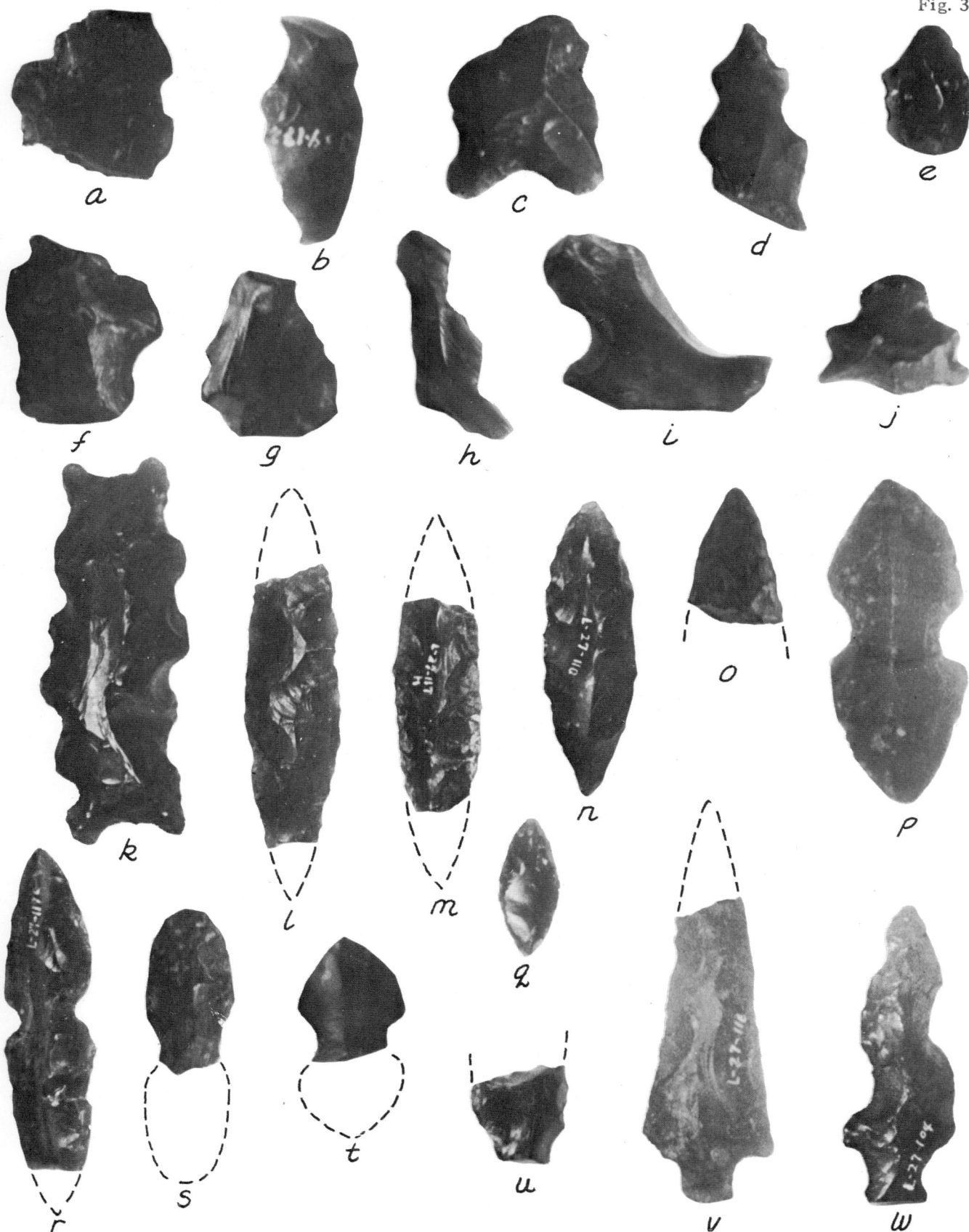

Fig. 35

FIGURE 36

CACHED OBSIDIANS
Natural size

DESCRIPTION		FIELD NO.	PROVENIENCE	DISPOSITION	REF. PAGE
		The following objects lack field numbers having been burned in the camp fire. They are believed to be from Str. O—13 caches (see also Fig. 35 k—w)			
a—c	Eccentric obsidians			UM	28
d	Eccentric obsidian			"	27
e	" "			"	27
f, g	Eccentric obsidians			"	28
h	Eccentric obsidian			"	28
i	" "			"	28
j, k	Eccentric obsidians			"	28
l	Eccentric obsidian			"	29
m	" "			"	28
n, o	Eccentric obsidians			"	26
p	Eccentric obsidian			"	27
q, r	Eccentric obsidians			NM	29
s	Eccentric obsidian			UM	29

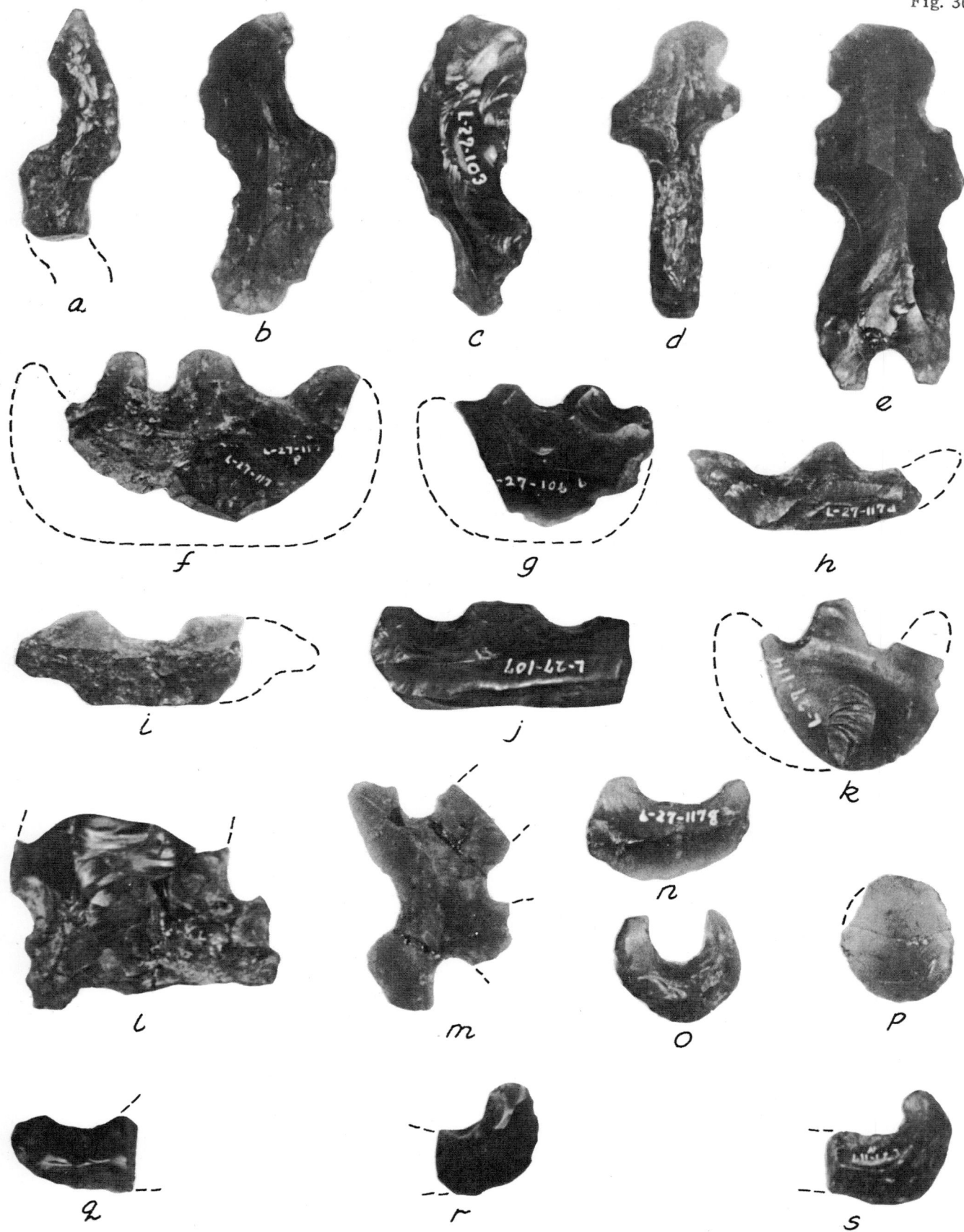

Fig. 36

FIGURE 37

MISCELLANEOUS OBJECTS, OBSIDIAN
Natural size

	DESCRIPTION	FIELD NO.	PROVENIENCE	DISPOSITION	REF. PAGE
a	Drill (?)	Unknown	Unknown	NM	14
b	Flake point	W—5—158	Str. K—5, plaza, surface debris	UM	14
c	Grooved core fragment	SE-1—43	Southeast Group, test pit	,,	14
d	Polisher	W—39—37	West Group, surface	,,	13
e	,,	Unknown	Unknown	NM	13
f	Core	,,	,,	,,	30
g	,,	Field number destoyed in camp fire, possibly from Str. O—13 cache		UM	30
h—j	Cores	See g		NM	30
k	Core	SE—1—9	Str. V—1, test pit	UM	14
l	,,	M—15—2	Surface	,,	14

Fig. 37

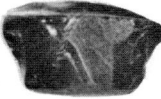

a

b

c

d

e

f

g

h

i

j

k

l

FIGURE 38

METATES

	DESCRIPTION	FIELD NO.	PROVENIENCE	DISPOSITION	REF. PAGE
a	Metate, basalt	S—15—21	Below plaza of Str. R—1 and above Burial 10 structure (see Fig. 66)	UM	34
b	Metate, sandstone	M—15—3	Surface, camp road	,,	34
c	Metate fragment	Unknown	Unknown	NM	34
d	,, ,,	Unknown	Unknown	NM ?	34

Fig. 38

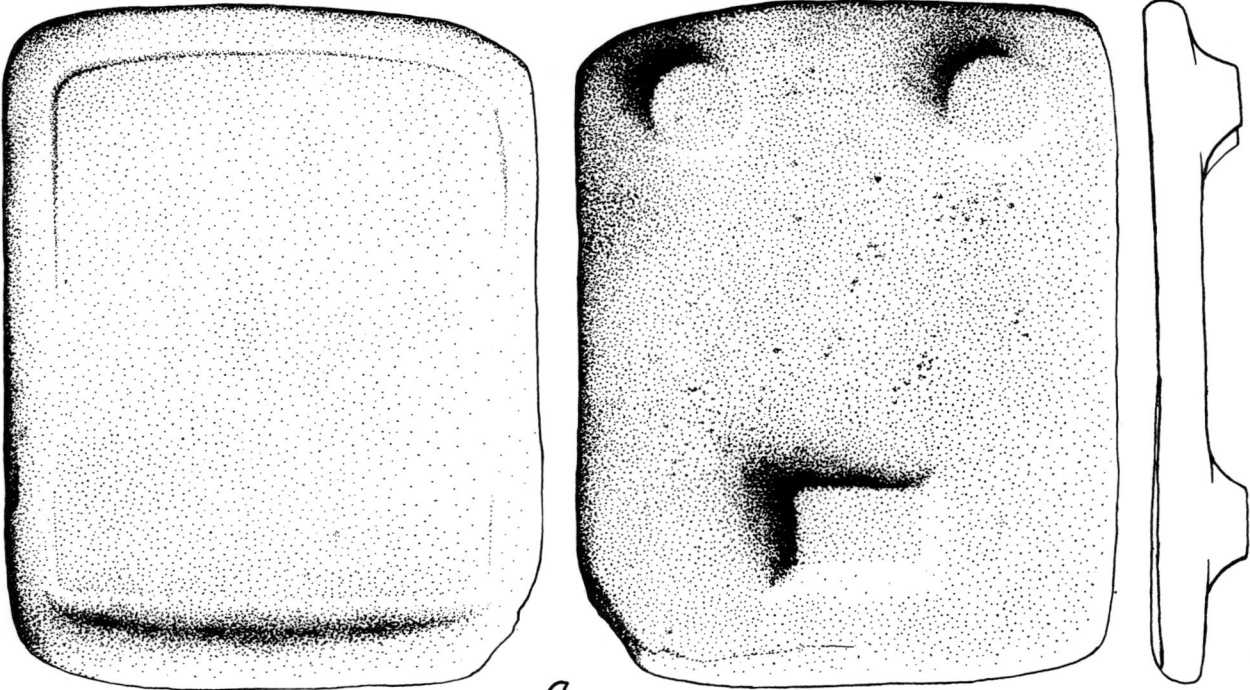

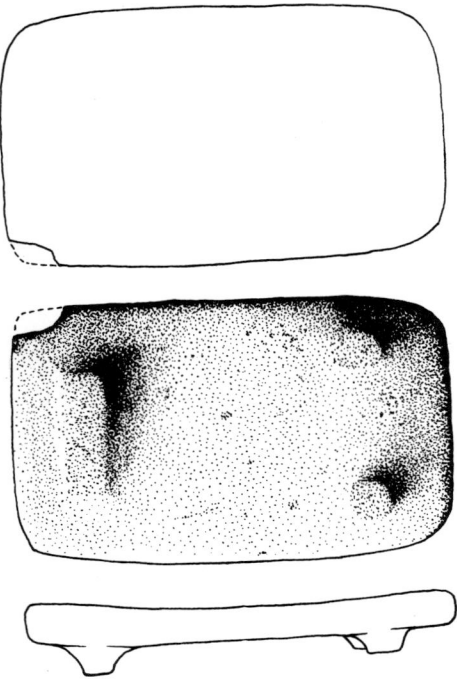

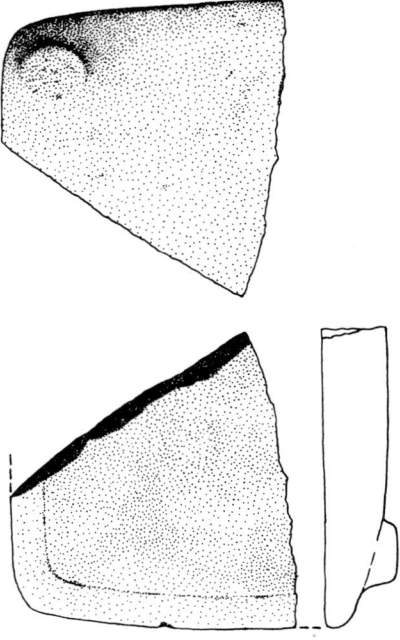

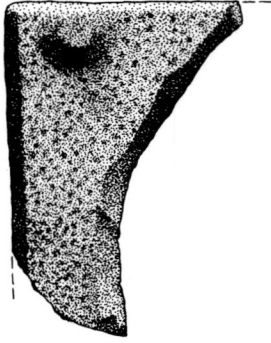

a

b

c

d

O 15 CM

FIGURE 39

MISCELLANEOUS STONE OBJECTS
All 1/2 scale except a

	DESCRIPTION	FIELD NO.	PROVENIENCE	DISPOSITION	REF. PAGE
a	Metates, large legless, troughed; whole and fragmentary	Uncatalogued. Collected from various parts of the site, including Str. J—17 and J—11		Discarded	34
b	Mano	S—2—37	Str. R—3, foot of stairway	NM	34
c	,,	M—15—4	Surface, camp road	,,	34
d	,,	S—1—22	Str. R—11	,,	34
e	,,	NE—4—76	Str. J—29, rear fill	,,	34
f	,,	W—3—11	Str. J—1	,,	34
g	Barrel-shaped stone	M—15—4	Surface, camp road	,,	38

Fig. 39

a

b

c

g

d

e

f

FIGURE 40

MISCELLANEOUS STONE OBJECTS
All 1/2 scale

	DESCRIPTION	FIELD NO.	PROVENIENCE	DISPOSITION	REF. PAGE
a	Hammerstone, discoidal	SE—11—2	Str. S—18, on floor	NM	36
b	,, ,,	W—5—112	Str. K—5—1st, front of stela terrace	,,	36
c	,, subspherical	E—1—89	Str. O—13, rear room	UM	36
d	,, ,,	S—17—3	Str. R—1, debris	,,	36
e	Hammerstone, discoidal	W—5—64	Str. K—5—1st, building plat-form surface	NM	36
f	Grinding stone, specialized	S—19—9	Str. U—15, test pit	UM	36
g	Hammerstone, subspherical	W—7—6	Str. K—6—b, alley debris	,,	36
h	Implement, problematical	S—22—35	Str. R—10, plaza floor	NM	37
i	Hammerstone, cuboidal	NE—3—7	Str. F—4, general debris	UM	36
j	,, subspherical	S—2—45	Str. R—3, debris left of main stairway	,,	36
k	Rubbing stone, pumice	W—5—48	Str. K—5, trench	,,	36
l	Implement, problematical	W—5—56	Str. K—5, trench	NM	37
m	Whetstone	S—22—34	Str. R—10, on plaza floor	,,	37
n	Implement, problematical	S—22—33	Str. R—10, on plaza floor	,,	37

Fig. 40

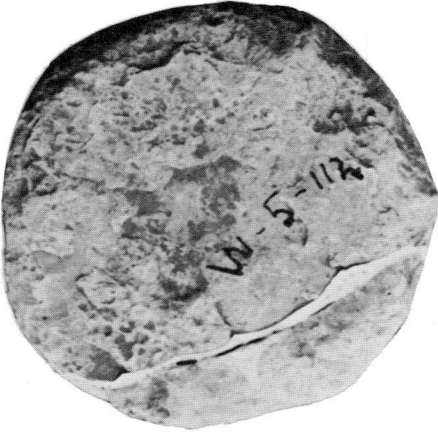

a

b

c

d

e

f

g

h

i

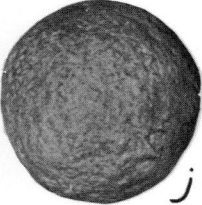

j

k

l

m

n

FIGURE 41

MISCELLANEOUS STONE OBJECTS

	DESCRIPTION	FIELD NO.	PROVENIENCE	DISPOSITION	REF. PAGE
a	Mano	W—7—5	Str. K—6—a, alley debris	UM	34
b	,,	M—31—1	Unknown	,,	34
c	,,	S—1—32	Str. R—11—a, debris	,,	34
d	,,	S—1—48	Str. R—11—a, summit	,,	34
e	Pecking tool	S—2—48	Str. R—3 and R—3—2nd, between floors	,,	37
f	Polishing stone	S—2—49	Str. R—3 and R—3—2nd, between floors	,,	36
g	Hammerstone, elongated	S—2—42	Str. R—3, debris	,,	36
h	,, ,,	M—32—1	Northeast section	,,	36
i	,, ,,	S—2—46	Str. R—3, debris left of main stairway	,,	36
j	,, ,,	E—1—88	Str. O—13, rear room	,,	36
k	,, ,,	W—5—108	Str. K—5—1st, stela terrace surface	,,	36
l	Rubbing stone, pumice	SE—1—36	Str. V—1	,,	36
m	,, ,,	E—2—7	Str. P—7, Northeast room	,,	36
n	,, ,,	W—5—108	Str. K—5—1st, stela terrace surface	,,	36
o	,, ,,	W—28—3	Str. K—5, east of, surface	,,	36
p	,, ,,	S—16—12	Str. R—5	,,	36

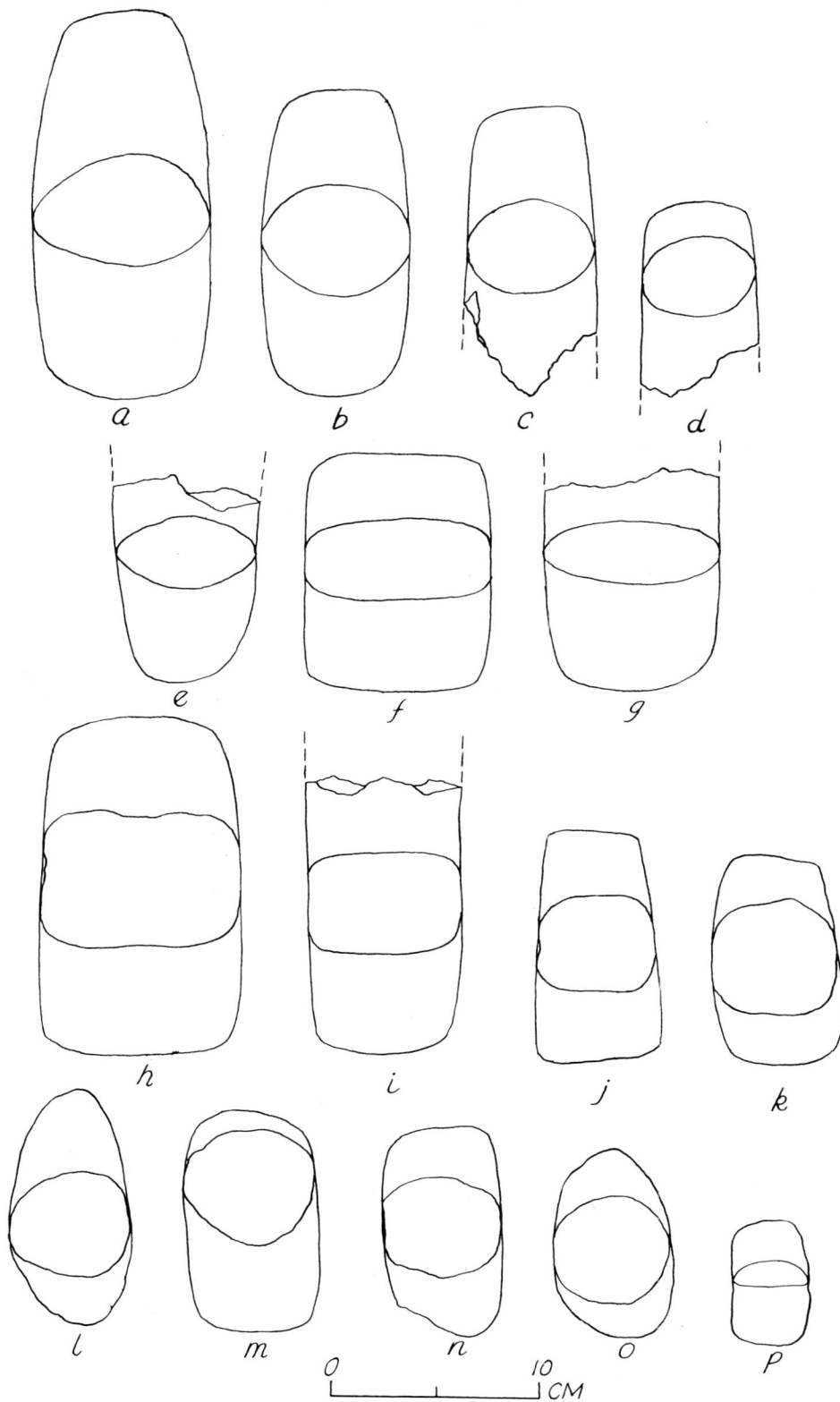

Fig. 41

a b c d

e f g

h i j k

l m n o p

0   10
|___|___|___|___| CM

FIGURE 42

MISCELLANEOUS STONE OBJECTS
f and g 1/4 scale

	DESCRIPTION	FIELD NO.	PROVENIENCE	DISPOSITION	REF. PAGE
a	Pestle (?)	W—3—17	Str. J—1, surface near Stela 2	UM	37
b	Problematical grindstone fragment	S—1—38	Str. R—11—a, summit (?)	,,	36
c	Barrel-shaped stone	E—1—12	Str. O—13, base of	,,	38
d	Metate (?) fragment	W—5—213	Str. K—5—1st, surface debris	,,	34
e	Bark-beater	SE—11—7	Str. S—18, surface debris	,,	37
f	Pyrite mosaic plaque	W—17—24	Burial 5, foot of Skeleton B	,,	42
g	Fillet, pyrite	W—17—86	Burial 5, Niche 1 (Fig. 64, 21)	,,	43

Fig. 42

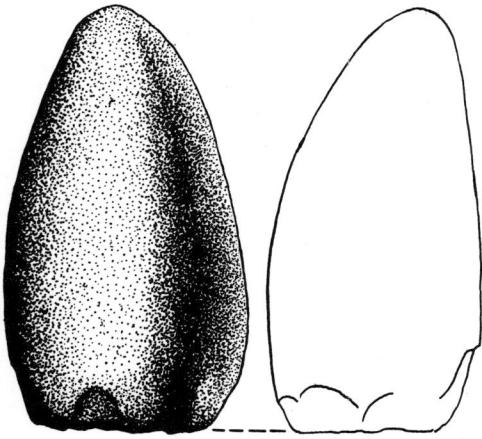

a

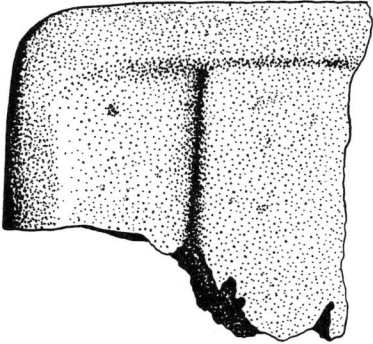

b

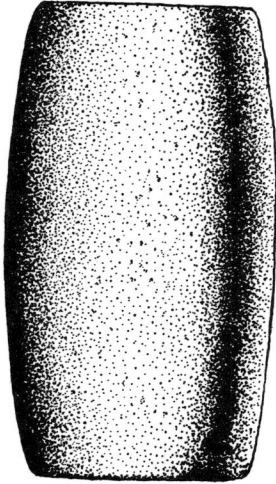

c

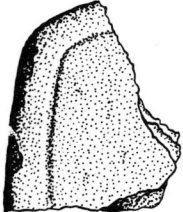

d

e

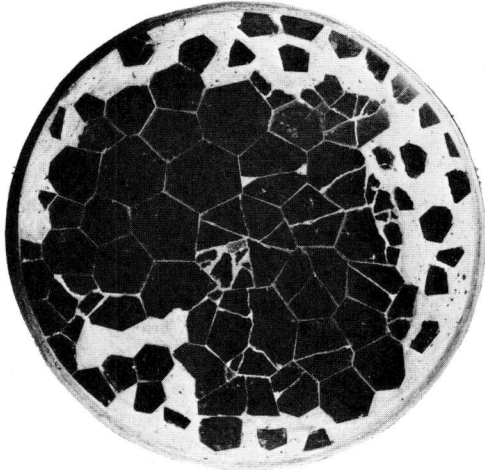

f

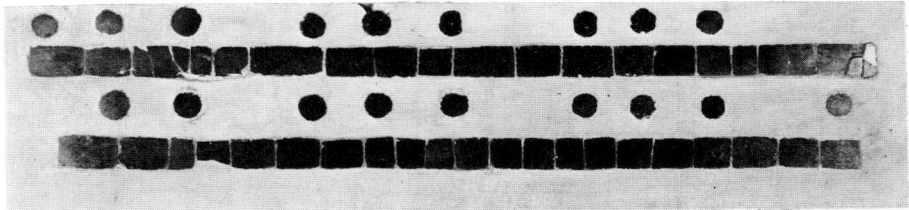

g

FIGURE 43

MISCELLANEOUS STONE OBJECTS

	DESCRIPTION	FIELD NO.	PROVENIENCE	DISPOSITION	REF. PAGE
a	Spindle whorl	S—1—13	Str. R—11—a and b, surface debris	UM	39
b	,, ,,	E—1—198	Str. O—13, surface debris	,,	39
c	,, ,,	M—15—2	Surface, camp road	,,	39
d	Disc, limestone	S—2—61	Str. R—3—2nd floor	,,	39
e	,, ,,	E—1—109	Cache O—13—13	,,	39
f	,, ,,	E—1—204e	Cache O—13—17	,,	39
g	Minor sculpture, pumice	S—2—13	Str. R—3, base of southeast terrace wall	,,	39
h	Disc, pyrite	W—12—18	Cache J—6—5	,,	42
i	Mosaic element, pyrite	S—22—52	Str. R—10, surface	NM	42
j	,, ,, ,,	W—5—157	Str. K—5, plaza surface	UM	42
k	Incised oval, pyrite	W—2—33	Str. J—2, drain under Rooms 5 and 6	,,	43
l	Disc, hematite	W—1—40	Cache J—1—1	,,	43
m, n	Small carved pieces of hematite	W—40—13f	Cache O—16—1	NM	43
o, p	Celts, combined front and side view	No field numbers. Provenience ?		,,	40
q	Celt, combined front and side view	NE—8—11	Test pit on slope to river	UM	40
r	Celt, combined front and side view	W—6—21f	Cache K—5—2	,,	40
s, t	Celts, jadeite	NE—4—19d	Cache J—29—1	NM	51
u	Incised sphere	W—2—28	Str. J—2, floor debris, Room 1	UM	39

Fig. 43

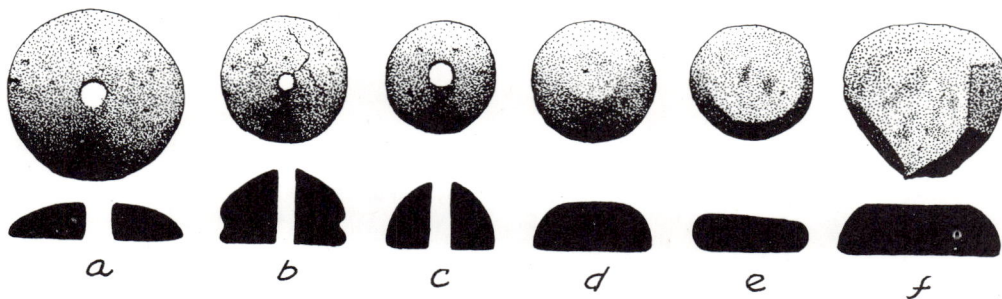
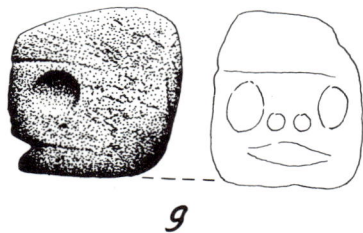
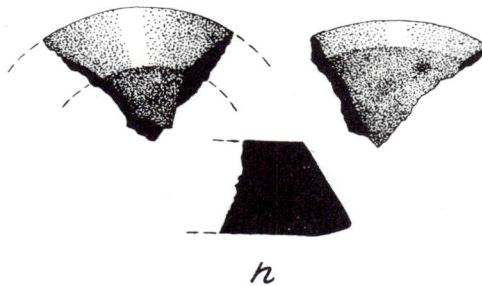

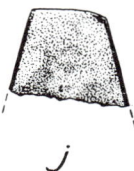
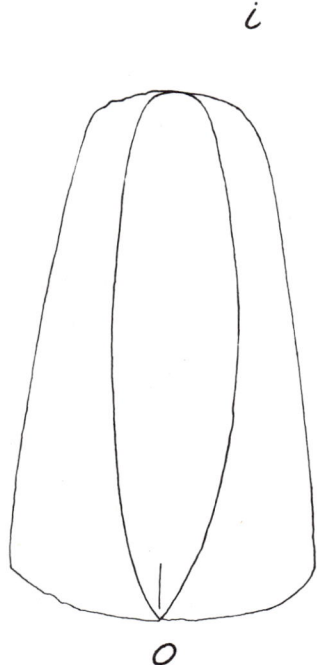
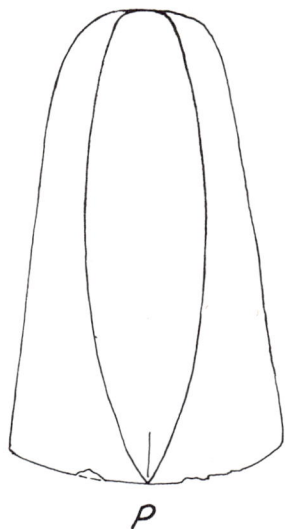
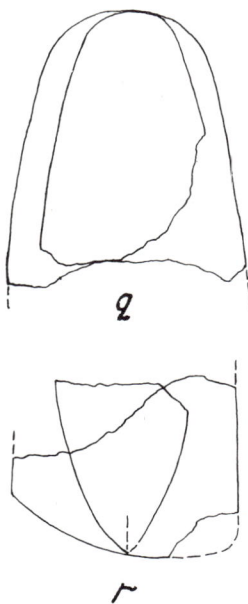
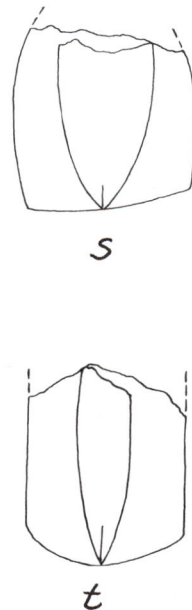

a   b   c   d   e   f

g   h

i   j   k   l   m   n

o   p   q   s

r   t

u

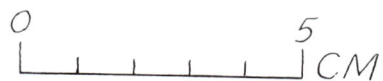

0   5   CM

FIGURE 44

MISCELLANEOUS STONE OBJECTS
Natural size

	DESCRIPTION	FIELD NO.	PROVENIENCE	DISPOSITION	REF. PAGE
a	Gouge	E—51—1	Str. O—12, room debris	UM	39
b	Gouge (?) or celt	W—1—40	Cache J—1—1	,,	39
c	Celt	W—7—8	Str. R—6—b, alley debris	,,	40
d	,,	W—12—105	Str. J—7, sub-plinth debris	,,	40
e	,, , jadeite	W—5—183	Cache K—5—6	,,	51
f	,,	W—34—10	Str. J—10, room debris	,,	40
g	Bead, jadeite	E—1—107	Cache O—13—12	,,	52
h	Ornament, jadeite (mate in Fig. 47 y)	W—17—32	Burial 5	,,	50
i	Flare, jadeite	E—1—10	Cache O—13—54	NM	50
j	Perforated disc, jadeite	W—17—4	Burial 5	UM	50
k	Wedge-shaped object, jadeite	W—17—8	Burial 5	,,	48
l	Pendant, jadeite (reworked bead)	S—2—13	Str. R—3, base of southeast terrace wall	,,	47
m	Ornament, jadeite	S—15—13	Burial 10	,,	50
n	,, ,,	S—15—15	Burial 10	,,	50
o	,, ,,	S—15—16	Burial 10	,,	50
p	,, ,,	S—15—17	Burial 10	,,	50
q	Fragmentary piece of incised decomposed jadeite	E—1—83	Cache O—13—47	,,	45

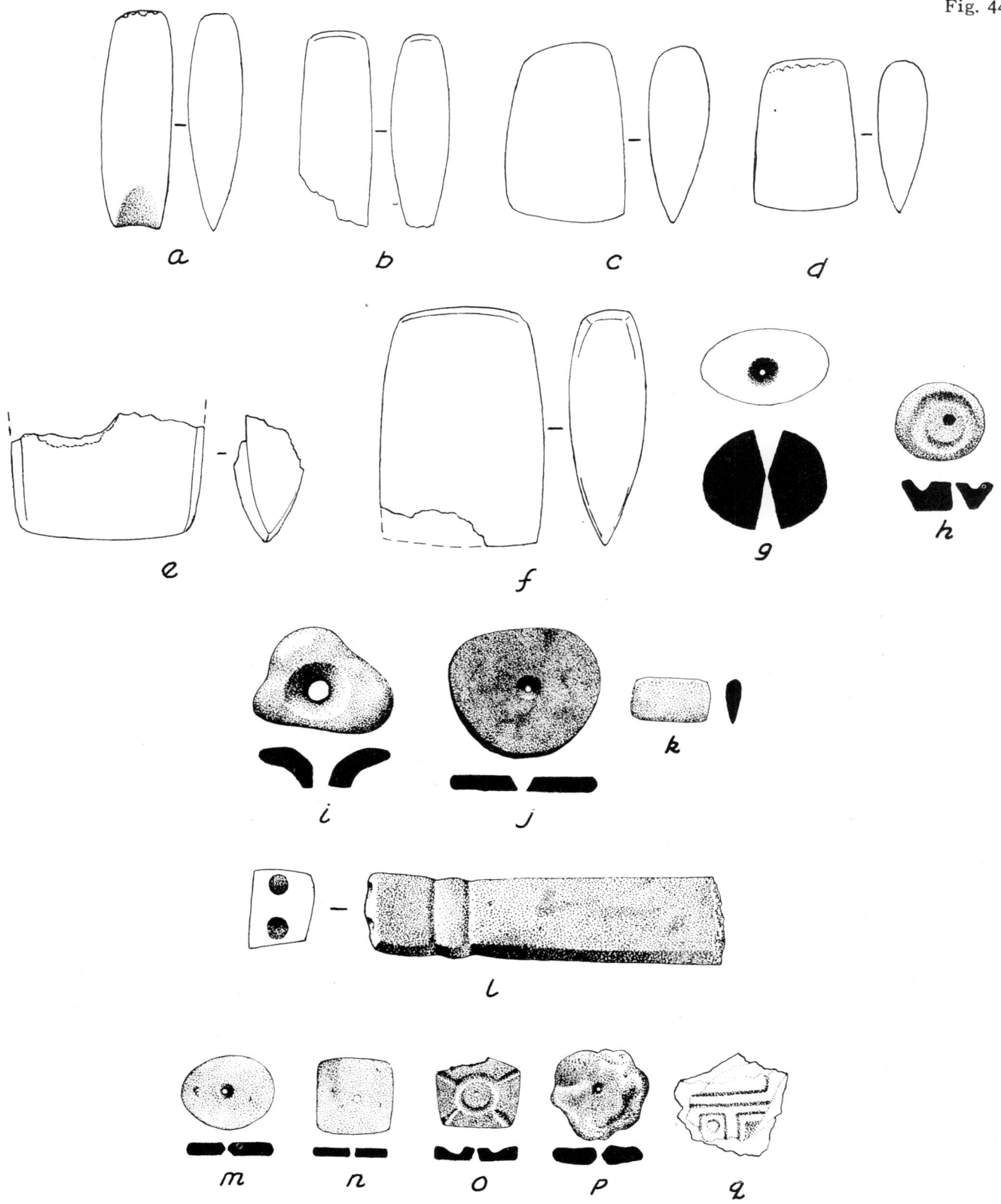

Fig. 44

FIGURE 45

OBJECTS OF JADEITE

	DESCRIPTION	FIELD NO.	PROVENIENCE	DISPOSITION	REF. PAGE
a—g	Incised objects	W—5—183d	Cache K—5—6	NM	44, 45
h—k	,, ,,	S—21—27c	Cache R—9—2	,,	44, 45
l	Incised object	E—1—92	Cache O—13—48	UM	44
m	Figurine	Field number lacking (camp fire) but from a Str. O—13 cache		,,	47
n, o	Figurines	See m		NM	47
p, q	,,	,, ,,		UM	47
r, s	,,	,, ,,		NM	47
t	Hook-shaped object, incised	E—1—83	Cache O—13—47	UM	48
u	,, ,, ,, ,,	See m		,,	48
v	Incised plaque (see Fig. 50 s)	E—1—85	Cache O—13—50	,,	46
w	,, ,,	E—1—84	Cache O—13—51	,,	46
x	Diagonally banded object	See m		,,	48
y	Carved pendant	S—15—2	Burial 10	NM (not located, from a field photo)	46
z	Saw-marked surface of polished jadeite shown in Fig. 48 d¹	E—1—11	Cache O—13—4	UM	52
a¹	Carved human head	,,	,, ,,	,,	47
b¹	Polished, perforated object	,,	,, ,,	,,	50
c¹	Carved pendant	See m		,,	46
d¹	Celtiform object	S—21—20c	Cache R—9—1	,,	48
e¹	Loaf-shaped object	W—1—40	Cache J—1—1	,,	48
f¹	Disc	S—22—1	Str. R—10, debris	,,	48
g¹	Conoidal object	See m		,,	48

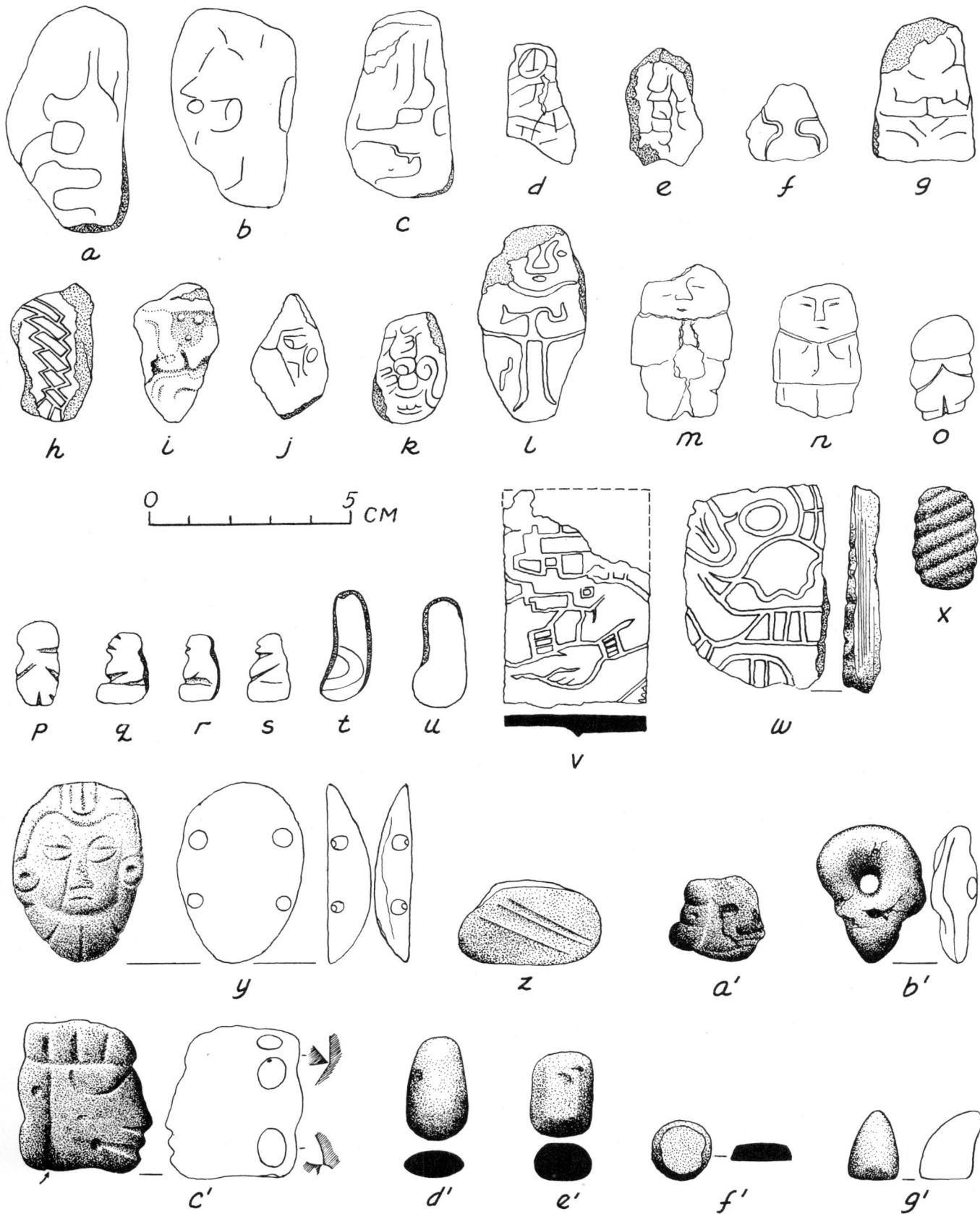

Fig. 45

FIGURE 46

OBJECTS OF JADEITE

	DESCRIPTION	FIELD NO.	PROVENIENCE	DISPOSITION	REF. PAGE
a	Incised object, with saw marks (see Fig. 50 q)	E—1—204c	Cache O—13—17	UM	44
b	Incised object	,,	,, ,,	,,	44
c	,, ,,	E—1—153	Cache O—13—16	,,	44
d	,, ,,	E—1—122	Cache O—13—6	,,	45
e—g	Incised objects	,,	,, ,,	,,	44
h	Incised object	Field number lacking (camp fire) but from a Str. O—13 cache		,,	44
i	,, ,,	E—1—119	Cache O—13—7	,,	44
j	,, ,,	E—1—22	Cache O—13—27	,,	45
k	,, ,,	E—1—83	Cache O—13—47	,,	44
l—n	Incised objects	W—5—275e	Cache K—5—8	,,	44
o	,, ,,	,,	,, ,,	,,	45
p	,, ,,	W—6—21	Cache K—5—2	,,	44
q—t	Incised objects	See h		NM	44
u	Incised object	E—1—93 (?)	Probably Cache O—13—49	,,	44
v	,, ,,	See h		,,	44
w	,, ,,	E—1—10	Cache O—13—54	,,	45
x	,, ,,	See h		,,	44
y	,, ,,	,, ,,		UM	44
z	,, ,,	W—40—13	Cache O—16—1	,,	45
a'	,, ,,	See h		,,	45
b', c'	Incised objects	,, ,,		,,	44
d'	Incised object	,, ,,		NM	45
e'	,, ,,	,, ,,		UM	44

Fig. 46

a   b   c   d   e   f

g   h   i   j   k   l   m

n   o   p   q   r   s

t   u   v   w   x   y   z

a'   b'   c'   d'   e'

0   5 CM

FIGURE 47

OBJECTS OF JADEITE
Natural size

	DESCRIPTION	FIELD NO.	PROVENIENCE	DISPOSITION		REF. PAGE
a, b	Sub-spherical beads	W—17—8	Burial 5	NM	(majority not located)	51
c	Rectangular bead (see Fig. 49 g)	W—17—68	,, ,,	UM		51
d	Rectangular bead	,,	,, ,,	NM		51
e	Carved pendant	W—17—57	,, ,,	,,	(not located)	46
f	Jaguar effigy pendant (see Fig. 49 a)	W—17—71	,, ,,	UM		46
g	Earplug (see Fig. 49 b)	W—17—63	,, ,,	,,		49
h	,,	,,	,, ,,	NM	(not located)	49
i	Problematical object (see Fig. 49 d for mate)	W—17—40e	,, ,,	,,		48

The following jadeite ornaments comprised a fillet around the head of Skeleton B, Burial 5 (Fig. 64, 4). Correct sequence and sections are given in Fig. 48 a—t

	DESCRIPTION	FIELD NO.	PROVENIENCE	DISPOSITION		REF. PAGE
j	See Fig. 48 o	W—17—55		NM		49
k	See Fig. 48 c	,,		UM		49
l	See Fig. 48 l	,,		NM		49
m	See Fig. 48 h	,,		UM		49
n	See Fig. 48 j	,,		NM	(not located)	49
o	See Fig. 48 t. Note plug (arrow)	,,		UM		49
p	See Fig. 48 d	,,		,,		49
q	See Fig. 48 g	,,		NM	(not located)	49
r	See Fig. 48 e	,,		UM		49
s	See Fig. 48 f	,,		NM		49
t	See Fig. 48 r	,,		UM		49
u	See Fig. 48 b (broken in transit ?)	,,		NM	(not located)	49
v	See Fig. 48 s	,,		UM		49
w	See Fig. 48 p	,,		,,		49
x	See Fig. 48 k	,,		,,		49
y	Ornament (see Fig. 44 h, for mate)	W—17—32	Burial 5	NM		50
z	Ornament	W—17—37	,, ,,	,,		50
a!	Sub-spherical bead	W—17—78 (?)	,, ,,	,,		51
b!, c!	Sub-spherical beads	W—17—65	,, ,,	,,		51
d!	Cylindrical bead	W—17—74	,, ,,	,,		51
e!	,, ,,	W—17—73	,, ,,	UM		51

Fig. 47

FIGURE 48

OBJECTS OF JADEITE

All 1/2 scale

DESCRIPTION	FIELD NO.	PROVENIENCE	DISPOSITION	REF. PAGE

The following jadeite ornaments comprised a fillet around the head of Skeleton B, Burial 5 (Fig. 64, 4). Photographs of certain of these sre shown in Fig. 47

	DESCRIPTION	FIELD NO.	PROVENIENCE	DISPOSITION	REF. PAGE
a		W--17—55		NM (not located)	49
b	See Fig. 47 u (broken in transit ?)	,,		,, (not located)	49
c	See Fig. 47 k	,,		UM	49
d	See Fig. 47 p	,,		UM	49
e	See Fig. 47 r	,,		,,	49
f	See Fig. 47 s	,,		NM	49
g	See Fig. 47 q	,,		,, (not located)	49
h	See Fig. 47 m	,,		UM	49
i		,,		NM ?	49
j	See Fig. 47 n	,,		NM (not located)	49
k	See Fig. 47 x	,,		UM	49
l	See Fig. 47 l	,,		NM	49
m		,,		NM ?	49
n		,,		NM (not located)	49
o	See Fig. 47 j	,,		,,	49
p	See Fig. 47 w	,,		UM	49
q		,,		NM (not located)	49
r	See Fig. 47 t	,,		UM	49
s	See Fig. 47 v	,,		,,	49
t	See Fig. 47 o	,,		,,	49
u	Sub-spherical beads, amazonite	W—17—8	Burial 5	,,	53
v	Sub-spherical beads	,,	,, ,,	,,	51
w	Sub-spherical bead, amazonite	,,	,, ,,	,,	53
x, y	Spherical beads	S—15—5b	Burial 10	,,	51
z	Sub-spherical beads	S—15—5a	,, ,,	,,	51
aᶦ	,, ,,	W—17—58	Burial 5	,,	51
bᶦ	,, ,,	S—15—4	Burial 10	,,	51
cᶦ	,, ,,	S—15—3	,, ,,	,,	51
dᶦ	Halved and polished pebble (see Fig. 45 z)	E—1—11	Cache O—13—4	,,	52
eᶦ	Halved and polished pebble	E—1—107	Cache O—13—12	,,	52
fᶦ	Two cylindrical beads (larger shown also in Fig. 49 l left)	W—17—58	Burial 5	,,	51
gᶦ	Sub-spherical beads	SE—1—10a	Burial 2	,,	51
hᶦ	,, ,,	S—15—5a	Burial 10	NM	51
iᶦ	,, ,,	S—15—4	,, ,,	,,	51
jᶦ	,, ,,	S—15—3	,, ,,	,,	51
kᶦ	Perforated ornament	S—15—8	,, ,,	,,	50
lᶦ	Spherical bead	S—15—5b	,, ,,	,,	51

Fig. 48

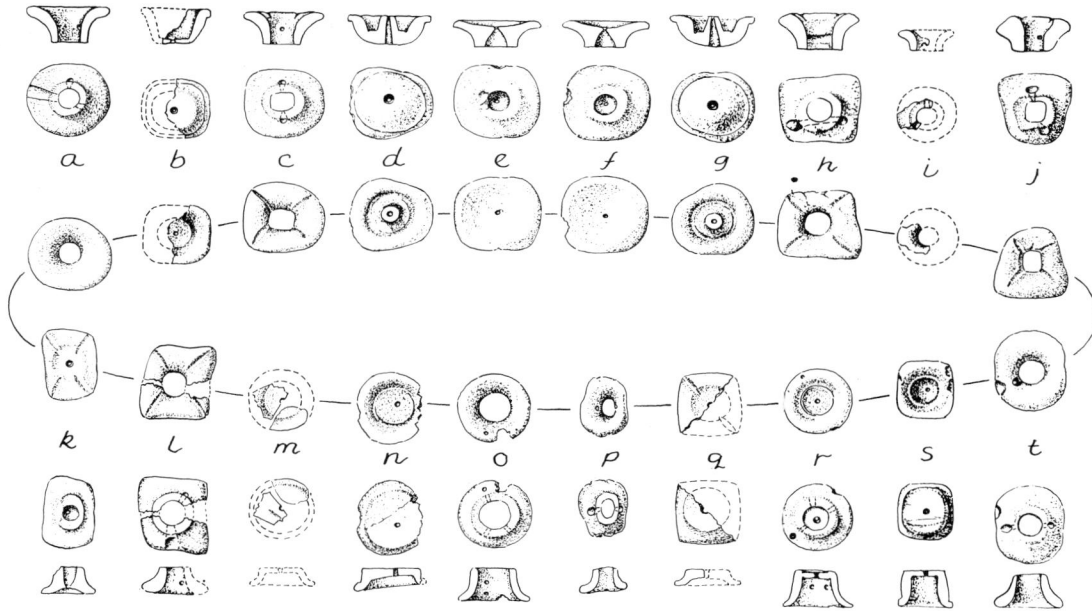

a　b　c　d　e　f　g　h　i　j

k　l　m　n　o　p　q　r　s　t

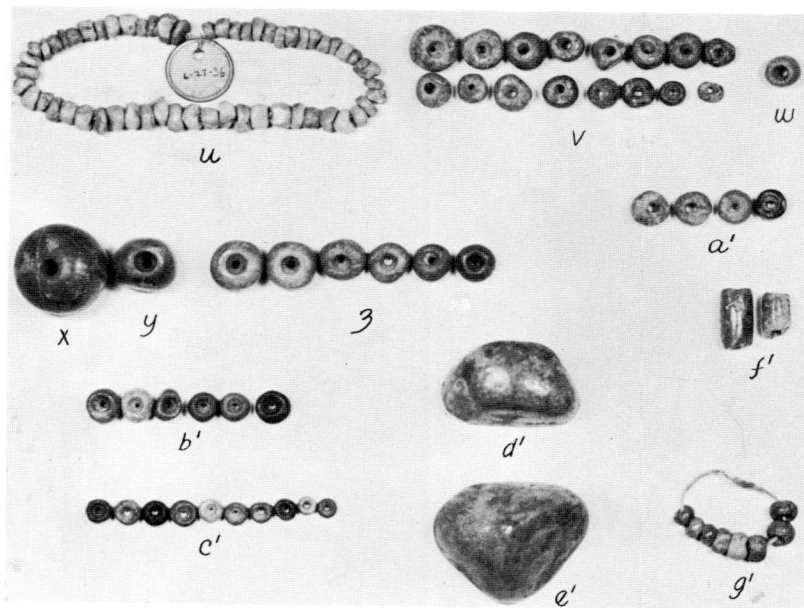

u　　v　　w

a'

x　y　3

f'

b'

d'

c'

e'　g'

h'　i'　j'

k'　l'

FIGURE 49

OBJECTS OF JADEITE
Scale about 1/2

	DESCRIPTION	FIELD NO.	PROVENIENCE	DISPOSITION	REF. PAGE
a	Jaguar effigy pendant, with inscription (see Fig. 49 f)	W—17—71	Burial 5	UM	46
b	Earplug (see Fig. 47 g)	W—17—63	,, ,,	,,	49
c	Bead	W—17—65	,, ,,	,,	51
d	Problematical object (see Fig. 47 i for mate)	W—17—40e	,, ,,	,,	48
e	Scalloped ornament	W—17—66	,, ,,	,,	50
f	Flare	W—17—43	,, ,,	,,	50
g	Rectangular bead (see Fig. 47 c)	W—17—68	,, ,,	,,	51
h	Rectangular bead	W—17—72	,, ,,	,,	51
i	Effigy stingray spine	W—17—70	,, ,,	,,	48
j	Tabbed ractangular plaque	W—17—40d	,, ,,	,,	48
k	Beads, synoptic series (as shown in Fig. 48 v, a')	W—17—(8, 58)	,, ,,	,,	51
l	*Ibid.*, but includes Fig. 48 f'	W—17—(8, 58)	,, ,,	,,	51

Fig. 49

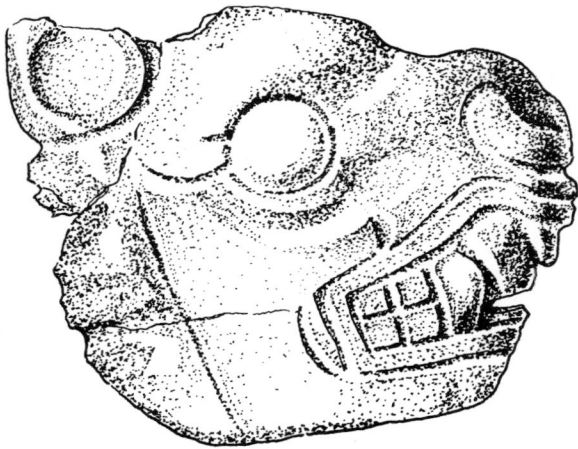
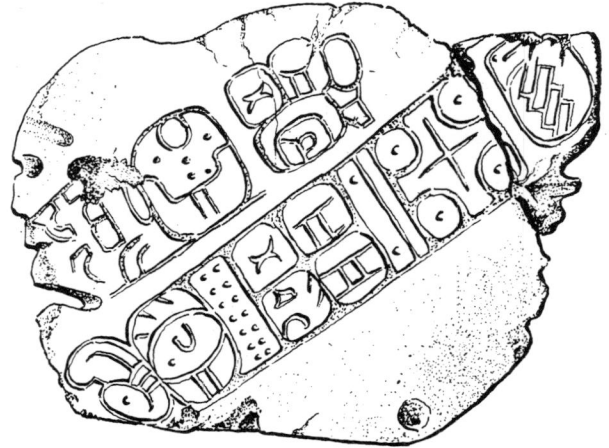

a

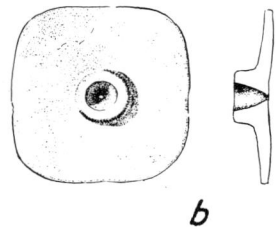

b

c

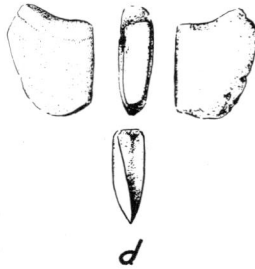

d

g

h

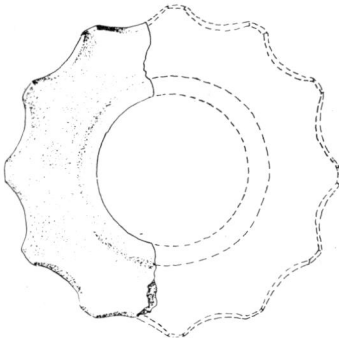

e

f

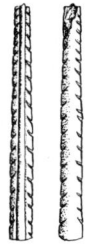

i

j

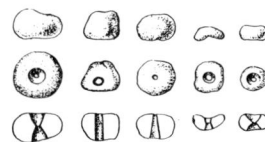

k

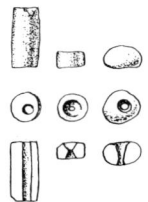

l

FIGURE 50

OBJECTS OF JADEITE
All 1/2 scale

	DESCRIPTION	FIELD NO.	PROVENIENCE	DISPOSITION	REF. PAGE
a	Slightly worked pieces	E—1—83	Cache O—13—47	UM	52
b	,, ,, ,,	E—1—42	Cache O—13—37	,,	52
c	,, ,, ,,	E—1—204d	Cache O—13—17	,,	52
d	,, ,, ,,	W—1—40	Cache J—1—1	,,	52
e	,, ,, ,,	E—1—39	Cache O—13—35	,,	52
f	,, ,, ,,	E—1—92	Cache O—13—48	,,	52
g	,, ,, ,,	E—1—33	Cache O—13—36	,,	52
h	Unworked piece	S—2—65	Cache R—3—2	,,	52
i—m	Unworked and slightly worked pieces	Field numbers lacking (camp fire) but some or all from Str. O—13 caches.		,,	52
n	Slightly worked pieces	W—1—40	Cache J—1—1	,,	52
o, p	,, ,, ,,	W—14—13c	Cache O—16—1	,,	52
q	Obverse of Fig. 46 a, showing unpolished surface of pebble and sawed groove	E—1—204c	Cache O—13—17	,,	44
r	Slightly worked pieces	S—21—20c	Cache R—9—1	,,	52
s	Obverse of Fig. 45 v, showing saw scars and septum	E—1—85	Cache O—13—50	,,	46
t	Slightly worked pieces	E—1—17	Cache O—13—21	NM	52
u	Unworked and slightly worked pieces	E—1—20	Cache O—13—8	,,	52
v	Rough spheres	S—21—27	Cache R—9—2	,,	52
w	Slightly worked pieces	W—6—21	Cache K—5—2	,,	52
x	Unworked pieces	NE—4—19	Cache J—29—1	,,	52

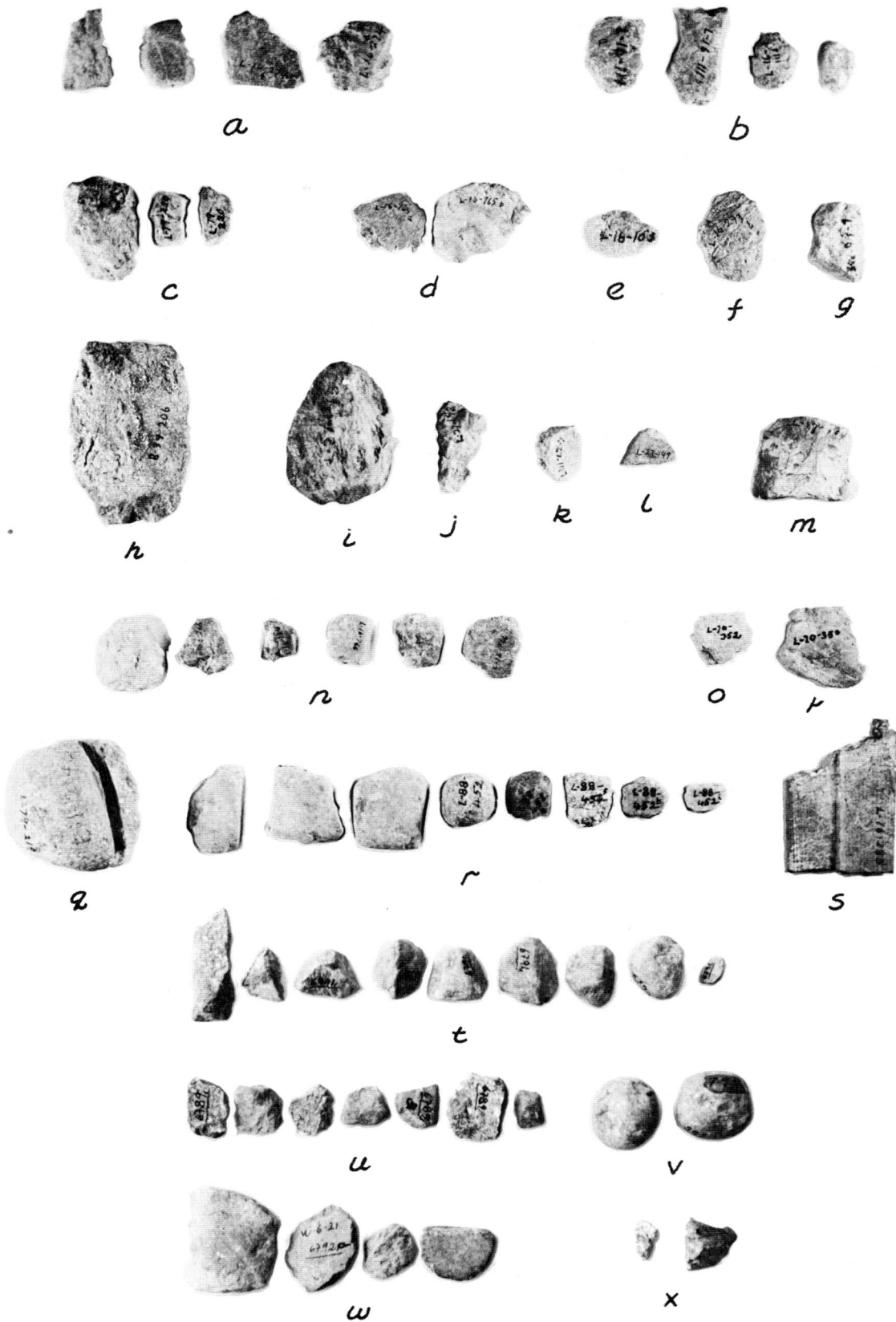

Fig. 50

FIGURE 51

OBJECTS OF SHELL

	DESCRIPTION	FIELD NO.	PROVENIENCE	DISPOSITION	REF. PAGE
a	Incised, silhouette-cut piece	W—6—21	Cache K—5—2	UM	56
b, c	Incised, silhouette-cut pieces	W—5—275	Cache K—5—8	,,	56
d, e	,, ,, ,, ,,	W—1—40	Cache J—1—1	,,	56
f, g	Small grooved figurines	E—1—109	Cache O—13—13	,,	56
h	Small grooved figurine	E—1—154	Cache O—13—23	,,	56
i	Incised and cut piece	W—1—40	Cache J—1—1	,,	57
j	,, ,, ,, ,,	E—1—119	Cache O—13—7	,,	57
k—n	Incised and cut pieces	W—5—145	Cache K—5—5	,,	57
o	Small grooved figurine fragment	No field number (camp fire)		,,	56
p	Incised and cut piece	E—1—42	Cache O—13—37	,,	57
q	Bead (in group in Fig. 52 g')	S—15—6	Burial 10	,,	59
r	Incised pendant	No field number (camp fire)		,,	57
s	Incised and cut piece	W—1—40	Cache J—1—1	,,	57
t	Incised disc	E—1—154	Cache O—13—23	,,	57
u, v	Incised discs (also shown in Fig. 52 b')	E—1—109	Cache O—13—13	,,	57
w	Hollow-drilled disc	W—5—218	Str. K—5, plaza, surface	,,	59

Fig. 51

a

b

c

d

e

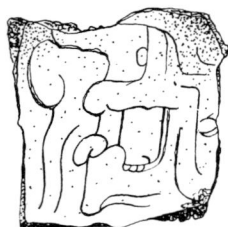

f

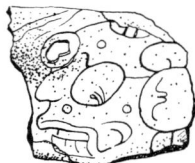

g

h

i

j

k

l

m

n

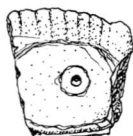

O

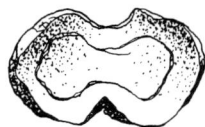

p

q

r

s

t

u

v

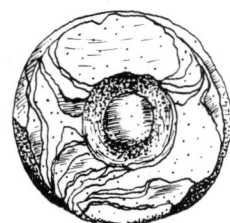

0   5

CM

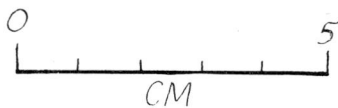

w

FIGURE 52

OBJECTS OF SHELL
All 1/2 scale

	DESCRIPTION	FIELD NO.	PROVENIENCE	DISPOSITION	REF. PAGE
a	Perforated valve	E—1—10	Cache O—13—54	NM	56
b	Perforated and cut piece	,,	,, ,,	,,	57
c	Cut piece	,,	,, ,,	,,	57
d	Coral branch	Field number lacking. Surely from a Str. O—13— cache		,,	60
e, f	Small, grooved figurines	*Ibid.*		,,	56
g	Unfinished (?) figurine	,,		,,	56
h	Unworked bivalve	E—1—104	Cache O—13—11	,,	55
i	Plain discs	Same as d		,,	57
j	Unworked valve	W—17—40b	Burial 5	,,	55
k, l	Bivalve fragments	W—17—40	,, ,,	,,	59
m	Perforated ornament (for mate, see Fig. 53 h)	W—17—42	,, ,,	,,	59
n	Tinklers (see t)	W—17—60	,, ,,	,,	57
o	Perforated valve	W—17—52	,, ,,	,,	56
p	Dentate ornaments (continued in x)	W—17—67	,, ,,	,,	58
q	Drilled univalve	S—1—40	Cache R—11—6	UM	56
r	Perforated valve	E—1—11	Cache O—13—4	,,	56
s	Tinkler	SE—1—6	Str. V—1, in debris surrounding Burial 1	,,	57
t	Tinklers (see n)	W—17—60	Burial 5	,,	57
u	Perforated fragment	E—1—42	Cache O—13—37	,,	59
v	Cut rectangular piece	W—30—5	Str. J—9, on floor	,,	59
w	Worked piece of freshwater clam shell	W—5—232	Str. K—5	,,	59
x	Dentate ornaments (see p)	W—17—67	Burial 5	,,	58
y, z, a'	Cut shell objects	E—1—11	Cache O—13—4	,,	57
b'	Incised discs (two also shown in Fig. 51 u, v)	E—1—109	Cache O—13—13	,,	57
c'	Plain disc	,,	,, ,,	,,	57
d'	Small, thin disc, perforated	W—8—135	Str. J—12, on floor	,,	58
e'	Beads (see Fig. 53 m)	W—17—8	Burial 5	,,	59
f'	,,	SE—1—10a	Burial 2	,,	59
g'	,,	S—15—6	Burial 10	,,	59
h'	Sharpened piece	,,	,, ,,	,,	59
i'	Perforated piece	,,	,, ,,	,,	59

Fig. 52

FIGURE 53

OBJECTS OF SHELL
e—m 1/2 scale

	DESCRIPTION	FIELD NO.	PROVENIENCE	DISPOSITION	REF. PAGE
a—d	Perforated inscribed plates. Natural size	W—17—42	Burial 5	a, b in NM; c, d in UM	59
e—i	Perforated pieces believed to be part of a mask (for mate of h, see Fig. 52 m)	,,	,, ,,	UM	59
j—1	Examples of perforated plates believed to have formed a shell-plated cloak (these two, asterisked, are shown in Fig. 54)	,,	,, ,,	,,	59
m	Details of typical beads shown in Fig. 52 e!	W—17—8	,, ,,	,,	59

Fig. 53

a

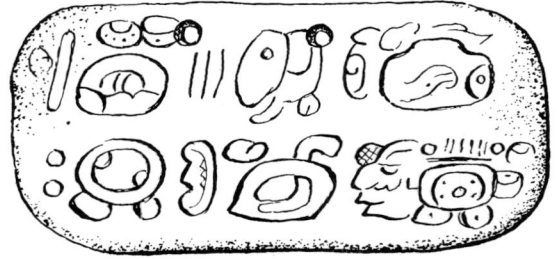

b

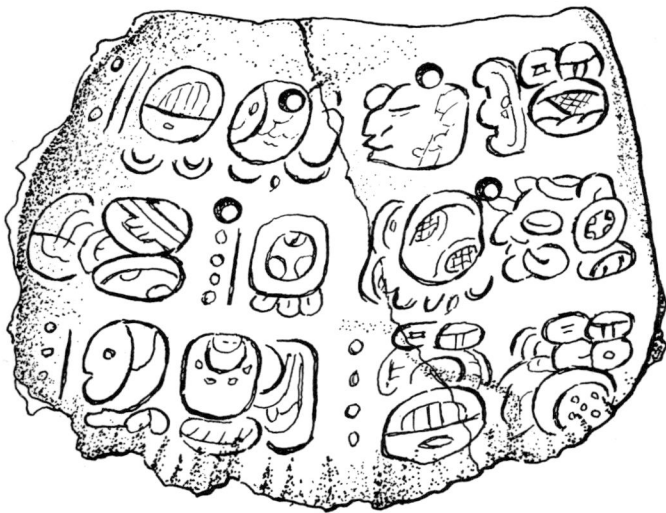

c

d

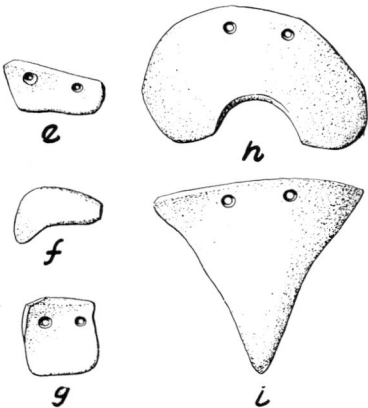

e

f

g

h

i

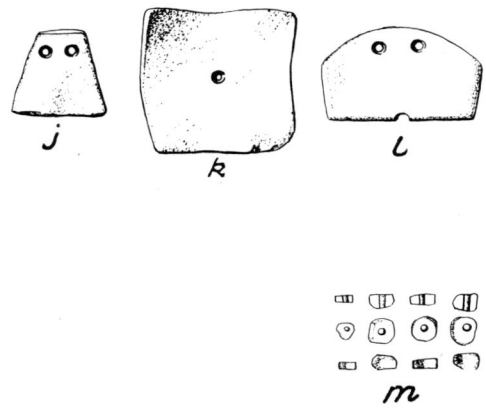

j

k

l

m

FIGURE 54

SHELL ELEMENTS OF CLOAK
1/2 scale

DESCRIPTION	FIELD NO.	PROVENIENCE	DISPOSITION	REF. PAGE
Perforated plates believed to have formed a cloak. (Others not shown here are in NM. Two asterisked pieces also illustrated in Fig. 53 j, l. Other related shell objects are shown in Figs. 52 m, 53 a—i)	W—17—42	Burial 5	UM	59

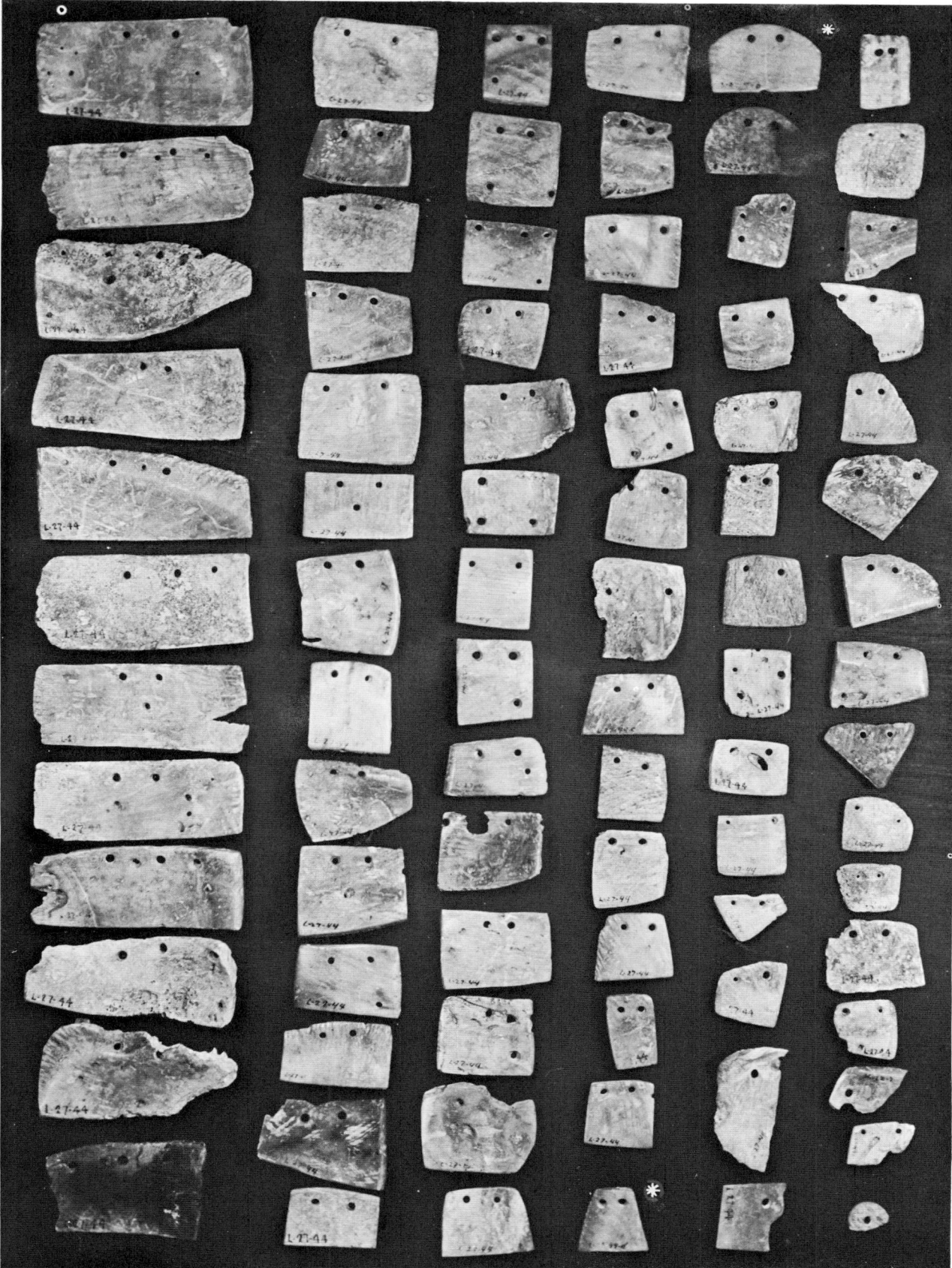

Fig. 54

FIGURE 55

OBJECTS OF BONE AND SHELL

	DESCRIPTION	FIELD NO.	PROVENIENCE	DISPOSITION	REF. PAGE
a	Awl, bone	NE—1—15	Northeast section, test pit	UM	62
b	Perforator, bone	SE—1—32	Str. V—1, in fill of Units D—E	,,	62
c	Split and worked stingray spine	W—1—40	Cache J—1—1	,,	64
d	Bone replica of stingray spine	W—5—275	Cache K—5—8	,,	65
e	Bone replica of stingray spine	W—6—21k	Cache K—5—2	,,	65
f	Grooved stingray spine	W—1—40	Cache J—1—1	,,	64
g	Pendant made from vertebra	W—6—3	Str. J—23, surface debris	,,	62
h	Tube, bone	SE—1—35	Str. V—1, in fill of Units D—E	,,	62
i	Perforated tube, bone	E—1—24	Cache O—13—29	,,	62
j	Awl, bone	W—5—209	Str. K—5—1st, surface debris	NM	62
k	Pendant from animal mandible	W—40—13g	Cache O—16—1	UM	62
l	Grooved bone	W—5—202	Str. K—5—1st, interior of secondary wall	,,	64
m	Rasper, bone	W—5—167	Str. K—5—1st, basal terrace hearting	,,	61
n	,, ,,	S—7—5	South section, test pit	,,	61
o	,, ,,	NE—1—12	Northeast section, test pit	,,	61
p	Perforated shell ornament	SE—1—10a	Burial 2	,,	58
q	Problematical ornament, shell	W—17—62	Burial 5	,,	58
r	Problematical ornament, shell (drawn from field photo)	W—17—61	,, ,,	NM (not located)	58
s	Problematical ornament, shell	M—43—1	Acropolis, precise source unknown	UM	58
t	Problematical ornament, shell	SE—1—10a	Burial 2	,,	58

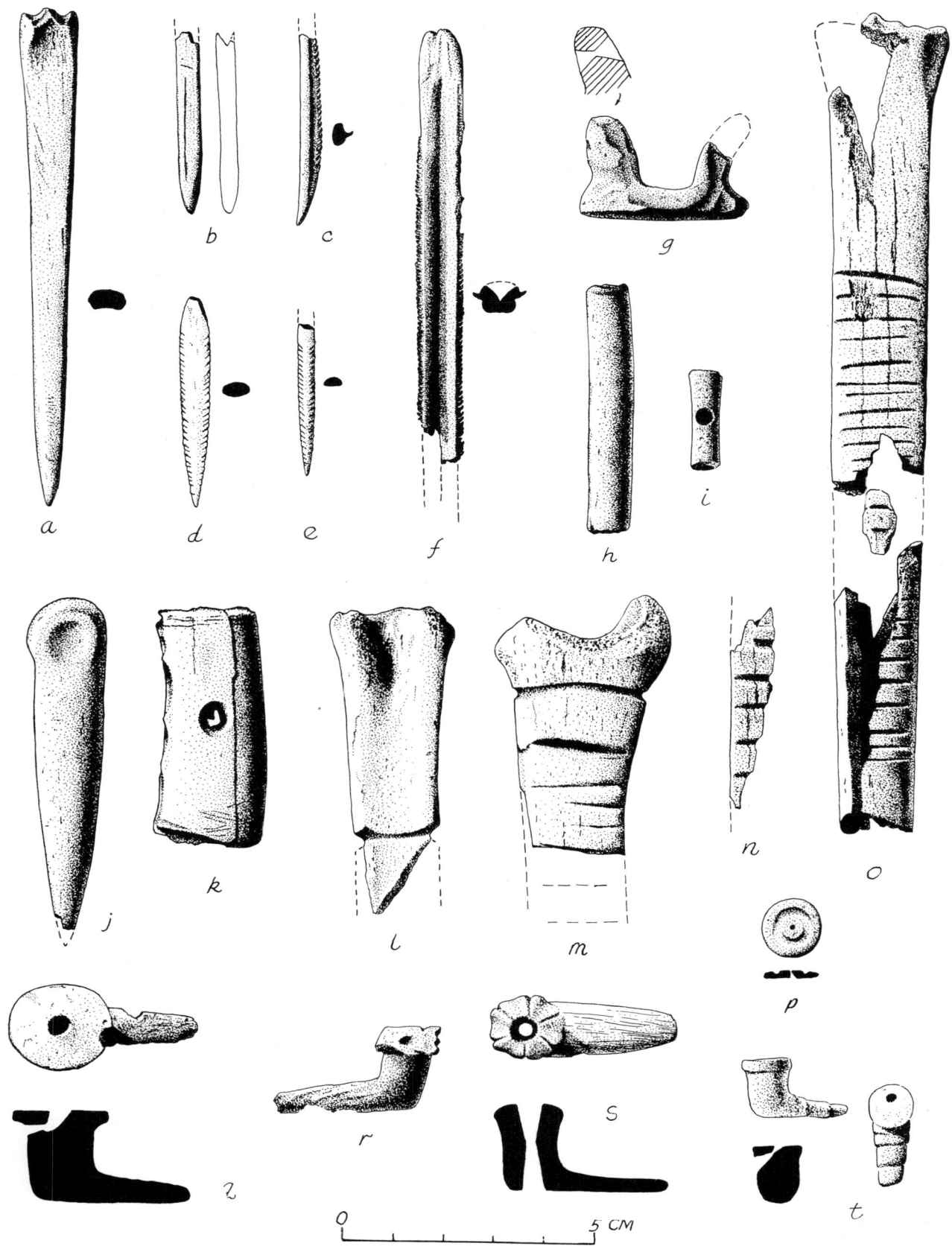

Fig. 55

a *b* *c* *d* *e* *f* *g* *h* *i* *j* *k* *l* *m* *n* *o* *p* *q* *r* *s* *t*

0   5 CM

FIGURE 56

INCISED STINGRAY SPINES

Twice natural size

DESCRIPTION	FIELD NO.	PROVENIENCE	DISPOSITION	REF. PAGE
Four fragmentary stingray spines with incised inscriptions	W—17—49	Burial 5	UM	65

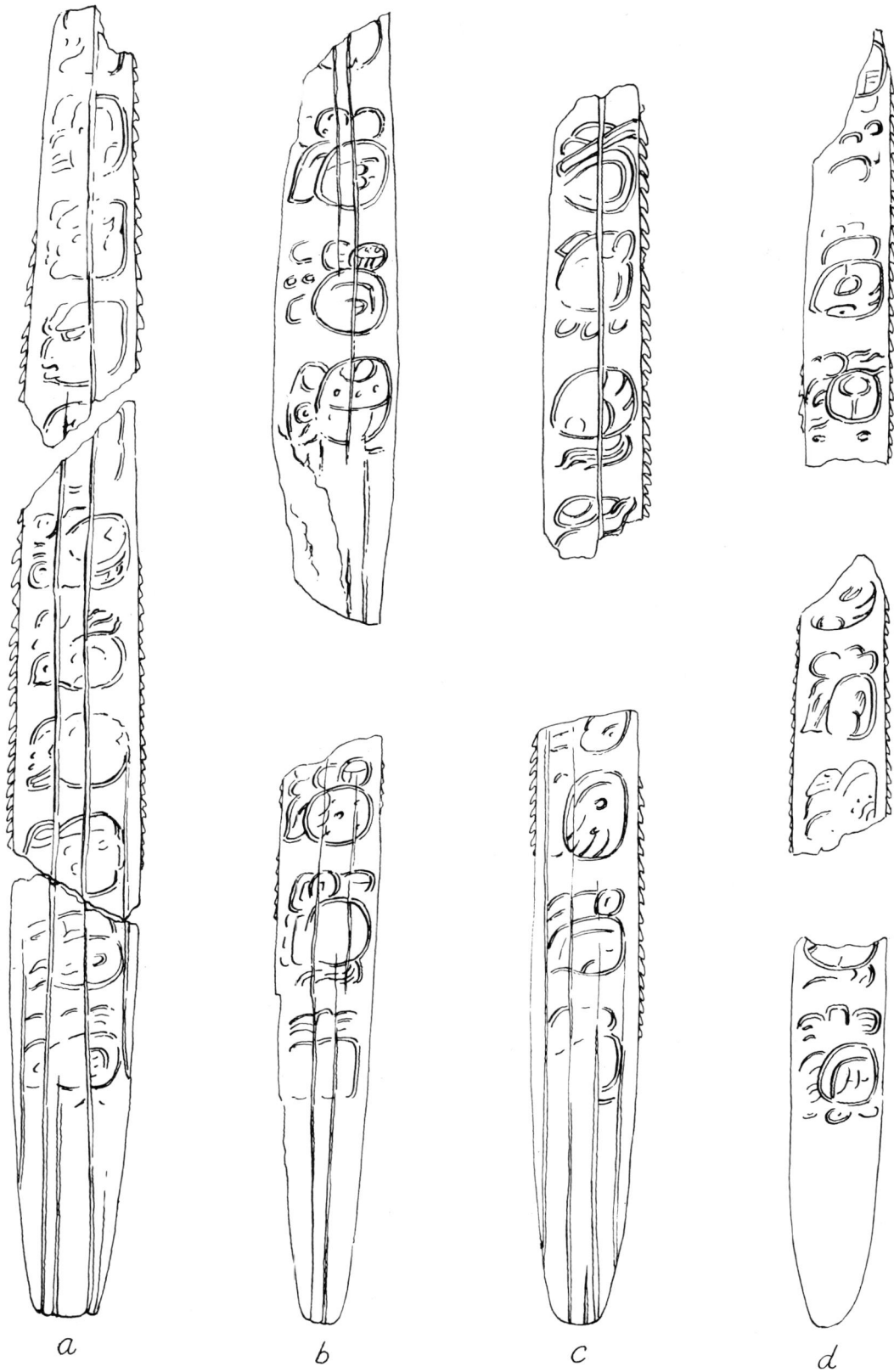

Fig. 56

a   b   c   d

FIGURE 57

MISCELLANEOUS BONE OBJECTS

	DESCRIPTION	FIELD NO.	PROVENIENCE	DISPOSITION	REF. PAGE
a	Human femur, sawed (note arrow)	W—43—5	See Lot 21 under Burials	UM	67
b	Antler tip	W—2—30	Str. J—2, surface debris	,,	63
c, d	Antler tips	S—22—14	Str. R—10, trench left side of stairway		63
e	Antler tip	W—8—81	Str. J—11, throne debris	,,	63
f	,, ,,	Same as b		,,	63
g	Shark tooth	E—1—42	Cache O—13—37	,,	63
h	Jaguar ulna, carved (L 8.8 cm.)	W—17—85	Burial 5	,,	63
i	Bone pin, carved (L 6.9 cm.)	W—31—25	Str. J—11, surface debris	,,	62

Fig. 57

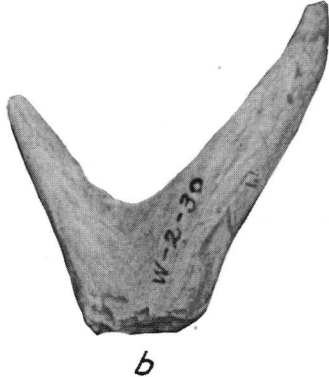

a

b

c

d

e

f

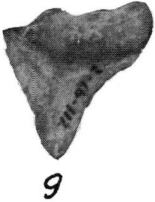

g

0   5 *CM*

h

i

FIGURE 58

OBJECTS OF CLAY
All 1/2 scale

	DESCRIPTION	FIELD NO.	PROVENIENCE	DISPOSITION	REF. PAGE
a	Spherical clay beads	W—17—7	Burial 5	UM	71
b, c	Clay replicas of bivalve shells with perforations near hinges	W—17—45, 47	,, ,,	,,	71
d	*Ibid*.	W—17—46	,, ,,	NM	71
e	,, fragmentary	W—17—84	,, ,,	,,	71
f	Large clay bead (?)	W—17—50	,, ,,	,,	71
g	,, ,, ,,	,,	,, ,,	UM	71
h, i	Large clay beads	SE—1—2	Str. V—1—1st, above cover stones of Burial 1 and among skeletal remains described as Lot 18 (see under Burials)	,,	71
j	Clay problematical object	W—17—34	Burial 5	,,	71
k, 1	Decorated clay beads	?	?	NM	71
m	Small clay sphere	Field number lacking		,,	72
n	Clay problematical object	,, ,, ,,	(camp fire)	UM	72
o	Rounded multiply drilled potsherd	S—1—45	Str. R—11—a, summit	,,	70
p	Rounded perforated potsherd	S—2—17	Str. R—3, plaza	NM	69
q	,, ,, ,,	S—19—1	Str. U—15, test pit	UM	69
r	,, ,, ,,	S—1—7	Str. R—11—a, bench trench	NM	69
s	Rounded potsherd	SE—1—32	Str. V—1, rubble west of Burial 3	UM	70
t	,, ,,	W—7—11	Str. K—6—b, surface debris	,,	70
u	,, ,,	W—29—68	West Group, surface	,,	70
v	,, ,,	W—5—9	Str. K—5, trench	,,	70
w	,, ,,	S—1—37	Str. R—11, court surface	,,	70
x	,, ,,	W—12—23	Str. J—6—2nd	,,	70
y	Irregularly edged pottery slab	NE—1—17	Cave, Northeast section, sub-surface	,,	70

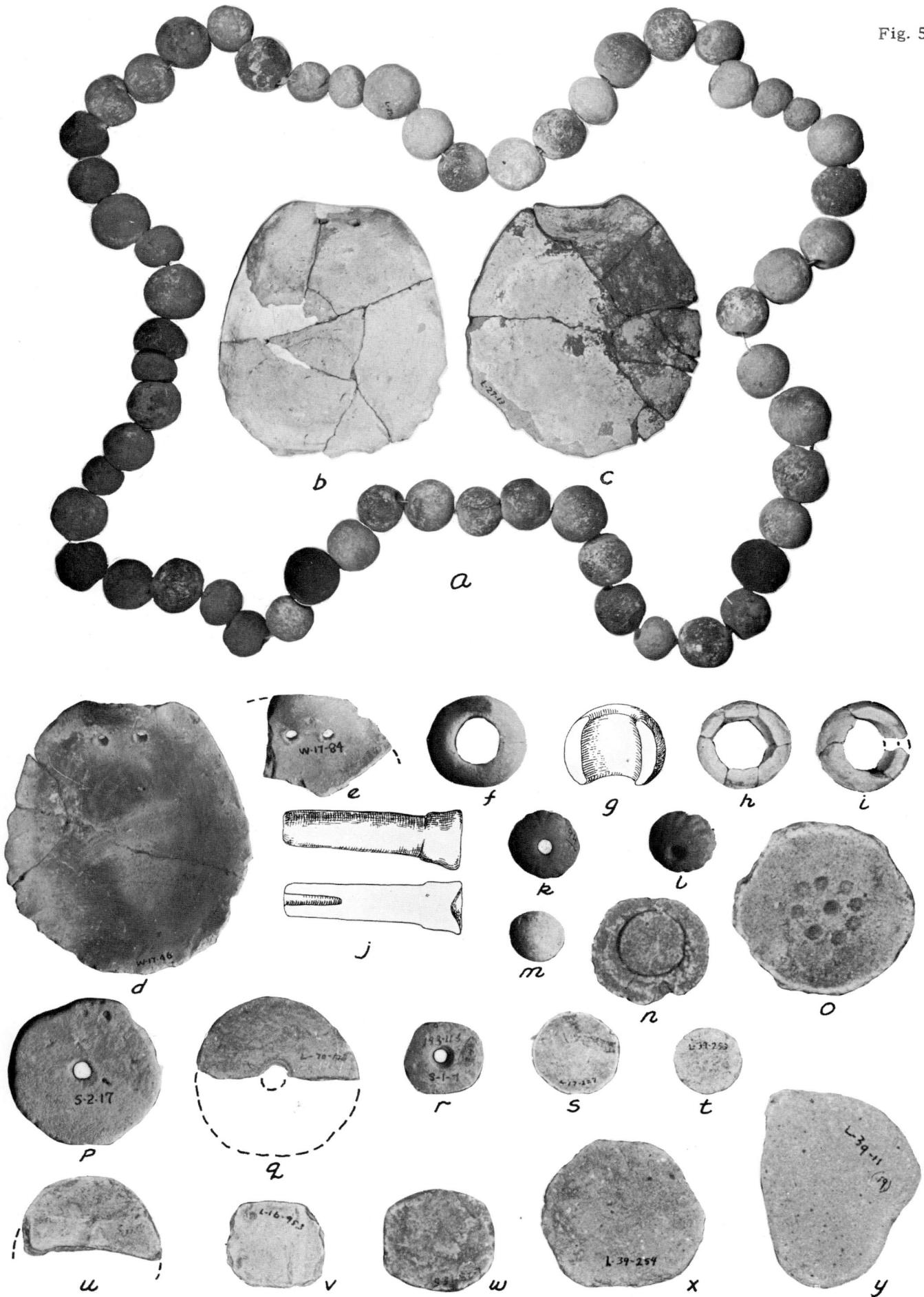

Fig. 58

FIGURE 59

OBJECTS OF CLAY

	DESCRIPTION	FIELD NO.	PROVENIENCE	DISPOSITION	REF. PAGE
a	Incised reworked sherd	W—5—119	Str. K—5, trench	UM	70
b	Partially perforated reworked sherd	W—5—223	Str. K—5—1st—B, below	,,	69
c	Incised pendant, with grooved edge, made from sherd	S—1—14	Str. R—11, debris	,,	70
d	Bar pendant	S—22—15	Str. R—10, trench, sub-surface	,,	71
e	Perforated cylindrical pendant	W—29—59	West Group, surface	,,	71
f	Flare	S—2—23	Str. R—3, left terrace base	,,	70
g	Spindle whorl	S—22—24	Str. R—10, probably surface	,,	69
h	,, ,,	SE—1—27	Str. V—1—1st, on floor of Unit D	,,	69
i	Bead, section	Same as d		,,	71
j	Problematical object	W—29—18	West Group, surface	,,	72
k	,, ,,	?	Str. R—11 (?)	,,	72
l	,, ,,	W—6—2	Str. J—23, probably surface debris	,,	72
m	Whetstone, fine-grained stone	E—50—3	East Group, surface	,,	37
n	Ear spool, fragmentary	E—1—143	Str. O—13, deep excavation	,,	70
o	,, ,, ,,	W—1—27	West Group, plaza trench	,,	70
p	,, ,, ,,	E—1—159	Str. O—13, surface	,,	70
q	,, ,, ,,	W—2—61	Str. J—2, test pit, just above bedrock	,,	70

Fig. 59

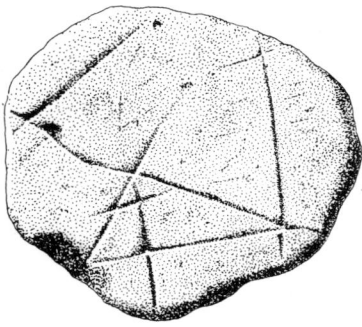

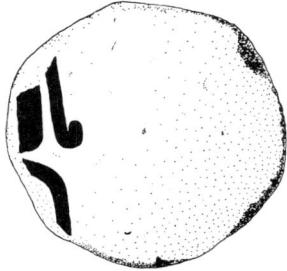

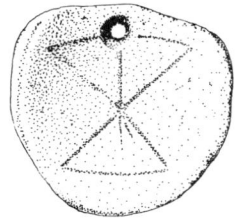

a

b

C

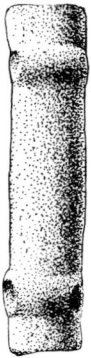 

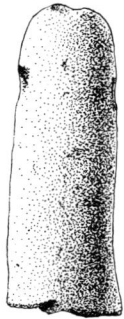

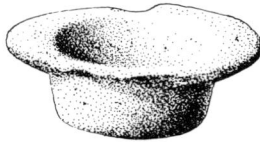

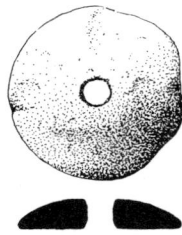

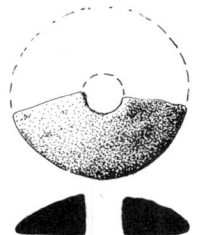

d

e

f

g

h

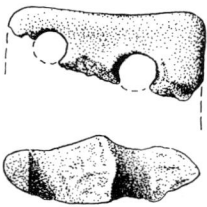

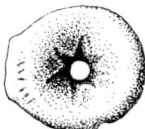

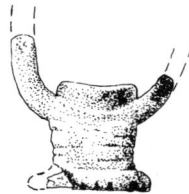

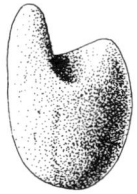

i

j

k

l

m

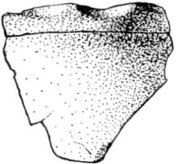

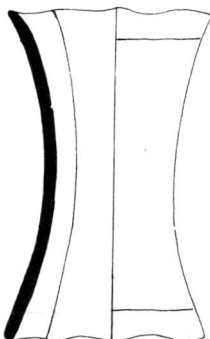

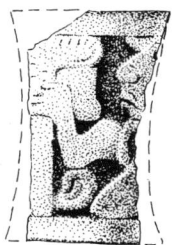

n

o

p

q

0   5 CM

FIGURE 60

MISCELLANEOUS POTTERY VESSELS
All 1/4 scale except f and g

	DESCRIPTION	FIELD NO.	PROVENIENCE	DISPOSITION	REF. PAGE
a	Orange slipped bowl with slipped orange lid. 38 parallel flutings. Black band interior and exterior of rim, encircled by 15 black painted glyphs (1 a ^{1}, 14 a ^{2}); traces of lime paste in lower half of bowl	NE—4—114 (lid) NE—4—113 (bowl)	Cache J—29—2	NM	104
b	Black slipped tripodal bowl. Hollow legs lacking. Identical bowl was inverted and lip-to-lip	S—2—62	Cache R—3—2	NM and UM (illustrated)	104
c	Polychrome E bowl. Mat design in specular hematite, with light orange filler, rim interior painted (specimen described and illustrated by Butler, 1935, pp. 6—7)	S—1—19	Cache R—11—3	UM	104
d	Polychrome E bowl. Specular hematite paint (heavy stippling) with dark orange filler (light stippling) and light orange wash (no stippling). 9 specular red glyphs (1/2 scale) with Chuen and Kin identifiable (d^8 is totally effaced). Rim interior painted. See also Butler (*ibid.*)	,,	,, ,,	,,	104
e	Spiked unslipped gray censer. Lid knob vertically perforated to interior. See also Butler (*ibid.*, p. 15) and Satterthwaite (1936, p. 14; 1946 a)	W—4—2	Cache J—3—2	,,	104
f	Small double-chambered object (1/2 scale)	W—2—73	Str. J—2, substructure above and outside J—2—2nd, below or inside latest construction	,,	72
g	Small double-chambered object, fragmentary (1/2 scale)	*Ibid.*			72
h	Dark-on-light orange cylinder jar. 6 bars grouped in pairs. See also Butler (*ibid.*, p. 8)	E—1—19	Cache O—13—25	,,	104
i	Polychrome C cylinder jar. Black and red on light yellow. Surface broken by two sets of paired vertical red lines, one section enclosing a black painted glyphic design, and the other vertical arrangements of faded black daubs. Rim interior painted. See also Butler (*ibid.*, pp. 4—5)	E—1—23	Cache O—13—28	,,	104

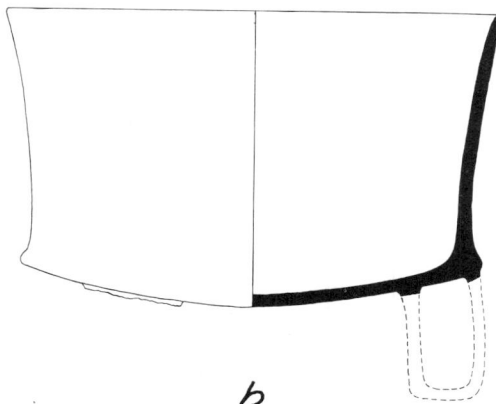

Fig. 60

a'

a^2

a

b

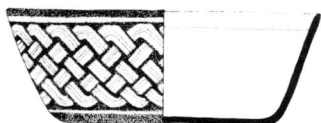

c

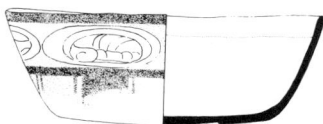

d

d'

d^2

d^3

d^4

d^5

d^6

d^7

d^8

d^9

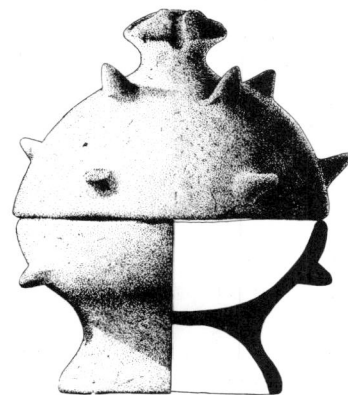

e

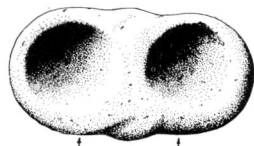

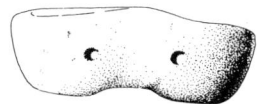

f

g

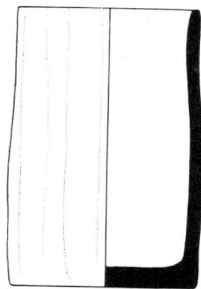

h

i

FIGURE 61

ORANGE 2 CACHE VESSELS
All 1/4 scale

	DESCRIPTION	FIELD NO.	PROVENIENCE	DISPOSITION	REF. PAGE
a	Bowl and lid. Lime paste covers lower third of bowl	W—5—183a	Cache K—5—6	NM	101
b	Bowl and lid	W—5—145d	Cache K—5—5	UM	101
c	Bowl and lid. Interior of bowl was covered with thick layer of lime paste to 6 cm. above bottom	W—5—275a	Cache K—5—8	,,	101
d	Bowl and lid. Lime paste covers bottom of bowl	W—1—40a	Cache J—1—1	,,	101
e	Bowl and lid. Lime paste covers lower half of bowl. Also illustrated by Butler (1935, Pl. VI, 7)	W—6—21a, b	Cache K—5—2	,,	101
f	Bowl and lid	W—3—5	Cache J—1—2	,,	101
g	,, ,, ,,	E—1—17	Cache O—13—21	,,	101
h	,, ,, ,,	W—40—12	Cache O—16—1	,,	
i	Bowl and lid, fragmentary	E—1—108	Cache O—13—19	,,	101
j	,, ,, ,, ,,	W—5—5	Cache K—5—1	,,	101
k	Lid	E—1—104	Cache O—13—11	,,	101
l	Bowl. Two-thirds of interior coated by lime paste	E—1—118	Cache O—13—8	,,	101
m	Bowl with textile impressions	S—1—16	Cache R—11—1	,,	74, 101
n	Bowl, originally with lid	NE—4—18	Cache J—29—1	NM	101
o	Bowl. Lime paste covers lower two-thirds of interior	E—1—117	From general position of Caches O—13— (6—9)	UM	101
p	Bowl. Lime paste covers entire interior to rim	E—1—122	Cache O—13—7	,,	101
q	Bowl. Half of interior coated with lime paste	E—1—(117—118)	Probably Cache O—13—6	,,	101
r	Bowl. Lime paste covers lower two-thirds of bowl	E—1—117	Probably Cache O—13—9	,,	101
s	Bowl. Two-thirds of interior coated by lime paste. Probably covered by an inverted, similar bowl	E—1—10	Cache O—13—54	,,	101
t	Bowl, fragmentary. Half of interior coated by lime paste. Lid not shown	E—1—203	Cache O—13—17	,,	101
u	Lid, inverted to hold cache contents. Lime paste coating to 2.5 cm. of rim	S—21—18	Cache R—9—1	,,	101

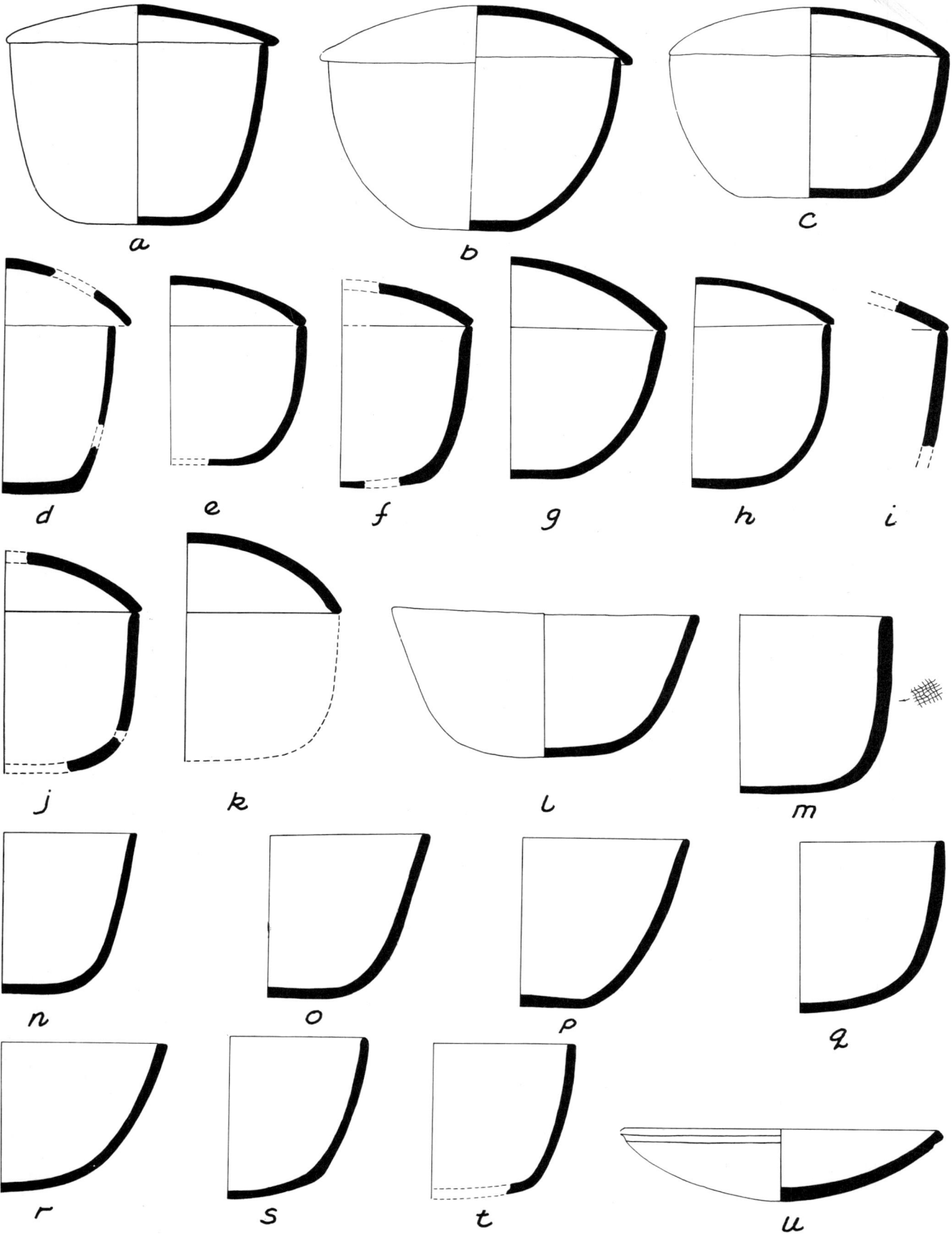

Fig. 61

a

b

c

d

e

f

g

h

i

j

k

l

m

n

o

p

q

r

s

t

u

FIGURE 62

MISCELLANEOUS CACHE VESSELS
All 1/4 scale

	DESCRIPTION	FIELD NO.	PROVENIENCE	DISPOSITION	REF. PAGE
a	Orange 2 bowl with flaring sides (covered by mate, as in c)	E—1—11	Cache O—13—4	UM	101
b	Orange 2 bowl with flaring straight sides. Lime paste coats entire interior to rim	E—1—113	Probably Cache O—13—13	,,	101
c	Pair of lip-to-lip Orange 2 bowls with flaring straight sides. Also illustrated by Butler (1935, Pl. VI, 8)	E—1—(104—105)	Cache O—13—12	,,	101
d	Orange 2 bowl, flat base, flaring sides (cf. R. E. Smith, 1955, Fig. 19 b, 10)	S—2—55	Cache R—3—1	,,	101
e	Orange 2 bowl, flat base, flaring straight sides	E—1—149	Cache O—13—55	,,	101
f	Orange 2 bowl, flat base, flaring sides	E—1—95	Possibly associated with Cache O—13—10	,,	101
g	Unslipped small bowl, orange to brick red	E—1—155	Cache O—13—18	NM	104
h	Unslipped buff paste jar with blue painted rim (dotted line), fragmentary	?	Str. O—13, cache assignment uncertain	UM	101
i	*Ibid.*	E—1—64	Cache O—13—46	,,	101
j	,,	E—1—55	From Str. O—13, rear room caches	,,	101
k	,,	E—1—26	From Str. O—13, rear room caches	,,	101
l	Unslipped buff paste jar sherd. Profile relates to jars in o—q	E—1—38	From Str. O—13, rear room caches	,,	101
m	*Ibid.*	E—1—25	From Str. O—13, rear room caches	,,	101
n	,,	E—1—26	From Str. O—13, rear room caches	,,	101
o	Unslipped buff paste jar with plain lid. Jar also illustrated by Butler (*ibid.*, Pl. VI, 20)	E—1—53	Cache O—13—42	,,	101
p	Unslipped, fire-clouded buff jar with lid and imprints of 3 leaves on underside. Also illustrated by Butler (*ibid.*, Pl. VI, 22)	E—1—(35—36)	Cache O—13—33	,,	101
q	Unslipped buff paste jar with lid	E—1—48	Cache O—13—41	NM	101
r	Unslipped, thin walled, buff paste jar	W—12—17a	Cache J—6—4	UM	104
s	Unslipped, light buff paste jar, constricted neck, everted rim. Disc lid not shown	W—12—6	Cache J—6—1	NM	104
t	Smooth unslipped jar. Also illustrated by Butler (*ibid.*, Pl. VI, 21)	E—1—40	Cache O—13—36	UM	104

Fig. 62

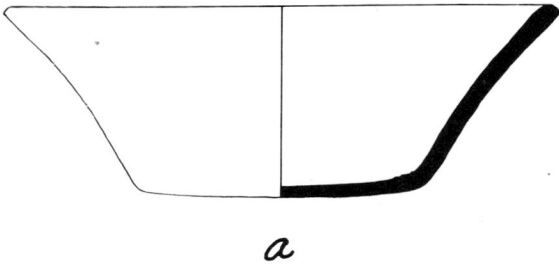

a

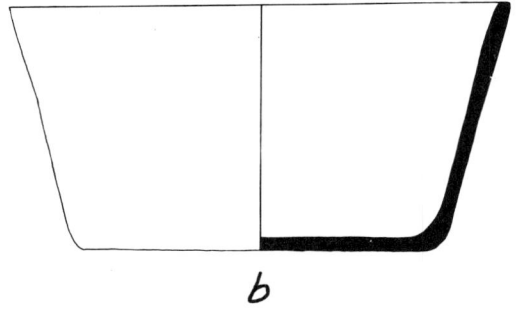

b

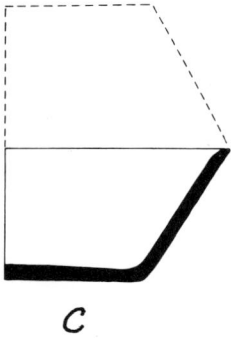

c

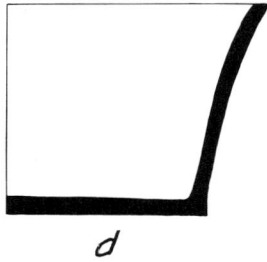

d

e

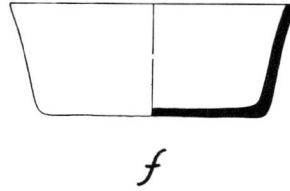

f

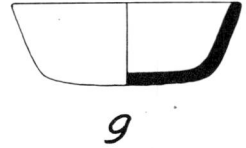

g

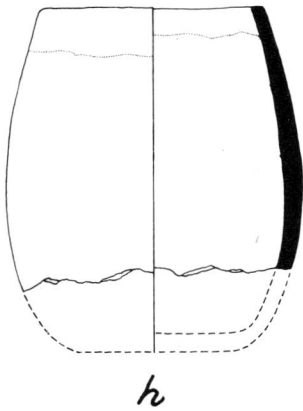

h

i j

k

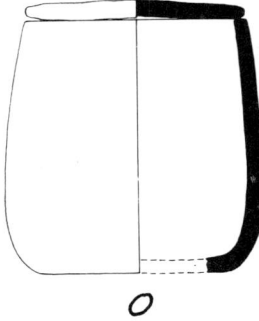

l m n

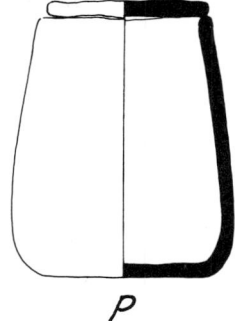

O P

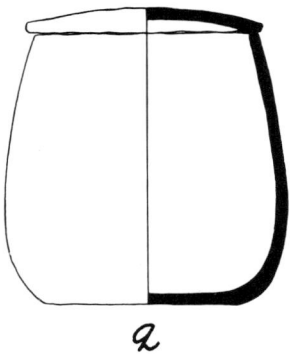

q

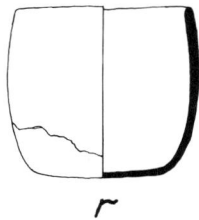

r

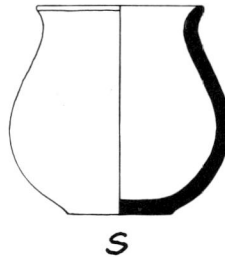

s

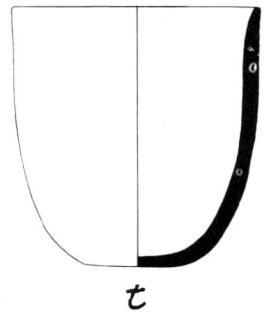

t

FIGURE 63

BURIALS 1, 2, and 3 (see pp. 121—123)

a   Burial 1

b   Burial 2: 1. 17 jadeite beads (8 shown in Fig. 48 g¹)
                    15 shell beads (6 shown in Fig. 52 f¹)
                    Shanked shell ornament (Fig. 55 t)
                    Perforated shell disc (Fig. 55 p)

            2. Shanked shell ornament (as in 1); see p. 58)

            3. Shark (?) tooth (see p. 63)

            4. Stingray spine, unworked (see p. 65)

c   Burial 3

Fig. 63

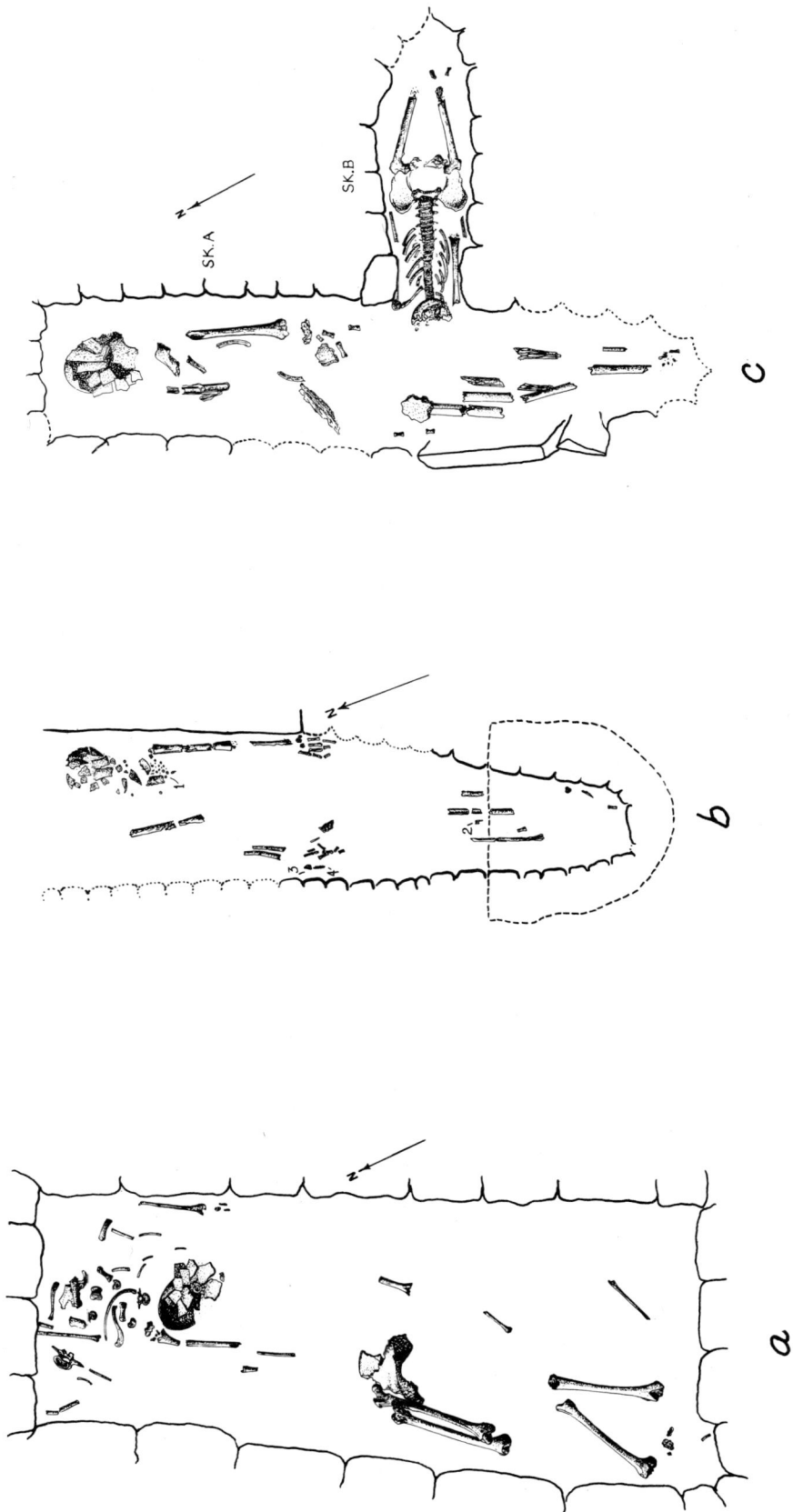

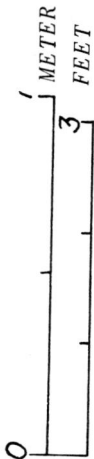

FIGURE 64

BURIAL 5, PLAN OF FLOOR (see pp. 124—125)

1   209 *Spondylus limbatus* perforated plates (Figs. 53 j—1; 54)
4 inscribed *Spondylus limbatus* perforated plates Fig. 53 a—d)
6 cut white shell elements (Figs. 52 m; 53 e—i)
2 (sub-spherical?) jadeite beads (see p. 51)
Perforated jadeite disc (Fig. 44 j)
Jadeite earplug flare (Fig. 49 f)
"Bird bones" (see p. 64)

2   Blue-painted clay pot cover
Cuffed, cylindrical clay object (as in 20)

3   Valve of perforated *Spondylus limbatus*, set partially beneath skull (see p. 56)

4   Fillet of 22 jadeite ornaments (Figs. 47 j—x; 48 a—t)

5   Pair of jadeite earplugs (Figs. 47 g, h; 49 b)

6   Clay effigy shell (Fig. 58 d)

7   Clay effigy shell (Fig. 58 b)

8   124 plain clay beads (Fig. 58 a)

9   Carved jaguar ulna (Fig. 57 h)

10 4 fragmentary inscribed stingray spines (Fig. 56)
11 fragments of unworked stingray spines (see p. 64)
3 pieces of bird (?) bone (see p. 64)

11 Teeth of Skeleton A
"Various jadeite beads" (sub-spherical?) (see p. 51)

12 Jadeite jaguar pendant (Figs. 47 f; 49 a)

13 Comal sherd (see Butler, 1935, p. 65, M20)

14 Perforated valve of *Spondylus limbatus*, spines removed (Fig. 52 o)

15 2 large clay beads (?) (Fig. 58 f, g)

16 Sherds

17 Pyrite mosaic plaque with shale backing, set on angle (Fig. 42 f)

18 Orange 2 plate (see Butler, 1935, p. 10)
Oval, flat, perforated jadeite ornament (Fig. 47 z)

19 2 whole *Quadrula quadrata* (see p. 55)
Whole *Spondylus limbatus* (see p. 55)
Knife-like implement (Fig. 3 v)
Rectangular, tabbed jadeite object (Fig. 49 j)
7 small pieces of worked and polished jadeite (see p. 52)
"Small jadeite sphere" (see p. 48)
Pair of jadeite problematical objects (Figs. 47 i; 49 d)
Pyrite discoidal plaque (see p. 42)
6 unworked stingray spine tips (see p. 65)
5 "phalanges" (see p. 64)

20 Cuffed, cylindrical clay object (Fig. 58 j)

21 Pyrite mosaic bands (Fig. 42 g)

22 Pyrite mosaic bands (mate of 21)

23 2 univalve shells

24 Stalactite, fragmentary

Objects not located by number include: A. Skeleton B, area of lower face: 10 sub-spherical (4 shown in Fig. 48 a') and two cylindrical beads (Figs. 48 f'; 49 l, left)—Cylindrical jadeite bead, "medium" (see p. 51)—Carved jadeite figurine pendant (Fig. 47 e)—A shanked shell ornament on either side of jaw (Fig. 55 q, r)

B. Skeleton B, right shoulder: Fragmentary (sub-spherical?) jadeite beads (see p. 51)

C. Skeleton B, slightly north of right orbit: Jadeite effigy stingray spine (Fig. 49 i)

D. Skeleton B, area of chest: Pair of large rectangular jadeite beads (Figs. 47 c, d; 49 g)—Scalloped jadeite ornament, fragmentary (Fig. 49 e)—7 jadeite beads (Figs. 47 a'—c'; 49 c)—2 cylindrical jadeite beads (see p. 51)—Clay effigy shell (Fig. 58 c)—13 dentate *Spondylus* objects (Fig. 52 p, x)

E. Skeleton B, abdomen and pelvis: 4 shell tinklers (Fig. 52 n, t)—Many small shell beads (Fig. 52 e'; 53 m)—Small cylindrical jadeite bead (Fig. 47 d')

F. Skeleton B, under left hand bones: Large rectangular jadeite bead (Fig. 49 h)

G. Skeleton B, under right hand bones: Large cylindrical jadeite bead (Fig. 47 e')

H. Skeleton B, near right knee: Pair of perforated jadeite ornaments (Figs. 44 h; 47 y)

I. On chamber floor, particularly scattered about Skeleton B: 128 sub-spherical jadeite beads (Figs. 47 a, b; 48 v)—66 amazonite beads (Fig. 48 u, w)—Wedge-shaped jadeite object (Fig. 44 k)—Clay effigy shell fragment (Fig. 58 e)—Bone awl (see p. 62)—White shell fragments—Flint chips—Sherds— Carnivore canine   (see p. 64)

Fig. 64

FIGURE 65

BURIAL 5, PLAN AND ELEVATIONS OF TOMB (see pp. 124–125)

Fig. 65

SURFACE, STR. J-5-1st

SURFACE, STR. J-5-2nd
SLABS, APPROX. LEVEL

0   1   2 METER
    3   6 FEET

—?

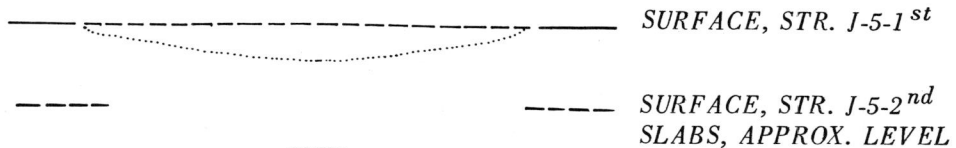

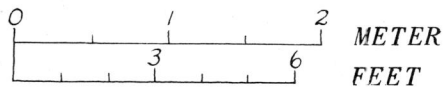

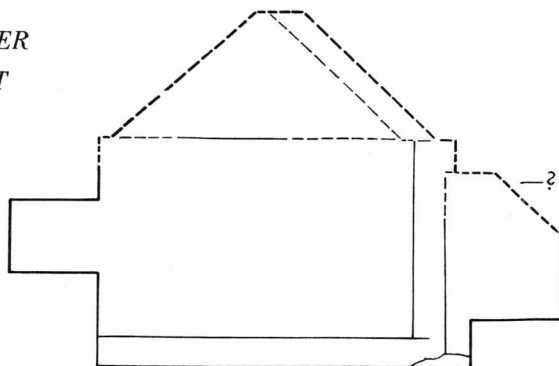

SECTION c-d, AND ELEVATION OF S.W. END

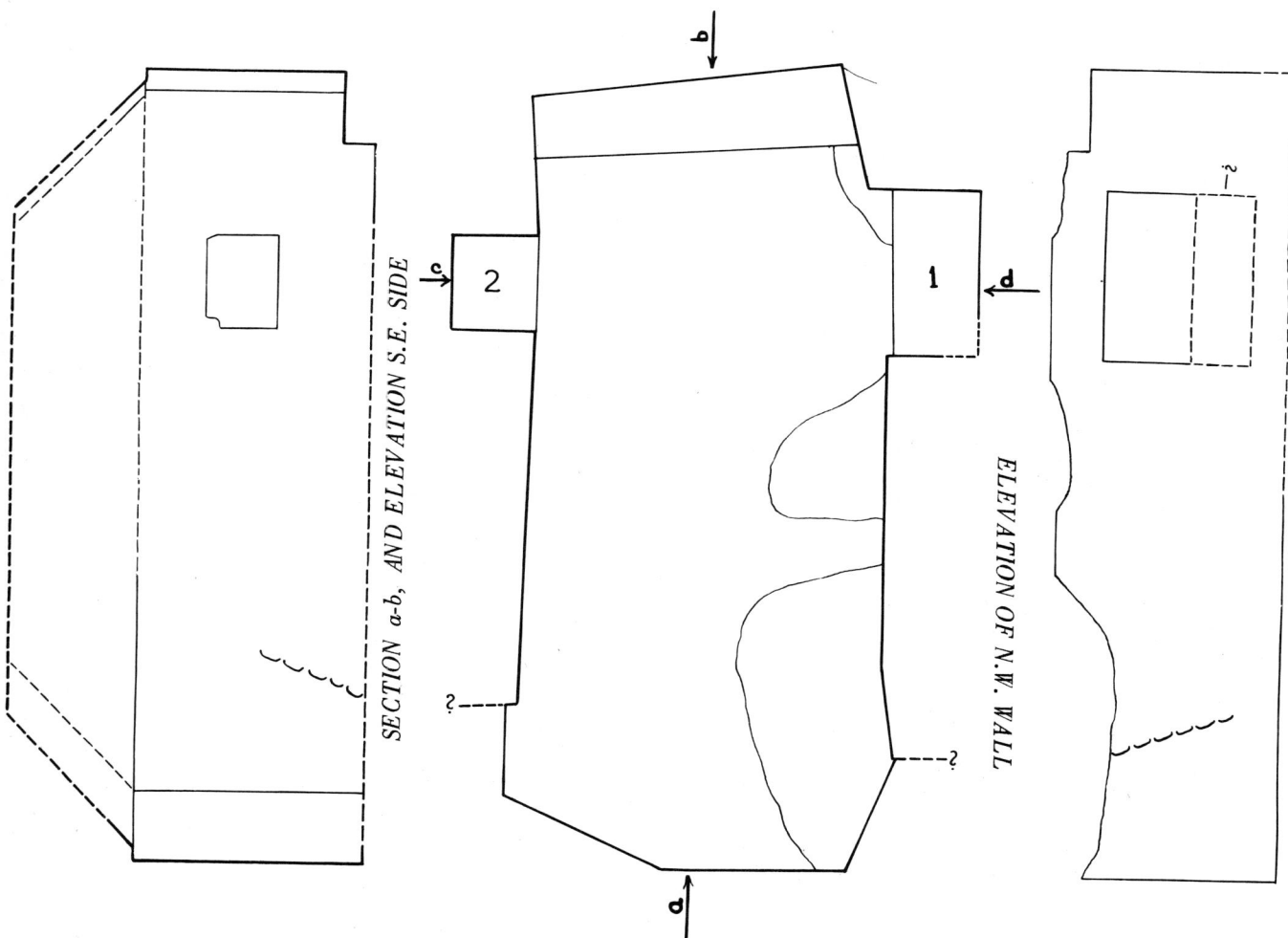

SECTION a-b, AND ELEVATION S.E. SIDE

ELEVATION OF N.W. WALL

b

c   2   1   d

?

a

?

?

FIGURE 66

BURIAL 10, PLAN AND ELEVATIONS OF TOMB (see pp. 126—127)

FIGURE 67

BURIAL 10, PLAN OF FLOOR (see pp. 126—127)

1   3 Class 1 jadeite beads   (Fig. 48 c', j')
    3 Class 2 jadeite beads   (Fig. 48 b', i')
    4 shell beads (Fig. 52 g')
    Animal canine tooth (see p. 64)
    Human molar tooth
    2 pieces of perforated shell

2   1 Class 1 jadeite bead   (Fig. 48 c', j')

3   1 Class 1 jadeite bead   (Fig. 48 c', d')
    1 Class 3 jadeite bead   (Fig. 48 x, y, h')
    2 shell ornaments (Fig. 52 h', i')

4   3 Class 1 jadeite beads   (Fig. 48 c', j')
    2 Class 3 jadeite beads   (Fig. 48 x, y, h')
    Shell fragments

5   1 Class 4 jadeite bead   (Fig. 48 x, l')

6   Carved jadeite pendant (Fig. 45 y)

7   2 Class 1 jadeite beads   (Fig. 48 c', j')

8   Small perforated shell disc (Fig. 52 d')

9   Perforated jadeite oval (Fig. 44 m)

10 1 Class 1 jadeite bead   (Fig. 48 c', j')
    1 Class 3 jadeite bead   (Fig. 48 x, y, h')

11 Bird claws (see p. 64)

12 1 Class 3 jadeite bead   (Fig. 48 x, y, h')

13 2 Class 1 jadeite beads   (Fig. 48 c', j')

14 1 Class 4 jadeite bead   (Fig. 48 x, l')
    1 Class 1 jadeite bead   (Fig. 48 c', j')
    Bird claws (see p. 64)

15 1 Class 2 jadeite bead   (Fig. 48 b', i')

16—30
     6 Class 1 jadeite beads   (Fig. 48 c', j')
     6 Class 2 jadeite beads   (Fig. 48 b', i')
     3 Class 3 jadeite beads   (Fig. 48 x, y, h')

31 Perforated jadeite ornament (Fig. 44 n)

32 Perforated jadeite ornament (Fig. 48, k!)

33 Perforated jadeite ornament (Fig. 44 o)

34 1 Class 1 jadeite bead   (Fig. 48 c', j')

35 Perforated jadeite ornament (Fig. 44 p)

36 1 Class 3 jadeite bead   (Fig. 48 x, y, h')

37 2 Class 1 jadeite beads   (Fig. 48 c', j')

38 2 Class 2 jadeite beads   (Fig. 48 b', i')

39 Shell fragments

40 Human skeletal fragments (UM) (see p. 127)
    Fragmentary cruciform problematical jadeite
    object (UM, not located) (see p. 48)

41 Child's mutilated cranial vault (Fig. 68 c, c')
    mandible, and fragmentary long-bone

42 Redware tripod bowl, broken (UM) (see pp. 126—127)

43 Flint flakes arranged as a drum (see p. 12 "Blank
    (?)" and p. 127)
    Chopper (Fig. 1 a)
    Blank (?) (Fig. 1, 1)

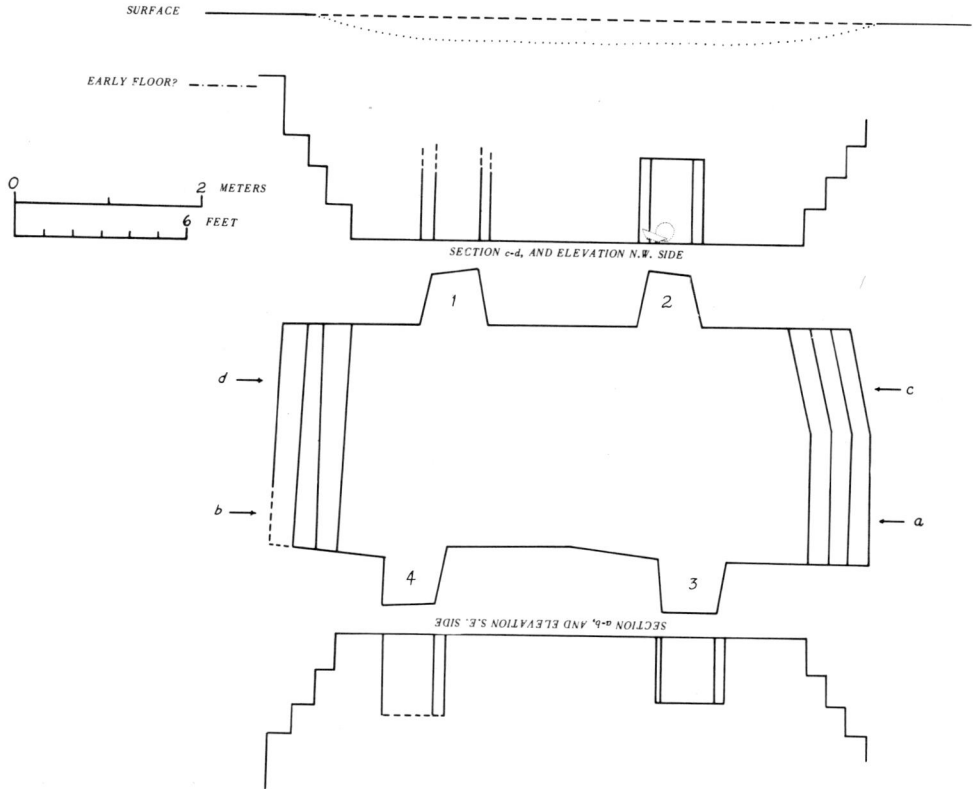

Fig. 66

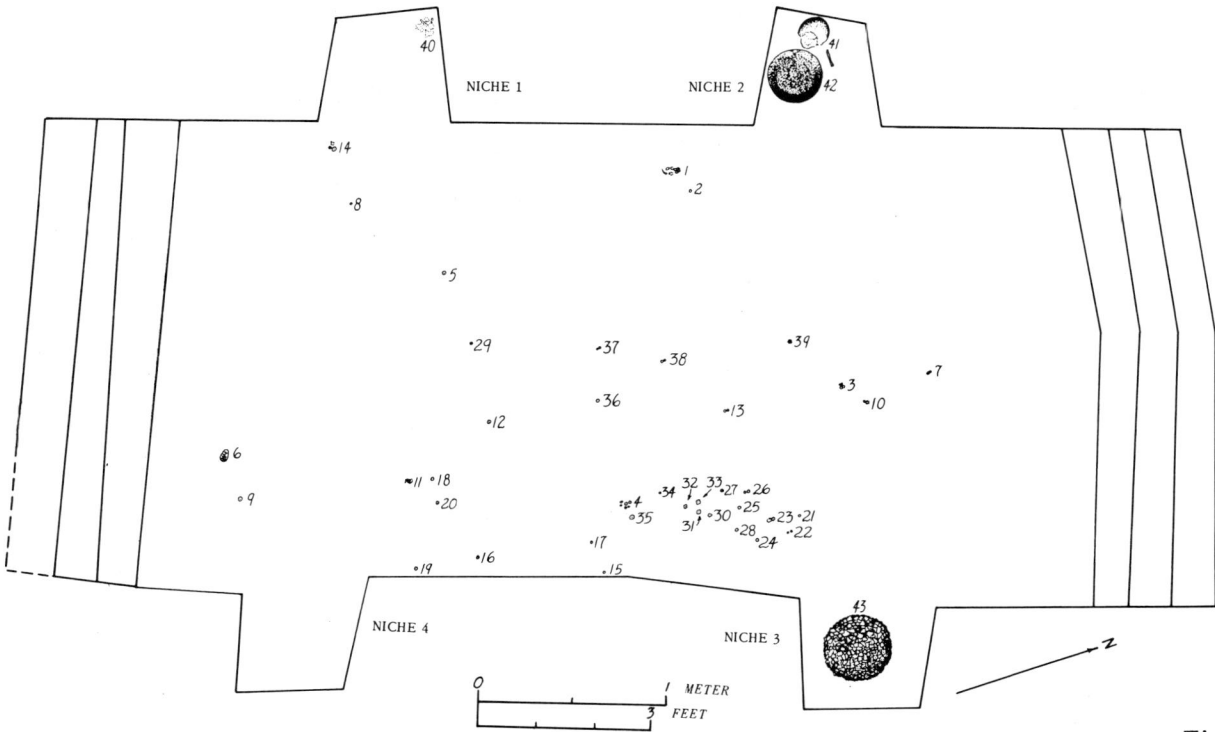

Fig. 67

FIGURE 68

MODIFIED HUMAN CRANIAL MATERIAL

	DESCRIPTION	FIELD NO.	PROVENIENCE	DISPOSITION	REF. PAGE
a, aʹ	Deformation	SE—1—1	Burial 1	UM	121
b, bʹ	,,	S—2—26	Burial 8	,,	126
c, cʹ	Post-mortem mutilation (arrows)	S—15—19	Burial 10, Niche 2	,,	127
d, dʹ	Deformation	W—43—1	Lot 1 (under Burials)	,,	128
e	Deformation	S—2—21	Burial 7	,,	126

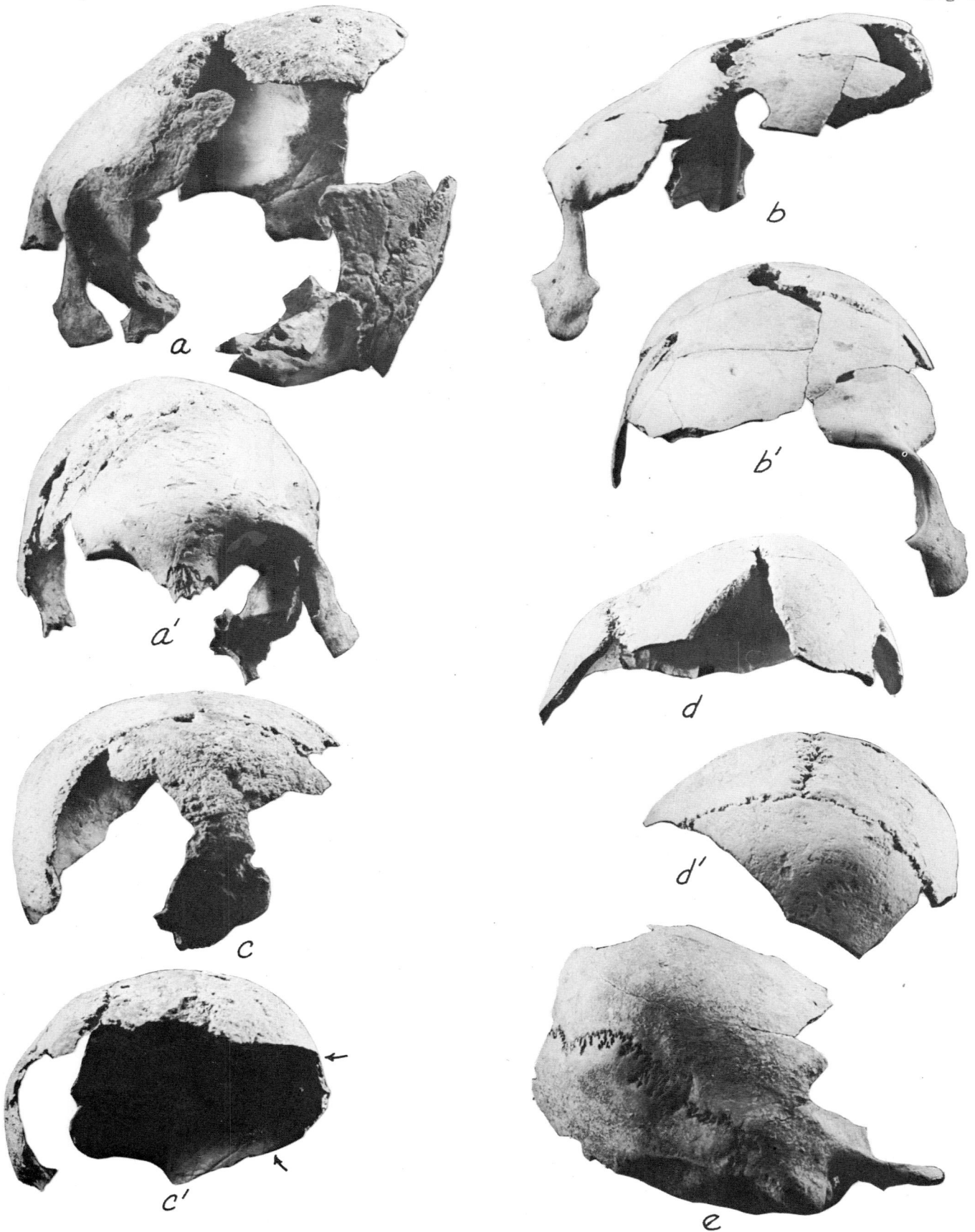

Fig. 68

FIGURE 69

MODIFIED HUMAN TEETH

	DESCRIPTION	FIELD NO.	PROVENIENCE	DISPOSITION	REF. PAGE
a	Filed and unmutilated, with jadeite and pyrite inlays	W—17—54	Burial 5, Skeleton B	UM	43, 52, 136
b	Filed, with jadeite inlay	SE—1—10a	Burial 2	,,	52, 136
c	Filed	NE—6—3	Lot 2 (under Burials)	,,	128, 136
d, e	Filed	W—7—1	Burial 4	,,	123, 136

Fig. 69

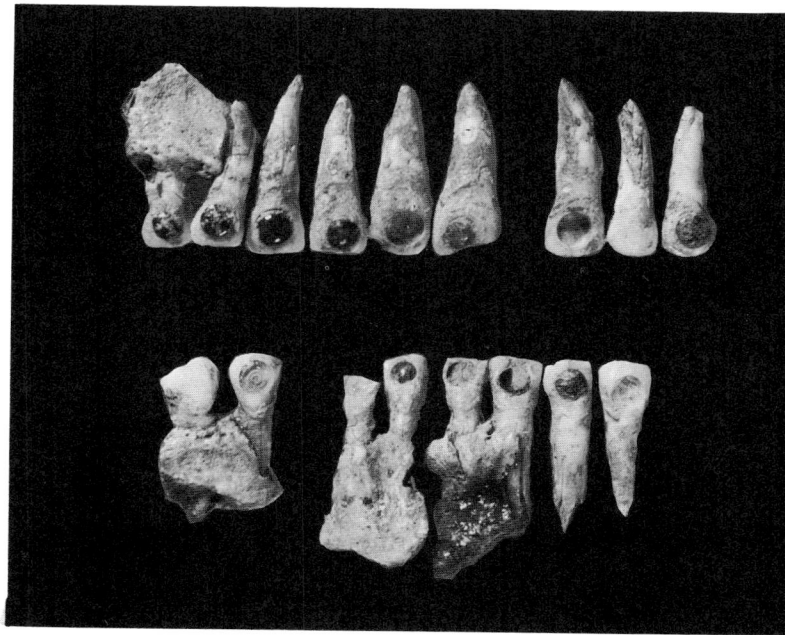

a

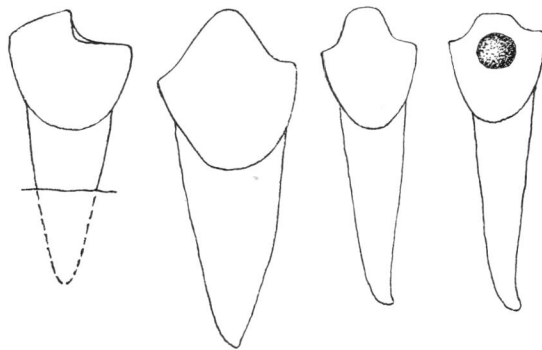

b   c   d   e